AF735473

Flying in the Face of Criminalization

Flying in the Face of Criminalization examines the critical intersection between aviation safety investigations and criminal proceedings. This comprehensive analysis reveals how the legal system's punitive approach often conflicts with aviation's core objective of learning from mistakes to enhance safety.

The new edition significantly expands coverage through 2025, documenting the increase in litigation against aviation professionals and organizations following accidents and serious incidents. It provides crucial insights into recent developments in corporate criminal liability, manslaughter charges, and corporate homicide cases that have transformed accountability standards across the industry. With an unparalleled collection of cases from January 2010 to June 2025, with updates to the Boeing 737 MAX and AF 447 litigation until 30 November 2025, the book explores how varying legal systems worldwide apply liability principles inconsistently and create uncertainty for aviation professionals operating across jurisdictions.

A diverse audience will benefit from this book, including legal professionals, aviation consultants, pilots, air traffic controllers, safety officers, airline managers, and accident investigators.

"*Flying in the Face of Criminalization* is a pivotal work in just culture. This book brilliantly bridges the gap between legal systems and safety investigations. It will transform the perspective on how to navigate the complexities of safety in a litigious world. It's a must-read for anyone in the safety and judiciary field, offering invaluable insights. Highly recommended!"

Tony Licu, *Head of DTO-Digital Transformation Office and CTO-Head of Technology Division, Eurocontrol*

"Sofia and Andreas Mateou deliver an exceptional work in *Flying in the Face of Criminalization*. Their unique blend of research, professional expertise, and industry insight provides clarity on the complex relationship between law and aviation safety. A must-read, it empowers professionals to navigate accountability while fostering stronger safety leadership."

Tzvetomir Blajev, *Director Europe and Global Operational Safety, Flight Safety Foundation*

"*Flying in the Face of Criminalization* is a landmark contribution to aviation literature and an indispensable resource for professionals at every level of the industry. Drawing on decades of hands-on experience and academic expertise, the authors illuminate one of the most urgent challenges in aviation today – the complex intersection of safety and criminal liability. This book not only analyzes the issue with clarity but also empowers the aviation community to transform concerns about liability into proactive safety leadership. It is a must-have reference for aviation managers, policymakers, and safety leaders worldwide."

Abdulelah Felemban, *EVP Safety Investigations & Research, The National Transport Safety Center, KSA*

"*Flying in the Face of Criminalization* is essential reading. It highlights the risks of criminalising air accidents and incidents, and the lessons to be learned. Clear, authoritative, and timely, and a vital contribution to air safety."

Joanna Kolatsis, *Aviation Lawyer, Director, Themis Advisory*

Flying in the Face of Criminalization

Navigating Personal and Corporate Liability in Aviation

Second edition

Andreas Mateou and Sofia Mateou

Routledge
Taylor & Francis Group
LONDON AND NEW YORK

Designed cover image: Shutterstock; iStock

Second edition published 2026
by Routledge
605 Third Avenue, New York, NY 10158

and by Routledge
4 Park Square, Milton Park, Abingdon, Oxon, OX14 4RN

Routledge is an imprint of the Taylor & Francis Group, an informa business

© 2026 Andreas Mateou and Sofia Mateou

The right of Andreas Mateou and Sofia Mateou to be identified as author[/s] of this work has been asserted in accordance with sections 77 and 78 of the Copyright, Designs and Patents Act 1988.

All rights reserved. No part of this book may be reprinted or reproduced or utilised in any form or by any electronic, mechanical, or other means, now known or hereafter invented, including photocopying and recording, or in any information storage or retrieval system, without permission in writing from the publishers.

For Product Safety Concerns and Information please contact our EU representative GPSR@taylorandfrancis.com. Taylor & Francis Verlag GmbH, Kaufingerstraße 24, 80331 München, Germany.

Trademark notice: Product or corporate names may be trademarks or registered trademarks, and are used only for identification and explanation without intent to infringe.

First edition published by Ashgate 2010 and by Routledge 2016

Library of Congress Cataloging-in-Publication Data
Names: Mateou, Andreas author | Michaelides-Mateou, Sofia, 1965- author
Title: Flying in the face of criminalization : navigating personal and corporate liability in aviation / Andreas Mateou and Sofia Mateou.
Description: [2nd edition]. | New York, NY : Routledge, 2026. | Includes bibliographical references and index.
Identifiers: LCCN 2025048418 (print) | LCCN 2025048419 (ebook) | ISBN 9781041209232 hardback | ISBN 9781041209218 paperback | ISBN 9781003724872 ebook
Subjects: LCSH: Aircraft accidents--Investigation | Liability for aircraft accidents | Airplanes--Piloting--Law and legislation | Aeronautics, Commercial--Law and legislation | Aircraft industry--Law and legislation | Aeronautics--Safety measures
Classification: LCC TL553.5 .M38 2026 (print) | LCC TL553.5 (ebook)
LC record available at https://lccn.loc.gov/2025048418
LC ebook record available at https://lccn.loc.gov/2025048419

ISBN: 978-1-041-20923-2 (hbk)
ISBN: 978-1-041-20921-8 (pbk)
ISBN: 978-1-003-72487-2 (ebk)

DOI: 10.1201/9781003724872

Typeset in Times
by Deanta Global Publishing Services, Chennai, India

Contents

Foreword

According to the International Air Transport Association (IATA), 4.8 billion people traveled by commercial airlines in 2024. The overwhelming majority of those passengers did so without even needing to think about the safety performance of the industry. They arrived safely at their destination without incident. In 2024, IATA recorded only 7 fatal accidents among 40.6 million flights resulting in 244 fatalities.

The safety performance of commercial aviation is remarkable, and yet, the hazards that the industry must manage are complex and varied. Safety has been achieved through international collaboration, strict regulation, engineering brilliance, intensive training, and more. The industry realized a long time ago that bitter lessons learned through accidents and serious incidents needed to be properly understood, acted upon, and shared. An industry-wide culture was nurtured by the International Civil Aviation Organization through the standards and recommended practices contained in Annex 13 – Aircraft Accident Investigation, that the purpose of safety investigation was not the allocation of blame or liability, but the prevention of future accidents.

While such an approach allows the industry to learn from its mistakes, it does not always fulfill the desire or need of an individual or a judicial system to identify someone to blame or an organization to hold accountable. For a loved one or family member of someone seriously injured or killed as a result of an aircraft accident, it is surely understandable. Their anger or grief is a natural reaction to an unimaginable tragedy, especially when such events dominate news coverage often with shocking imagery.

For a judicial system, holding individuals or organizations to account for their actions or inactions is at the heart of the process. Indeed, there is a strong argument that a robust and fair legal system is the best way to decide whether a sanction is appropriate. Even in the case of civil litigation, there is an argument that where damages are awarded, they are merely to compensate for the harm and loss suffered by others.

However, the two views – of learning by a "not for blame" approach to investigation or by achieving justice through a judicial process – are not necessarily compatible. The former system is dependent on trust to ensure that people are willing to share information without self-implicating themselves or fearing punishment for genuine errors. Information collected for the purposes of improving safety should not be used against someone in pursuit of prosecution or compensation. Protecting those principles has been of prime concern for aviation safety professional investigators for many years. Where prosecutions have taken place, they have had a negative effect on the willingness of others to engage in reporting or investigations.

While aircraft accidents remain an incredibly rare event, they can happen to any operator and in any part of the world. The nationalities of those on board can vary hugely and as a consequence, the response to that occurrence can be hard to predict. Regardless of whether a State is a signatory to the ICAO Annexes, judicial systems can interpret a particular accident as a criminal act and take primacy in the investigation. In countries where protections are in place to ensure that a safety investigation takes precedence, this does not prevent a quasi-judicial process such as a coronial one from recommending a prosecution, or indeed civil litigation from taking place.

These factors make *Flying in the Face of Criminalization* an essential text for all of those involved in aviation safety. It was my privilege to be the external examiner of Andreas and Sofia's PhD on the topic, and I was delighted when they developed their work further into such an important and timely book. Their insights are extremely valuable to those who are attempting to navigate a complex field of competing perspectives. Knowing the positive impact that the first book had, and recognizing that the impact of criminalization of aircraft accidents is continuing to evolve, I was excited to hear they had updated their text into a second *Flying in the Face of Criminalization* book with the subtitle *Navigating Personal and Corporate Liability in Aviation.*

The second book provides rich examples of recent cases from around the world, ranging from the prosecution of individuals under health and safety laws to high-profile litigation involving corporations following fatal accidents. They provide expert commentary on how legal frameworks have evolved, how court decisions have influenced the landscape, and how amendments to ICAO Annex 13 have attempted to protect the integrity of not-for-blame safety investigations. For such a globalized industry, it is refreshing to find a text that covers multiple legal jurisdictions and provides examples from around the world. It is another reason why this text is so important and will be useful to a wide audience.

The authors' dedication to ensuring that the highest standards of aviation safety are maintained is clear. While they are careful to ensure that different perspectives are considered and that the important role of the judiciary is respected, they never lose sight of the formula that has helped aviation to achieve such an enviable safety record. The importance of managing risk as part of a safety management system is highlighted, along with the legal implications of a deficient system. The aim is to provide those involved in safety management (which arguably encompasses most leadership roles in the aviation industry) with the insight to find the right balance between learning and holding someone or an organization to account.

Professor Graham Braithwaite,
Director of Aerospace and Aviation -
Cranfield University

Preface

When we first wrote *Flying in the Face of Criminalization: The Safety Implications of Prosecuting Aviation Professionals for Accidents,* our primary aim was to provide an analysis of the intermingling between the safety investigation and the judicial process subsequent to high-profile accidents that impacted aviation globally in the 1990s and early 2020s. The realization that aviation professionals, airlines, and legal entities found themselves in a court of law after an aviation accident was very concerning, given that the legal system is designed to punish rather than promote learning and safety improvements.

Our first book was primarily based on our doctoral research, which collected data to determine how pilots and ATCs in the European Union perceive aviation accident investigations, the intermingling between technical and judicial investigations, and the impact that criminalization has on aviation safety.

The response was overwhelming. Readers from various sectors of the aviation industry, including flight crew, air traffic controllers, engineers, postholders, managers, accident investigators, auditors, regulators and inspectors, legal scholars, lawyers, and judges, reached out to let us know that they found the book helpful, enlightening, and, at the same time, alarming.

Our insight into the areas of criminalization has been enriched through our continuous research and academic teaching at reputable universities. Our professional development and industry experience with civil aviation authorities, senior management positions in various airlines, and our involvement as consultants in litigation in several aviation accidents, the just culture task force, and other aviation safety organizations have enabled us to examine the current developments regarding the criminalization of individuals and organizations in a spherical and practical way and to share our knowledge and insight with our readers.

The aviation landscape has undergone significant changes since our first book, particularly in terms of criminalization and corporate manslaughter, and this area has remained the focus of our research over the last fifteen years. Our continuous engagement with aviation professionals, senior managers, and other postholders, as well as the judiciary and aviation lawyers, together with our analysis of many criminal cases after aviation accidents, has demonstrated that the dimensions of criminalization have evolved and become more complex and are increasingly being considered by aviation professionals in performing their daily duties.

This book emphasizes the increasing importance of continuing to examine the philosophy, purpose, and approach of the judiciary in criminalizing individuals and corporations after an aviation accident. It provides a new dimension to criminalization, raises awareness, and promotes a stronger, more profound, and thought-provoking analysis of arguments between the need for accountability and justice, and aviation safety.

This book emphasizes the increasing focus on the duties, responsibilities, and accountabilities assigned to aviation professionals and potential legal consequences, to help aviation professionals transform their fears of liability into effective safety leadership.

Our ongoing commitment to aviation safety is demonstrated by our dedication to publishing a second book titled *Flying in the Face of Criminalization*, with the subtitle, *Navigating Personal and Corporate Liability in Aviation*. In this book, we go beyond merely examining cases of professional negligence and the criminal litigation and prosecution of aviation professionals. We question whether these concepts are applied consistently and explore how different legal systems impact aviation professionals, organizations at the corporate level, and aviation safety as a whole, and explore the shift in accountability and blameworthiness, and the judiciary's approach to evaluating when a risk assessment's effectiveness can transition to gross negligence and a criminal act.

Directed at a diverse range of stakeholders in the aviation industry, including, but not limited to, international safety organizations, air traffic control service providers, unions, safety experts, pilots, air traffic controllers, engineers, safety officers, airline managers, airport and ground handling managers, air accident investigators, judges, prosecutors, lawyers, scholars, and aviation consultants, the book can be utilized in various ways, either as a complete read or as a reference text that can be consulted as needed.

Our aim is that our book will:

- provide an analysis of the evolution of criminal liability in various jurisdictions by examining key aviation accidents and subsequent litigation against key aviation professionals
- advance awareness of possible civil and criminal ramifications in the aftermath of aviation accidents
- strengthen aviation professionals' understanding of their duties, responsibilities, and accountabilities, as well as the correlation between occurrences, non-conformities, safety risk assessment, and effective implementation of mitigating controls and possible legal ramifications
- provide insight into corporate criminal liability
- foster an understanding of risks and accountability to mitigate fear, enhance adherence to safety standards, and promote a proactive and predictive safety culture
- promote safety as the primary goal and value of every aviation organization, including aviation executives, postholders, and professionals, while also encouraging safety leadership

Acknowledgements

Writing this book while being actively engaged in our demanding and highly dynamic professional lives could not have been possible without the encouragement of so many people who, over the years, supported us and believed in the need for *Flying in the Face of Criminalization: Navigating Personal and Organizational Liability* to be published.

We express our thanks to:

Each other, for our life together and our family. For sharing our passion for aviation safety and the law, and the intellectual collaboration that shaped this book. For the continuous emotional support, motivation and patience, and the enjoyable, hearty discussions that were critical to completing the book.

Our daughter Evgenia and son Stephanos: You are so precious to us both. We thank you for being who you are and for being our pride and joy.

Chris, for always being there

Andreas and Michael, our two beautiful grandchildren, for lighting up our lives.

Our brother and sisters, for their love, support, and for always believing in us.

Our parents for being our role models, giving us such inspiration, their love, and support.

Our friends and all aviation professionals, for their invaluable insight, guidance, endless support, encouragement, and unwavering belief in us.

Our publishers for their support and guidance, their patience, and for helping us to make this book a reality.

About the Authors

Captain Andreas Mateou holds a PhD from the University of Middlesex, UK, an MSc in Aviation Management from the University of New South Wales, Australia, and a Law Degree (LLB) from the University of London. He started his career as an Airbus A320 pilot and held the position of Safety Manager at Cyprus Airways. He continued his career as a Flight Operations Inspector at the UAE General Civil Aviation Authority (GCAA) before joining a major airline, initially as the Chief Pilot of the A320 fleet and is now VP Safety and Quality at a major airline in the Middle East. He is also a TRI/TRE, GACA Check Airman with more than 20,000 flying hours experience and an IOSA Risk Based Auditor. Andreas is a Visiting Professor at Emirates University and has written extensively on aviation topics and participated in a number of aviation conferences. He is an Associate Member of ISASI, a member of the Eurocontrol Just Culture Task Force, and has been an aviation safety and legal consultant in a number of aviation litigation cases.

Sofia Mateou holds a PhD from the University of Middlesex, UK, a BA, and a Law Degree (LLB) from the University of Witwatersrand, South Africa. She practiced law in South Africa before returning to Cyprus to start her academic career. She is a Professor of law and aviation and has lectured full time at the University of Nicosia and the University of Lancashire (UCLan) Cyprus, the University of Abu Dhabi, Abu Dhabi, UAE, Prince Sultan University, Riyadh, KSA and as a part-time guest lecturer at Cranfield University, UK., and a Visiting Professor at Emirates University, Dubai, United Arab Emirates. Sofia, as an aviation-legal consultant, has participated in several court proceedings against pilots, ATCs, and engineers after a number of high-profile aviation accidents. She was an advisor to the Cyprus Air Accident and Incident Investigation Board (AAIIB). She is a member of the Just Culture Task Force of Eurocontrol and an Associate Member of ISASI. Sofia is an avid speaker and presenter at international conferences, has published numerous articles and chapters on key areas impacting aviation safety and security. She is also the author of the book, *Air Law: A Practical Perspective*.

List of Abbreviations

AAIB	Air Accidents Investigation Branch
ACARS	Aircraft Communications Addressing and Reporting System
ACSAA	Aircraft Certification, Safety, and Accountability Act
AEG	Aircraft Evaluation Group
AIGP	Accident Investigation Panel
ALT	Alternate Law
ANO	Air Navigation Orders
AoA	Angle of Attack
ARAIB	South Korean National Aviation and Railway Accident Investigation Board
ARMS	Aviation Risk Management Solutions
ASR	Air Safety Report
ATC	Air Traffic Controllers
AWOS	Automated Weather Observation System
BALPA	The British Air Line Pilots Association
BEA	Bureau of Enquiry and Analysis for Civil Aviation Safety
CBA	Collective Bargaining Agreement
CEO	Chief Executive Officer
CIAIAC	Civil Aviation Accident and Incident Investigation Committee
CJIP	Convention judiciaire d'intérêt public
CPS	Crown Prosecution Service
CVR	Cockpit Voice Recorder
CVRA	Crime Victim's Rights Act
DEI	Diversity, Equity and Inclusion
DFT	Department for Transport
DGAC	Dirección General de Aeronáutica Civil
DME	Distance Measuring Equipment
DOJ	Department of Justice
DPA	Deferred Prosecution Agreement
EASA	European Aviation Safety Agency
ECAA	Egyptian Civil Aviation Authority
EGPWS	Enhanced Ground Proximity Warning System,
EST	Eastern Standard Time
EAFR	Enhanced Airborne Flight Recorders
ENCASIA	European Network of Civil Aviation Safety Investigation Authorities
ERC	Event Risk Classification
FCOM	Flight Crew Operating Manual
FCPA	Foreign Corrupt Practices Act
FCU	Flight Control Unit
FDR	Flight Data Recorder

FL	Flight Level
FO	First Officer
GCAA	General Civil Aviation Authority of the UAE
GTA	Air Transport Gendarmerie
GPWS	Ground Proximity Warning System
HSWA	Health & Safety at Work Act 2015 – NZ
IAC	Russian Interstate Aviation Committee
IATA	International Air Transport Association
IAS	Indicated Airspeed
ITAR	International Traffic in Arms Regulations
ICR	Investigative Committee of Russia
ILS	Instrument Landing System
IMC	Instrument Meteorological Conditions
ISIL	Islamic State of Iraq and the Levant
JIAAC	Junta de Investigación de Accidentes de Aviación Civil Argentine (Civil Aviation Accident Investigation Board
KNKT	Transportation Safety National Committee of Indonesia
KPIs	Key Performance Indicators
MED	Mid-Exit Door
MCAS	Maneuvering Characteristics Augmentation System
MC	Montreal Convention
MCC	Maintenance Control Centre
MDA	Minimum Descent Altitude
MED	Mid-Exit Door Plug
MLIT	Ministry of Land, Infrastructure, Transport and Tourism
MOC	Management of Change
MOC	SRA Management of Change Safety Risk Assessment
MS	Management System
NBAAI	National Bureau of Air Accidents Investigation of Ukraine
NTSB	National Transportation Safety Board
NTSC	The National Transportation Safety Committee, Indonesian: Komite Nasional Keselamatan Transportasi, KNKT
OCC	Operations Control Centre
OIG	Office of the Inspector General
PALPA	Pakistan Airline Pilots' Association
PCBU	Person Conducting A Business Or Undertaking
PIA	Pakistan International Airlines
PIC	Pilot in Command
PTSD	Post-Traumatic Stress Disorder
PNF	Parquet National Financier
QMS	Quality Management System
QRA	Quick Reaction Alert
QSA	Quality System Audit
RA	Resolution Advisory
RAT	Ram Air Temperature

RBI	Risk-Based IOSA
RESA	Runway End Safety Area
RVR	Runway Visual Range
SAIB	Swiss Accident Investigation Board
SAR	Search and Rescue
SDCP	Safety Data Collection And Processing Systems
SERA	Standardised European Rules of the Air
SFO	Serious Fraud Office
SMS	Safety Management System
SMM	Safety Management Manual
SMICG	Safety Management International Collaboration Group
SOPs	Standard Operating Procedures
SWAPA	Southwest Airlines Pilot Association
TASS	Court of Social Security Affairs (Argentina)
TAWS	Terrain Awareness and Warning System
TCAS	Traffic Alert And Collision System
TNT	Trinitrotoluene
TSB	Transportation Safety Board of Canada
VFR	Visual Flight Rules
VOR	Omnidirectional Range
VMC	Visual Meteorological Conditions
VRRA	Victims' Rights and Restitution Act
WHO	World Health Organization
WSH	Work Health and Safety

List of Cases

A

Adomako [1995] 1 A.C. 171.Australian National Airlines Commission v The Commonwealth of Australia & Canadian Pacific Airlines [1975] High Court of Australia, reported at (1974-5) 132CLR 582

B

R v Bateman [1925] Cr. App R. 8.Blyth v Birmingham Waterworks Co [1856]11 Ex 781.Bolam v Friern Hospital Management Committee [1957] 1 WLR 583.Brooks v United States [5th Circ. 1983] 695 F. 2d 984, 987.The Bywell Castle [1879] 4 PD 219.

C

Canada (Transportation Safety Board) v Carroll-Byrne, 2021 NSCA 34Coatney v Berkshire [1974] 500F 2d 290 (8th Circ).Cohen et al v Northern Thunderbird Air Inc, 2017 BCSC 315

D

Delta Airlines Inc. v US [1977] 561 F2d 381 (1st Circ).Overseas Tankship (UK) Ltd v Morts Docks & Engineering Co. Ltd. [1961] UKPC 1, [1961] AC 388, [1961] 1 All ER 404.DPP v Newbury [1977] AC 500.

F

FAA v NTSB [1991] Columbia Circuit) argued April 8, 1999 Decided September 21, 1999 No. 98-1365.

G

Goldman v Thai Airwys International Ltd [1983] 1 WLR 118.

H

Hartz v United States [1965] 249 F.Supp.119.Hayes v United States [5th Cir. 1990] 899 F.2d 438.Hoyle v Rogers & Anors, 2014

I

In re Air Crash Near Clarence Ctr., N.Y., 09-md-2085 (W.D.N.Y. Oct. 19, 2010)

K

Kack v United States [D.Minn. 1977] 432, F.Supp. 633,624-35

L

Lochgelly Iron & Cool Co. v M'Mullan [1934] AC. 1

N
Nettleship v Weston [1971] 2 QB. 691.

O
Overseas Tankship (UK) Ltd v Morts. Docks & Engineering Co. Ltd [1961] AC 388

P
People v Crossan 87 Call. App. 5, 261 p531 (Cal. Dist. Ct. App.1927)

R
R v Caldwell [1982] A.C. 341 354.R v Dr Errol Cornish [2015] EWHC 2967 (QB).R v P & O Ferries (Dover) Ltd [1990] 93 Cr App R 72.R v Woolin [1999] 1 A.C. 82; [1998] 3 W.L.R. 382; [1998] 4 All E.R. 103.Rogers v Hoyle (EWHC/QB, 2013)

S
Saif Ali v Sydney Mitchell & Co. [1980] AC 198.Shankle v United States [5th Cir. 1986] 796 F. 2d 742, 745.Susanne Yvonne Andrews v British Airways [2008] EWCA Civ 1308

T
Taylor v Alidar Ltd [1976] IRLR 420 & [1978] IRLR 82 CA.The Chief Constable of Sussex Police v The Secretary of State for Transport [2016] EWHC 2280 (QB) The Queen v Her Majesty's Senior Coroner for Norfolk [2016] EWHC 2279 (Admin)

V
Voli v Inglewood Shire Council [1963] 110 CLR 74.

W
Wagon Mound (The), The No. 1) [1961] see Overseas Tankship (UK) Ltd v Morts Docks & Engineering Co [1961] UKPC 1, [1961] AC 388, [1961] 1 All ER 404.

Y
Yates v US [1974] 497 F 2d 878 at 882-3 (10th Circ).

1 Introduction

1.1 OUR PERSPECTIVE

As aviation safety continuously improves and is enhanced through the effective implementation of a Safety Management System (SMS), improved oversight, risk-based audits, and technological advancements, when an aviation accident or serious incident occurs, public perception and media attention shift to identifying those responsible and apportioning blame and accountability. Major aviation accidents such as the Boeing 737 MAX 8 and Air France 447 accidents, the Germanwings 9525 pilot suicide, and the Shoreham Airshow accident have become landmark cases with significant legal implications for individuals and organizations involved, while also revealing the legal complexities of criminalization in different legal systems.

The number of litigation cases arising from aviation accidents or serious incidents against individuals and corporations has increased in recent years. Recent developments concerning liability and accountability highlight how professionals, senior managers, and organizations can face manslaughter and corporate homicide charges. This marks a major shift in society and the legal system's approach to holding individuals and organizations accountable for actions or omissions that lead to or contribute to accidents or serious incidents. In some cases, these criminal cases can take years, resulting in extended legal battles and a lot of uncertainty.

The significant change in corporate criminal liability and corporate homicide, which has increased accountability for organizations and senior managers after an accident, results not only from admitting the accident investigation report and sensitive aviation data into a court of law but also from the increasing focus of prosecutors and judges on examining core elements of a Safety Management System, such as hazard identification, safety risk assessment processes, and the discharge of duties and responsibilities, when they determine liability and accountability of organizations such as CEOs, accountable executives, postholders, and other senior managers. As a result, there is a need for a thorough analysis of current liability issues in the aviation industry, along with an examination of court proceedings following aviation accidents.

The comprehensive collection of cases from January 2010 to June 2025, with updates to the Boeing 737 MAX and AF 447 litigation until 30 November 2025 which cannot be accessed in any single resource, examines the criminalization of aviation accidents, with the primary objective of highlighting and drawing attention to the legal complexities and consequences for aviation professionals, airlines, organizations, and the aviation industry as a whole.

The book emphasizes the increasing focus on corporate liability and accountability for unintentional but negligent or reckless acts that cause death and offers a

DOI: 10.1201/9781003724872-1

detailed comparative analysis of recent legislation on corporate homicide in various jurisdictions. It highlights the global trend toward increased accountability for senior executive managers and aviation organizations.

The connection between the safety management system, hazard identification, risk assessment process, and the organization's and individuals' assigned duties, responsibilities, and accountabilities for maintaining safety standards was central to recent high-profile criminalization cases.

The contradiction in how different jurisdictions' legal systems and their laws are applied after the Air France 447 and Boeing 737-MAX accidents, and the consequences for both individuals and organizations, is not only highly concerning but has also renewed focus on this sensitive issue.

Courts are increasingly assessing corporate safety cultures, senior managers' corporate and safety leadership, and the effective implementation of an SMS by scrutinizing the hazard identification process, the risk assessments conducted, and the implementation of the mitigating controls that create a new judicial approach in dealing with blameworthiness and accountability subsequent to an aviation accident or serious incident.

Aviation organizations and aviation professionals must be aware of this shift so that they discharge their duties, responsibilities, and accountabilities in accordance with the strictest legal standards set by the courts, irrespective of the jurisdiction in which they operate.

In Chapter 2, we expand our discussion of the legal principles underlying liability and negligence. It reviews several recent cases, including, among others: the first instance where a pilot was criminally prosecuted in the UK in March 2025 for failing to maintain radio communication; the first case in New Zealand where a pilot was prosecuted as an officer under the 2015 Health and Safety at Work Act; a 2025 case in the US where a flight instruction company's owner was charged with multiple conspiracy offenses and the pilot with involuntary manslaughter after an accident causing the death of a student pilot, as well as the Germanwings and Concorde accident where charges were filed for criminal negligence and manslaughter against individuals and organizations. We broaden the discussion by providing a detailed, comparative analysis of recent legislation on corporate homicide across various jurisdictions, highlighting the international trend toward greater accountability for organizations and senior managers. Recent cases where corporations have been charged and found liable for acts resulting in death are also briefly discussed.

Chapter 3 provides an overview of the legal framework for aviation accident investigations at both the International and European levels. This sets the stage for discussing the admissibility of safety data obtained during safety investigations and the use of accident investigation reports in subsequent litigation arising from serious aviation accidents. Court decisions from various jurisdictions, including the UK, Canada, the USA, and France, are discussed to highlight key legal principles related to the protection of safety data, the disclosure of materials and records held by safety investigators, and the admissibility of safety data – such as cockpit voice recorder transcripts, flight data recorder information, or the Final Report – as evidence in court. The second part of the chapter provides a comprehensive overview of significant developments and amendments at the international and European levels related to the legal issues discussed. Amendments to ICAO Annex 13 from 2010 to 2024 are highlighted, specifically, the 10th edition (2010), the 11th edition (2016), the 12th edition (2020), and the most recent 13th edition (2024). At the European level, EU Regulation 996/2010 (repealing Directive 94/56), as amended by EU Regulation 376/2014, is also discussed.

In Chapter 4 we discuss three serious incidents involving near midair collisions that took place in Switzerland and the subsequent criminal proceedings against the air traffic controllers involved who were charged with negligent disruption of public transport and endangering the lives of passengers and crew. In each of the three cases, appropriate avoidance action was taken, and there were no injuries or deaths. The recent midair collision between an American Airlines passenger jet and a military helicopter on 25 January 2025 at the Reagan Washington National Airport, resulting in the death of 67 persons, highlights the very different approaches to holding individual aviation professionals liable and apportioning accountability in jurisdictions with other legal systems. The chapter continues with an in-depth overview and analysis of the Boeing 737 MAX 8 Lion Air Flight 610 and Ethiopian Airlines Flight 302 accidents, the Alaska Airlines Flight 1282 incident on 5 January 2024, and the Air France Flight 447 accident, the safety investigations conducted, the subsequent civil and criminal lawsuits against individuals, the airlines as well as Boeing and Airbus as corporate entities.

Chapter 5 explores the key differences in the legal philosophies and overall structures of the French and U.S. legal systems, as well as their contrasting approaches to managing potential criminal conduct and apportioning accountability in serious aviation accidents. Specifically, it discusses the steps taken by the French judiciary following the Concorde Flight 4590, Air Inter Flight 148, and Air France 447 accidents, as well as the prosecution of Airbus for bribery schemes aimed at securing and maintaining business. The chapter then examines the actions of the U.S. Department of Justice following the two Boeing 737 MAX 8 crashes and the Alaska Airlines MAX 9 incident, to highlight the differences between the two jurisdictions. The analysis of legal recourse and consequences following aviation accidents reveals several significant differences in prosecuting professionals and corporations involved in aviation accidents, as well as in holding them criminally accountable.

In Chapter 6 we review and discuss some of the suggestions made in our first book regarding the establishment of an EU accident investigation body to investigate major aviation accidents and serious incidents within the EU without being limited by resources, experience, skills, or the influence of potential external factors, as well as an Aviation Tribunal or Aviation Court serving as a central forum for the criminal prosecution of aviation personnel. This forum would have a uniform set of rules and procedures specifically focused on the complexities of aviation accidents and serious incidents, addressing the trials of aviation professionals more fairly, equally, with certainty, and predictability. Notable developments such as the establishment of the European Network of Civil Aviation Safety Investigation Authorities (ENCASIA) aimed at further improving the quality of investigations conducted by air safety investigation authorities of the Member States and to strengthen their independence; the establishment of several Regional Accident and Incident Investigation Organizations (RAIOs); the Shanghai International Aviation Court of Arbitration (SIACA); the Hague Court of Arbitration for Aviation (HCAA); and the Aviation Expertise Centre of the PPS in the Netherlands are highlighted.

Chapter 7 emphasizes the importance of aviation organizations implementing an effective SMS, with robust hazard identification, risk assessment, and mitigation controls to address and reduce serious safety risks and emerging concerns such as runway incursions and excursions, on-board fires, and midair collisions. It discusses the legal ramifications following the AF 447 accident and explores the connection between the safety management system, hazard identification, risk assessment process, and the organizations and individuals' assigned duties, responsibilities, and accountabilities. This highlights the legal complexities of when a risk assessment's effectiveness can transition to gross negligence and a criminal act. Comparing the legal proceedings by the U.S. Department of Justice following the Boeing 737 MAX accidents demonstrates two very different legal approaches and outcomes. It is vital for aviation professionals and organizations to understand the legal complexities and potential inconsistencies that can arise when a judge or jury assesses the effectiveness of risk assessments and mitigation controls. The chapter also discusses whether the balance between financial performance, profitability, and maintaining safety standards – through sometimes costly mitigations – as well as the shift in the courts assessing risk, can be a positive development in safeguarding the traveling public and aviation safety standards.

In Chapter 8, we provide updates on the legal proceedings of the accidents discussed in our previous book up to 2010. Then, in chronological order, we present a discussion of accidents or serious incidents from January 2010 to June 2025, along with an often extensive analysis of the criminal investigations and legal proceedings following those accidents. This highlights the increasing criminalization of individuals and aviation organizations, as well as the differing judicial approaches across various jurisdictions.

CONCLUSION

During the writing of the book, we had to make some conscious decisions that defined its boundaries and limitations, primarily based on our ability to have access to critical court proceedings and legal arguments. As an active flight crew and senior manager in an airline, and as an academic and consultant, we have approached the various issues in our book from our aviation industry and academic perspective as research, and not from an aviation lawyer or judicial perspective. Our limited access to legal arguments, court decisions, and transcripts may also result in a narrower analysis of some court decisions. While every effort was made to ensure impartiality, we encourage our readers to seek further legal analysis, obtain additional information, and form their own perspective. We acknowledge that this may differ from our views, as our primary objective is to re-ignite interest in the highly sensitive and controversial issue of criminalization in aviation.

The aviation industry will continue to expand and contribute to the economic development of the world, making our planet a smaller village year after year. Borrowing from and paraphrasing the famous preamble of the 1944 Chicago Convention, we would like to set the scene by stating that:

Whereas the future development and safety and operational standards of international civil aviation could be improved through an effective implementation of a robust and mature safety management system, positive safety reporting based on a safety corporate culture, and values and lessons learned from accident and incident investigations can significantly help to create and preserve a just culture environment and understanding among the nations and peoples of the world, aviation organizations and aviation professionals with regard to criminalization of aviation accidents, yet its abuse can become a threat to general aviation safety.

Whereas it is desirable to avoid friction and to promote cooperation between aviation organizations and professionals and nations and peoples, upon which the balance between safety and society's demand for accountability can be achieved.

Therefore, the authors, having agreed on certain principles and information available to us, hereby present to the aviation industry our book to contribute to the further development of the aviation industry in a safe and orderly manner, and that international air transport services may be established based on equal opportunity, operated soundly and economically, safely, and when needed, are justly evaluated.

2 What the Black Box Cannot Tell You
Liability in Law

2.1 INTRODUCTION

Aviation accidents have social, political, and economic implications, drawing significant media attention, which ultimately directs attention to the errors and omissions of certain parties and/or organizations, fueling public demand for accountability and the need to bring those responsible to justice.

"Accountability" refers to accepting one's responsibility and giving an account for one's actions and is often used to denote responsibility, answerability, blameworthiness, and liability. It is a concept that encompasses various forms of accountability, such as inter alia, moral, administrative, political, managerial, market, legal, and professional.[1] Following an aviation accident, instinctively, we believe that someone's fault or wrongdoing caused the accident, and hence, the party(s) or organization must be identified and blamed.

Legal accountability assigns responsibility for a legal wrong, which may be in the form of a violation of an individual's rights or non-performance of a legal duty. Failure by a person or organization to meet the imputed legal responsibility paves the way for a lawsuit for damages, as in cases where an airline is ordered to pay compensation to passengers or the relatives of the deceased. Liability also applies to alleged criminal acts, making the defendant subject to criminal prosecution, conviction, and punishment.

Legal liability is therefore the liability that a court imposes on a party for his acts or inactions (omissions) and for which the court will impose a form of redress, such as pecuniary damages in a civil matter and criminal sanctions in a criminal case. Subsequent to an aviation accident, a number of aviation professionals may be faced with both civil and criminal liability. Civil actions may be initiated by the injured party or the relatives of the deceased to recover compensation, while criminal actions may be commenced by judicial authorities when the accident has resulted in death or situations of violations of local, regional, and international laws, policies, and regulations.

Legal liability arises from three general classes of legal wrongs: Breach of contract for which financial compensation will be sought; Tort, a civil wrong where a tortfeasor (wrongdoer) breaches a duty imposed by law and causes injury or damage to another person, resulting in financial compensation; Crime, an action or omission which constitutes an offense and is punishable by law. In some cases, the law imposes strict liability without the need to prove fault by the wrongdoer, as in when

DOI: 10.1201/9781003724872-2

manufacturers are held strictly liable for their defective products. There are also situations where one party may be held liable for the torts committed by another party, such as when an employer is held vicariously liable for the torts of its employees committed during the course of employment.

There are two main branches of the law, namely Civil and Criminal. Civil law is concerned with an individual's rights and duties, which are enforceable by the individual. The purpose of civil law is to remedy the wrong and to compensate the victim for the loss or damages suffered as a result of the wrong. Breach of contract and negligence (constituting a tort) are civil wrongs. Criminal law regulates the conduct of individuals in a society and is therefore concerned with wrongs committed against society at large. The purpose of criminal law is essentially to punish the wrongdoer and to deter similar acts.

Even though the purpose of each of these two branches of law and their rules and procedures differ, it often happens that an individual's action or inaction can give rise to both a civil and a criminal action. A pilot who flies his aircraft disregarding the rules of navigation, resulting in the injury of a passenger, may be faced with criminal charges brought against him by the State as well as a civil claim brought by the injured passenger for compensation. An air traffic controller (ATC) who speaks on his mobile telephone when responsible for air traffic control, and as a result of his negligence, two aircraft collide, may be faced with criminal as well as civil proceedings.

Criminal law is largely statutory law passed by the legislature. Civil law, which is essentially case law, is influenced by historical, social, and economic factors, as well as technological advancements. Well-established and entrenched common law principles of decades ago may still apply to situations that arise today. A pertinent example can be illustrated by the case of *The Bywell Castle*[2] decided in 1879, which established the principle that a person who professes to have a certain skill has a duty in law to exercise their duties in accordance with those skills, by stating: "captains of ships are bound to shew such skill as persons of their positions with ordinary nerve ought to shew under the circumstances" (per Brett LJ, p. 226).

2.2 CIVIL LIABILITY – NEGLIGENCE

The legal basis for accountability, barring terrorism and willful misconduct, following an aviation accident, is negligence. Simple negligence is the least culpable level of legal liability. Negligence can be defined as 'the breach of a legal duty to take care, which results in damage, undesired by the defendant to the plaintiff.[3] The following definitions are provided by case law.

In the case of *Blyth v Birmingham Waterworks Co* (1856),[4] it was stated that negligence is the omission to do something which a reasonable man, guided by those considerations which ordinarily regulate the conduct of human affairs, would do; or doing something which a prudent and reasonable man would not do.

A further definition is that provided in the case of *Lochgelly Iron & Cool Co v M'Mullan* (1934),[5] where negligence was described as the infliction of damage as a result of a breach of a duty of care owed by the defendant to the plaintiff.

Liability in tort (negligence) may be imposed as the legal consequence of a person's act or omission to act in accordance with a legal duty imposed on him. When a person suffers loss as a result of negligent conduct, that loss is shifted onto the party who caused the loss by bringing an action in negligence against that party. In nearly all aviation accidents, the actions or inactions of those involved will be investigated in relation to any negligent conduct, either for ignoring regulations or for failing to exercise due care.

Under English law, for a claimant to prove that the defendant was negligent, it must be shown that (Winfield and Jolowitz 2002):

(1) the defendant owed the claimant a duty of care
(2) the damage suffered was a foreseeable result of the wrongful act of the defendant
(3) the defendant breached this duty or failed to conform to the standard of care
(4) that as a result of this breach, the claimant suffered damages that are not too remote and that there is some relation or proximity between the parties

The duty of care was first established in 1932 by Lord Atkin in the case of *Donoghue v Stevenson*,[6] when he stated:

> The rule that you are to love your neighbour becomes, in law, you must not injure your neighbour; and the lawyers' question, (Who is my neighbour?) receives a restricted reply. You must take reasonable care to avoid acts or omissions which you can reasonably foresee would be likely to injure your neighbour. Who, then, in law, is my neighbour? The answer seems to be the persons who are so closely and directly affected by my act that I ought reasonably to have them in contemplation as being so affected when I am directing my mind to the acts or omissions which are called in question.
>
> **(per Lord Atkin, p. 580)**

The "neighbor principle" which established the duty of care, has since developed. To establish a duty, the defendant must have reasonably foreseen that any careless act or omission on his part may cause damage, injury, or loss to the claimant; the defendant must in some way be proximate to the claimant; and it must be fair, just, and reasonable to impose such a duty.[7] When determining the fairness and reasonableness of imposing a legal duty, the courts take into account policy considerations such as arguments that extending negligence liability would open the floodgates to litigation. The courts now consider more recent arguments such as the possible commercial or financial consequences, the prospect of indeterminate liability, the possibility of risk-spreading (for example, through insurance), and potential conflicts with rights in property or other social or moral values.

The courts have clearly stated that the question of how far the duty of care can be imposed in a given situation is more of a policy question. In *Hedley Byrne & Co v Heller & Partners Ltd* [1964],[8] the court stated: How wide the sphere of the duty of care in negligence is to be laid depends ultimately upon the court's assessment of the demands of society for protection from carelessness of others (per Lord Pearce, page 536).

"Proximity" is shorthand for Lord Atkin's neighbor principle. It means that there must be legal proximity, that is, a legal relationship between the parties from which the law will attribute a duty of care. "Foreseeability" means whether a hypothetical "reasonable person" would have foreseen damage in the circumstances. The foreseeability test followed is that expounded in the case of *The Wagon Mound* (1961).[9] In other words, a defendant will only be liable for the damages suffered by the plaintiff if the damages arising from the defendant's breach of duty are not too remote. The test of remoteness of damage is one of foreseeability, namely, whether the defendant could have foreseen the kind of damage that occurred. It is important to note that it is not a requirement that the exact details or the exact extent or degree of damage or injury should have been foreseen (*The Wagon Mound,* 1961). A pilot or ATC, therefore, who may be negligent will only be held liable for the resulting damage that he could reasonably foresee.

To establish a breach of duty, it must generally be shown that the defendant failed to meet the standard of care set by law, which is that of the hypothetical reasonable person. A breach of duty, therefore, involves either failing to do something that a reasonable person would do or doing something that a prudent or reasonable person would not do. The reasonable person is a fictitious, hypothetical individual who "eliminates the personal equation and is independent of the idiosyncrasies of the particular person whose conduct is in question and who is presumed to be free from both over-apprehension and over-confidence." The test is objective and does not consider the personal characteristics of the person involved. It asks what a reasonable person would have done in the defendant's position. It is not about whether the defendant acted reasonably but whether a reasonable person in the defendant's position would have acted as the defendant did.

Outlined thus far is the general test laid down by the law regarding an ordinary, reasonable person. Professionals are judged according to the standard that the law requires of that particular profession. When considering whether a person is negligent and another is injured as a result, the question to be decided is whether the tortfeasor (the wrongdoer) was in breach of his duty of care to the injured party, thus committing a tort. The general principles of tort law are applicable irrespective of whether the wrongdoer or tortfeasor is a surgeon (*Bolam v Friern Hospital Management Committee* (1957)),[10] a driver (*Nettleship v Weston* (1971)),[11] an architect (*Voli v Inglewood Shire Council* (1963)),[12] a lawyer (*Saif Ali v Sydney Mitchell & Co.* (1980)),[13] a pilot, or any other professional. This indicates an increase over the years in the category of professionals being held accountable for their professional negligence.

Where a person practices a profession or holds himself out as having professional skills, the law requires that person to show the amount of competence associated with performing the duties of that profession and if the conduct of that person falls short of that, and someone is injured as a result, he could be found to be acting negligently and therefore be held liable.

It is clear, therefore, by applying the general principles outlined above, that a pilot, ATC, engineer, or other aviation professional must be judged for their reasonableness through the eyes of a reasonable pilot, ATC, engineer, and so on.

In relation to pilots, the courts have held that the standard of care required of a pilot is that of a competent, prudent, and qualified pilot. In the case of *McInnerny v McDougall*[14] the courts held that in the absence of statute, the ordinary rules of negligence apply to the operation of an aircraft and that the pilot is required to exercise that degree of care and skill which a competent, prudent, and qualified pilot would use under the circumstances. The courts have also held that a professional is not required to have an extraordinary degree of expert skill, but only the standard degree of competence common to that profession. Justice McNair, in *Bolam v Friern Hospital Management Committee* (1957), stated that:

> Where you get a situation which involves the use of some special skill or competence, then the test as to whether there has been negligence or not is not the test of the man on top of the Clapham Omnibus because he has not got any special skill. A man need not possess the highest of expert skill; it is well established in law that it is sufficient if he exercises the ordinary skill of an ordinary man exercising that particular art.
>
> **(page 587)**

An American court, in the case of *Long v Clinton Aviation Co.* (1950), discussing the standard of skill the law requires of a pilot, stated that, in the absence of a statute providing otherwise, a pilot is not required to exercise extreme care and caution in operating an airplane but only ordinary care given the circumstances. "Ordinary care" of an airplane pilot means doing or failing to do what an experienced pilot, considering the safety of himself and others, would do or fail to do under similar conditions.

In *Saif Ali v Sydney Mitchell & Co.* (1980),[15] Lord Diplock stated that:

> No matter what profession it may be, the common law does not impose on those who practice it any liability for damage resulting from what … turn out to be errors of judgment, unless the error was such as no reasonably well informed and competent member of that profession could have made it.

It can be argued from the cases that the degree of skill and the duty of care imposed on pilots are high and perhaps higher than that imposed on many other professions. As such, it can be said that it would be easier to find a pilot negligent for even the slightest degree of error than it would be for a slight error on the part of many other professionals. The leading statement of the duty of care owed by aircrew is found in the English case of *Taylor v Alidair Limited* (1976), which dealt with a pilot who was dismissed subsequent to an accident in which a very heavy touchdown and the collapse of the nose wheel assembly resulted in damage.[16] The court held that the pilot was not unfairly dismissed and stated:

> there are activities in which the degree of professional skill which must be required is so high and the potential consequences of the smallest departure from that high

> standard are so serious, that one failure to perform in accordance with those standards is enough to justify dismissal.
>
> **(per Bristow J., page 423)**

The matter went on to the Court of Appeal, which concurred with this statement:

> Not every error of judgment by a pilot constitutes negligence. Similarly, not every negligent act by a pilot will place the airline under a positive duty to dismiss him. But the airline may have to justify its decision not to dismiss in proceedings arising out of any accidents attributable to further errors by the same pilot.[17]

In an Australian case concerning the standard of care expected of a pilot, Judge Mason in *Australian National Airlines Commission v The Commonwealth of Australia & Canadian Pacific Airlines* (1975) stated that the standard of care expected of a pilot is that of a reasonable pilot, which is a reasonable person with the additional qualities or skills of airmanship. He also highlighted that the pilot's responsibility increases with the number of lives under his care. Since the case above explicitly recognizes that the standard of care for a pilot includes airmanship skills, it is essential to consider the concept of airmanship briefly.

Airmanship, like seamanship, is a vague concept and cannot be easily defined (Kane and Pyne 1995).[18] It would be difficult to get any number of aviators to agree on precisely what constitutes airmanship. Airmanship can be said to comprise training, human and operational factors, combined into a single entity. Often operational errors and aviation mishaps, of which approximately 80% involve human error (ICAO Human Factors Training Manual 1998),[19] are frequently linked to poor airmanship.

The question that follows is whether poor airmanship in relation to the standard of professionalism required of a pilot would constitute a breach of the duty of care, thus amounting to negligence.

While pilots can demonstrate poor airmanship in certain situations, such as bending standard operating procedures and the Minimum Equipment List (MEL), it does not automatically mean they have been negligent, even though in some cases the line can be hard to define. In today's operation of advanced technology like fly-by-wire aircraft, the law recognizes that the cockpit crew cannot and is not expected to check everything personally. However, failing to check a malfunctioning piece of equipment or not obtaining necessary information could be seen as poor airmanship.

In *Hayes v United States*,[20] the court clearly stated that the ordinary rules of negligence apply to aviation accidents[21] and that for the plaintiff to succeed in a negligence claim, s/he must prove the existence of a duty of care that the defendant owed to him, that the defendant breached the duty, and that damages resulted from the breach. The court affirmed that it is a question of law whether a duty of care does exist and the extent of the duty, [22] and that it is a question of fact to be decided by the courts whether the duty was in fact breached. On the facts of this case, the Supreme Court affirmed the earlier decision, holding that the required test of negligence was met in that the FAA inspector in charge of the flight had a duty to conduct the flight examination with due regard for the safety of the aircraft and its passengers. It went on to say that this duty was breached by failing to give a pre-flight briefing, failing to stop the test after the first attempt to perform the maneuver, negligently allowing a second attempt, and that the negligence was the proximate cause of the injuries suffered by the plaintiffs/appellees. The court also held that the safety pilot had a duty to ensure the safety of the flight and that this duty was breached when he failed to stop the inspector and the flying pilot from proceeding with the second maneuvre attempt, and that this was a proximate cause of his own injuries as well as of the injuries to others.[23]

In the case of *Goldman v Thai Airways International Ltd.*,[24] the court had to decide whether the pilot had acted recklessly to determine whether the airline was entitled to limit its liability in accordance with Article 25 of the Warsaw Convention.[25] A passenger on board a Thai Airways flight from Heathrow to Bangkok with scheduled landings at Amsterdam and Karachi sued the airline for injuries suffered when the aircraft encountered turbulence. While the plaintiff wanted to fasten his seat belt, he was thrown from his seat and struck the ceiling. The plaintiff passenger was among other passengers and crew members who were also injured when thrown against the roof. The pilot landed the aircraft at Karachi, the plaintiff was given an injection and then continued his flight to Bangkok. The trial judge held that the plaintiff had successfully brought his claim under Article 25 and therefore there was no limit to the claim. With regards to the pilots alleged recklessness, the judge found that the pilot violated the specific instructions contained in the flight operator's manual which stated that the "fasten seat belts" sign should be lit during taxiing, take-off, and landing, during all flying in turbulent air and when turbulence can be expected by not illuminating the seat belt signs ten minutes before entering the specific area.[26] The judge quoted the words of Lord Diplock in *R v Caldwell*,[27] who stated:

> In my opinion, a person charged with an offfence under section 1(1) of the Criminal Damage Act 1971 is "reckless as to whether any such property would be destroyed or damaged" if (1) he does an act which creates an obvious risk that property will be destroyed or damaged and (2) when he does the act he either has not given any thought to the possibility of there being any such risk or has recognized that there was some risk involved and has nonetheless gone on to do it.

The judge found that the pilot was reckless in disregarding the safety instructions specified in the manual. With reference to the requirement "with knowledge that damage would probably result," the judge stated that "*The probability of the result must be read as qualifying the nature of the act, and if the nature of the act is to make the damage probable – I agree it is not possible, but probable--- provided the concurrent circumstances for impact or damage are there, then the probability of damage is fulfilled.*" He concluded that as the accident occurred in that particular area, it was probable that damage would almost inevitably result. As it is not required that the actual damage suffered is foreseen, only that some damage is foreseen, the pilot also satisfied this requirement. Based on the facts of the case and the law as outlined, the trial court held that the pilot was reckless for not illuminating the seat belt signs when he should have done so. On appeal, however, the court held that the plaintiff had the burden of proving that his personal injuries resulted from the Captain's reckless act or omission, with knowledge that damage would probably result. As the plaintiff had not successfully proved that the Captain knew that damage would probably result, he did not discharge this burden and did not prove that the pilot had, in fact, acted recklessly.

In the UK, the court in *Susanne Yvonne Andrews v British Airways*[28] refused to grant compensation for personal injuries incurred by a cabin crew member who was injured while on duty in an aircraft that encountered turbulence during its descent at O'Hare Airport, Chicago. As a result of severe thunderstorms, the aircraft encountered some turbulence, and the passengers and crew were required to wear their seat belts. The pilot had instructed the cabin crew to ensure the passengers had their safety belts on, but no special instruction was given to the cabin crew. The applicant thus continued her duties and was thrown around as a result of the turbulence. The District Court found that, as the severe turbulence encountered was unforeseeable due to the wind blowing from the west and the aircraft being northeast of the storm core, the Captain was not negligent in failing to instruct the crew to wear their safety belts. The question of foreseeability depended on whether the aircraft was flying downwind of the storm core. The judge accepted the evidence presented by the expert with the most recent flying experience whose opinion aligned with the published guidance. The expert stated that because the flight path was not under the anvil at a downwind position relative to the storm, there was some risk of turbulence, but it was not severe enough to require the pilot to order the crew to be seated with their seat belts fastened. Therefore, there was no risk of severe turbulence. The Court of Appeal agreed with these findings and did not grant the appeal.

For an airline to be held liable for injuries caused by turbulence, the injured passenger(s) must prove that the airline or its crew acted negligently, which includes inter alia, failing to warn passengers about anticipated turbulence, not activating the seatbelt sign when the turbulence was foreseeable, and not properly securing items that became projectiles during turbulence.

A recent case involving allegations of airline negligence during a turbulent flight is that of Singapore Airlines' Boeing 777, flight SQ321, on 21 May 2024. Flight SQ321, traveling from *London Heathrow Airport* to Singapore Changi with 211 passengers and 18 crew on board, hit severe turbulence while flying over Myanmar's Irrawaddy Basin and was forced to make an emergency landing. *One passenger died from a suspected heart attack*, and several others suffered minor and severe injuries. Passengers sued the airline for pilot negligence. They alleged that other aircraft had avoided the turbulence and changed direction, and that the pilots of flight SQ321 knowingly flew too close to a thunderstorm as it passed over the Irrawaddy Basin in Myanmar at 37,000 feet during a meal service, sending passengers, crew, and unattended items flying around the cabin. A lawyer representing many of the passengers stated that the passengers are entitled to substantial compensation and not just the expense payments the airline offered them by way of inviting passengers to apply for advance medical expense payments, with the signing of a final release. He said that "We are convinced the true facts will show there was crew responsibility for the accident and that the airline's compensation liability to passengers is therefore unlimited. Many passengers will be entitled to seven-figure compensation."[29]

Dealing with air traffic controllers, it is clear that Air Traffic Services owes a duty of care to anyone who uses or relies on the services they provide. This duty of care emanates from the legal regulations governing the provision of their services as well as from the legal relationship that the controller has with the pilot (*Yates v US* 1974).[30] A breach of this duty will give rise to an action for negligence, and the relevant government or ATC service provider will be the defendant. Generally, the tasks of ATCs relate to the safe operation of aircraft and maintaining the expeditious flow of air traffic (*Delta Airlines Inc. v US* 1977).[31] When exercising their duties, ATCs should follow the procedures outlined in official manuals, such as Doc 4444, Procedures for Air Navigation Services.[32] It should be noted that in some jurisdictions, such manuals and the regulations contained therein carry the weight of the law. Not every breach of the official procedure automatically constitutes negligence, nor will strict compliance automatically preclude negligence, as in some cases, it may be reasonably expected of the ATC to do more than the minimum officially stipulated.

The duty of care owed by controllers has been described as taking reasonable care to provide all necessary instructions and advice to promote the safety of aircraft within their area of responsibility (*Nicole v Simmonds* 1975).[33] ATCs owe this duty to all aircraft that may be within the zone being controlled. As is often the case, there are many aircraft within that zone at a given time, and as such, the controller must share his time according to the needs of the moment. An example can be provided by the case of *Coatney v Berkshire* (1974),[34] where the court said that a controller cannot be expected to check upon the pilot's full compliance when other aircraft call upon his attention.

This duty of care arises because the proximity or closeness of controllers and pilots is determined by the degree of reliance existing in the relationship; in other words, pilots are reliant upon the acts, advice, or information provided by controllers. The difficulty, which often creates great confusion in establishing the legal liability of each party, is differentiating the respective responsibilities of pilots and controllers. Hopkin (1995)[35] offers a clarification by stating that the pilot is legally responsible for the safety of the aircraft and its passengers, whereas the controller is legally responsible for the safety of the air traffic control instructions.

The three main categories of duty that a Controller has, that if breached, can lead to potential liability, can be described as:

(1) a duty to provide information that is accurate and not misleading;
(2) a duty to warn of known dangers; and
(3) a duty to warn of potential dangers (Bartsch 1996).

ICAO Doc 4444 (PANS-RAC 1996), supplemented by each country's legal enactments and the local procedures of each country's air traffic control system, creates the proper manner in which to conduct ATC communication. The corresponding legal duty imposed on pilots to conform and comply with the relevant legislation, regulations, procedures, and training regarding ATC creates a safe flying environment.

Additionally, a special relationship of trust is established, and it is assumed that each party will adhere to the relevant procedures and fulfill their individual duties. However, when there is reasonable cause that makes it evident that either the controller or the pilot is not conforming to his/her duties, then this relationship of trust should no longer be assumed.

A controller using non-standard phraseologies and words may be faced with legal action against him if an accident results from consequent miscommunication. If a controller knowingly violates safe operating procedures, he will be more culpable as this may increase both the likelihood of inducing an error and the chances of serious consequences resulting therefrom.

An example to illustrate possible miscommunication is that of a Canadian Pacific Douglas DC-8, which had landed at Sydney's Kingsford-Smith Airport in 1971.[36] The pilot requested permission to backtrack along Runway 16, and the air traffic controller gave the instruction "take taxiway right." The pilot mistook that for "you can backtrack if you like." In the resulting confusion, a Trans Australian Airlines (TAA) Boeing 727 was cleared for take-off on the same runway. Due to a lump in the runway, the TAA crew was unable to see the DC-8. The fin and rudder of the DC-8 were torn off in the collision with the airborne B727's belly, but there were no fatalities. The High Court found that both defendants, the controllers and the Canadian Pacific crew, were negligent, with contributory negligence on the part of the TAA crew. Justice Mason referred to the failure of the air traffic controller to keep a proper lookout and for issuing a clearance for immediate take-off without maintaining adequate visual and radio observations as being "a serious departure from the standards of a reasonable man" (Bartch 1996).[37]

The case clearly demonstrated that an air traffic controller might be held negligent if he or she provides misleading information upon which the pilot relies that subsequently causes damage. It also showed that pilots are not relieved of responsibility to maintain situational awareness by gathering information from their own eyes, ears, and instruments. The Canadian Pacific crew was found to be negligent for, inter alia, not paying attention to the controller's instruction, not querying or seeking confirmation of that instruction, and failing to call the surface movements controller promptly after receiving the instruction to do so (Boughen 1994).[38]

The second duty that can give rise to possible legal liability, if breached, is the duty of the controller to warn pilots of known dangers. This could include the duty to provide information regarding, inter alia, midair collision, wake turbulence, and weather-related hazards. The controller's duty to warn of a potential midair collision depends on the controller's and the pilot's knowledge of the traffic situation. Controllers owe a duty of care to pilots and passengers, even when pilots are generally responsible for their own separation. Furthermore, if a controller issues a late warning, this does not absolve the controller of liability, as warnings must be both timely and adequate to alert the pilot to the extent and severity of the potential danger (*Nicole v Simmonds* 1975). Justice Wallace of the Australian Supreme Court stated:

> In my view, where there is a duty to submit and obey, there is a corresponding duty to, inter alia, warn of danger within the limits of practicability in the performance of the controller's duty and having regard to circumstances prevailing in each particular case.
> **(Page 655)**

In some instances, the Controller may have an additional duty beyond that prescribed by the ATC manual (*Hartz v United States* 1965)[39] where improper phraseology was used in a warning given to the pilot of a Beechcraft Bonanza about a departing Douglas DC-7. The court found that the controller's warning of "prop-wash" (instead of "wake turbulence") was insufficient to adequately warn the pilot of the degree of hazard created by the DC-7 and that the controller had an additional duty, beyond that prescribed by the ATC manual, to delay the take-off clearance of the Bonanza for as long as reasonably necessary to permit the DC-7's turbulence to dissipate.

In March 2025, the Swiss Second Military Court of Appeals found an air traffic controller guilty of negligent homicide after a fatal F/A-18 military jet accident in Switzerland on 29 August 2016. The Appeals Court upheld the verdicts of the lower court over eight and a half years after the accident in which the pilot was killed when his military jet collided with the mountainside of Hinter Tierberg during a training flight after take-off from Meiringen. The lower court found him guilty on the grounds that he had not informed the pilot that he was flying too low, and sentenced him to a suspended fine of CHF11,400 ($12,900). Both the air traffic controller and the prosecutor had appealed that sentence. The Appeals Court presiding judge stated that if the air traffic controller had ordered the specified minimum flight altitude of 15,000 feet instead of the incorrect 10,000 feet, the collision with the mountain would not have occurred, and that he could have corrected the order later. He said that it was the air traffic controller's radio message that triggered the maneuver and the collision. He went on to say that the radio message was an instruction and that the pilot could have trusted it. The court did, however, acknowledge that there had been a "chain of unfortunate circumstances," including "the stressful situation, the level of training, and the over 60-year-old radar in Meiringen." The Second Military Court of Appeals upheld the acquittal of the second fighter pilot, who was acquitted of the charge of negligent homicide by a first court of appeals in early 2024. The Second Military Court of Appeals found that, although he had not complied with all the regulations regarding his flight on short notice, he had corrected the deviations.[40]

A recent midair collision, the deadliest in the US since 2001, occurred on 29 January 2025. American Eagle Flight 5342, a Bombardier CRJ-701ER operated by PSA Airlines, took off from Wichita, Kansas, with 60 passengers and 4 crew members. At approximately 9:00 p.m. Eastern Time, the aircraft collided in midair with a US Army Sikorsky UH-60 Black Hawk helicopter (PAT 25), carrying three soldiers, and crashed into the Potomac River near Washington-Ronald Reagan National Airport, DC. There were no survivors. Both American Eagle and PSA Airlines are subsidiaries of American Airlines. The Black Hawk, which was on a training flight, was flying at low altitude over the Potomac River from north to south while on a combined annual and night vision goggle check ride for the pilot flying. It is believed that the crew were wearing their night vision goggles at the time of the accident.[41]

It is noteworthy that the ATC tower communicated simultaneously on two VHF frequencies, and that the PAT 25 and the CRJ700 were communicating separately on one of those frequencies. They could both hear the tower, and vice versa, but the CRJ700 and the helicopter could not hear each other's communication. The NTSB Chairwoman Jennifer Homendy told reporters that the recording from the UH-60 Black Hawk helicopter cockpit suggested an incomplete radio transmission may have left the crew without understanding how it should shift position seconds before the crash. "That transmission was interrupted, it was stepped on," she said, leaving them unable to hear the words "pass behind the" because the helicopter's microphone key was pressed at the exact moment.[42]

The NTSB's 14 February press briefing, which provided preliminary information obtained from aircraft data and voice recorders and air traffic control sources, states:

> The last radio altitude recorded for the CRJ was 313 ft and was recorded two seconds prior to the collision. The CRJ pitch at this time was, again, 9 degrees nose up, and roll was 11 degrees left wing down. The CRJ was descending at 448 feet per minute.
>
> The radio altitude of the Blackhawk at the time of the collision was 278 feet and had been steady for the previous 5 seconds. The Blackhawk pitch at the time of the crash was about a half degree nose up with a left roll of 1.6 degrees. Examination of wreckage will assist in determination of the exact angle of the collision.
>
> We are confident that the radio altitude of the Black Hawk at the time of the collision was 278 feet. I want to caution that this does not mean this is what the Black Hawk crew was seeing on the barometric altimeters in the cockpit.
>
> We are seeing conflicting information in the data, which is why we aren't releasing altitude for the Blackhawk's route.[43]

ATCs have a duty to pass on information to pilots when it is available to them. Liability could arise if the information was inaccurate, incomplete, or provided too late. The question then is what duty a controller has regarding information that they should have had but did not obtain or pursue. When establishing the individual liability of a controller or pilot, it is important to determine which party was better positioned to evaluate the situation. If the controller should have known such information but did not acquire it, and if the information could have been obtained through other means by a pilot exercising due care, it may be possible for the controller to avoid liability if the lack of information by the controller was not the primary cause of the resulting accident or was not one of the events that caused the accident or serious incident.

In *Kack v United States*[44] a student pilot claimed damages against the United States for negligent conduct of the air traffic controllers on the basis that the controllers, (employees of the Federal Aviation Administration), failed to: provide him with adequate and timely notice of the existence of wake turbulence that caused his accident while he tried to land the aircraft; provide adequate separation between his aircraft and the aircraft landing before him that caused wake turbulence; and warn him of his dangerously low altitude in relation to the wake turbulence hazard that was created by the other aircraft. The District Court denied the plaintiff's claim and held: Controllers do have the duty to warn pilots of the existence of wake turbulence and that the controller had given a warning that would have been timely if the plaintiff was not negligent in failing to maintain the proper altitude; the controllers did not fail to provide adequate space between the two aircraft, and that if the plaintiff had maintained a proper altitude the accident would have been avoided; the controllers had no special duty to warn the plaintiff of his precariously low altitude as the plaintiff, even as a student pilot, had the primary responsibility for the safe operation of his aircraft.[45] The Appeal Court, affirming the decision of the lower court, stated that the court had correctly held that the pilot has the primary responsibility to see and avoid the hazard of wake turbulence and that the law is clear that under Visual Flight Rule conditions, the primary responsibility for the safe operation of the aircraft rests with the pilot, irrespective of the traffic clearance. The Appeal Court affirmed that traffic controllers do have some duty of care toward pilots and the aircraft they direct, and that in some situations this duty may be violated. Still, the facts of the case did not present such a situation, and therefore, the accident did not occur as a result of the controller's breach of their duty, but as a result of the plaintiff's negligence.

The general principles of negligence law and civil liability were outlined; however, a deeper examination is required into the principles of criminal liability. This can include prosecuting aviation professionals or organizations for violations of relevant regulations, provisions, and other aviation legislation, or the more serious criminal offense of manslaughter if negligent acts or omissions resulted in death.

All aviation professionals and aviation organizations should be aware of the increased risk of facing criminal liability for failing to exercise their duties and responsibilities in accordance with the standard of care required by the law.

In the words of an Administrative Law Judge in the case of *FAA v NTSB* (1999).[46]

> [A]viation is....particularly unforgiving of carelessness or neglect.

2.3 CRIMINAL NEGLIGENCE

Aviation professionals can be criminally prosecuted for their negligent, albeit unintentional acts or omissions, as is evidenced by the case of *People v Crossan* in 1927,[47] which is the first reported case of the prosecution of an aviator in which the defendant was convicted of involuntary manslaughter when the aircraft he operated struck and killed two girls.

Article 12 of the Chicago Convention, which deals with the Rules of Air, states:

> Rules of the Air: Each contracting State undertakes to adopt measures to ensure that every aircraft flying over or maneuvering within its territory and that every aircraft carrying its nationality mark, wherever such aircraft may be, shall comply with the rules and regulations relating to the flight and maneuver of an aircraft there in force. Each contracting State undertakes to keep its regulations in these respects uniform, to the greatest possible extent, with those established from time to time under this Convention. Over the high seas, the rules in force shall be those established under this Convention. Each contracting State undertakes to ensure the prosecution of all persons violating the regulations applicable.

It is therefore clearly stated that the provisions establishing criminal liability are set out in the domestic legislation of each contracting party, which differs from state to state. For example, pilots and ATCs can be criminally liable for contravening, permitting the contravention of, or for noncompliance with the relevant Air Navigation Orders (ANO) and Rules of Air. In accordance with the Air Navigation Orders, criminal liability may also be imposed on any person who endangers an aircraft, persons, or property in the air or on the ground. For example, the Cyprus Civil Aviation Law 2001[48] outlines specific offenses related to endangering the aircraft or its passengers, including those arising from negligence, and results in both criminal and administrative sanctions.

The UK Air Navigation Order 2009[49] states that criminal charges may be filed if a person: recklessly or negligently acts in a manner likely to endanger an aircraft, or any person therein, and on conviction on indictment will be liable to a fine or imprisonment of a maximum of five years; recklessly or negligently causes or permits an aircraft to endanger any person or property, or enters an aircraft when drunk or to be drunk on an aircraft and on conviction on indictment for both these offenses will be liable to a fine or imprisonment of up to two years; or smokes on board an aircraft when smoking is forbidden. The more recent Air Navigation Order 2016[50] has similar provisions in sections 240–243. It also includes two other important provisions: section 244, which states that persons on board the aircraft must obey the pilot's lawful safety and security commands; and section 245, which deals with acting in a disruptive manner and unruly passengers.

A pilot who acts below the standard required of him may be negligent and held accountable for violating the ANO, the Rules of Air, and/or the endangering offenses. However, in nearly all the cases where aviation accidents or serious incidents involve the loss of life, aviation professionals have found themselves charged with various offenses such as, inter alia, involuntary homicide, involuntary manslaughter, professional negligence, interruption of air traffic, and face criminal prosecution.

2.3.1 Criminal Negligence

Generally, however, a person may not be convicted of a crime unless the prosecution has proved beyond a reasonable doubt firstly, that the accused caused a particular act and that he is responsible for that act which is forbidden by criminal law, namely the *actus reus* (conduct, circumstances, consequences), and secondly, that the accused had a defined state of mind in causing that act, namely the *mens rea* (intention, recklessness, or negligence) (Smith and Hogan 2002).[51]

Criminal negligence is defined differently by the laws of each country; however, it can be said that certain elements of this offense are common, viz, that the actor does not comprehend the consequences of his behavior and is unaware of the risk he creates, or that he is aware of the risk, but chooses to ignore it.

In Canada, for example, according to the Penal Code (amended in January 2025)[52] offenses are separated into causing death by criminal negligence, causing bodily harm by criminal negligence, and homicide, namely, directly or indirectly, by any means, causing the death of a human being, which may take the form of culpable and non-culpable homicide. Culpable homicide can be murder or manslaughter, and is committed when a person causes the death of a human being by, inter alia, means of an unlawful act and by criminal negligence.[53] Criminal negligence is defined as doing anything, or omitting to do anything, that it is his legal duty to do, showing wanton or reckless disregard for the lives or safety of other persons.[54] To prove that the defendant showed a wanton or reckless disregard for the lives or safety of others, the prosecution must prove beyond a reasonable doubt that (a) the defendant's conduct showed a marked departure from the conduct of a reasonable person in the circumstances; and (b) that a reasonable person in the same circumstances would have foreseen that this conduct posed a risk of bodily harm, which is defined as any hurt or injury that interferes with a person's health or comfort and is more than brief or minor. The defendant's individual characteristics are not taken into account when determining what a reasonable person would have done or foreseen. The 2025 amendment provides that a person who is found guilty of causing bodily harm to another person by criminal negligence is guilty of a) an indictable offence and liable to imprisonment for a term of not more than 10 years; or (b) an offence punishable on summary conviction.[55]

A general outline of some relevant categories provided in the German Penal Code[56] is as follows: Homicide, which carries a prison sentence of 10 to 20 years; qualified homicide, 15 to 25 years; extremely grave homicide, 15 to 25 years or life imprisonment; infanticide, 2 to 7 years, and negligent or accidental homicide. A killing that is not a murder may be either manslaughter (*Totschlag*) or negligent homicide (*fahrlässige Tötung*). Negligent or accidental homicide has the following aggravating circumstances: (a) caused by a professional in connection with his job (2 to 7 years); (b) by a vehicle driver with blood alcohol concentration above the legal limits or who is in a drunken state (5 to 15 years); (c) by a professional in a drunken state in connection with his job duties (five to 15 years); and (e) when causing the death of two or more persons (5 to 15 years).

The French Penal Code[57] categorizes offenses according to their seriousness as felonies, misdemeanors, or petty offenses. Article 121-3[58] states that there is no felony or misdemeanor in the absence of an intent to commit it and that the deliberate endangering of others is a misdemeanor where the law so provides. It goes on to provide that a misdemeanor also exists, where the law so provides, in cases of recklessness, negligence, or failure to observe an obligation of due care or precaution imposed by any statute or regulation, where it is established that the offender has failed to show standard diligence, taking into consideration, where appropriate, the nature of his role or functions, his capacities and powers and the means then available to him. In such cases, natural persons who have not directly contributed to causing the damage but who have created or contributed to creating the situation that allowed the damage to happen, and who have failed to take steps to prevent it, are criminally liable. It must be shown that they have broken a duty of care or precaution laid down by statute or regulation in a manifestly deliberate manner or have committed a specified piece of misconduct which exposed another person to a particularly serious risk of which they must have been aware.

The Penal Code further provides that causing the death of another person by clumsiness, rashness, inattention, negligence, or breach of an obligation of safety or prudence imposed by statute or regulations, in such circumstances, constitutes manslaughter, punished by three years' imprisonment and a fine of €45,000. In cases of a deliberate violation of an obligation of safety or prudence imposed by statute or regulations, the penalty is increased to five years' imprisonment and a fine of €75,000.[59] In addition, Article 221-7 provides that a legal person may incur criminal liability in such circumstances.

The Code also creates the offense of endangering other persons.[60] In particular, it provides that the direct exposure of another person to an immediate risk of death or injury likely to cause mutilation or permanent disability, by the manifestly deliberate violation of a specific obligation of safety or prudence imposed by any statute or regulation, is punished by one year's imprisonment and a fine of €15,000.[61] A legal person may also incur such criminal liability.[62]

In Taiwan, Article 276 of the Criminal Code specifies that:

(1):A person who negligently kills another shall be punished with imprisonment for not more than two years, detention, or a fine of not more than 2,000 yuan.
(2) A person who, in the performance of his occupation, commits an offense specified in the preceding paragraph by neglecting the degree of care required by such occupation shall be punished with imprisonment for not more than five years. In addition, a fine of not more than 3,000 yuan may be imposed.

Article 284 states that:

(1):A person who negligently causes bodily harm to another shall be punished with imprisonment for not more than six months, detention, or a fine of not more than 1,000 yuan; if serious bodily harm results, he shall be punished with imprisonment for not more than one year, detention, or a fine of not more than 500 yuan.
(2) A person who, in the performance of his occupation, causes bodily harm to another by neglecting the degree of care required by such occupation shall be punished with imprisonment of not more than one year, detention, or a fine of not more than 1,000 yuan. If serious bodily harm results, he shall be punished with imprisonment of not more than three years, detention, or a fine of not more than 2,000 yuan.[63]

It is noteworthy that, according to Article 276, if criminal negligence causes the death of more than one person, the maximum penalty to be imposed is five years. Several recent cases involving a negligent act caused multiple fatalities and injuries, resulting in public outcry that the punishment is not commensurate with the crime. As a result, several amendments to the law were proposed on multiple occasions. One of the amendments suggested after, inter alia, a man was charged in the Taroko Express accident killing 49 and injuring 213 people in 2021 and was sentenced to only five years in prison, was to increase the punishment for those who cause the death of three or more people due to gross negligence. Further attempts to amend the law were made after a fire at a golf ball factory owned by a manufacturing company in Pingtung County killed nine and injured over 100 people in 2023. In 2024, a 15-year-old illegally drove his grandfather's sports utility vehicle and crashed into a roadside eatery, killing three and injuring two people.[64] In November 2023, the following draft amendment to Article 276 of the Criminal Code, to increase the penalty for negligent homicide, was announced:

> Those who commit the crime in the preceding paragraph, depending on the severity of the circumstances and consequences, shall be sentenced to a minimum of one year or a maximum of seven years in prison. If the circumstances are serious and more than three people are killed as a result, they shall be sentenced to prison for a minimum of three years or a maximum of 10.[65]

The bill to amend the Criminal Code passed a third reading in the Legislative in May 2024.[66]

Provisions in the Italian Penal Code (*Codice Penale)* provide that manslaughter occurs when death is caused by fault, i.e., when death is not intended but has occurred. Involuntary manslaughter is governed by Article 589 of the Italian Penal Code,[67] which states that it is a crime to cause the death of a person by negligence, imprudence, or malpractice. The penalty varies depending on the specific circumstances. Generally, it consists of imprisonment ranging from six months to five years. However, the code provides for specific aggravating factors that can increase the penalty, such as in cases of violations of traffic or workplace safety regulations. If the same act causes more than one death, the multiple counts can be added up to 12 years in prison.[68]

Although the classifications and details may vary between them, generally, criminal penalties are imposed for negligent or reckless conduct that leads to injury or death.

2.3.2 Manslaughter

Despite the differences in the criminal law of each country, there are generally three common levels of criminal charges:

(1) "Criminal negligence," or "unintentional/involuntary manslaughter" alleges the creation of a risk to others' lives and that the risk had foreseeable consequences. The person may recognize the danger that their act or omission creates, but fails to do anything about it.
(2) "Manslaughter" alleges the defendant knows that the risk of his or her actions may result in death for others, ignores the risk, and continues the behavior anyway.

(3) "Third degree murder," which applies to the US, holds the defendant responsible for causing the death of another while the defendant was committing another felony.

Generally, there are three forms of unlawful homicide: murder, voluntary manslaughter, and involuntary manslaughter. The state of mind of the defendant at the time of committing the act determines the type of homicide.

For murder, the mens rea is malice aforethought, meaning either an intention to kill or an intention to inflict grievous bodily harm. It is generally assumed that in aviation accidents, excluding terrorism, no one will have the necessary intention to kill or cause grievous bodily harm (although under UK law (*R v Woolin*),[69] where a person foresees death or grievous bodily harm as a virtually certain consequence of his actions, a jury is free to find intention that would suffice for a murder conviction). Therefore, a discussion on manslaughter is more relevant.

Unlawful and dangerous manslaughter occurs where one sets out to commit a less serious offense but kills a person in the process. In this particular offense, death must be caused by an act, not an omission, the defendant must have acted dangerously, and the unlawful and dangerous act must have caused the death of another. The mens rea is the mental element of the crime constituting the unlawful act, and can be either intention or recklessness, depending on the definition of the particular offense. To amount to constructive manslaughter, the defendant must firstly commit an unlawful act amounting to a criminal offense and have the mens rea of intention or recklessness;[70] secondly, the act must be dangerous. This is objectively judged,[71] the defendant need not be aware that the act is dangerous,[72] and the act need not be directed at the victim.[73] Thirdly, the act must cause the death of the victim.

Criminal negligence occurs when the defendant recognizes the danger that their act or omission creates but fails to take any action to prevent it. Criminal negligence becomes gross negligence when a failure to foresee involves a wanton disregard for human life. Gross negligence, which is the test for manslaughter, has been described as follows:[74] *In explaining to juries the test which they should apply to determine whether the negligence, in the particular case, amounted or did not amount to a crime, ... to establish criminal liability the facts must be such that, in the opinion of the jury, the negligence of the accused went beyond a mere matter of compensation between subjects and showed such disregard for the life and safety of others as to amount to a crime against the State and conduct deserving punishment.*

Gross negligence, which may take the form of an act or omission, is therefore a failure to exercise a reasonable level of precaution, and the defendant may be found guilty if he fails to meet the standard of care expected from a reasonable person of the same profession. To be found guilty, the prosecution must prove that the defendant owed a duty of care to the deceased; the defendant breached this duty; the breach caused the death; and the defendant's negligence was gross, meaning it demonstrated such a disregard for the life and safety of others that it amounted to a crime and deserved punishment.[75]

For gross negligent manslaughter to arise, the jury must be satisfied that the accused has satisfied the degree of fault required for manslaughter, as was stated in the case of *Adomako* (1995)[76] namely: "*whether, having regard to the risk of death involved, the conduct of the defendant was so bad as in all the circumstances as to amount in [the jury's] judgment to a criminal act or omission*"

The elements for this offense are a duty of care, which has the same meaning as that in civil law, and the breach of that duty by the defendant. The basic test for gross negligence is an objective one, where it is questioned whether the defendant's conduct has fallen below the standards of a reasonable man. The courts will therefore examine the defendant's thoughts, a reasonable person's thoughts, and the defendant's acts or omissions.

It was made clear in the *Adomako* case that to be guilty of gross negligence manslaughter, there has to be a risk of death.

Several recent cases are discussed below to illustrate how the courts in various jurisdictions apply the above legal principles to individuals charged with criminal offenses after an aviation accident and/or violations of aviation rules and procedures.

2.4 RECENT CASES

2.4.1 UK – Loss of Communications Triggering a Security Alert

In March 2025, in the first prosecution for such an incident, a pilot was criminally prosecuted for failing to maintain radio communication with air traffic control during a flight from Oslo to Manchester in February 2024. Air traffic control provider, NATS, reported that the aircraft with fifty-eight passengers on board had no communication with the Hollands ATC for over half an hour. This triggered a Quick Reaction Alert (QRA), a response to threats such as unresponsive aircraft or suspected hijackings. Two RAF Eurofighter Typhoons intercepted the passenger jet over the North Sea, communications were soon re-established, and they escorted the A320Neo aircraft to Manchester airport to land at a remote stand.[77]

Following an investigation by the UK's Civil Aviation Authority (CAA), the pilot was charged in the Manchester Magistrates' Court with violating Article 265(7) of The Air Navigation Order 2016, and the Standardized European Rules of the Air (SERA.8035),[78] which states that:

"An aircraft operated as a controlled flight shall maintain continuous air-ground voice communication watch on the appropriate communication channel of, and establish two-way communication as necessary with, the appropriate air traffic control unit."

Pilots who fail to do so can be prosecuted and sentenced to a fine and/or a prison term of up to two years. The pilot pleaded guilty and was sentenced to a fine of £4,511.[79]

The CAA's head of flight operations said in a statement, "We continue to work with pilots, airlines, and the Government to reduce similar incidents, including by prosecuting offenders when appropriate to maintain confidence in UK aviation's safety and security."[80]

2.4.2 New Zealand – Recklessly Engaging in Conduct with a Risk of Death or Serious Injury

In New Zealand, a pilot who was flying a Robinson 22 helicopter with his business partner on board was prosecuted under the Health and Safety at Work Act (HSWA) 2015[81] after the helicopter crashed on 30 April 2016, near Lindis Pass, New Zealand. In this, the first case where someone was prosecuted as an "officer" under the HSWA, he was found guilty of engaging in conduct that recklessly exposed a person to the risk of serious injury or death under s 47 of the HSWA by the Queenstown District Court in 2019. He was convicted of two of the five charges, namely:

(1) that as an officer of the company, AgWorks, the earthmoving business he co-owned with his partner, who died in the accident, and
(2) as a worker of that business, he, without reasonable excuse, engaged in conduct that exposed the deceased to the risk of death or serious injury, and was reckless as to that.

The pilot appealed both convictions, and the Civil Aviation Authority appealed the amount of damages awarded as consequential losses for the victim's family. In December 2020, the High Court dismissed both appeals.

The decision of the High Court provides the authority regarding the following important points under the Health & Safety at Work Act 2015, namely, the liability of "officers" of a person conducting a business or undertaking (PCBU); when a person is "at work" for the HSWA; clarification of the elements of the "recklessness" offense (s 47 of the HSWA); and, the correct calculation of reparation for consequential loss for family members of the victim of a fatal workplace incident.

Relevant to our discussion is the following analysis regarding two key points: the clarification of the elements of the offense of "recklessness" under s47 and the liability of "officers" of a person conducting a business or undertaking under the HSWA.

2.4.2.1 The Elements of Recklessness

Under the HSWA, reckless conduct in respect of a duty imposed by the Act is the most serious health and safety offense. The offense of recklessness under s47 of the Act carries a maximum sentence of:

(a) five years imprisonment or a fine not exceeding $300,000 (or both) for an individual who is not a PCBU or an officer of a PCBU;
(b) five years imprisonment or a fine not exceeding $600,000 (or both) for an individual who is a PCBU or an officer of a PCBU; and
(c) a fine not exceeding $3 million for any other person (including a company).

The District Court stated that the offense of recklessness under the HSWA includes the following elements:[82]

(a) the defendant must have a duty under subpart 2 or 3 of part 2 of the Act (in this case, as an officer or, in the alternative, as a worker);
(b) the defendant must engage in conduct that exposes an individual to whom that duty was owed to a risk of death or serious injury;
(c) there was no reasonable excuse for such conduct; and
(d) the defendant was reckless as to the risk to an individual of death or serious injury.

The court went on to state that recklessness has both a subjective and objective element and that for the prosecution to prove that the defendant was reckless, it must show that:

(a) The defendant recognized there was a real possibility that:
  (i) their actions would bring about the proscribed result; and/or
  (ii) that the proscribed circumstances existed; and

(b) Considering that risk, those actions were unreasonable.

The first ground of the pilot's appeal centered upon the elements of the offense, namely, whether failure to comply with a duty imposed by the HSWA was a necessary element of the recklessness offense under s 47 of the Act. The pilot argued that the trial court did not consider this element of the offense and that, as he had complied with his duty as an officer of the PCBU, he could not have been found guilty of that charge.

In December 2020, the High Court[83] dismissed the appeal. It clarified that failing to comply with a duty imposed by the HSWA is an implicit element of the offense and approved the District Court's explanation of the remaining elements.

There are three levels of offenses under the heading "[o]ffences relating to duties" are set out in HSWA in subpart 4 of part 2, ranging in seriousness as follows: S 47 is the most serious offense and has an element of recklessness as to the risk of death or serious injury; s 48 adds the aggravating aspect of the failure exposing a person to the risk of death or serious injury; and the least serious is outlined in s 49, which only requires proof of a person being subject to a duty and the failure to comply. It was agreed in the appeal that s 47 does not state that to be found guilty of the offense, a defendant must have failed to comply with the identified duty imposed on them by the HSWA. The pilot argued in his appeal that proof that he failed to comply with a relevant duty imposed on him by the HSWA was an essential element of the charge. The High Court agreed that to be found guilty of a charge under s 47, the defendant must have failed to comply with a duty which they owed under subpart 2 or 3 of part 2 of the HSWA. The Court stated that the element was "implicit in the words of s 47(1) (b) that require the person to have engaged in conduct that exposes an individual to whom 'that duty' is owed to a risk of death or serious injury" and the Court could not foresee a circumstance where someone having a duty could engage in conduct which knowingly exposes another person to the risk of death or serious injury without breaching their duties under HSWA. In other words, if a person having a duty under the HSWA recklessly and without excuse, by their conduct, exposes the person to whom they have that duty to a risk of death or serious harm, they will necessarily have breached their duty. The High Court held that the pilot failed to comply with the identified duty under the HSWA, dismissed his appeal on this ground, and upheld his conviction.[84]

The second ground of appeal was with regard to the scope of the duties imposed by the HSWA on "officers"[85]. The High Court rejected the pilots' argument that the duties imposed on officers by the HSWA are limited to obligations of governance and clarified what duty of due diligence is imposed on "officers" of a PCBU. The High Court held that due diligence depends on the nature of the PCBU and the role the officer occupies and is not limited to obligations of governance.

One of the aims of the HSWA is to "protect workers and other persons against harm to their health, safety, and welfare by eliminating or minimizing risks arising from work or prescribed high-risk plant, and to do so, it imposes specific duties on a PCBU. Referring to the primary duty of care of a PCBU, s36 (1)[86] stipulates:

> A PCBU must ensure, so far as is reasonably practicable, the health and safety of—
> (a) workers who work for the PCBU, while the workers are at work in the business or undertaking; and (b) workers whose activities in carrying out work are influenced or directed by the PCBU, while the workers are carrying out the work

The court went on to say that an officer of a PCBU must exercise due diligence to ensure that the PCBU complies with that duty or obligation and that due diligence includes:[87]

(a) to acquire and keep up to date, knowledge of work health and safety matters; and
(b) to gain an understanding of the nature of the operations of the business or undertaking of the PCBU and generally of the hazards and risks associated with those operations; and
(c) to ensure that the PCBU has available for use, and uses, appropriate resources and processes to eliminate or minimize risks to health and safety from work carried out as part of the conduct of the business or undertaking; and
(d) to ensure that the PCBU has appropriate processes for receiving and considering information regarding incidents, hazards, and risks and for responding in a timely way to that information; and
(e) to ensure that the PCBU has, and implements, processes for complying with any duty or obligation of the PCBU under this Act; and
(f) to verify the provision and use of the resources and processes referred to in paragraphs (c) to (e).

In exercising due diligence, an officer is required to exercise the care, diligence, and skill that a reasonable officer would exercise in the same circumstances, taking into account (without limitation) the nature of the business or undertaking and the position of the officer and the nature of their responsibilities.

An officer is defined in s18.[88] The definition differs according to the nature of the PCBU.

If the PCBU is a:

i. company, it means any person occupying the position of a director of the company (by whatever name called).
ii. partnership (other than a limited partnership), it means any partner
iii. limited partnership, it means any general partner; and
iv. body corporate or an unincorporated body (other than a company, partnership, or limited partnership), it means any person occupying a position in the body that is comparable with that of a director of a company.[89]

The definition includes "any other person occupying a position in relation to the business or undertaking that allows the person to exercise significant influence over the management of the business or undertaking (for example, a chief executive) and excludes a Minister of the Crown acting in that capacity; and anybody who only advises or makes recommendations to a person referred to in paragraph (a) or (b)." [90]

In this case, the pilot was an officer, as per point (b) above, since he was in a partnership. He argued that the duties imposed on officers by the HSWA were limited to governance obligations – that is, that the duty of an officer to ensure the PCBU complies with its obligations is confined to functions of governance or directorial oversight. The High Court disagreed, noting that because the Act includes governance-type obligations as part of due diligence, it is clear that due diligence extends to officers who are removed from the day-to-day operations of a PCBUs business. The court also stated that directors of a large company may have a supervisory or oversight role that limits their due diligence duties to governance-related responsibilities. However, this is not necessarily the case for smaller companies, where officers are more likely to be directly involved in the daily activities of the PCBU. As a result, their activities can have immediate health and safety implications. Therefore, if an officer engaged in operational conduct fails to exercise due diligence and endangers workers' health and safety, they could face prosecution. Additionally, being prosecuted in their capacity as workers does not alter their duties and obligations as officers.

It can be said that by depicting due diligence in taking reasonable steps, the court intended to extend the responsibility to ensure health and safety to those who are at the head of large organizations. As the due diligence duty depends on "the nature of the business or undertaking; and the position of the officer and the nature of the responsibilities undertaken by the officer," "the obligation of due diligence on officers will apply across a spectrum of PCBUs, and is designed to apply to a wide range of businesses and organizations, small and large, with both flat and hierarchical structures."[91]

The High Court's ruling provides significant clarity on the responsibilities of "officers" under the HSWA. The responsibilities are not confined only to governance-related duties and can include a broad spectrum of actions. In certain circumstances, the obligation of "due diligence" can extend to the measures an officer undertakes in the daily operations of the PCBU's activities. This decision underscores the importance of context. Officers should therefore thoroughly assess their specific role within a PCBU and the influence they can exert on managing hazards and risks tied to its operations, as neglecting to fulfill the resulting due diligence responsibilities adequately could lead to prosecution.[92]

2.4.3 USA – Involuntary Manslaughter

On 28 September 2022, a single-engine Piper PA-28 with a flight instructor and a student onboard was destroyed in an accident near Allentown, Pennsylvania. According to the NTSB report, after a pre-flight inspection and pre-takeoff engine run-up, the flight instructor asked the student to perform a soft-field takeoff. Shortly after takeoff, they encountered engine problems, and the flight instructor took control of the plane from the student, maintaining airspeed. He then raised the flaps and continued flying the aircraft but was still unable to climb. He noted that the airplane was approximately 200 feet above ground and approaching rising terrain, but he was unable to find a suitable area to land. The aircraft descended into trees, and soon afterward crashed and caught fire, killing the student (K.K.), initially identified as K.K., and seriously injuring the pilot.[93]

On 1 August 2024, the pilot, McPherson was indicted for involuntary manslaughter and serving as an airman without a certificate. He was arrested on 5 August and was charged with manslaughter under 18 U.S.C. § 1112, 40 counts of serving as an airman without a certificate, and illegally flying with passengers contrary to 49 U.S.C. § 46306(bX7).[94] The federal grand jury indictment filed in Allentown, Pennsylvania, Federal Court, alleged gross negligence because he was not competent to fly an aircraft as a pilot in command safely. The indictment refers to the pilot as allegedly being "such a menace in the air." The charges carry a maximum sentence of 128 years in prison and fines exceeding $10 million. He pleaded not guilty to the charges and was released on bail.[95] The indictment states that he acted intentionally, and with wanton and reckless disregard for the life of his student pilot, and that he acted without malice but with gross negligence in the commission of an act which might produce death. Referring to the requirements of causation and the legal principles of involuntary manslaughter, the indictment states that

> But for [the defendant's] intentional and grossly negligent disregard for the safety of K.K., knowing he was not competent to safely fly the aircraft as the pilot in command since he had never mastered the skills necessary to operate the aircraft safely, K.K. would not have died.[96]

Regarding counts two to forty one, the indictment states that on the dates specified

> [the defendant] knowingly and willfully served and attempted to serve as an airman without an airman's certificate authorizing him to serve in that capacity, that is, on

> each of these occasions, [defendant] flew and served as pilot-in-command of an aircraft with passengers without possessing an FAA pilot's certificate permitting him to do so.[97]

The indictment referred to an incident where an FAA safety inspector, evaluating his skills, had to grab the controls mid-flight to avoid disaster, and outlines his career path. It notes that he earned his student pilot's certificate in January 2018, and about a year later, he began trying for his full pilot's license. In December 2019, he finally qualified for his commercial pilot's certification, with an instrument rating, "[a]fter multiple failed practical exams," according to the indictment. In March 2020, he obtained his flight instructor certificate. According to the indictment, on two separate occasions, while in the air with student pilots in November 2020 and March 2021, he veered off the runway while attempting to land, avoiding serious injuries but leaving the plane "substantially damaged." "Following these accidents, the FAA received a Safety Hotline complaint about [him]" and "Based on this investigation, the [inspector] concluded that the FAA had reason to question defendants [ ] 'competence as a certificated airman' and that 'reexamination of [his] qualification to be the holder of an airman certificate' is necessary in the interest of safety."The FAA then contacted him by mail, requesting that he appear in May 2021 for a reexamination; however, he did not respond. In July, the FAA "began calling" him about taking the retest, but the indictment asserts that it took months for him to appear, and that during that time, he continued to fly and instruct students.

The indictment states that when he tried to obtain the FAA reexamination on 29 September 2021, he failed the go-around portion of his reexamination, and that "In fact, the [safety inspector] had to assume control of the aircraft that [he] was flying or the plane could have crashed." Choosing not to request a second reexamination attempt, he then surrendered his pilot's license on 7 October 2021. He was given a Temporary Airman Certificate, which permitted him only to fly solo or with an instructor. The indictment stresses that the physical certificate clearly states, "PASSENGER CARRYING PROHIBITED." His restricted temporary license expired on 8 November 2021. Despite that, he continued to give lessons through a now-defunct Pennsylvania flight school called Proflite Aero LLC until "at least" 28 September 2022, according to the indictment.

On 13 February 2025, a federal grand jury in the Eastern District of Pennsylvania returned a superseding indictment that charged the pilot, McPherson, and the company owner, Saleem, in connection with the accident and the death of the student. McPherson was charged with involuntary manslaughter, conspiracy to commit an offense against the United States, conspiracy to commit wire fraud, obstruction of an administrative proceeding, and serving as an airman without a certificate. Saleem was charged with conspiracy to commit an offense against the United States, conspiracy to commit wire fraud, and obstruction of an administrative proceeding. The superseding indictment further alleges that between October 2021 and September 2022, Saleem and McPherson conspired to provide flight instruction to students even though he did not possess an FAA pilot certificate permitting him to do so. It further stated that they allegedly communicated through text messages, agreeing to hide his check ride failure from students, and that they conspired to obstruct an administrative proceeding by submitting false affidavits to the FAA stating they were told by FAA personnel that McPherson could continue to instruct students.[98]

In addition to potential individual criminal liability, cases including the Germanwings and the Concorde accident discussed below, as well as the Air France 447 accident, the Lion Air and Ethiopian Airlines accidents involving the Boeing 737 MAX aircraft, discussed in the following chapters, have put the spotlight on the liability and accountability of corporations for the unintentional but negligent or reckless causing of death.

2.5 CORPORATE MANSLAUGHTER/HOMICIDE

Prosecuting corporations for manslaughter has been fraught with difficulties, mainly because it was necessary to demonstrate that the corporation had acted through the controlling mind of one of its agents. To convict a company of manslaughter, the prosecution had to establish that individual defendants could be held accountable for the company's actions and that they were guilty of manslaughter.

In several European countries, corporate criminal liability is not a recent development. The French penal code has provided for this since March 1994. It is stated explicitly in the Code that "Causing the death of another person by clumsiness, rashness, inattention, negligence or breach of an obligation of safety or prudence imposed by statute or regulations, [...] constitutes manslaughter"[99] and that a legal person may incur criminal liability for this offense.[100] Portugal, Spain, Norway, Finland, and Denmark have all enacted or amended existing laws to provide criminal punishments against criminally culpable corporations.[101]

In Italy, for example, in 1996, a court in Turin sentenced nine owner-managers of an asbestos factory to between seven and eight years imprisonment with a fine of $12 million compensation award after 32 employees were killed and 11 others became ill.[102]

The legal system in Germany also holds corporations criminally accountable for their actions. In 1998, two German rail managers and an engineer were charged with manslaughter and causing bodily harm through negligence for the death of 101 passengers who died in a high-speed train accident.[103]

In Australia, a company was convicted and fined £700,000 for the death of an employee who had died after crashing her go-kart into a barrier during her employment duties. However, as the company had already gone into liquidation, no one was held accountable for her death.[104]

2.5.1 United Kingdom

In English law, criminal law requires the presence of both the criminal act, the actus reus, as well as criminal intent, the mens rea. Recklessness and gross negligence are sufficient to be included within the definition of criminal intent for manslaughter, be it voluntary or involuntary manslaughter. Involuntary manslaughter occurs when there is an unlawful killing without the intent to kill someone or cause grievous bodily harm. Involuntary manslaughter can be classified as either "unlawful act" manslaughter or "gross negligence" manslaughter. Unlawful act manslaughter (or constructive manslaughter) occurs when the unlawful or criminal act of a person causes death. The act itself must be unlawful, and it must be dangerous in that it is likely, in the circumstances of the case, to cause some physical injury to another person.[105] Whether or not it is "likely" will be determined by examining whether a reasonable or sober person would foresee the risk. It should be noted that, as this offense can be committed unintentionally, it is irrelevant whether the accused knows the act is unlawful and criminal, and whether s/he realized any risk. In gross negligence manslaughter, the following elements must be proven: a duty of care owed to the victim and a breach of that duty. The breach must be characterized as gross negligence or recklessness, and the breach must have caused the death of the victim. Whether or not the accused's actions are so bad as to amount to criminal liability, in other words, to be grossly negligent, is a question of fact that the jury must decide. Being indifferent to an obvious risk, as well as being aware of such a risk, coupled with disregarding it, can amount to recklessness. Failure to recognize that the risk exists on its own will not suffice. A company cannot be charged with voluntary manslaughter or unlawful act manslaughter, but it can be found guilty of manslaughter through gross negligence or recklessness. Under common law, an organization could only be successfully prosecuted for manslaughter if the guilt of a specific company director or officer could be attributed to the company. Identifying grossly negligent or reckless conduct by a specific company director or officer who acts as the guiding mind of the company was easier in small companies, but it proved more difficult in larger, more complex organizations.

2.5.1.1 Corporate Manslaughter

Corporate manslaughter, also referred to as corporate homicide or corporate killing, is the act of a corporation or organization causing the death of a person due to its negligence, gross negligence, or a serious management failure.

The following are just a few examples of unsuccessful attempts over the years to hold corporations criminally accountable in the UK, subsequent to accidents resulting in fatalities.

The MS Herald of Free Enterprise was a passenger ferry on route to Dover, which capsized on 6 March 1987 shortly after departing from the Belgian port of Zeebrugge. The bow doors had been left open, and water flooded the car decks, resulting in the death of 192 passengers and crew. In 1987, a coroner's inquest returned the verdict of unlawful killing.[106] As a result, five company managers were charged with gross negligence manslaughter and the operating company, P&O European Ferries, with corporate manslaughter. The judge in *R v P&O Ferries* (Dover) Ltd[107] stated that a corporation that commits an act fulfilling the prerequisites for the crime of manslaughter through the controlling mind of one of its agents is indictable for the crime of manslaughter. However, the jury was instructed to find the defendants not guilty on the basis that there was insufficient evidence to prove that any of the managers had the necessary mens rea, and that mens rea could not be attributed to the company.

Other unsuccessful manslaughter prosecution cases include the 1997 Great Western Railway Southall rail disaster, in which seven people were killed. In this case, only the company was charged. The prosecution did not file charges against any of the directors or managers; the Kings Cross underground fire, which resulted in 31 deaths, the Clapham rail accident, which caused 35 fatalities, and the Paddington rail disaster in 1999, with 31 deaths.

Four corporate manslaughter prosecutions that were successful in the UK are OLL Limited (formerly Active Leisure and Learning Ltd), the first company in English legal history to be convicted of the crime of manslaughter in December 1994 after the deaths of four teenage schoolchildren in a canoeing disaster. The company was fined £60,000, and the owner of the company was sentenced to three years' imprisonment because he was directly in charge of the activity center where the children were staying. In 1996, Jackson Transport (Ossett) Limited was convicted of corporate manslaughter and fined £22,000. The company director was convicted of manslaughter following the death of an employee who inhaled chemicals[108] and was sentenced to prison for a year and fined £1500.00. In 2001, English Brothers Ltd, a construction company, was convicted of corporate manslaughter. A director was also charged with manslaughter, but after the company pleaded guilty to manslaughter, the charges were dropped. In 2003, Teglgaard Hardwood Ltd was convicted of corporate manslaughter. The director was also found guilty of manslaughter and was sentenced to 15 months' imprisonment, suspended for two years.[109]

The Corporate Manslaughter and Corporate Homicide Act 2007, which came into force on 6th April 2008 in the United Kingdom, was a landmark law introducing a new offense, as, for the first time, companies and organizations could be found guilty of corporate manslaughter as a result of serious management failures resulting in a gross breach of a duty of care. Prior to the Act, organizations could be charged with the same manslaughter charges as individuals only if the prosecution could show that a senior individual within the organization who "embodied" the company was guilty of the offense. If this 'controlling mind' was not personally guilty of gross negligence manslaughter, then the company could not be found guilty of the offense.

The offense was established largely to fill the common law gap of not effectively dealing with death resulting from corporate negligence by widening the scope of corporate criminal liability to ensure that corporations and other organizations could be held accountable for their failures which resulted in the death of their employees. Under the Act, an organization could be guilty of committing corporate manslaughter if the manner in which its operations were managed or organized, including a significant contribution by its "senior management," amounted to a gross breach of a relevant duty of care owed by the organization toward the victim, resulting in death. The main elements of the offense are that the defendant is a qualified organization; the organization owed the victim a duty of care; presence of a gross violation of the responsibility by the organization; the way in which the organization's activities are conducted and managed by its seniors; management was a key component in the violation; the grave violation of the responsibility of the organization caused or contributed to the death. The prosecution needs to be able to prove that the breach of the duty of care caused the death, and here, it needs to be shown that the violation contributed to the death more than minimally. A jury hearing a corporate manslaughter case would need to examine the company's health and safety culture and assess how its management regulations, codes of practice, and guidelines measure up against the Health and Safety at Work Act 1974 to determine whether there was a gross breach of duty by the company or gross negligence manslaughter by a senior manager.[110] In accordance with the Act, corporate manslaughter can be proven only if the management failures are committed by the senior management of the organization which, under Section 1(4) of the Act, is a person in an organization who has a significant role in the decision-making process of how to manage or organize the entire or a substantial portion of their activities or the actual management or coordination of the entire activity or the major portion thereof. It is crucial, therefore, for senior management to understand that the health and safety of employees and other individuals is an essential part of their risk management.

The Corporate Manslaughter and Corporate Homicide Act defines the crime as being caused by a "gross breach of duty of care" by the organization in the event of a person's death. It clarifies the criminal liabilities of companies, including large organizations, where serious failures in the management of health and safety have resulted in death. Under the Act, corporate bodies and organizations as legal entities, not the individuals working within them, will be prosecuted. The liability of directors, board members, or other individuals under health and safety law or general criminal law will be unaffected. In addition, both the organization and individuals can still be prosecuted for separate health and safety offenses, and individuals connected to any corporate manslaughter incidents can still be charged separately in their personal capacity. The immunity that the Crown had under the common law corporate manslaughter offense had been removed under the Act. Under the Act, it is not required to show that a person who was the organization's "control mind" was personally responsible for the crime, as now, responsibility for the offense is evaluated by considering the faults of the organization as a whole.

Corporate manslaughter charges can be brought against organizations that have been grossly negligent, resulting in death; however, it is often difficult to satisfy the burden of proof, as the prosecution has to show that the level of care the organization gave the victims fell far short of what could reasonably be expected in that specific situation, i.e., that the company's actions or failures were a result of gross negligence or serious management failures, and that the company's actions or failures directly led to a person's death. A company will therefore be judged on whether it met existing standards, and new standards cannot be applied retrospectively. The court will thus examine what policies an organization had in place to uphold its duty of care, how serious the breaches were that led to the death, whether the organizational failures fell far below the expected standard, and whether these failures were present at senior or operational levels.[111]

According to Section 1(6) of the Corporate Manslaughter and Corporate Homicide Act, an organization found to be guilty of corporate manslaughter or corporate homicide is liable for a fine. However, the court can also issue supplementary orders such as remedial orders and publicity orders requiring the organization to publicize the details of its conviction at its own expense. As of 1 February 2016, guidelines issued by the Sentencing Council state that the sentence level will depend on the organization's size and can be between £180,000 and £20 million.

2.5.1.2 Cases

The first prosecution of corporate manslaughter under the Act was in February 2010, when a geotechnical company and its director were charged with the unlawful killing of a young geologist by gross negligence, who died when soil collapsed in the trench he was examining. In 2009, the director appeared in court facing the charges on behalf of the company in his capacity as director. The company was found guilty and fined £385,000. The company appealed, and in 2011, the Court of Appeal upheld the original fine.[112] Other cases where a company was found guilty of corporate manslaughter include a Northern Ireland company convicted in 2012 when a farm employee was killed,[113] a company convicted after one of its workers fell through a fiberglass roof light and was found not to have carried out any safety training or a risk assessment with incorrect equipment and no supervision,[114] a sporting club in 2013 after a young girl who fell from a moving banana boat ride was killed when she collided with the propeller of the boat that was pulling it,[115] a specialist autoclave company after an explosion at the company's waste processing plant causing the death of a worker in which the court ruled that the majority of blame was at senior management level.[116] Cases in 2015 include: a kayak manufacturing company following the death of a worker who was trapped in an industrial oven;[117] a building and joining company following the death of an employee in a roof fall;[118] an Aerospace company after the death of a worker crushed when a dangerously high stack of Airbus parts delivered to the warehouse of Cambridge airport fell on top of him. In this case the judge said that there was a failure from top to bottom of the company;[119] a building company following the death of a worker when a wall fell onto him;[120] the first case that a national health service organization (the NHS Trust) as well as individuals were charged with corporate manslaughter, but found not guilty, after a woman died following postpartum hemorrhage;[121] and, a crane hire company following the death of an employee when the 16-wheel, 130-ton crane he was driving down an access road crashed.[122]

In February 2016, new guidelines aiming to provide a more consistent approach to the sentencing of convicted individuals and organizations were introduced. Under the guidelines, courts will first assess the seriousness of the offense based on the offender's culpability and the risk of serious harm, irrespective of whether any harm was caused, and then stipulate a range of possible fines based on the seriousness of the offense, depending on the size of the organization and based on the organization's turnover. The courts can consider mitigating factors, which include, inter alia, no prior convictions, steps taken to remedy the wrong, and a high level of cooperation with the investigation. Aggravating factors can include a history of relevant offenses and committing the offense for financial gain.[123]

The following sample of cases, albeit non-aviation related, illustrates the level of sentencing and fines imposed on corporations for corporate manslaughter offenses under the new guidelines. In July 2016, a construction company was fined £550,000 for two corporate manslaughter offenses, £50,000 for breaching the HSWA, and

£23,000 in costs, and was also subject to a publicity order after two workers fell into a 3.7m light well. The judge took into account the fact that the company was a "micro organization" with a turnover of much less than £2 million, as well as the company's good safety record, the remedial steps it had taken and the fact that it had no previous prosecutions.[124] In 2017, two companies were fined for corporate manslaughter following the death of a worker who fell through the roof of a warehouse. The one company, the owner of the warehouse, was fined £500,000 plus £53,000 costs and the other, a roofing company contracted to carry out the work, £100,000. The court found that there were no safety measures, no risk assessment, and no training. A director of the first company was sentenced to one year imprisonment and another was sentenced to 10 months' imprisonment. A director of the second company was sentenced to eight months' imprisonment. All three were disqualified from being directors for 10 years.[125] In 2017, a company was convicted and fined £1.2 million after two workers fell from a balcony.[126] In 2020, a Cornish commercial waste recycling company was fined £200,000 after the death of an employee who became trapped in a bailing machine in 2017. The three-year investigation highlighted several systemic failings, which included failures in training, risk assessments, and supervision.[127] In 2021, owners of a care home were fined £1.04 million, and suspended prison sentences were given to its former manager and a member of staff after the death of a 93-year-old dementia patient who died in 2015 after being scalded in a hot bath.[128] In 2022, a company was fined £2 million after two workers drowned in a slurry tanker.[129] In 2024, a company that pleaded guilty to corporate manslaughter and breaching the 1974 HSWA was fined £450,000 for corporate manslaughter and ordered to pay £167,601 costs. The principal director was sentenced to 23 weeks' imprisonment, suspended for 18 months, and the site foreman received a community order of 130 hours of unpaid work.[130]

2.5.1.3 Reforms

In 2023, the UK government passed the Economic Crime and Corporate Transparency Act 2023 (ECTA) to modernize the identification doctrine for economic crimes.[131] The Act allows senior managers to be brought within the scope of who can be considered the "directing mind and will" of a business. If they commit an economic crime, the company could also be held criminally liable and fined for the offense. A senior manager is defined as an individual who plays a significant role in:[132]

"a) the decision making about how the whole/substantial part of the activities of the body corporate are to be managed or organized; or
b) the actual managing or organizing of the whole or a substantial part of its activities."

A further step to extend corporate criminal liability beyond economic offenses to all types of crime is the introduction of the Crime and Policing Bill which had its second reading in the House of Commons on 10 March 2025. Clause 130 of the Bill, if enacted, would extend this statutory basis for corporate criminal liability further to include all criminal offenses.[133]

2.5.2 New Zealand

In New Zealand, the current legal framework dealing with holding organizations and their senior managers accountable for deaths that occur in the workplace includes the Health and Safety in Employment Act 1992, which focuses more on prevention than accountability and punishment. The Act creates a general duty on every employer to "take all practicable steps to ensure the safety of employees while at work" and examines whether the harm was foreseeable and preventable.

Section 49, which deals with offenses likely to cause serious harm, states that if a person knows that any action or omission is reasonably likely to cause serious harm to someone and takes that action or fails to act, contrary to the provisions of the Act, they are liable on conviction to a maximum of two years' imprisonment, a fine of up to $500,000, or both. It must be proven that the offender failed to take all practicable steps and was aware of the reasonable likelihood of serious harm. Section 50 makes it an offense to breach the duties stipulated in the Act, but does not require that the offender had knowledge of the likely harm.

On 19 November 2010, 29 of the 31 miners who were working in New Zealand's Pike River Mine were killed by an explosion caused by the ignition of built-up methane gas. Due to the absence of relevant legislation, none of the individuals responsible for the operation of the Pike River Mine or the design of the building were charged or held accountable for the deaths, which could have been prevented if effective safety standards had been applied.[134] The Independent Taskforce on Workplace Health and Safety made the following recommendations after the Pike River disaster:

> The Taskforce recommends extending the existing manslaughter offence to corporations and revising the corporate liability framework that applies to all offences (including manslaughter). This would be the most effective way to maximize the denunciatory and deterrent effect of the criminal law in influencing the behavior of corporations. The recommended revision to existing law would need to address two issues. First, it would need to allow the attribution of criminal liability to a corporation as a result of the acts and omissions of a greater range of officers and employees within that corporation, provided they are acting within the scope of their authority. Second, it would need to provide that liability could be attributed to a corporation if two or more individuals of the required seniority within the company engaged in conduct that, if it had been the conduct of only one of them, would have made them personally liable for the offence. This would allow conduct and states of mind to be aggregated to attribute corporate liability in a way not permitted under current New Zealand law.[135]

To deal with the gap in the legislation, the Health and Safety at Work Act 2015 (HSWA) was passed. Despite the HSWA, there were still gaps in the legislation with regard to corporate manslaughter, as was highlighted by the eruption of the Whakaari volcano in December 2019. No person was sentenced to prison in this case. A fine of $1,045,000 was imposed on Whakaari Management Ltd which licensed tours to the island, with $4,880,000 compensatory damages for the families.[136]

On 4 April 2016, the Health and Safety Reform Bill came into effect, and the Health and Safety at Work Act 2015 is the workplace health and safety law. The

HSWA 2015 sets out the principles, duties, and rights concerning workplace health and safety, and it shifts the focus on monitoring and recording health and safety incidents to proactively identify and manage risks. It states that the responsibility for safety lies with businesses that have the primary responsibility for the health and safety of their employees and any other workers they influence or direct and of people at risk from the work of their business; officers (company directors, partners, board members, chief executives) who have the responsibility to do due diligence to ensure that the business is meeting its health and safety responsibilities; workers who must take reasonable care for their own health and safety and who do not negatively affect the health and safety of others; and other people who come into the workplace, such as visitors or customers, who also have some health and safety duties to ensure that their actions don't adversely affect the health and safety of others.[137] In accordance with the Act there are four categories of persons that hold a duty, namely, PCBUs, defined as a "person conducting a business or undertaking" and this may be an individual person such as a sole trader or an organization, officers, workers and other persons at workplaces, officers, workers and other persons at workplaces.

The primary purpose of the 2015 HSWA is to provide a balanced framework to ensure the health and safety of workers and workplaces. The penalties under the Bill can reach a maximum fine of $3,000,000 and/or a term of imprisonment not exceeding five years. Directors or senior managers who have been found at fault are not disqualified from holding such positions.[138]

Despite the HSWA 2015, many organizations were not prosecuted for reckless behavior or gross negligence, causing the death of a person in the workplace. To try to bridge the gap, the Crimes (Corporate Homicide) Bill was introduced in April 2024. The Bill provides that a person will commit the offense of corporate homicide if:

(i) s/he has a relevant legal duty of care,
(ii) s/he engages in conduct that exposes any individual to whom that duty is owed to a risk of death or serious injury; and intends to cause the individual's death or serious injury, or is reckless as to the risk to the individual of death or serious injury, and
(iii) their conduct results in the death of the individual.

The Labour Party's workplace relations and safety spokesperson introduced the Crimes (Corporate Homicide) Amendment Bill, saying it would hold companies that are knowingly reckless with health and safety accountable, and most importantly, it would encourage and improve a good health and safety culture and save lives. Citing the 57 workplace fatalities in 2023, the three fatalities in the first two weeks of 2024 and New Zealand's track record of workplace deaths, said to be one of the worst in the developed world with three times the fatality rate of the United Kingdom and nearly twice the rate of Australia, as highlighted by the International Labour Organization, the safety spokesperson stated that the Bill was one of the most effective ways of preventing workplace deaths.[139] The Bill provides for imposing either life imprisonment for an individual or, in any other case, a fine of $10 million. The Bill aims to bring New Zealand at par with international best practices, and it remains to be seen if and when the Bill becomes law.

2.5.3 Australia

In Australia, industrial manslaughter refers to the offense where a person conducting a business or an undertaking (PCBU) recklessly or negligently fails to ensure the safety of workers, or others who are affected by their business or undertaking, resulting in death. An individual or a PCBU has a duty of care to provide their workers with a safe working environment. Industrial manslaughter charges can arise if the person having this duty under the safety laws engages in conduct that breaches the duty of care and that conduct causes the death of an individual, in circumstances where the person engages in such conduct, knows it is likely to cause the death or serious harm to an individual, or disregards that likelihood.

In 2022, 195 Australian employees were killed in a workplace accident. In another case in 2023,[140] 175 workers lost their lives. In October 2023, the work health and safety ministers from the states, territories, and Commonwealth acknowledged that more had to be done to prevent workplace deaths and serious injuries and to develop a harmonized industrial manslaughter offense with corresponding penalties of heavy fines and terms of imprisonment for individuals who breach their duty of care and negligently or recklessly cause the death of a worker.[141]

Almost all jurisdictions require, as part of the offense, that the PCBU or officer who owes such a duty to the worker engages in conduct that breaches this duty, and that this conduct causes the worker's death. However, the degree of fault required for the offense of industrial manslaughter, as well as the penalties, varies between each State and Territory. Additionally, some states, such as Western Australia, Victoria, and New South Wales, impose bans on obtaining insurance protection or indemnity for WHS penalties, so employers cannot insure against the large fines that may result from committing industrial manslaughter.[142]

The following outlines the law regarding industrial manslaughter, the conduct that could give rise to an offense by individuals and organizations, as well as the maximum penalties imposed.[143]

In the Commonwealth, the Fair Work Legislation Amendment Bill 2023 was introduced on 4 September 2023, aiming to propose changes to the Fair Work Act 2009 and the Work Health and Safety Act (WHSA) 2011, and to make industrial manslaughter an offense at a federal level. The offense commenced on 1 July 2024 under a new section 30A of the WSHA 2011, but has limited application as it will only apply to the Commonwealth public sector. The test required is "actions of gross negligence or recklessness" and individuals can face a maximum imprisonment for up to 25 years and a body corporate a maximum fine of up to $18 million.[144]

In the Australian Capital Territory, industrial manslaughter has been an offense since 2004. It was initially introduced under the Crimes Act 1900 and was then adopted in S 34A of the 2011 Work Health and Safety Act 2011 and the 2021 Work Health and Safety Amendment Act 2021. The test is conduct that is "reckless or negligent about causing the death" and the maximum penalty for an individual is imprisonment for up to 20 years and for a body corporate a fine of up to $16.5 million. The offense of industrial manslaughter has, as of the beginning of 2025, not yet been prosecuted.[145]

In New South Wales, the NSW Parliament passed the Work Health and Safety Amendment (Industrial Manslaughter) Bill 2024 in June 2024, which introduced a new offense of industrial manslaughter into the Work Health and Safety Act 2011 (WHS) applicable to persons conducting a business or undertaking (PCBU) and individuals in respect of workplace deaths involving gross negligence. The industrial manslaughter offense is committed when a person who is a PCBU or an officer of a PCBU with a health and safety duty engages in conduct, either by an act or omission, that breaches their duty and causes the death of a worker or another individual to whom the person's duty is owed, and the conduct is engaged in with gross negligence. The penalty for such an offense is imprisonment for up to 25 years and, for a body corporate, fines of up to $20 million.[146]

In the Northern Territory, the offense of industrial manslaughter came into effect on 1 February 2020 under S34B of the Work Health and Safety (National Uniform Legislation) Act 2011. The test is "reckless or negligent conduct" and the law imposes a maximum penalty of life imprisonment for an individual and, for a body corporate, a fine of up to $11.5 million. Charges of industrial manslaughter were filed in two cases. Darwin's largest privately owned construction company was charged after a man was killed when a chain allegedly failed and struck him during an excavator towing operation. The charges were later withdrawn; however, the company is still facing penalties for not complying with its health and safety duties. The second case involves charges laid against an individual who was trading as a construction company after the death of one of his workers who fell approximately 3.2 meters through an unguarded void while moving cabinets. In this case, the individual will be tried.[147]

In Queensland, the offense of industrial manslaughter was introduced in 2017 under section 34C of the Work Health and Safety Act 2011. The test here is "negligence" and individuals can be imprisoned for up to 20 years and a body corporate fined up to $15.48 million. Queensland is the first state to convict a body corporate and an individual for industrial manslaughter.[148] In the first case, a worker was killed by a reversing forklift truck which was being driven by an unlicensed driver with no traffic management safety systems in place. In 2020, the company was convicted and fined $3 million. Two directors were convicted and sentenced to 10 months imprisonment, with a suspended sentence.[149] In the second case, in 2022, an individual was convicted and sentenced to a five-year prison sentence, suspended after 18 months, after he negligently caused the death of a worker who was crushed by a generator that fell on him from a moving forklift.[150]

In South Australia, the Work Health and Safety (Industrial Manslaughter) Amendment Bill 2023 was passed on 29 December 2023, introducing a new offense of industrial manslaughter under section 30A of the Work Health and Safety Act 2012. The Act requires "grossly negligent or reckless conduct" to amount to the offense and the maximum penalty for an individual is 20 years imprisonment, and for a body corporate it is a fine of $18 million.[151]

In Western Australia, industrial manslaughter became an offense on 31 March 2022 under section 30A of the Work Health and Safety Act 2020. The conduct required for the offense is that of "knowing that the conduct was likely to result in death or serious harm and disregarding that likelihood." Individuals can have a maximum sentence of up to 20 years imprisonment and a fine of up to $5 million imposed, and a body corporate, a fine of up to $10 million. [152] The first conviction for industrial manslaughter was against a director of a company who was sentenced to 2 years and 2 months imprisonment.[153]

In Victoria, workplace manslaughter is an offense according to section 39G of the Occupational Health and Safety Act 2004, which was introduced under the Workplace Safety Legislation Amendment (Workplace Manslaughter and Other Matters) Bill 2019, commencing on 1 July 2020. The test is that of "negligence" and offenders can get a maximum penalty of imprisonment for up to 25 years for an individual and for a body corporate, fines of up to $19.23 million. The first conviction of workplace manslaughter was in February 2024 against a stonemasonry business after a subcontractor died when a loaded forklift operated by the director tipped and landed on the worker, killing him. The company was convicted and fined $1.3 million. The sole director was also convicted. He received a two-year Community Corrections Order, 200 hours of unpaid community work, and was ordered to complete a course in forklift operation. Three other charges of workplace manslaughter were filed in the last four years. The first is against a centenary bakehouse for the death of a worker who fell about four meters while removing suspended ceiling panels at a warehouse. The second and third charges of industrial manslaughter were filed after the death of an apprentice electrician who was electrocuted while working.[154]

In Tasmania, industrial manslaughter is not an offense; however, in June 2024, the industrial manslaughter Bill was passed by the lower House. The Upper House must then approve the Bill for approval before it becomes law. The proposed Bill states that the offense will be committed by an individual or PCBU who "engages in conduct that is negligent" and provides for a maximum penalty of imprisonment of up to 21 years for an individual and a fine of up to $18 million for a body corporate.[155]

It is clear that many jurisdictions are improving, amending, and even enacting legislation to create laws aiming at apportioning accountability on individuals and organizations who breach their duty of care and whose negligent or reckless conduct results in the death of workers.

In addition, there is more focus on directors and officers prioritizing risk assessment and risk management to effectively identify hazards and mitigate risks, and also encourages reporting. Safety Management Organizations must ensure that they have effective safety systems in place, and that they are regularly assessed, reviewed, audited, and tested.

The preceding overview of corporate manslaughter illustrates the international trend of increasing accountability for organizations and senior managers. This will be further expanded in relation to aviation accidents, with a particular focus on France and the US, in light of the Air France 447 accident and the two Boeing 737 MAX accidents discussed in Chapter 4.

2.5.4 France

Corporate criminal liability refers to the vicarious liability of a legal person for the acts of its stakeholders (i.e., directors, officers, employees, and agents) if they commit an illegal act within the scope of their duties with the intention to benefit the undertaking.

Until the reform of French criminal law in 1994, French statutory law recognized corporate criminal liability only in limited cases. Between 1994 and 2005, the liability of legal persons was restricted to offenses explicitly permitted by law. Since 31 December 2005 (Law No. 2004-204 of 9 March 2004), this principle of specificity has been removed, and legal persons can be held liable for any criminal violation of French law. Currently, French law bases corporate criminal liability on Article 121-2 of the French Criminal Code, which states that legal persons other than the French State may be held liable for crimes committed on their behalf by any of their representatives or organs. Therefore, corporate liability applies not only to natural persons but also to legal entities, except for the French State. A legal entity or company can be held criminally responsible for actions taken on its behalf or for its benefit by responsible individuals, who are referred to as the organs or representatives of the entity in the code.

A "representative" is generally someone to whom the entity has delegated certain responsibilities. A body of a legal person is any entity that can take decisions on behalf of the legal person, whether its existence is *de jure,* namely provided for by law or the bylaws, the articles of association, as is the case of the board of directors, directors, managers, general managers and presidents, who are vested with the power to administrate, manage and control the entity; *de facto* directors or managers, but also persons, vested with delegation of powers (including employees) or acting within a specific mission for the company (such as liquidators).[156] Some Supreme Court cases refer to the status or quality of the employee to determine whether they are acting as representatives of the legal person.[157] Recent case law has confirmed that an employee who does not have a written delegation of powers can be considered a representative of the legal entity if they have a de facto delegation of powers, implying the status and powers to make decisions on behalf of the legal entity.[158]

The act must have been committed on behalf of the legal person. The law does not clearly define this concept, but it would cover all acts that are in the interest of the legal person. The courts have held a legal person liable where the offense simply occurred in the conduct of its activity, even though the entity gained no benefit, and this would apply to cases where the offense is a failure to act in accordance with safety or supervision regulations. Generally, it can be said that whenever the representative or body committing the offense did not pursue its own personal interest, it can be considered that it was done for the legal persons' interest.[159] An offense would be deemed to have been committed on behalf of the legal person when it is committed in the exercise of activities whose purpose is to ensure the organization, operation, or objectives of the legal person, even if the legal person has no interest therein, or has not benefited therefrom.[160] Another point that was settled was whether the courts had to precisely identify who committed the offense on behalf of the company to hold the legal entity liable. Initially, the courts held that the judge had to unambiguously identify the natural person who committed the offense. Later, judges were relieved of the duty to precisely identify the physical person who committed the offense if it appeared from the circumstances that the offense could only have been committed or sanctioned by the bodies or representatives of the legal person. The Supreme Court then returned to its earlier case law. Judges must specify how the offenses held against the legal person were committed on its behalf, by one of its bodies or representatives.[161]

If a company is found liable for a criminal offense committed on its behalf by its bodies or representatives, the courts may apply a range of sanctions such as: (a) monetary fines; (b) restraining measures; (c) confiscation measures; or (d) compliance-related measures in the case of conviction for corruption or influence peddling offenses. Whether the offense is a felony, a misdemeanor, or a minor offense will determine the severity of the sanctions. As it is not possible for a company to serve a prison sentence, fines are the most common sentence handed down by the courts. Penalties for minor offenses usually are fines and specific restraining measures, as well as indemnificatory sanctions, depending on the circumstances of each case.[162]

The maximum monetary fine applicable to legal persons is five times the fine incurred by individuals for the same offense. Where there is an offense for which no fine is provided to individuals, by law, the fine incurred by legal persons is set at €1 million, pursuant to Article 13, 1-38 of the *French Criminal Code*. Other sanctions that can be imposed in accordance with the *French Criminal Code* include, inter alia:

- Dissolution of the company where the legal entity was created to commit an offense or was diverted from its corporate objects to commit a felony or other offense punishable by a prison sentence of three years or more (not applicable to public bodies and other specific bodies such as workers' unions and political parties)
- Prohibition on exercising (up to five years or permanently), directly or indirectly, one or more corporate or professional activities
- Placement under judicial supervision for a maximum period of five years (not applicable to public bodies and other specific bodies such as workers' unions and political parties)
- Closure (up to five years or permanently) of the establishment or facility that was used to commit the offense
- Debarment (up to five years) from public procurement
- Prohibition (up to five years or permanently) on making public offerings and listing securities on the stock exchange.[163]

In addition, the penalty of confiscation can be incurred in cases provided by law and for offenses of certain severity. Confiscation includes any profit or revenue or goods used in the commission of the offense and covers all movable or immovable property, whatever the nature, used to commit the offense or the intended offense, as well as all direct or indirect proceeds of the commission of the offense, with the exception of property subject to restitution to the victim. The law also provides that for some offenses, there is no limitation set as to the origin or the use of goods that may be confiscated. The fourth possible sanction is compliance-related under the *Sapin II Law*, which introduced a new compliance-related sanction under Article 131-39-2 of the *French Criminal Code*.[164]

With regards to corruption offenses, implementing a compliance model or policy will not exempt or reduce criminal liability; however, the courts may take this into account when determining the appropriate sanction to impose. The *Sapin II Law* imposes an obligation on companies having a minimum of 500 employees (or companies belonging to a group of companies whose parent company is headquartered in France and whose workforce includes at least 500 employees) and with revenues over €100 million (consolidated revenues in case of a group) to manage corruption risks actively. Accordingly, the presidents, managing directors, directors, and managers of such companies have a legal obligation to take appropriate measures to prevent and detect acts of corruption both in France and abroad. Fines of up to €200,000 for individuals and €1 million for legal persons may be imposed for non-compliance. In the event that a compliance program is mandatory, the company must implement it effectively to avoid liability or penalties. Legal entities falling under the ambit of the *Sapin II Law* are required to implement: (i) an ethics code; (ii) an internal whistleblowing procedure; (iii) a regular risk-mapping exercise; (iv) assessment procedures for customers, major suppliers and intermediaries; (v) accounting checks; (vi) training programs for employees exposed to high risks of corruption and influence peddling; (vii) disciplinary sanctions; and (viii) an internal check and assessment system regarding the implemented measures. The requirement to implement these measures entered into force on the first day of the sixth month following the enactment of the *Sapin II Law*, that is, 1 June 2017.[165]

In addition, the French *Vigilance Law* passed in March 2017 created an obligation for certain companies to implement and publish a vigilance program aimed at controlling the activities of their subsidiaries, subcontractors, and suppliers. The vigilance plan shall include: (i) a risk mapping that identifies, analyzes, and ranks risks; (ii) procedures to regularly assess, in accordance with the risk mapping, the situation of subsidiaries, subcontractors, or suppliers with whom the company maintains an established commercial relationship; (iii) appropriate action to mitigate risks or prevent serious violations; (iv) an alert mechanism that collects reporting of existing or actual risks; and (v) a monitoring scheme to follow up on the measures implemented and assess their efficiency. Violations may result in civil liability toward those who have suffered damage as a consequence.[166]

The Sapin II Law recently replaced the French Central Service for the Prevention of Bribery (SCPC) with the French Anti-Corruption Agency, which operates under the auspices of the French Minister of Justice and the Minister of Budget. Its mission is to assist the relevant authorities in preventing and identifying acts of corruption, influence peddling, extortion, misappropriation of public funds, and other related misconduct. The Agency is similar to the U.S. Department of Justice and will, among other things: help relevant public and private entities prevent and detect corruption by, notably, adopting recommendations on compliance programs that are required to be implemented; report potential offenses to the French public prosecutor; oversee the enforcement of the French "Blocking Statute" created by Law No. 68-678 of July 1968, – which prohibits individuals or companies in France from sharing certain information with non-French authorities for judicial or administrative proceedings without following an internationally approved process such as the Hague Convention – in the context of compliance programs mandated by foreign authorities for companies based in France; review the quality and effectiveness of companies' anti-corruption programs; monitor the implementation of compliance programs imposed as penalties; and publish an annual report detailing its activities.[167]

Under French law, there are three different types of plea bargain procedures applicable to legal persons. The first is a criminal out-of-court settlement where the prosecutor may offer the accused the option to pay a fine instead of starting criminal proceedings, provided the person pleads guilty. The fine cannot exceed the maximum fine for the relevant offense. For legal persons, this option is only available for offenses listed under IV of the French Commercial Code, which do not carry imprisonment penalties. These offenses can also be settled before criminal prosecution begins through the so-called procedure for criminal settlement if the accused pleads guilty. In such cases, the French General Directorate for Competition Policy, Consumer Affairs, and Fraud Control suggests a proportionate fine, which must be approved by the state prosecutor and accepted by the accused. The second is the prior guilty plea procedure, allowing a prosecutor to propose an alternative sanction to the accused contingent upon a guilty plea. This is not an out-of-court process and applies to misdemeanors, with a fine or up to a five-year prison sentence. The fine amount should not surpass the maximum for the relevant offense. According to the Ministry of Justice Circular dated 2 September 2004, this procedure also applies to legal persons.[168]

The third is the Judicial Public Interest Agreement (CJIP), which was introduced under Article 41-1-2 of the French Code of Criminal Procedure by the Sapin II Law. This new form of French deferred prosecution agreement allows legal entities suspected of international or national corruption offenses, influence peddling, money laundering, tax fraud, and environmental crime to avoid prosecution and criminal sanctions by entering into an agreement with a court. This new procedure is very similar to the US Deferred Prosecution Agreement, but does not apply to natural persons. The public prosecutor may propose that companies settle, either: (a) during the course of criminal proceedings, in which case the company would have to plead guilty; or (b) before criminal proceedings are initiated, to avoid criminal conviction, and the legal person must execute the obligations to which it has committed itself in the agreement which can be either or both of the following:

- paying a public interest fine, the amount of which cannot exceed 30% of the average annual turnover, increased by damages to the victim and certain expenses incurred by the new French Anti-Corruption Agency within its mission;

- implementing an internal anti-corruption compliance program to be monitored by the French Anti-Corruption Agency for a maximum period of three years.

Additional requirements are that a judge must approve the fine imposed and/or the compliance program in a public hearing, and the settlement order, agreement, and the amount of the fine imposed must be published on the agency's website. The charges will then be dropped, and the company will not be required to make any admission of liability. This deferred prosecution agreement is only available to corporate entities, and individual offenders remain subject to criminal sanctions even if the company enters into a deferred prosecution agreement. Judicial Public Interest Agreements are beneficial for settling large-scale cases such as the following recent cases rapidly. On 31 January 2020, the Paris Criminal Court validated a CJIP concluded between the National Financial Prosecutor's Office and Airbus S.E. after the National Financial Prosecutor's Office imposed a fine of €2.8 billion on Airbus to resolve allegations of bribery and corruption related to the sale of aircraft and satellites between 2004 and 2016. The CJIP was part of a wider settlement with authorities in France, the UK, and the US.[169]

The National Financial Prosecutor's Office highlighted the importance of this agreement for France as it has raised it

> to the level of the leading judicial authorities in this area, alongside the United States (Department of Justice / DOJ) and the United Kingdom (Serious Fraud Office / SFO), insofar as it was the responsibility of the PNF to coordinate the French CJIPP with the two Deferred Prosecution Agreement in this case. The total amount of the fine imposed on Airbus by the three judicial authorities reached the sum of 3.6 billion euros.[170]

Establishing corporate criminal responsibility does not preclude individual responsibility for the same facts.

2.5.4.1 Directors' or Managers' Individual Criminal Liability

Article 121-3 of the Criminal Code states that there is no crime without the intention to commit it; however, where the law provides so, there is a crime if the person of another is deliberately endangered. It also provides that an offense is committed

> where the law provides so, in the case of recklessness, negligence or failure to comply with an obligation of prudence or safety laid down by law or regulation, if it is established that the perpetrator did not take the normal precautions, taking into account, where appropriate, the nature of his duties or functions, his competences and the power and means at his disposal. In the case provided for by the preceding paragraph, natural persons who have not directly caused the damage, but who have created or contributed to creating the situation which allowed the damage to occur or who have not taken the measures to avoid it, are criminally liable if it is established that they have either violated, in a manifestly deliberate manner, a particular obligation of prudence or safety

> provided for by the law or the regulations, or committed a serious fault which exposed others to a risk of particular gravity which they could not ignore.[171]

An individual can commit a misdemeanor for an intentional offense in the case of recklessness, imprudence, negligence, or a failure to meet a duty of care as set out by law or regulation, if it is established that the person did not exercise normal care, taking into account the nature of his or her duties, functions and competence, and the powers and available means. Those who have not indirectly caused the harm but who created or contributed to creating the situation that caused the harm or did not take the measures necessary to prevent it may be held criminally liable only if: (i) he or she violated, clearly and deliberately, a particular legal or regulatory obligation of prudence or care (deliberate fault or *faute délibérée*); or (ii) he or she committed a grossly negligent act that resulted in particularly serious risk to others, which he or she could not have ignored (grave fault or *faute caractérisée*).

2.5.4.2 Manslaughter

In France, manslaughter is the act of causing the death of a person unintentionally, through clumsiness, recklessness, inattention, negligence, or failure to observe a duty of care or safety, and it is considered to be an offense and not a crime, as the intention to kill is absent. Three elements are required for this offense, namely, the death of a victim; the commission of a fault; and the existence of a specific causal link between the fault committed and the death of the victim. The nature of causality, whether it is direct or indirect, will determine the type of fault that may give rise to criminal liability. Law No 2000-647 of 10 July 2000, which defines unintentional offenses, introduced a distinction between "direct" and "indirect" causality. It provides that a simple fault is sufficient to engage the criminal liability of the direct author of the damage; and a qualified fault is required (i.e., a fault of a higher degree of seriousness) to engage the criminal liability of the person who has only indirectly caused the damage. [172]

Article 221-6 of the Criminal Code defines the offense of unintentional injury and provides the corresponding punishment for committing the offense as follows:

> The act of causing, under the conditions and according to the distinctions provided for in Article 121-3, by clumsiness, imprudence, inattention, negligence or failure to comply with an obligation of prudence or safety imposed by law or regulation, the death of another person constitutes involuntary manslaughter punishable by three years of imprisonment and a fine of 45,000 euros. In the event of a manifestly deliberate breach of a particular duty of care or safety imposed by law or regulation, the penalties incurred are increased to five years' imprisonment and a fine of 75,000 euros.

The manslaughter charges against individuals and corporations in the Germanwings Flight 9525 and Concorde Flight 4590 accidents are discussed below, providing insight into the German and French judiciary's approach after an aviation accident.

2.5.4.3 Germanwings Flight 9525

On 24 March 2015, Germanwings Flight 9525 took off from Barcelona-El Prat, Spain, destined for Düsseldorf Airport in Germany with 150 passengers and crew on board. The aircraft, an A320, crashed into the French Alps, killing all persons on board.

Many of the civil suits filed against the Lufthansa Group, which owns the low-cost Germanwings airline, as well as the Lufthansa training school in the US were centered on allegations that the "defendants, together negligently, carelessly and recklessly breached their duty of care to passengers by failing to maintain, operate, maneuver, handle, control, equip, manage, and pilot Germanwings Flight 9525, and by failing to properly and safely train, educate, prepare, inform, alert, monitor, guide, or tutor its pilots, crew, and other personnel to operate a passenger aircraft." In addition, they argued that "the defendants did not have known policies in place that would have timely and safely responded to or prevented emergency situations, including an unaccompanied, solitary, crew member in the cockpit. As a direct and proximate result of the defendants' gross negligence, [the passengers] suffered unspeakable horrors before their lives were tragically cut short."[173]

In the criminal proceedings, French and German prosecutors assigned to investigate the crash determined that the co-pilot deliberately caused the crash.[174] Prosecutors considered filing involuntary homicide charges against the airline due to negligence. In France, the Marseille prosecutor stated that, as the co-pilot had died in the crash, it was not possible under French law to charge him posthumously and that they would therefore examine the airlines and Lufthansa's potential criminal liability. He also clarified that, in accordance with European regulations, only an individual can request health records to be handed over to their employer, and this could have prevented the airline from being aware of his medical conditions. As the co-pilot had seen 41 doctors in the past five years, including seven doctors during the month before the crash in March, the investigation would focus on how medical secrecy laws prevented the company from knowing about the doctor's visits. He stated, "How can we reconcile medical secrecy with the info that an employer like an airline needs to make a determination on the aptitude of its employee to fly a plane?"[175]

In March 2022, the French court in Marseille announced that it was dropping the criminal proceedings for involuntary manslaughter. The judges had to consider whether any culpability for negligent homicide could be attributed to the airline or doctors for not having foreseen the danger that the co-pilot posed to the safety of the passengers. The court held that the airline had not been told why the co-pilot had been off work, and that neither the aviation medical service, the pilots, nor the airline was informed of the trouble he had been having. The three judges concluded that no one could have foreseen that the co-pilot would have acted the way he did despite his mental illness, and therefore, the criteria for the criminal offense of negligent homicide had not been met. The managing directors of Germanwings, now Eurowings, the parent company, Lufthansa, as well as the doctors consulted by the co-pilot before the crash, did not have any criminal liability.[176] In Germany, prosecutors also conducted a criminal investigation, focusing on whether any doctors who treated the co-pilot had been criminally negligent in not reporting him to authorities. The investigation determined that his doctors knew he was "suffering psychologically" in the months before the disaster, but that he had not been diagnosed as clinically depressed. In addition, they established that "the co-pilot did not tell the doctors treating him or anyone else in his personal life about his suicidal thoughts so that none of these people could have been expected to tell his employer or the authorities." They concluded that Germanwings had "no knowledge of psychological ailments" he suffered and that "The investigation has shown no sufficient evidence of guilt by anyone still alive in connection with the Germanwings crash."

On 9 January 2017, the Düsseldorf public prosecutor's office announced that they had closed their criminal investigation as they had concluded that the co-pilot was solely responsible for the death of all those on board.[177]

Even though the Concorde accident occurred in 2000, the court proceedings against the defendants charged with manslaughter and corporate manslaughter commenced in 2010. It is a significant case illustrating the application of negligence and manslaughter principles as well as the new approach by the court in evaluating the safety risk assessments, but also the effectiveness of the mitigating controls implemented and actions taken by the manufacturer and the oversight by the civil aviation authority.

2.5.4.4 Concorde Flight 4590

On 25 July 2000, Air France Flight 4590, operated by Concord aircraft registration F-BTSC, departed from Paris Charles de Gaulle Airport runway 26R at 16:42:31 following the departure of a Continental Airlines D-10-30, Flight C055. During the Continental Airlines DC-10 aircraft's takeoff roll, a titanium wear strip fell from one of the aircraft's engines onto the runway. During the takeoff roll of the Concord, the aircraft suffered a tire blowout after running over the titanium strip on the runway. Debris from the tire ruptured a fuel tank, causing a severe fire and the failure of two engines. The aircraft crashed into a hotel in Gonesse, resulting in the deaths of all 100 passengers and 9 crew members on board, as well as 4 individuals on the ground.

The judicial investigation by the French authorities, parallel to the BEA accident investigation, resulted in the filing of manslaughter charges against the following defendants.

1. Continental Airlines, as a legal entity, for allowing engineers to use banned titanium during engine repairs.
2. A Continental mechanic who fitted the titanium strip that fell onto the runway.
3. A Continental maintenance supervisor for approving engine repair.
4. The former Concorde chief engineer at Aerospatiale for not taking action to strengthen the fuel tanks following previous incidents.
5. The former head of the Concorde program at Aerospatiale for underestimating the gravity of previous tire and fuel tank incidents and failing to demand design changes.

6. A former senior official at the French Civil Aviation Directorate for underestimating previous tire and fuel tank incidents and failing to demand design changes.

The judge explained that, under French law, if a natural person has committed a serious misconduct, which is an "unacceptable failing, or an accumulation of recklessness and negligence showing prolonged incompetence," the court must determine that the offender exposed others to a particularly serious risk and that they could not have been unaware of the risk caused by the misconduct. Legal entities, on the other hand, incur criminal responsibility for the actions committed on their behalf by their entities or representatives, and the test to be applied here is ordinary negligence, not serious misconduct.

The Court found the Continental mechanic who fitted the titanium strip guilty of manslaughter and unintentional injuries and sentenced him to a 15-month suspended sentence and two fines of €1,000. Continental Airlines was found guilty of involuntary manslaughter and unintentional injuries by a legal entity and fined 200,000 Euros. The other defendants were acquitted.[178]

It is essential to highlight that the court considered the charges of misconduct against the three natural persons involved in certification and airworthiness and the supervision of the Concorde aircraft in relation to the handling of the following four risks:[179]

(i) tires bursting,
(ii) the risk of perforation and the wing reinforcement,
(iii) fire risk,
(iv) loss of thrust from both engines.

The Court examined the possible liability of the manufacturer for neglecting existing technology and not encouraging additional research to deal with the increasing incidents of tire bursts. It held that the manufacturer could not be blamed for failing to equip the Concorde with radial tires. It further stated that the causes of the tire bursts were dealt with in an acceptable manner, but that the manufacturer may have been overconfident about their degree of control of the risk.

Regarding the risk of perforation and wing reinforcement, the court examined the test and the consequences of the choices made by the manufacturers following a 1979 incident. It held that the manufacturer could be blamed for not having pushed the investigation to its limits to deal with this risk. The court concluded, however, that this did not amount to recklessness or negligence and that the manufacturers' missed opportunity did not amount to a criminal offense.

Referring to the risk of handling the fire, the Court said that the manufacturers were negligent in that they did not further analyze the consequences that could result from a fuel leakage caused by a perforation of the lower surface of a tank following a burst tire, but the degree of negligence was not so serious as to constitute serious misconduct.

Concerning the risk of loss of thrust from the engines, the Court ruled that the manufacturers and the administrative authorities could not be held criminally liable for not having envisaged, when the aircraft received its certification, the breakdown from the loss of both engines on the same side at take-off or for failing to assess the risk of loss of thrust during the operation of the Concorde aircraft.

Acquitting the three defendants, the Court held that there was no causal link between the actions of these three defendants and the accident, and the manner in which the fire risk was handled amounted only to misconduct and not serious misconduct.

The Court considered the mechanic's misconduct regarding the material used for the manufacture of the wear strip. It held that the first error he committed was using titanium, which was unsuitable. This was not the cause of the loss of the wear strip, but it contributed to the damage as the hardness of this material systematically generates the bursting of tires of the Concorde aircraft, which other materials did not do. It went on to say that he did not: fill in the holes, thus weakening the cowling; follow the rules applicable for fixing the strip; follow the rules of repair; use the recommended template to fix the strip; assess the requirement of using a shim, and that by omitting to use the shim, he was not made aware of the problem that existed by the mounting of the strip. The Court concluded that this amounted to negligence. It went on to say that he could not have been unaware of the state of the substrate and the problems this would likely cause, and that he should have referred this to his supervisor or taken the necessary steps to prepare the substrate so that the strip could be correctly repaired. This amounted to serious misconduct, and the Court thus found him guilty of negligence on several counts.

With regards to the mechanic, the court clearly stated that based on the mechanic's job, his professional qualities, his knowledge and experience in aeronautics and its associated dangers, he could not have been unaware of the risks that such a strip could pose to others if it had fallen off as a result of being poorly fixed. Nor could he have been unaware of the risk of objects on the runway and of the serious risks of death/injury. As the loss of the wear strip contributed to the accident, there was a causal link between the serious misconduct and the resulting damage.

Regarding the supervisor, the Court held that he was not obliged to specifically inspect the repair carried out before signing the aircraft release, but that as a result of his professional training and role as supervisor, he had noticed the wear strip protruding. He therefore had the responsibility to use all reasonable means to understand the exact nature of the problem and the extent of the repair. The Court held that failing to do this amounted to negligence, but not to serious misconduct, and it acquitted the supervisor.

Referring to Continental Airlines and applying the test that ordinary negligence, not serious misconduct on behalf of the company, entities, and representatives is required, the Court held that the serious misconduct of the mechanic could not be charged to the airline as he was only an employee of the airline. However, it did say that the ordinary offense of negligence of the supervisor did incur the legal responsibility of Continental Airlines as its representative.[180]

It is important to highlight that the Court assessed the quality of the maintenance carried out. It is significant to emphasize that the Court examined in great detail the risk assessment process and then critically evaluated each risk assessment carried out by the individuals charged.

The Court's decision is a landmark decision regarding the extent and depth of the court's examination of the risk assessment process and the evaluation by the judiciary of the resulting actions taken to mitigate the risks. Central to aviation safety is an effective safety management system, with recorded data, risk assessment processes, and mitigating controls. However, the same SMS processes can provide facts and recorded evidence to a court that will carry out its own evaluation of actions taken within the SMS.

Two years later, in 2012, the Appeal Court found Continental Airlines, which by then had merged with United Airlines, and the supervising engineer not guilty. The Court, however, held that Continental Airlines still had civil liability for the accident.

2.5.4.5 Other Cases of Corporate Manslaughter Include

In June 2022, in a significant development, the Criminal Chamber of the *Cour de Cassation* (French Supreme Court) overruled its previous case law and held that to establish the liability of a legal entity, it is necessary to explicitly identify the body or the representative having committed the offense on behalf of said legal entity.[181] An employee of a company specializing in the production of cotton wool (Company A) suffered an accident at work on an "opener-crusher" machine. Company A was owned by a holding company. Company A, the holding company, and its site manager were prosecuted for unintentionally injuring an employee who became totally incapacitated for more than three months, as well as for failing to comply with health, safety, and working conditions measures. All three defendants were convicted by the first instance court but appealed against the judgment. On 24 November 2020, the Paris Court of Appeals imposed a €20,000 fine on Company A and a €40,000 fine on the holding company for unintentional injury, and two fines of €5,000 each on Company A for breaches of applicable health and safety regulations. Company A and the holding company then appealed to the *Cour de Cassation,* which had to decide two questions: Whether a legal entity could be considered as a body or representative of another legal entity and thus allow for the latter to be convicted; and, whether a holding company for which judges have not identified any body or representative could be held criminally liable.

In its decision, the *Cour de Cassation* held that the holding company of a prosecuted company could be considered as an organ of the latter. It also ruled that the Court of Appeals does not disregard the requirements of Article 121-1 of the French Criminal Code when it convicts the prosecuted company for breaches committed by its organ or representative. The *Cour de Cassation* did, however, overturn the part of the decision that concerned the liability of the holding company due to the lack of identification of said company's organ or representative.[182] This case, therefore, confirmed the need for a precise identification of the body or representative and that a legal entity can be the body or representative of another legal entity.

In 2022, in one of the biggest health scandals in France, a company was found guilty of manslaughter and deception over the Mediator pill, which was on the market for 33 years and was blamed for hundreds of deaths. Prosecutors asked for nearly €15 million in fines for the company and a three-year prison sentence and fine for the only surviving executive accused. The judge stated that the company had been aware of the risks for many years but had never taken the necessary measures. The company's former deputy boss was sentenced to a 4-year suspended sentence. The chairman was indicted but died in 2014 before the trial. The company was fined €2.7 million for aggravated deceit, manslaughter, and causing unintentional injury and was acquitted of fraud. In addition, France's medicines agency was told that it had seriously failed in its role as health watchdog and fined €303,000 for delaying the suspension of the pill.[183] The 6,500 claimants involved in the case sought €1 billion in damages, and the company was ordered to pay victims an estimated €160 million in compensation.[184]

In 2024, two of Nestlé's French subsidiaries were charged with unintentional manslaughter after E. coli-contaminated pizzas were suspected of having led to the death of two children and acute kidney failure in many others in May 2022. French investigative magistrates commenced an investigation for involuntary manslaughter and unintentional injuries after dozens of customers fell sick from eating pizzas containing E. coli bacteria. The Nestlé units managing the factory in northern France that produced the Buitoni-branded pizzas, as well as Nestlé France, were indicted, and charges were filed against Nestlé France and Société des Produits Alimentaires de Caudry (SPAC), a subsidiary of the company.[185]

2.5.5 USA

2.5.5.1 Liability of an Entity

In the US, the concept of a legal entity's liability is based on the premise that a corporation, as a separate and independent legal entity, should be held responsible for its liabilities. In the US, civil and criminal corporate liability is generally vicarious, as it depends on the behavior of the organization's directors, officers, employees, or agents. Under the "respondeat superior doctrine," which literally means "let the master answer," an employer is accountable for the actions of its employees performed during their employment and can be held liable for negligence or wrongdoing committed by them. The doctrine, applied by U.S. courts, makes a corporation liable for the criminal acts of its employees if those acts are committed within the scope of employment and intended, even partially, to benefit the company.

The doctrine, first established in England in the late 17th century to prevent employers from avoiding financial responsibility for their employees' actions, was generally applied to civil cases until the case of New York Central & Hudson River Company in 1909. The court reasoned that since the corporation could be attributed with the knowledge of its employees' actions during their employment, any criminal liability for employees' acts that violate the law could also be attributed to the corporation. Removing the immunity from criminal prosecution that corporations previously enjoyed, the court extended the civil liability principle. It held that the unlawful acts of an agent acting within the authority delegated to him can be attributed to his employer, and the court can impose penalties on the corporation for such acts. In accordance with New York Central & Hudson River Railroad Co. v United, the corporation can be held liable for its agents' criminal misconduct or actions even if the agents' actions go against corporate policy or directly ignore explicit orders from the corporation. The court added that criminal law cannot ignore how business is conducted today, and if corporations continue to enjoy prosecutorial immunity for their actions, it will undermine nearly all the government's means to regulate and correct its abuses.

According to U.S. federal law, corporate criminal liability generally applies to offenses (a) committed by the corporation's officers, employees, or agents; (b) within the scope of their employment; and (c) at least partly for the benefit of the corporation. Whether an activity falls within an individual's scope of authority depends on whether they engage in activities "on the corporation's behalf in performing [their] general line of work, and these acts must be motivated, at least partially, by an intent to benefit the corporation." If this standard is met, the corporation can be held liable even if it explicitly told its agent, employee, or officer not to commit the offense. The 1985 Model Penal Code, along with many state penal codes, states that corporate criminal liability may depend on the misconduct of senior management officials because misconduct by lower-level employees might not suffice, even if they act within their scope of authority for the benefit of the corporation. Generally, corporations can be held liable for specific intent offenses based on the 'knowledge and intent' of their employees, and this only applies when the employee or agent acted, or acquired knowledge, within the scope of their employment, at least partly to benefit the corporation. When liability depends on the knowledge, intent, or actions of multiple individuals, determining corporate criminal liability becomes more complex and challenging.

The 1985 Model Penal Code, Section 2.07[186] states:

1. A corporation may be convicted of the commission of an offense if:
   i) the offense is a violation or the offense is defined by a statute other than the Code in which a legislative purpose to impose liability on corporations appears and the conduct is performed by an agent of the corporation acting in behalf of the corporation within the scope of his office or employment, except that if the law defining the offense designates the agents for whose conduct the corporation is accountable or the circumstances under which it is accountable, such provisions shall apply; or
   ii) the offense consists of an omission to discharge a specific duty of affirmative performance imposed on corporations by law; or
   iii) the commission of the offense was authorized, requested, commanded, performed or recklessly tolerated by the board of directors or by a high managerial agent acting in behalf of the corporation within the scope of his office or employment.

(2) When absolute liability is imposed for the commission of an offense, a legislative purpose to impose liability on a corporation shall be assumed, unless the contrary plainly appears.

(3) ……

(4) As used in this Section:

(a) "corporation" does not include an entity organized as or by a governmental agency for the execution of a governmental program;

(b) "agent" means any director, officer, servant, employee or other person authorized to act in behalf of the corporation or association and, in the case of an unincorporated association, a member of such association;

(c) "high managerial agent" means an officer of a corporation or an unincorporated association, or, in the case of a partnership, a partner, or any other agent of a corporation or association having duties of such responsibility that his conduct may fairly be assumed to represent the policy of the corporation or association.

A corporation, therefore, is criminally liable for the federal crimes its employees or agents commit in its interest. Corporate directors, officers, employees, and agents are individually liable for the crimes they commit and conspire to commit. Statutes establishing the offense of corporate criminal liability do not generally release the officers, employees, or agents from any liability they may have. Prosecuting a corporation is not a substitute for prosecuting criminally culpable individuals within or outside the corporation. Corporations and individuals, if convicted, may face the same penalties. With the exception that corporations cannot be physically imprisoned, they can be ordered to pay a fine and restitution, placed on probation, have their property confiscated, and be barred from engaging in some commercial activity. The federal Sentencing Guidelines determine the sentencing consequences for an organization that has been convicted. For example, the corporate fine Guidelines start with the assertion that if the statutory maximum permits, a corrupt corporation should be fined to the extent that it is put out of business. If a corporation operated for criminal purposes or by criminal means, the amount of the fine should strip it of all of its assets. In other cases, the Guidelines recommend fines and other sentencing options by the nature and seriousness of the crime and the level of corporate culpability.[187] In the USA, it is the Department of Justice (DOJ) that decides whether to prosecute a corporation, any culpable employees, or both.

In 2019, two Bills that would impose several substantial changes were introduced. The Corporate Executive Accountability Act would primarily target white-collar crime and would allow for prosecuting corporate executives for their negligent conduct. The Bill would do away with the requirement that the defendants must have knowledge of the conduct constituting the crime and proposes that executives of large companies could be criminally prosecuted if they are found to have acted negligently in failing to prevent criminal acts committed by the companies they supervise. The Corporate Executive Accountability Act expands criminal liability to negligent executives of corporations with more than $1 billion in annual revenue who: "Are found guilty, plead guilty, or enter into a deferred or non-prosecution agreement for any crime; Are found liable or enter a settlement with any state or federal regulator for the violation of any civil law if that violation affects the health, safety, finances, or personal data of 1% of the American population or 1% of the population of any state; Are found liable or guilty of a second civil or criminal violation for different activity while operating under a civil or criminal judgment of any court, a deferred prosecution or non-prosecution agreement, or settlement with any state or federal agency."[188] The proposed law would apply to executives of companies, the company's president, vice presidents, and any other officer or person who has the authority to make a policy decision, as long as "by reason of the position of the individual in the corporation, [he or she] has the responsibility and authority to take necessary measures to prevent or remedy violations."[189] Senator Warren who proposed the Bill stated "the bill would "expand[] criminal liability to any corporate executive who negligently oversees a giant company causing severe harm to U.S. families," "[and that i]f top executives knew they would be hauled out in handcuffs for failing to reasonably oversee the companies they run, they would have a real incentive to better monitor their operations and snuff out any wrongdoing before it got out of hand."[190] The Bill has not, to date, been enacted.

The second Bill announced is the "Ending Too Big to Jail Act," which was initially introduced in 2018, aiming to introduce three changes, namely: to create a permanent unit within the Treasury Department mandated with investigating fraud committed by financial institutions; require executives of financial institutions with assets greater than $10 billion to annually certify that they "have conducted due diligence and found that there is no criminal conduct or civil fraud in the financial institution … that has not been disclosed in full to the Department of Justice or the applicable regulator"; and require the courts first to determine whether a deferred prosecution agreement is in the public interest before approving them. [191] Despite being endorsed by Public Citizen, Americans for Financial Reform, Take on Wall Street, and the Consumer Federation of America, the Bill did not go through the committee stage and was not enacted into law.[192]

CONCLUSION

The detailed and in-depth analysis of recent and updated legislation regarding corporate homicide in several countries, including the UK, Australia, New Zealand, the USA, and France, highlights the significant steps and developments taken by various legislative bodies to strengthen laws related to corporate manslaughter. It also demonstrates the different approaches taken by multiple jurisdictions in holding individuals, aviation organizations, and other organizations accountable for accidents that have resulted in loss of life.

NOTES

1. Jabbra, J.G. and Dwivedi, O.P. (eds.). 1989. *Public Service Accountability: A Comparative Perspective.* Hartford, CT: Kumarian Press.
2. *The Bywell Castle* [1879] 4 PD 219.

3. Rogers, W.V.H. 2002. *Winfield & Jolowitz on Tort.* 16th Edition. London: Sweet & Maxwell.
4. per Baron Anderson in *Blyth v Birmingham Waterworks Co* [1856] 11 Ex 781.
5. per Lord Wright in *Lochgelly Iron & Cool Co v M'Mullan* [1934] AC. 1.
6. *Donoghue v Stevenson* [1932] AC 562.
7. *Caparo Industries Plc v Dickman* [1990] 2 A.C. 605. 'What emerges is that, in addition to the foreseeability of damage, a necessary ingredient.
8. *Hedley Byrne & Co. v Heller & Partners Ltd* [1964] 2 QB 412.
9. *The* Wagon *Mound, The No. 1* [1961] See *Overseas Tankship (UK) Ltd v Morts. Docks & Engineering Co. Ltd.* [1961] UKPC 1, [1961] AC 388, [1961] 1 All ER 404.
10. *Bolam v Friern Hospital Management Committee* [1957] 1 WLR 583.
11. *Nettleship v Weston* [1971] 2 QB. 691.
12. *Voli v Inglewood Shire Council* [1963] 110 CLR 74.
13. *Saif Ali v Sydney Mitchell & Co* [1980] AC 198.
14. *McInnerny v McDougall* [1938] 1 DLR 22, [1937] 3 WWR 625, 7 FLJ (Can) 227.
15. *Saif Ali v Sydney Mitchell & Co.* [1980] AC 198.
16. *Taylor v Alidar Ltd* [1976] IRLR 420 and [1978] IRLR 82 CA.
17. Shawcross and Beaumont. 2002. *Air Law.* 4th edition. Reissue. London: Butterworth.
18. Kane, R., and Pyne, T., The legal status and liability of the copilot' Part II, Air & Space Law Vol XX. Number 1, 1995.
19. ICAO. *Human Factors Training Manual 1998 Doc 9683-AN/950.*
20. *Hayes v United States* [5th Cir. 1990] 899 F.2d 438.
21. See *Brooks v United States* [5th Circ. 1983] 695 F. 2d 984, 987. Cited in Hayes at 17. *Hayes v United States* [5th Cir. 1990] 899 F.2d 438.
22. See *Shankle v United States* [5th Cir. 1986] 796 F. 2d 742, 745. (And City *of New Orleans, Etc. v American Commercial, Etc.* [5th Cir. 1981] 662 F 2d 1121, 1123. Cited in *Hayes* at 17. *Hayes v United States* [5th Cir. 1990] 899 F.2d 438.
23. *Hayes v United States* [5th Cir. 1990] 899 F.2d 438.
24. *Goldman v Thai Airways International Ltd* [1983] 1 WLR 118.
25. The 1929 Convention for the Unification of certain rules relating to international carriage by air, commonly known as the Warsaw Convention.
26. *Goldman v Thai Airways International Ltd* [1983] 1 WLR 118.
27. *R v Caldwell* [1982] A.C. 341 354, cited in Goldman's case. *Goldman v Thai Airways International Ltd* [1983] 1 WLR 118.
28. *Susanne Yvonne Andrews v British Airways* [2008] EWCA Civ 1308.
29. Nelson, J., "Singapore Airlines 'lowballing' turbulence passengers, says lawyer," 24 September 2024. Available at https://australianaviation.com.au/2024/09/singapore-airlines-low-balling-turbulence-passengers-says-lawyer/.
30. *Yates v US* [1974] 497 F 2d 878 at 882-3 (10th Circ).
31. *Delta Airlines Inc. v US* [1977] 561 F2d 381 (1st Circ).
32. Doc 4444-RAC/501 Procedures for Air Navigation Services, Rules of the Air and Air Traffic Services.
33. *Nicole v Simmonds* [1975] WAR 1 W Aust SC.
34. *Coatney v Berkshire* [1974] 500 F 2d 290 (8th Circ).
35. Hopkin, D.V. 1995. *Human Factors in Air Traffic Control.* 1st edition. London: Taylor and Francis.
36. *Australian National Airlines Commission v The Commonwealth of Australia and Canadian Pacific Airlines* [1975] High Court of Australia. 1974-5 132CLR 582.
37. Bartsch, R. 1996. *Aviation Law in Australia. LBC Information Services.* Sydney: Airline Operations Management Course, UNSW.

38. Boughen, D. 1994. *Air Traffic Controller Liability- The Australian Perspective.* Aviation Law Association of Australia and New Zealand Annual Conference.
39. *Hartz v United States* [1965] 249 F.Supp.119.
40. SWI, "Swiss military jet crash: Air traffic controller found guilty," Translated from German by DeepL/sb, 28 March 2025. Available at https://www.swissinfo.ch/eng/swiss-politics/swiss-military-jet-crash-air-traffic-controller-found-guilty/89081549.
41. ASN, Bombardier CRJ-701ER (CL-600-2C10), 29 January 2025. Available at https://asn.flightsafety.org/wikibase/474365.
42. Ibid.
43. NTSB, "Briefing points on mid-air collision near DCA," 14 February 2025. Available at www.ntsb.gov/investigations/Documents/Feb.14.2025_Briefing_Mid-air_Collision%20near%20DCA.pdf.
44. *Kack v United States* [D.Minn. 1977] 432, F.Supp. 633,624-35.
45. *Kack v United States* [D. Minn. 1977] 432, F. Supp. 633,624-35. At 635.
46. *FAA v NTSB* [1991] (Columbia Circuit) Argued April 8, 1999 Decided September 21, 1999. No. 98-1365.
47. *People v Crossan* [Cal. Dist. Ct. App. 1927] *87 Call. App. 5, 261* page 531.
48. Cyprus Civil Aviation Law 2001.
49. Air Navigation Order (ANO) 2009 which came into force on 1st January 2010.
50. Air Navigation Order 2016 (as amended) No 765 which came into force on 25th August 2016. It was amended by the Air Navigation (Amendment) Order 2017 No 1112 coming into force 14 December 2017, and the Air Navigation (Amendment) Order 2024 No 990 (adding important updates regarding UAS) which came into force on 4th November 2024.
51. Smith and Hogan. 2002. *Criminal Law.* 10th edition. London: Butterworths.
52. *Criminal Code (R.S., 1985, c. C-46).* Available at http://laws.justice.gc.ca/eng/C-46/index.html [accessed: 5 November 2009].
53. S222 (4) (5) (a) and (b).
54. S219((1) 2).
55. See S 221. The 2025 amendment adds part (b) of the section.
56. *German Penal Code, Strafgesetzbuch (StGB).* Online: date. Available at http://bundesrecht.juris.de/englisch_stgb/englisch_stgb.html#StGB_000G6 [accessed: 22 November 2009].
57. *French penal code.* Available at http://195.83.177.9/upl/pdf/code_33.pdf [1 December 2009].
58. Act no. 1996-393 of 13 May 1996. Article 1 *Official Journal* of 14 May 1996; Act no. 2000-647 of 10 July article 1 *Official Journal* of 11 July 2000.
59. Article 221-6 (Act no. 2000-647 of 10 July 2000 Article 4 *Official Journal* of 11 July 2000) (Ordinance no. 2000-916 of 19 September 2000 Article 3 *Official Journal*, 22 September 2000 into force 1 January 2002).
60. Chapter III Endangering other persons, Articles 223-1 to 223-30.
61. Risks caused to other persons, Articles 223-1 to 223-2.
62. Article 223-2.
63. Yang, H. December 2003. *Legal Challenges in Patient Safety in Taiwan.* Department of Health Care Management, CGU. Available at: http://psi.tmu.edu.tw/file/Legal%20Challenges%20in%20Patient%20Safety%20in%20Taiwan-920409%E6%A5%8A%E7%A7%80%E5%84%80.pdf [accessed: 4 March 2008].
64. Hsuey-wen, C., "Reforming justice for young people," Taipei Times, 24 November 2024. Available at https://www.taipeitimes.com/News/editorials/archives/2024/11/07/2003826501.

65. Hsuey-wen, C., “Criminal code should be revised,” Focus Taiwan, 14 October 2023. Available at https://www.taipeitimes.com/News/editorials/archives.
66. Hsuey-wen, C., “Amendment criminalizing contempt of Legislature passes into law,” Focus Taiwan, 28 May 2024. Available at https://focustaiwan.tw/politics/202405280024.
67. Articles 589 Codice Penale.
68. Article 589.
69. *R v Woolin* [1999] 1 A.C. 82; [1998] 3 W.L.R. 382; [1998] 4 All E.R. 103.
70. *R v Franklin* [1883] 15 Cox CC 163.
71. *R v Church* [1966] 1 QB 59, R v Dawson (1985) 81 Cr App R 150.
72. *DPP v Newbury* [1977] AC 500.
73. *AG's Reference (No. 3 of 1994)* [1997] 3 WLR 421.
74. *Lord Hewart CJ in R v Bateman* [1925] 28 Cox's Crim Cas 33.
75. *R v Bateman* [1925] Cr. App R. 8.
76. *Adomako* [1995] 1 A.C. 171.
77. Lancefield, N., “Pilot fined for failing to communicate during flight,” The Independent, 20 March 2025. Available at https://www.independent.co.uk/news/uk/crime/civil-aviation-authority-pilot-nats-oslo-aviation-b2718845.html.
78. Annex I – Rules of the Air, Section 8 Air traffic control service, Standardised European Rules of the Air. SERA.8035 Communications.
79. UK Civil Aviation Authority, Prosecutions, “Commercial pilot fined after RAF intercepted flight,” 20 March 2025. Available at https://www.caa.co.uk/newsroom/news/commercial-pilot-fined-after-raf-intercepted-flight/.
80. Ibid.
81. Health and Safety at Work Act 2015, Public Act 2015 No 7. Available at https://www.legislation.govt.nz/act/public/2015/0070/latest/DLM5976660.html.
82. Hesketh, H., “Recklessness” under the Health and Safety at Work Act 2015, 19 February 2021. Available at https://www.heskethhenry.co.nz/insights-opinion/recklessness-under-the-health-and-safety-at-work-act-2015/.
83. *Sarginson v Civil Aviation Authority* [2020] NZHC 3199.
84. Ibid.
85. Hesketh, H., “When is someone ‘at work’ under the Health and Safety at Work Act?,” 18 February 2021. Available at https://www.heskethhenry.co.nz/insights-opinion/the-high-court-clarifies-the-liability-of-officers-under-the-health-and-safety-at-work-act-2015/.
86. HSWA 2015 op cit., Subpart 2 – Duties of PCBUs.
87. Hesketh, H., op cit.
88. HSWA, S18 Meaning of Officer.
89. HSWA s18 (a) Meaning of Officer.
90. HSWA s18 (b) (c) (d).
91. Ibid.
92. Hesketh, H., op cit.
93. NTSB, Aviation Investigation Final Report, Accident number CEN22FA436, Registration number N7329F, 5 June 2024. Available at Report_CEN22FA436_106014_11_16_2024%206_01_01%20AM.pdf.
94. United States District Court for The Eastern District of Pennsylvania, Case 5:24-cr-00277-JMG Document 1 Filed 08/01/24 Page 1 of 11. 1 August 2024. Available at https://s3.documentcloud.org/documents/25032746/mcpherson-indictment.pdf.
95. Rohrlich, J., “‘Grossly negligent’ flight instructor charged in plane crash that killed student pilot,” 5 August 2024. Available at https://www.independent.co.uk/travel/news-and-advice/pennsylvania-plane-crash-flight-instructor-manslaughter-b2591638.html.

96. Ibid., pp. 7–8.
97. Ibid., p. 9.
98. Haley Davoren, H., "Unlicensed flight instructor, school owner charged with conspiracy, fraud in connection to deadly 2022 crash," GlobalAir, 5 March 2025. Available at https://www.globalair.com/articles/unlicensed-flight-instructor-school-owner-charged-with-conspiracy-fraud-in-connection-to-deadly-2022-crash?id=8647.
99. French Penal Code Section 11 – Involuntary Offences against life, Article 221-6.
100. Article 221-7.
101. Crown Prosecution Service, "CPS advises first corporate manslaughter charge under new act." 2009. Available at http://www/cps.gov.uk/news/press_releases/124_09.
102. Lowery, J. and Wilson, P. 2002. *These Workers Should Not Have Died. Their Only Mistake Was to Turn Up at Work that Day.* [Online]. Available at http://www.vthc.org.au/your-rights-at-work/ohs/industrial-manslaughter/case-studies/case-studies/index.cfm [accessed on: 10 March 2003].
103. Lowery, J., and Wilson, P. 2002. *These Workers Should Not Have Died. Their Only Mistake Was to Turn Up at Work that Day...* [Online]. Available at http://www.vthc.org.au/your-rights-at-work/ohs/industrial-manslaughter/case-studies/case-studies/index.cfm [accessed on: 10 March 2003].
104. Fogarty, D. 2009. *Auscarts Convicted Over Go-kart Death. Available at* www.news.com.au AAP [accessed on: 10 March 2003].
105. *DPP v. Newbury* [1977] A.C. 500.
106. "Zeebrugge disaster was no accident," BBC, 8 October 1987. Available at http://news.bbc.co.uk/onthisday/hi/dates/stories/october/8/newsid_2626000/2626265.stm [accessed: 4 October 2004].
107. *R v P & O Ferries (Dover) Ltd* [1990] 93 Cr App R 72.
108. "Putting directors in the dock," BBC News, 22 January 2001. Available at http://news.bbc.co.uk/2/hi/uk_news/1130544.stm [accessed: 3 January 2004].
109. Welham, M.C. 2003. Corporate Manslaughter: The proposed offence of Corporate Killing and the potential impact in the EU. Available at http://www.sheilapantry.com/oshworld/focus/2003/200312.html#footnotes [accessed: 17 February 2005].
110. Transportsfriend, Health and Safety, "Corporate Manslaughter & Corporate Homicide," 2024. Available at https://www.transportsfriend.org/health-safety/manslaughter/.
111. Byrne, D., "What is corporate manslaughter?," Corporate Governance Institute, 2024. Available at https://www.thecorporategovernanceinstitute.com/insights/guides/what-is-corporate-manslaughter/.
112. CQMS Safety-Scheme, "Corporate Manslaughter," 2024. Available at https://cqms-ltd.co.uk/blog/category/corporate-manslaughter/page/3/.
113. Ibid.
114. Thompsons Solicitors, "Worker killed falling through roof," 4 October 2012. Available at https://www.thompsons.law/services/personal-injury-claims.
115. Croneri, "Corporate manslaughter and Homicide Act 2007," 13 February 2024. Available at https://app.croneri.co.uk/topics/corporate-manslaughter-and-corporate-homicide-act-2007/indepth?section=3554&topic=4001.
116. CQMS, op cit.
117. Croneri, "Corporate manslaughter and Homicide Act 2007," 13 February 2024. Available at https://app.croneri.co.uk/topics/corporate-manslaughter-and-corporate-homicide-act-2007/indepth?section=3554&topic=4001.
118. Ibid.
119. The Guardian, "CAV Aerospace fined £600,000 for death of worker crushed by Airbus parts," 31 July 2015. Available at https://www.theguardian.com/uk-news/2015/jul/31/cav-aerospace-fined-600000-death-worker-crushed-airbus-parts.

120. Croner, op cit.
121. *R v Dr Errol Cornish* [2015] EWHC 2967 (QB). Available at https://vlex.co.uk/vid/r-v-dr-errol-79270438.
122. Ibid.
123. Elson, S., "Company fined £550,000 in first corporate manslaughter sentencing under new guideline," Out-Law News, 20 July 2016. Available at: https://www.pinsentmasons.com/out-law/news/company-fined-550000-in-first-corporate-manslaughter-sentencing-under-new-guidelins.
124. Croner, op cit.
125. Ibid.
126. Croneri, "Corporate manslaughter and Homicide Act 2007," 13 February 2024. Available at https://app.croneri.co.uk/topics/corporate-manslaughter-and-corporate-homicide-act-2007/indepth?section=3554&topic=4001.
127. Liversedge, B., "Recycling firm fined for manslaughter of 23-year-old man," Safety Management, 8 December 2020. Available at https://www.britsafe.org/safety-management/2020/recycling-firm-fined-for-manslaughter-of-23-year-old-man#:~:text=A%20Cornish%20waste%20recycling%20company,He%20died%20at%20the%20scene.
128. Quinn, B., "'Grossly negligent' care home fined £1m after death of woman, 93," The Guardian, 8 October 2021. Available at https://www.theguardian.com/uk-news/2021/oct/08/grossly-negligent-care-home-fined-1m-after-death-of-woman-93.
129. Croneri, "Corporate manslaughter and Homicide Act 2007," 13 February 2024. Available at https://app.croneri.co.uk/topics/corporate-manslaughter-and-corporate-homicide-act-2007/indepth?section=3554&topic=4001.
130. Campbell, U., and Taylor, P., "Company and director sentencing for corporate manslaughter offences," Health and Safety / Corporate Manslaughter – Q1 2024, Kingsley Napley, 4 April 2024. Available at https://www.kingsleynapley.co.uk/insights/blogs/criminal-law-blog/health-and-safety-corporate-manslaughter-q1-2024.
131. UK Government, "More action to fight fraud, bribery and other economic crime," 15 June 2023. Available at https://www.gov.uk/government/news/more-action-to-fight-fraud-bribery-and-other-economic-crime.
132. S.196(4) Economic Crime and Corporate Transparency Act 2023.
133. Ivanovs, A., "UK government proposes to extend corporate criminal liability to all crimes," 17 March 2025. Available at https://www.ashurst.com/en/insights/uk-government-proposes-to-extend-corporate-criminal-liability-to-all-crimes/.
134. Blumenfeld, 2018; NZ Police, 2017, cited in Camila, B., "Why Aotearoa New Zealand needs a corporate Homicide Bill," New Zealand Journal of Health and Safety Practice; Vol 1, Ed 2, July 2024. Available at https://ojs.victoria.ac.nz/nzjhsp/article/view/9549.
135. Camila, B., ibid.
136. Ibid.
137. Worksafe, "Health and Safety at Work Act 2015," 4 September 2017. Available at https://www.worksafe.govt.nz/laws-and-regulations/acts/hswa/
138. Camila, B., "Why Aotearoa New Zealand needs a corporate Homicide Bill," New Zealand Journal of Health and Safety Practice; Vol 1, Ed 2, July 2024. Available at https://ojs.victoria.ac.nz/nzjhsp/article/view/9549.
139. Camila, B., "Why Aotearoa New Zealand needs a corporate Homicide Bill," New Zealand Journal of Health and Safety Practice; Vol 1, Ed 2, July 2024. Available at https://ojs.victoria.ac.nz/nzjhsp/article/view/9549.

140. Ciara Donnelly, C., "Understanding industrial manslaughter laws: Where is Australia at in 2024?," Marsh Advisory, Pacific, Updated 22 July 2024 (Originally published 30 November 2023). Available at https://www.marsh.com/au/services/risk-consulting/insights/industrial-manslaughter-laws-australia-2023-update.html.
141. Lander & Rogers, "Industrial manslaughter soon to be an offence in almost every jurisdiction," November 2023. Available at https://www.landers.com.au/legal-insights-news/industrial-manslaughter-soon-to-be-an-offence-in-almost-every-jurisdiction.
142. Biling, S., and Biling, S., "Industrial manslaughter offence in Australia: A state-by-state analysis," HFW, 9 July 2024. Available at https://www.hfw.com/insights/industrial-manslaughter-offence-in-australia-a-state-by-state-analysis/.
143. Ciara Donnelly, C., Understanding industrial manslaughter laws: Where is Australia at in 2024?, Marsh Advisory, Pacific, Updated 22 July 2024 (Originally published 30 November 2023). Available at https://www.marsh.com/au/services/risk-consulting/insights/industrial-manslaughter-laws-australia-2023-update.html.
144. Selinger, M., and Hamer, C., "Update: Industrial manslaughter offences across Australia," 21 February 2024. Available at www.holdingredlich.Com/Update-Industrial-Manslaughter-Offences-Across_Australia#:~:Text=Industrial%20manslaughter%20became%20an%20offence,A%20fine%20of%20%2410%20million.
145. Ibid.
146. Banks, D. et al., Gilbert and Tobin, "New South Wales creates new industrial manslaughter offence," 10 July 2024. Available at https://www.gtlaw.com.au/insights/new-south-wales-creates-new-industrial-manslaughter-offence.
147. Ibid.
148. Ibid.
149. Ibid., see R v Brisbane A*uto Recycling Pty Ltd* [2020] QDC 113.
150. Ibid., see *R v Jeffrey Owens* [2022] QD CSR 168.
151. Ibid.
152. Ibid.
153. Ciara Donnelly, C. op cit.
154. Banks, D. et al., op. cit.
155. Ciara Donnelly, C., "Understanding industrial manslaughter laws: Where is Australia at in 2024?" Marsh Advisory, Pacific, Updated 22 July 2024 (Originally published 30 November 2023). Available at https://www.marsh.com/au/services/risk-consulting/insights/industrial-manslaughter-laws-australia-2023-update.html.
156. Cass. Crim., 17 December 2003, n°00-87.872, cited in Bomm, P., et al., "Corporate criminal liability under French law, a decade of dramatic change," Novacelle, 19 April 2022. Available at https://navacelle.law/corporate-criminal-liability-under-french-law-a-decade-of-dramatic-change/.
157. Lasry, E., "Corporate liability in France," Baker McKenzie France, 2024. Available at https://www.globalcompliancenews.com/white-collar-crime/corporate-liability-in-france/.
158. Cass. Crim., 21 November 2017, n°16-86.667.
159. Lasry, E., op cit.
160. Bomm, P., et al., op cit.
161. Ibid.
162. Lasry, E., op cit.
163. Ibid.
164. Ibid.
165. Ibid.
166. Ibid.
167. Ibid.

168. Ibid.
169. Hepher, T., "Airbus faces UK criminal probe over potential export control breach," Reuters, 31 July 2024. Available at https://www.reuters.com/business/aerospace-defense/airbus-faces-uk-criminal-probe-over-export-control-rules-2024-07-30/.
170. "National Prosecutor's Office, summary 2020," National Prosecutor's Office, p. 3. Available at PNF-brochure_A5_2201.pdf (justice.fr) cited in Bomm, P., et al., op cit.
171. Article 121-3 of the French Criminal Code.
172. LeTutour Avocats, "Manslaughter & unintentional injury: French law firm intervening in manslaughter and unintentional injury cases." Available at https://letutour-avocats.fr/en/skills/manslaughter-and-unintentional-injury/.
173. Baum Hedlund Aristei & Goldman PC, "Baum Hedlund files Germanwings crash lawsuit for two Americans killed," 30 January 2017. Available at https://www.wisnerbaum.com/blog/2017/january/baum-hedlund-files-germanwings-crash-lawsuit-for/.
174. The Associated Press, "Germanwings flight 4U9525 co-pilot Andreas Lubitz deliberately crashed jet: Prosecutor," 26 March 2015, last updated 27 March 2015. Available at https://www.cbc.ca/news/world/germanwings-flight-4u9525-co-pilot-andreas-lubitz-deliberately-crashed-jet-prosecutor-1.3010045.
175. ABC News, "Germanwings could face involuntary Homicide charges in Alps Crash." 11 June 2015. Available at https://abcnews.go.com/International/germanwings-face-involuntary-homicide-charges-alps-crash/story?id=31694798#:~:text=%E2%80%94%20%2D%2D%20The%20criminal,to%20negligence%2C%20investigators%20announced%20today.
176. Timothy Jones, T., "France drops Germanwings crash inquiry," 3 March 2022. Available at https://www.dw.com/en/germanwings-crash-france-drops-manslaughter-proceedings/a-61000671.
177. Vietnam Investment Review, "Germany closes Germanwings crash probe," 10 January 2017. Available at https://vir.com.vn/germany-closes-germanwings-crash-probe-46871.html.
178. BBC, "Concorde crash: Continental Airlines killings verdict quashed," 29 November 2012. Available at https://www.bbc.com/news/world-europe-20545201.
179. Maud, M., "The Concorde accident criminal trial in France," Air & Space Law Journal, Volume 36, Issue 2 (2011) pp. 131–138. Available at https://kluwerlawonline.com/journalarticle/Air+and+Space+Law/36.2/AILA2011017.
180. Lauter, D., "Continental, mechanic guilty of manslaughter in Concorde crash," Los Angeles Times, 7 December 2010. Available at https://www.latimes.com/archives/la-xpm-2010-dec-07-la-fg-concorde-crash-ruling-20101207-story.html.
181. Criminal Chamber of the *Cour de Cassation*, 21 June 2022, No. 20-86.857.
182. Soulier Avocats, "For a legal entity to be held criminally liable, it is necessary to identify said entity's body or representative who has committed the offense," Legal Insights, 11 August 2022. Available at https://www.soulier-avocats.com/en/for-a-legal-entity-to-be-held-criminally-liable-it-is-necessary-to-identify-said-entitys-body-or-representative-who-has-committed-the-offense/.
183. Casassus, B., "Drug company Servier is found guilty of manslaughter and aggravated deceit over Mediator diabetes drug," 31 March 2021. Available at https://www.bmj.com/content/372/bmj.n873.full.
184. Coex, T., "French company convicted of manslaughter over deadly diet pill," AFP, 29 March 2021. Available at https://www.aljazeera.com/news/2021/3/29/french-court-convicts-fines-pharma-firm-for-deadly-diet-pill.
185. News Desk, Food Safety News, "Nestlé France faces charges in Buitoni case," 9 July 2024. Available at https://www.foodsafetynews.com/2024/07/nestle-france-faces-charges-in-buitoni-case/.

186. Model Penal Code, §2.07, Liability of Corporations, Unincorporated Associations and Persons Acting, or Under a Duty to Act, in Their Behalf 1985. Available at https://www.law.upenn.edu/faculty/paul-robinson/clrgcodes/MPC.html.
187. Doyle, C., "Corporate criminal liability: An abbreviated overview of federal law," Updated 30 October 2013. Available at https://crsreports.congress.gov/product/pdf/R/R43294/2.
188. Corporate Executive Accountability Act Summary, 1 April 2019. Available at www.warren.senate.gov/imo/media/doc/2019.4.1%20Corporate%20Executive%20Accountability%20Act%20Summary.pdf.
189. Dassin, L.L., et al., "Bill proposal-corporate executives criminally accountable for negligent conduct," Harvard Law School Forum on Corporate Governance, 18 April 2019. Available at https://corpgov.law.harvard.edu/2019/04/18/bill-proposal-corporate-executives-criminally-accountable-for-negligent-conduct.
190. Ibid.
191. Ibid.
192. Op cit., Corporate Executive Accountability Act Summary.

3 The Greying of the Black Box

Aviation Accident Investigation

3.1 INTRODUCTION

Investigating an accident may have various purposes depending on the type of accident. The objective of conducting the technical safety investigation into an aviation accident under ICAO Annex 13 is to establish the course of events leading up to the accident, (that is to identify "what, where and when"), to determine the direct and root causes or the contributing factors (that is the "why") and to identify any measures that ought to be taken to prevent similar future accidents from occurring. The legal approach to an investigation involves identifying the parties at fault and apportioning blame and liability to them, either in the form of criminal or civil liability. In aviation investigations, the investigation takes on a completely different turn, as the purpose of investigating aviation accidents is to enhance safety by identifying the circumstances that led to the accident and making safety recommendations to prevent similar accidents from recurring.

The responsibility for investigating an accident rests with different people, depending on the type of investigation and its purpose. In aviation accidents, this responsibility rests with the relevant accident investigation body, as established by ICAO's rules and procedures. However, in an investigation to evaluate the potential for criminal prosecution, the responsibility rests with the police and the prosecuting authorities, and the courts have the ultimate responsibility for passing the appropriate sentence once liability and blameworthiness have been proved.

The technical, safety investigation should identify all the factors that may have had an impact on the sequence of events leading up to the accident and analyze the weight of each of these factors, ranging from the aircraft manufacturers, the technical/maintenance/engineering systems, the air traffic controllers, the crew, their managers, regulators, and the government.

DOI: 10.1201/9781003724872-3

3.2 THE LEGAL FRAMEWORK OF AN AVIATION ACCIDENT INVESTIGATION

3.2.1 International Level – ICAO Annex 13

The investigation of international aviation accidents and incidents is governed by the accident investigation standards and recommended practices established by the International Civil Aviation Organization (ICAO), as mandated by the Chicago Convention in 1944. The Convention applies only to civil aircraft, not to state aircraft, and it is one of the most essential aviation instruments.

Annex 13 to the Convention deals with the procedures to be adopted in the event of an aviation accident or incident and contains "Standards" and "Recommended Practices" which provide the background for the investigation. The aim of Annex 13 is to "standardize the procedures of reporting aircraft accidents and incidents; to establish procedures ensuring the participation of experts in accident and incident investigation; and to ensure the expeditious publication of important safety and airworthiness information." The technical investigation is a process conducted for the purpose of accident prevention, which includes the gathering and analysis of information, the drawing of conclusions, including the determination of causes, and, when appropriate, the making of safety recommendations.

In the event of an accident to an aircraft of a contracting State occurring in the territory of another contracting State and involving death or serious injury or indicating a serious technical defect in the aircraft or air navigation facilities, the State in which the accident occurs will institute an inquiry into the circumstances of the accident.

The terms "accident," "incident," and "serious incident" are defined in Annex 13 to ICAO (ICAO 2001)[1] as follows:

3.2.1.1 Accident

An occurrence associated with the operation of an aircraft that takes place between the time any person boards the aircraft with the intention of flight until such time as all such persons have disembarked, in which:

(a) a person is fatally or seriously injured as a result of:
- being in the aircraft, or
- direct contact with any part of the aircraft, including parts which have become detached from the aircraft, or
- direct exposure to jet blast, *except* when the injuries are from natural causes, self-inflicted or inflicted by other persons, or when the injuries are to stowaways hiding outside the areas normally available to the passengers and crew; or

(b) the aircraft sustains damage or structural failure which:
- adversely affects the structural strength, performance, or flight characteristics of the aircraft, and
- would normally require major repair or replacement of the affected component, *except* for engine failure or damage, when the damage is

limited to the engine, its cowlings or accessories; or for damage limited to propellers, wing tips, antennas, tires, brakes, fairings, small dents or puncture holes in the aircraft skin; or

(c) the aircraft is missing or is completely inaccessible.

Note 1. For statistical uniformity only, an injury resulting in death within thirty days of the date of the accident is classified as a fatal injury by ICAO.

Note 2. An aircraft is considered to be missing when the official search has been terminated and the wreckage has not been located.

3.2.1.2 Incident

An occurrence, other than an accident, associated with the operation of an aircraft that affects or could affect the safety of operation.

Note. The types of incidents which are of main interest to the International Civil Aviation Organization for accident prevention studies are listed in the Accident/Incident Reporting Manual (Doc 9156).[2]

3.2.1.3 Serious Incident

An incident involving circumstances indicating that an accident nearly occurred.

Note 1. The difference between an accident and a serious incident lies only in the result.

Note 2. Examples of serious incidents can be found in Attachment D of Annex 13 and the ICAO Accident/Incident Reporting Manual (Doc 9156).

In accordance with Annex 13, the State where the accident occurs is responsible for preserving the aircraft wreckage and its contents immediately and for initiating the investigation. It has the option to invite another government to participate in the investigation. Other States, the State of Registry, the State of Manufacturer and Design, the State of the Operator, and a State with an interest because of citizens on board are entitled to participate in the investigation by the appointment of "Accredited representatives" and Technical Advisers. Treaties and other special agreements between countries often include provisions allowing agents of a particular government to participate in the investigation of foreign accidents.

It is specifically stated that "The sole objective of the investigation of an accident or incident shall be the prevention of accidents and incidents. It is not the purpose to apportion blame or liability" (Annex 13 Chapter 3.1).

Even though it is mentioned explicitly that the purpose of this investigation differs from a normal legal investigation, the purpose of which is to determine criminal and/or civil liability, it does not ensure that, in practice, the evidence and results of the investigation are not used in subsequent legal consequences and litigation. Concurrent with the accident investigation carried out in accordance with Annex 13, police and judicial investigations will also be conducted to determine what offenses were committed, the exact nature of the offenses, and the parties allegedly involved. The precise details of the accident need to be established to assist the victims in establishing their claims. The person or persons who are allegedly blameworthy for the accident and the legal basis of their liability need to be determined.

The evidence, data, and other specific details gathered in the course of the investigation are also significant to the police authorities and the plaintiffs when establishing their claim. Annex 13, however, stipulates that the investigators shall not make the information available to those persons "unless the appropriate authority for the administration of justice determines that their disclosure outweighs the adverse domestic and international impact such action may have on future investigations" (Chapter 5.2).

The accident investigation authority has independence in conducting the investigation. The investigator-in-charge has unrestricted access to the wreckage and full control over it. Once the investigation has been completed, a final report must be published containing all relevant factual information relating to the circumstances of the accident (Chapter 6).

An analysis of this information, leading to an assessment of the causes as well as safety recommendations intended to reduce the likelihood of a similar accident occurring in the future, is also included. A draft of this report is first circulated to all States that participated in the investigation for their comments. Any comments made should then be taken into account by the state drafting the report. The report will then be amended, or it may include the dissenting comments, before the final report is issued.

3.2.2 European Level – Council Directive 94/56/EC

At an international level, Annex 13 lays down the international standards and recommended practices relating to aircraft accident and incident investigation. At a European level, in an effort to provide the competent authorities with an appropriate legal framework within which to investigate civil aviation accidents and incidents, the European Community adopted Council Directive 94/56/EC,[3] which established the principles of Annex 13 to the Chicago Convention into European law and provides the fundamental principles governing the investigation of civil aviation accidents and incidents. Directive 94/56/EC came into effect on 21 November 1994 and applies to investigations into civil accidents and incidents that occur in the territory of the European Community and accidents that occur outside the territory which involve aircraft registered in the EC when another State does not carry out an investigation.

Several significant changes are introduced by the Directive. In accordance with the Chicago Convention, a permanent and "independent" accident and investigation body is established in each State (Article 6). This introduced a change, as previously, the aviation regulatory authority mainly employed the accident investigators. In addition, a clear distinction is made between the judicial inquiry, aimed at establishing liability, and the technical investigation, the status of which was expanded. Another change brought about by the Directive is the provision of powers that enable the investigators, in cooperation with the authorities responsible for the judicial inquiry, to have, inter alia, free access to the accident site, the aircraft and all the other available evidence, immediate access to flight recorders, access to the results of examination of the bodies of victims or of tests made on samples taken from the bodies of victims, etc. Article 7(2) of the Directive further provides that the investigating body shall make the final accident report public as soon as possible, and stipulates that, where possible, this should be done within 12 months of the accident date. Another change was the provision of powers that enable free access to the accident site and all available evidence.

The purpose of the Directive is clearly stated to be to improve air safety by facilitating the expeditious holding of investigations, the sole objective of which is the prevention of future accidents and incidents, and not to apportion blame or liability. The Directive also clearly establishes the principle that a safety recommendation must in no case create a presumption of blame or liability for an accident or incident. Article 7.1 states that "The [investigation] report shall state the sole objective of the investigation….. and contain, where appropriate, safety recommendations."

This clearly reiterates the purpose of an accident investigation as stipulated by Annex 13; however, it needs to be examined whether, in practice, the technical investigation is used to apportion blameworthiness.

The Directive is very similar to Annex 13, and it has a mandatory nature that requires Member States to bring into force laws, regulations, and administrative provisions, providing a uniform legal framework for investigating aviation accidents in Member States. In particular, it imposes a specific obligation on Member States to investigate, determine the status of the investigation, conduct the investigation in the most expedient manner, and publish a report of the investigation. It is essential to emphasize that the Directive stipulates that Member States must define a legal status for the technical investigation of the accident and ensure cooperation with the judicial inquiry (Article 5.1). It is therefore up to each State to establish an "independent" accident and investigation body or entity to investigate civil aviation accidents and incidents "in order to avoid any conflict of interest and any possible involvement in the causes of the occurrences being investigated." The accident investigation committee should be totally impartial, owing no allegiance to the government or the industry, and should decide every case in relation to the air safety accident, the lessons to be learnt therefrom, aiming solely to prevent future similar accidents.

EU Directive 94/56 has been repealed and replaced by Regulation No. 996/2010,[4] amended by Regulation (EU) No 376/2014, Regulation (EU) 2018/1139 of the European Parliament and of the Council Regulation (EU) 2024/1230.

At a domestic level, individual states provide for accident investigation by enacting domestic legislation, constructed mainly within the framework of the guidelines laid down by ICAO. The regulations of any domestic legislation must conform to the international requirements of Annex 13 and the relevant EU Directives which apply to all 27 member states. The domestic laws have very similar wording reflecting the philosophy promulgated in the international treaty and the European Directive with regard to the purpose of investigating an aviation accident.

It is very clearly stipulated in each legal stratum that the purpose of an aviation investigation is to improve safety by investigating accidents to prevent their recurrence in the future. It is also explicitly stated that the purpose of the investigation is not to apportion blame or liability.

It is this thread that forms the background to examining the investigation of accidents, the final reports compiled, and the ultimate use of the reports in subsequent legal proceedings.

As the purpose of conducting the ICAO Annex 13 safety investigation into an aviation accident is to prevent future accidents by learning safety lessons from the accident investigated, the final report includes a number of safety recommendations. The safety recommendations must be supported by the evidence obtained from the investigation and other related sources. However, there is no framework in place to ensure that the safety lessons have been learnt or that corrective actions have been implemented.

The ICAO Manual of Aircraft Accident Investigation (Doc 9756 2000), updated,[5] refers to the purpose of the accident investigation through reference to the Group Organization, by stating that the primary purpose of the Group system is to establish the facts pertinent to an accident by making use of the specialized knowledge and practical experience of the participating individuals with respect to the construction and operation of the aircraft involved in the accident and of the facilities and services provided to the aircraft prior to the accident. It goes on to ensure that undue emphasis is not placed on any single aspect of the accident by neglecting other aspects that might be significant to the investigation, and that, whenever it is possible to establish a particular point using several methods, all those methods have been resorted to and coordination of results has been ensured.

There have been several significant amendments and developments regarding aviation safety data obtained during the official accident investigation, as well as the admissibility of the final investigation report in a court of law subsequent to an accident, which will now be discussed. An overview of the legal updates is provided at the end of this chapter.

3.3 ADMISSIBILITY OF ACCIDENT INVESTIGATION REPORTS

As stated above, aviation accidents are investigated in accordance with ICAO Annex 13[6] and the national legislation of each country. In addition, in the European Union, accident investigations are conducted in accordance with the 1994 EU Directive 94/56 establishing the fundamental principles governing the investigation of civil aviation accidents and incidents[7] which has been repealed and replaced by Regulation No. 996/2010,[8] amended by Regulation (EU) No 376/2014, Regulation (EU) 2018/1139 of the European Parliament and of the Council Regulation (EU) 2024/1230.

Each stratum of legislation stresses that the sole purpose of investigating an aviation accident or serious incident is not to determine or apportion blame or liability but to make safety recommendations to prevent future similar accidents. The technical investigation conducted in accordance with Annex 13 is non-punitive in nature, and the focus is on establishing the accident scenario by examining the events leading up to the accident in order to identify corrective measures and make safety recommendations to enhance aviation safety. On the other hand, a judicial investigation is often initiated subsequent to an aviation accident or serious incident, seeking to determine the fault and liability of a party and to then apportion blame. The judicial investigators focus on determining the cause of the accident for the sole purpose of determining blameworthy parties, gathering evidence that can clearly establish their guilt and holding them accountable in a court of law for their conduct.

The two independent, often parallel investigations have different aims and objectives, and this frequently results in the judicial authorities and the technical investigators being at odds, particularly with regard to access and use of sensitive safety data such as the cockpit voice recorder (CVR) and Flight Data Recorder (FDR) and the admissibility of the final technical accident investigation report into a court of law in any subsequent civil or criminal proceedings.

Aviation professionals should in no way be exempt from liability for serious legal transgressions and criminal behavior. However, in the interest of justice, judicial authorities should strictly adhere to the correct procedures in their quest to uphold the law and hold wrongdoers accountable for their blameworthy behavior.

Despite the legal framework surrounding the use of aviation accident reports clearly stating that the sole purpose of conducting an investigation is to prevent the recurrence of similar occurrences and not to apportion blame or liability, claimants often seek to use such reports in litigation to support their allegations of blameworthiness. It should also be noted that in some cases, individuals accused of criminal conduct may seek to have the accident report admitted into evidence in a court of law to strengthen their defense.

3.3.1 United Kingdom

3.3.1.1 Rogers & Rogers v Hoyle EWHC/QB, 2013

In the subsequent litigation arising out of a fatal accident which occurred in May 2011, J Leggart had to decide whether the Air Accidents Investigation Branch (AAIB) final report was admissible as evidence in court. The claimants in *Rogers v Hoyle*[9] who were dependents of Mr. Rogers, a passenger in a Tiger Moth biplane piloted by the defendant, Mr. Hoyle, were Mr. Rogers, who was killed when the aircraft crashed on 15 May 2011. Mr. Hoyle survived the accident with serious injuries.

The claimants based their claim on part of the AAIB report which stated that a loop maneuver *"was carried out at too low a height for the pilot to be able to recover from the subsequent spin"* and, further, that as the pilot *"did not have sufficient knowledge or training on the Tiger Moth's correct spin recovery technique, it is probable that he would not have been able to recover from an unintentional spin, especially given the limited height available."*[10] They sought to attach the AAIB report to support several of their claims, inter alia, that he did not have sufficient knowledge or training in the correct spin recovery for that aircraft and that, shortly before the accident, the aircraft was observed pulling up into a loop. The defendant denied this and claimed that the rudder pedals jammed, and thus he could not prevent the aircraft from stalling and flipping over into a spin from which he could not recover.

The defendant contested the admissibility of the report and initiated an application for (1) an order that the parts of their claim relying on the AAIB report be struck out, and (2) a declaration that the report was inadmissible in the current proceedings.[11]

Mr. Justice Leggatt, at first instance, held that the AAIB report was admissible as evidence in civil proceedings, both as evidence of the facts stated in the report and as expert opinion evidence. The judge went on to state that the question regarding the evidential weight to be given to the report was a matter for the Court to decide and concluded that

> *the whole of the AAIB Report is admissible as evidence in these proceedings, with it being a matter for the trial judge to make such use of the report as he or she thinks fit. Even if I had concluded that the AAIB Report contains some inadmissible material, I would not have thought it sensible to engage in an exercise of editing out parts of the report. Even on that view, the whole report should be before the court, with the judge at trial taking into account what is admissible and ignoring the remainder.*[12]

The defendant appealed on three main grounds, namely:

1. The admission of the Report was contrary to the principle in *Hollington v Hewthorn [2943] KB 857*, which held that factual findings made by judges in civil cases cannot be admitted as evidence of fact in later civil proceedings to prevent the latter proceedings from being unduly influenced. The defendant argued that as the AAIB report contained findings of fact based on an evaluation of evidence, it fell within the ambit of this rule.
2. Insofar as the report contained expert evidence, it was inadmissible as it did not comply with the rules of court on expert evidence (CPR Part 35) and should thus be excluded; and
3. That if the AAIB report was found to be admissible, it should be excluded as a matter of discretion under CPR 32 as the first instance court had failed to properly take into account policy considerations when failing to exercise its discretion to exclude the report from evidence, including the prejudice that might be caused to future air accident investigations as a result of the use of AAIB reports in civil proceedings.

The Department for Transport (DFT), representing the interests of the AAIB, as well as the International Air Transport Association (IATA), supported the third argument. Both intervened in the appeal proceedings and made representations that the courts should use their discretion to exclude the report from evidence as its admission would impede future accident investigations and aviation safety.

In a precedent-setting case, the Court of Appeal rejected the appeal on all grounds. It confirmed the decision of the trial judge to admit the report in evidence both as to the facts it contains and as expert opinion evidence.

Clarke LJ delivering judgment on 13 March 2014, stated that

> The potential value of this material to anyone seeking to establish the cause of the accident (and any culpability therefore) is obvious. The inspectors are experienced and expert individuals fulfilling a public duty to investigate air accidents and incidents for the purposes of preventing further accidents or incidents in future. It is no part of their function to attribute blame or responsibility. …I agree with the judge when he said that a non-lawyer would be astonished that the report of the AAIB was not something to which a court could even have regard.[13]

The court held that as the findings in the report were unattributed and that the report did not include direct reporting of witness evidence, this went, in the opinion of the Court, to the weight to be given to the evidence in the report rather than admissibility and that as the report included statements or reported statements of fact, it was *prima facie* admissible.

Secondly, the court did not agree with the submission that the AAIB report fell within the ambit of the *Hollington v Hewthorn* rule. The Court stated that the AAIB was not acting in a judicial or quasi-judicial role, deciding on disputed facts, but that the report was a document containing the accident investigators' expert statements of opinion on statements of fact, and as such, was not rendered inadmissible by the rule. In addition, the court held that CPR Part 35 was not a comprehensive and exclusive code which regulated the admission of expert evidence in civil proceedings, but that it regulated the evidence of experts who were *"instructed to give or prepare expert evidence for the purpose of proceedings,"* and Part 35 therefore did not exclude the admissibility of other expert evidence, such as the AAIB report which was prepared for a different purpose, namely, to prevent accidents.

Addressing the third ground of appeal and the court's discretion over whether to admit the report into evidence, the judge emphasized the court's goal of resolving cases fairly and at a reasonable cost. The judge noted that the court generally favors admitting the report into evidence. The Court of Appeal rejected the arguments (supported by the DFT and IATA) that admitting the report would negatively impact future accident investigations and safety. Clarke LJ stated that, among other points, there is no good reason why the report's admissibility should hinder or restrict inspectors in their work, as they are professionals who are not focused on establishing liability. The court also highlighted the challenges faced by litigants who lack access to information available to investigators, as well as the costs involved in obtaining such information independently. It held that AAIB reports are accessible to litigants and can be used as a basis for a claim or defense. The judge rejected the argument that admitting the reports would harm the work of the AAIB and did not believe that admitting the reports would discourage people from providing information and assistance to accident investigators, as they have a vested interest in aviation safety. He concluded by stating, "I do not, however, regard the admissibility of AAIB reports as so likely to prejudice the interests which the AAIB is there to serve, that they should generally be excluded from consideration in court."

Before the judgment, AAIB's official technical safety reports were occasionally used as evidence in court proceedings following an aviation accident, sometimes assisting claimants in identifying areas and persons to focus on for potential liability or to highlight possible blameworthy actions and raise awareness of potential third-party liability to potential defendants. The Court of Appeal's judgment in this case will increase the courts' admissibility and reliance on the official Annex 13 technical report.

Regardless of the court stressing that nothing in its judgment *"should be taken to mean that anything in the [AAIB Report] is to be treated as conclusive or prima facie conclusive of anything; or as shifting the incidence of the burden of proof,"* the Court did recognize that the AAIB report can be used as direct evidence in litigation. As such, this could reduce the need for independent expert evidence to prove the cause(s) of the accident and any blameworthiness and accountability of those responsible. Despite the concerns raised that parties would be less likely to be transparent and honest during an investigation and that this practice would impede aviation safety, the Court admitted the AAIB report.[14]

3.3.1.2 The Chief Constable of Sussex Police v The Secretary of State for Transport (2016)

In a precedent-setting case relating to a substantive application for disclosure, the QBD in The Chief Constable of Sussex Police v The Secretary of State for Transport (2016)[15] the court had to consider whether or not to order the disclosure of material held by the AAIB arising out of an accident which occurred on 22 August 2015 at the Shoreham Airshow, West Sussex.

While performing a stunt at the Royal Air Force Association air show at the Shoreham Airshow, a Hunter Hawker crashed, killing 11 people on the ground and injuring others, including the pilot. In accordance with Annex 13 and EU Regulation 996/2010, the AAIB, as the competent authority, conducted the technical investigation into the accident. The Sussex Police also conducted their investigation into the accident. During the investigation, the Chief Constable of Sussex, relying on Regulation 18 of the Civil Aviation (Investigation of Air Accidents and Incidents) Regulations 1996, applied to the High Court for the disclosure of material that fell into three categories: First, the statements made in response to interviews or discussions with the pilot. Second, contemporaneous evidence from the flight itself, specifically film footage of the flight recorded by cameras that had been voluntarily installed on the aircraft, and third, material produced by various people after the accident, such as experiments conducted and tests done on various aspects of the flight.[16]

The Secretary of State for Transport, representing the AIIB, did not contest the application but argued that it was the High Court that had to exercise the discretion afforded by Regulation 18 and decide whether it would be in the public interest to order the disclosure of that material. The Secretary of State argued that there were policy considerations against disclosure and that an order to disclose the material would have a significant and adverse domestic and international impact on future safety investigations. In addition, the British Airline Pilots Association (BALPA), opposing the application, submitted that the Court could not order disclosure unless the criteria for making the production order in the Police and Criminal Evidence Act 1984 (PACE) were satisfied and that, in this case, they were not met.[17]

As this application was the first of its kind to be heard in the courts of England and Wales, the court had to devise appropriate procedures for such applications. As such, the first part of the hearing was publicly held in open court with members of the press. Part of the hearing was held in private, where factual matters that might prejudice possible future criminal trials were heard and where the court deemed that it was impossible or inappropriate for the representatives of the Chief Constable to be present. The hearing was conducted in the same manner as if it were considering an application for public interest immunity.[18]

It is important to stress that this case was the first one in which the courts in England and Wales considered such an application. A 2015 judgment of the Scottish Court of Session of the Outer House,[19] in which Lord Jones ordered the disclosure of the cockpit voice recorder and flight data recorder pursuant to Regulation 18 was cited by counsel; however, the court noted that the decision did not set a precedent.[20]

Lawyers cited the only other three cases in different jurisdictions which considered applications for disclosure of material in the context of air accidents; however, as those cases addressed their own set of facts in light of each jurisdiction's domestic law, the court stressed that they did not shed light on the principles of Regulation 18 of the 1996 Regulation and the issues to be dealt with in the present case.

In accordance with the relevant international, national, and local laws, the test that the court must apply is whether the benefits of disclosure outweigh the adverse domestic and international impact that such disclosure may have on the investigation or any future safety investigation. Applying this test, the court considered the three categories of material requested to be disclosed.

3.3.1.2.1 Judgment

With regards to the first category, the court stated that it was almost inconceivable that the witness statements made by the pilot to the AAIB could be ordered to be disclosed to the Chief Constable, and ruled in favor of non-disclosure for the following two reasons. First, Mr. Justice Sing pointed out that this would not only be contrary to Annex 13, the EU Regulation and the 1996 Regulations but that "there would be a serious and obvious chilling effect which would tend to deter people from answering questions by the AAIB with the candour which is necessary when accidents of this sort have to be investigated by it. This would seriously hamper future accident investigations and the protection of public safety by the learning of lessons which may help to prevent similar accidents." Second, it would be unfair to require such disclosure since the purpose of the AAIB interviewing witnesses during an accident investigation is to obtain the fullest possible information, and the powers of the AAIB are such that they compel witnesses to answer questions without the need to provide a caution to the interviewee. This was contrary to a police investigation, which is aimed at obtaining information to be used in a criminal prosecution, and to the powers of the police who can administer the caution and conduct their own interviews with the witnesses.[21]

It is important to note that with regard to the second category, namely the cockpit film footage from the camera which was voluntarily installed for leisure and private commercial reasons, the judge distinguished this material from data obtained by a CVR and FDR which are legally required to be on board an aircraft, and from the ruling in the Lord Advocate case. The British Air Line Pilots Association (BALPA), acting as intervener, raised concerns that if cockpit and image recording were permitted to be given to the police, pilots may be inhibited in what they say or do during an emergency situation and would also be hesitant to have such equipment, which can provide useful information on board, thus impeding the AAIB investigations. The judge was not persuaded by the submissions and ruled that the balance fell in favor of disclosure. As the film footage was a contemporaneous recording of the flight and had significant potential value to the investigation, disclosure of the material, with certain restrictions, was ordered.[22]

The third category related to specialist investigations carried out on behalf of the AAIB, including experiments and tests, as well as some hearings, which were held in private. During the private hearing, the Chief Constable dropped the application for disclosure of the speed calculation and the report of the Health and Safety laboratory. Noting that there was nothing to prevent the police from conducting their own independent investigations to obtain that information, and that all relevant reports, including the speed calculation report, would be annexed to the final AAIB report with names redacted and made publicly available, the judge consented to dropping the applications. What remained for the court to consider were the requests for disclosure of reports of test flights conducted by a specialist pilot and the engineering reports on the mechanical state of the aircraft. Mr. Justice Sing refused the request for disclosure and set out his reasons in the Confidential Annex to the judgment.[23]

The court therefore ruled in favor only of disclosing the cockpit film footage. The court stressed that all parties agreed that in the event of the court ruling in favor of the disclosure of any material, it would be subject to the following conditions: first, the material would be disclosed to the Chief Constable of Sussex for the criminal investigation into the accident; second, that he would retain overall responsibility for the material until the material was returned to the AAIB; third, that he would not further disclose the material except to any experts instructed by the police to further their investigation; the Crown Prosecution Service for the purposes of advising him and for any subsequent criminal prosecution and any solicitor or counsel engaged by them to act as their agents or representatives or any expert instructed by them; the pilot and any other defendant who is prosecuted as a result of the investigation and any solicitor or counsel they engage to ensure their procedural safeguards by way of disclosure in the case of an investigation and criminal prosecution; fourth, that the results of any analysis and any subsequent expert opinion shall be treated on the same confidential level as the rest of the material; and that fifth, the material in the schedule shall be returned to the AAIB once any criminal proceedings have been concluded.[24]

In the same year, 2016, the UK courts had to consider an application for judicial review of a coroner requiring the AAIB to disclose a cockpit flight and voice data recorder and/or a full transcript of that recording.

On 13 March 2014, a Westland Augusta AW139 helicopter crashed at Gillingham Hall, Norfolk, killing both pilots and the two passengers who were on board. The accident was investigated by the AAIB (falling under the Department of Transport), and the accident investigation report was submitted on 8 October 2015. Inquests into the deaths were heard before the Senior Coroner for Norfolk and a jury between 12 and 15 January 2016. Before the inquest, the Norfolk senior coroner required the AAIB's chief inspector to disclose the helicopter CVR and FDR and/or a complete transcript of the CVR. Despite receiving notices on four occasions (24 December 2015, 11, 12, and 13 January 2016) requiring disclosure, the chief inspector refused to comply, stating that the coroner did not have the powers to make such an order. On two occasions, the coroner fined him £100 for non-compliance. The Secretary of State for Transport, supported in substance by the Intervener, the British Airline Pilots Association, challenged the coroner's notices for disclosure as well as the fines imposed.

3.3.1.3 The Queen v Her Majesty's Senior Coroner for Norfolk (2016)

In *The Queen v Her Majesty's Senior Coroner for Norfolk*,[25] the Secretary of State for Transport applied for judicial review of the coroner's decisions.[26] Both sides provided arguments on the 14th and 15th July 2016, and Mr. Justice Singh gave judgment on 28 September 2016. The Secretary of State for Transport argued that the coroner had no power to make such orders as a matter of law and that only the High Court has the power to require such disclosure. The coroner argued that in accordance with the 2009 Coroners and Justice Act, she had the power to require disclosure. As the inquest had been concluded at the time of the judicial review, the court did not have to consider the question whether, if an order of the High Court was in fact required to order disclosure, it should make such an order in this case.[27]

The court referred to relevant local, national, and international law and provided an analysis of Regulation 1996, as outlined above, which implements the UK's obligations under Council Directive 94/56/EC (now repealed and replaced by Regulation (EU) No. 996/2010 and Annex 13). During the hearings, the 10th edition (2010) of Annex 13 was in force, even though reference was made to the 9th edition (2001).

Mr. Justice Singh noted that there is no material difference between the 9th and 10th editions with regard to the point in hand and that both specify that CVR and FDR and the CVR transcript *shall not be disclosed "for purposes other than accident or incident investigation" unless "the appropriate authority for the administration of justice" determines that "disclosure outweighs the adverse domestic and international impact such action may have on that or any future investigations."*[28]

The Lord Chief Justice referred to the trend that coroners often conduct their own investigations into accidents instead of relying on the conclusions of the accident investigating body that has the expertise in the matter and said:

> In the absence of credible evidence that the investigation into an accident is incomplete, flawed or deficient, a coroner conducting an inquest into a death which occurred in an aircraft accident should not consider it necessary to investigate again the matters

> covered or to be covered by the independent investigation of the AAIB. [...] [T]he findings and conclusions should not be reopened.[29]

The Court granted the application for judicial review. It concluded that only the High Court, and not the coroner, had the power to make an order requiring the AAIB to disclose the CVR and FDR and/or a complete transcript of the CVR, and that the coroner had exceeded her powers. The coroner's notices for disclosure, as well as the fine she had imposed for non-compliance, were quashed.[30]

3.3.1.4 Discussion

In the wake of the Court of Appeal decision in *Rogers v Hoyle* that the AAIB report was admissible in civil proceedings and the impact that this decision has had on the willingness of witnesses to provide their testimony to the AAIB in a frank and honest manner, the decisions in the Shoreham and Norfolk case provided some assurance regarding the degree of protection afforded to safety investigations conducted by the AAIB and their reports.

These important cases highlight several essential points. The Lord Chief Justice in Shoreham took the view that the public interest in encouraging frank cooperation with the AAIB outweighed the public interest in providing the information for use in a police investigation. Of particular note, and hopefully to be applied in future cases, is the observation "there would be a serious and obvious 'chilling effect' which would tend to deter people from answering questions by the AAIB with the candour which is necessary when accidents of this sort have to be investigated by it." In accordance with the Shoreham judgment, it is doubtful that witness interviews and statements provided during a safety investigation would be ordered to be disclosed. If there is a concurrent criminal investigation taking place subsequent to an aviation accident, the police would have to conduct a separate investigation and separate interview, and the witness must be afforded the same protection as any other witness in a criminal investigation. It should be noted that sensitive safety data, such as CVR/FDR data (not witness statements), can be ordered to be released for criminal investigation purposes if the High Court determines that the public interest balancing test is met.

The Norfolk case stresses that coroners do not have the power to re-open AAIB investigations and conduct their inquiries unless there is "credible evidence that the investigation is incomplete, flawed, or deficient," and may not demand access to sensitive CVR/FDR data not already published by the AAIB. In addition, AAIB inspectors may be required to provide additional supplementary information to a coroner, but they are unlikely to be cross-examined or forced to express opinions in a court, which may point to blameworthiness or be used in any potential civil or criminal litigation.

Supporters of the Just Culture approach will welcome these decisions, which attempt to have a more balanced approach between enhancing safety and determining liability and imposing accountability, as a just culture does not protect the individual from the consequences of his/her deliberate or reckless acts and the balancing test is conducted by the organization and not a court of law.

3.3.2 CANADA

3.3.2.1 Cohen et al v Northern Thunderbird Air Inc, 2017

On 27 October 2011, a Beechcraft King Air 100 operated by Northern Thunderbird Air Incorporated departed Vancouver International Airport for Kelowna, British Columbia. There were seven passengers and two pilots on board. Approximately 15 minutes after take-off, the flight diverted back to Vancouver due to an oil leak. No emergency was declared. When the aircraft was approximately 300 feet above ground level and about 0.5 statute miles from the runway, it suddenly banked left and pitched its nose down. The aircraft collided with the ground and burst into flames before coming to rest on a roadway just outside the airport fence. Passers-by assisted in evacuating six passengers, while fire and rescue personnel rescued the remaining passenger and the two pilots. The aircraft was destroyed, and all of the passengers were seriously injured. Neither pilot recovered from their injuries, and they died in the hospital.[31] Six of the passengers commenced a legal proceeding against Northern Thunderbird.[32]

The plaintiffs filed a motion before the British Columbia Supreme Court requesting an order granting them access to the CVR communication and a partial transcript of the CVR data. The Transportation Safety Board (TSB), the official body investigating the accident, did not oppose the access request but appeared before the court to "explain the enabling legislation and the policy reasons for the statutory privilege that pertains to such recordings." The TSB seized the cockpit voice recorder from the aircraft, extracted and analyzed four audio recordings from it, and prepared an incomplete transcript of the CVR and noise from the aircraft.[33]

The Canadian Transportation Accident Investigation and Safety Board Act (SC 1989) states:

> 28(2). Every on-board recording is privileged and, except as provided by this section, no person, including any person to whom access is provided under this section, shall:
>
> (a) knowingly communicate an on-board recording or permit it to be communicated to any person; or
> (b) be required to produce an on-board recording or give evidence relating to it in any legal, disciplinary or other proceedings...

32. Except for proceedings before and investigations by a coroner, an investigator is not competent or compellable to appear as a witness in any proceedings unless the court or other person or body before whom the proceedings are conducted so orders for special cause.33. An opinion of a member or an investigator is not admissible in evidence in any legal, disciplinary or other proceedings.The court referred to previous cases and emphasized that CVR and transcripts did not enjoy an absolute privilege from disclosure and that the court was required to carry out a balancing test when determining whether to uphold that privilege by considering the following factors:

- the nature and subject matter of the litigation;
- the nature and probative value of the evidence in the case and how necessary this evidence was for the proper determination of a core issue before the court;
- whether other ways of getting this information before the court existed; and
- the possibility of a miscarriage of justice.

The court also considered the case of *Société Air France v Greater Toronto Airports Authority* (2009 OJ 5337), relating to the accident of Air France 358 when the aircraft crashed into a creek at the end of the Toronto Airport runway in 2005. In *Société Air France*, Justice Strathy was faced with the same balancing exercise and ordered the production of the cockpit voice recorder on the following grounds:[34]

(a) The cockpit voice recorder contained highly relevant, probative, and reliable evidence that was central to the issues in the litigation.

(b) The circumstances of the case justified the production of the cockpit voice recorder: i) It was important and substantial litigation involving a class of some 300 people and damages in the hundreds of millions of dollars. ii) There was a large volume of evidence from other sources, including flight data recorder information, air traffic control data and evidence from the pilots. iii) There was some concern about the reliability of the pilots' evidence. iv) The cockpit voice recorder had already been used to refresh the pilots' recollections. v) One of the pilots consented to the release of the cockpit voice recorder, while the other, and Air France, took no position. vi) The cockpit voice recorder contained no personal communications or communications of a sensational or disturbing nature. vii) There were no pending disciplinary or criminal proceedings against the pilots. viii) Privacy concerns could be addressed pursuant to the existing confidentiality order and the limited scope of disclosure of the cockpit voice recorder.

It was important and substantial litigation involving a class of some 300 people and damages in the hundreds of millions of dollars.

There was a large volume of evidence from other sources, including flight data recorder information, air traffic control data and evidence from the pilots.

There was some concern about the reliability of the pilots' evidence.

The cockpit voice recorder had already been used to refresh the pilots' recollections.

One of the pilots consented to the release of the cockpit voice recorder, while the other, and Air France, took no position.

The cockpit voice recorder contained no personal communications or communications of a sensational or disturbing nature.

There were no pending disciplinary or criminal proceedings against the pilots.

Privacy concerns could be addressed pursuant to the existing confidentiality order and the limited scope of disclosure of the cockpit voice recorder.

(c) Without the cockpit voice recorder evidence in this case, there was a real risk of the parties and the trier of fact not having the best and most reliable evidence concerning the central issue in these cases.

(d) There was no basis on which to conclude that the release of the cockpit voice recorder in this case, under appropriate restrictions of confidentiality, would interfere with aviation safety, damage the relationship between pilots and their employers, or impede the investigation of aviation accidents.

Chief Justice Hinton then listened to the cockpit voice recording from the Northern Thunderbird aircraft to "*determine whether, in the circumstances of the case, the public interest in the proper administration of justice outweighs in importance the privilege attached to the on-board recording by virtue of s. 28 of the TSB Act.*"

The judge stated that even though there was "a large volume of evidence from other sources, the death of the two pilots makes their evidence unavailable and obviates any suggestion of reliability pertaining to their evidence," that the idle conversation between the pilots did not contain any personal communications, it was not of a sensational or disturbing nature, and that there were no disciplinary or criminal proceedings against the pilots.

Deciding in this case that it was not just in the interest of the litigants, but also in the public interest and the administration of justice to allow the disclosure of the cockpit voice recorder, the judge stated that he was "*satisfied that there is a real risk that the parties and the [trial judge] will not have the best and most reliable evidence concerning the central issues in [the] case if the [cockpit voice recorder] is not released to counsel for the plaintiffs.*"

Applying the balancing exercise, the court therefore ordered the disclosure of the cockpit voice recorder data, but not the transcript, with the following restrictions:

- The cockpit voice recorder data must be disclosed only to the parties and their experts, consultants, insurers, and lawyers.
- The cockpit voice recorder data must remain confidential and be used only for the purposes of the lawsuit.
- The cockpit voice recorder data must not be filed in court in any form in the litigation or any other action.[35]

3.3.2.2 Canada (Transportation Safety Board) v Carroll-Byrne, 2021

On 29 March 2015, Air Canada Flight 624 departed from Toronto Pearson International Airport on a scheduled passenger flight to Halifax with 133 passengers and five crew.

In its final approach to Halifax International Airport, the Airbus A320 aircraft suffered a landing accident. During the final approach, the aircraft severed power lines 250 m from the beginning of the paved surface of runway 05, struck snow-covered ground short of the runway and hit a localizer antenna array, causing the landing gear to separate. The aircraft bounced twice more and skidded on its belly before coming to a rest past the threshold. A power line was impacted, leaving the Halifax Airport without electricity for approximately 90 minutes. The aircraft was extensively damaged. The nose cone was ripped off in the accident sequence, and pieces of the antenna array were embedded in the nose of the plane. Part of the undercarriage was sheared off, and both engines separated. There was extensive damage to both wing leading edges, horizontal stabilizers, and lower fuselage. Twenty-four of the 133 passengers, including both pilots and a flight attendant, were taken to the hospital with non-life-threatening injuries. All but one were released the same day.[36]

After the accident, the passengers filed a class action against Air Canada, the pilot and first officer of Flight 624, Airbus, the airport, NAV Canada (which operates Canada's civil air navigation system), and the Canadian government.

During the proceedings, an application was made to have the contents of the cockpit recorder released to the parties. Airbus, joined by the plaintiffs, the airport authority, and Nav Canada, moved for an order requiring the Transportation Safety Board of Canada (TSB) to hand over the audio of the cockpit voice recording. Still, the TSB refused to do so and, claiming a statutory privilege over the materials, asked the court to deny the order. The Transportation Safety Board and the Air Canada Pilots' Association were granted leave to intervene and opposed the requested disclosure order, together with Air Canada.

Section 28(2) of the *Canadian Transportation Accident Investigation and Safety Board Act* prohibits the disclosure of the CVR or its contents except in accordance therewith. Section 28(6) allows a court to order the production and discovery of the CVR if the public interest in the proper administration of justice outweighs the importance of the statutory privilege attached to the CVR. It states:

> Power of court or coroner
>
> (6) Notwithstanding anything in this section, where, in any proceedings before a court or coroner, a request for the production and discovery of an on-board recording is made, the court or coroner shall
>
> (a) cause notice of the request to be given to the Board, if the Board is not a party to the proceedings;
> (b) in camera, examine the on-board recording and give the Board a reasonable opportunity to make representations with respect thereto; and
> (c) if the court or coroner concludes in the circumstances of the case that the public interest in the proper administration of justice outweighs in importance the privilege attached to the on-board recording by virtue of this section, order the production and discovery of the on-board recording, subject to such restrictions or conditions as the court or coroner deems appropriate, and may require any person to give evidence that relates to the on-board recording.

Section 28(6), therefore, permits disclosure if the court "concludes in the circumstances of the case that the public interest in the administration of justice outweighs in importance the privilege attached to the on-board recording."

The Supreme Court judge stated that in the specific circumstances of the case, the public interest in the administration of justice outweighed the importance attached to the statutory privilege protecting the cockpit voice recorder and ordered the TSB to release the CVR and ordered disclosure subject to confidentiality conditions. The TSB was required to produce a copy of the CVR and transcript to counsel for use only in the class litigation.[37] The TSB, supported by the Air Canada Pilots' Association and Air Canada, appealed against the disclosure decision, arguing that the court failed to allow it to make *in camera* representations with respect to the CVR, and further that the court erred in determining that the public interest in the proper administration of justice outweighed the importance of the privilege in the CVR. The Air Canada Pilots' Association argued that the disclosure of the CVR would compromise pilot privacy interests and public safety by discouraging honesty in flight crew communications.

On 16 April 2021, dismissing the appeal, the Court of Appeal upheld the lower court's authorization of the conditional release of the contents of the CVR to the parties to a class action. The appeal court unanimously affirmed the earlier decision that the public interest in the proper administration of justice outweighed the statutory privilege attached to the CVR.[38]

The judge had to consider the difference between "in camera" versus "ex parte" as the TSB argued that Section 28(6)(b) of the act, in its inclusion of the words "*in camera*," entitled it to make *ex parte* representations to the judge prior to any decision to release the contents of the CVR.

> Section. 28(2) of the *Act* protects against disclosure of the cockpit voice recorder or its contents:
>
> Privilege for on-board recordings
>
> (2) Every on-board recording is privileged and, except as provided by this section, no person, including any person to whom access is provided under this section, shall
>
> (a) knowingly communicate an on-board recording or permit it to be communicated to any person; or
>
> (b) be required to produce an on-board recording or give evidence relating to it in any legal, disciplinary or other proceedings.

Section 28(6) of the *Act* provides for disclosure of cockpit voice recordings if the public interest in the proper administration of justice outweighs the importance of the privilege:

> Power of court or coroner
>
> (6) Notwithstanding anything in this section, where, in any proceedings before a court or coroner, a request for the production and discovery of an on-board recording is made, *the court* or coroner shall
>
> (a) cause notice of the request to be given to the Board, if the Board is not a party to the proceedings;
>
> (b) *in camera, examine the on-board recording and give the Board a reasonable opportunity to make representations with respect thereto*; and
>
> (c) *if the court* or coroner *concludes in the circumstances of the case that the public interest in the proper administration of justice outweighs in importance the privilege attached to the on-board recording by virtue* of this section, *order the production* and discovery of the on-board recording, subject to such restrictions or conditions as the court or coroner deems appropriate, and may require any person to give evidence that relates to the on-board recording.

The TSB asserted that the motion judge should have allowed it to make submissions not only in the absence of the public (*in camera*), but also in the absence of any other adverse parties (*ex parte*). In detailed reasons, the Court of Appeal held that the TSB's interpretation was incorrect. In particular, the court held that the fact that Section 28(6)(b) of the Act uses the words "*in camera*" and not "*ex parte*" presented a considerable challenge to the TSB's argument. As noted by the court, there is a clear distinction between *in camera* and *ex parte*, and it can be assumed that Parliament will use ex parte when that is what it means, as it has in Section 19(3) of the Act and various other federal legislation. The court held that on a plain reading of Section 28(6) of the Act, it authorizes the Court and not the parties to listen to the cockpit recorder in camera and that the TSB, which was not a party in the ordinary sense, then had the opportunity to make representations with respect to the recording, something which non-parties could not ordinarily do.

With regards to favoring public interest and allowing the conditional release of the CVR, the Nova Scotia Court of Appeal held the following. The motion judge had not erred on this point and held that the CVR was reliable and material to the heart of the claim; that the flight crew's discovery evidence revealed gaps in their ability to provide facts about their conduct at material times in the flight which could be filled by production of the CVR; that the disclosure of the CVR under the stringent conditions proposed would not unduly compromise flight officer privacy, especially given that the most essential part of the recording occurred when the aircraft was below 10,000 feet when "sterile cockpit rules are in effect," meaning that only operational issues are to be discussed; and that disclosure of the CVR would not unduly compromise safety by having a "chilling effect" on pilot communication or witness cooperation with investigators, having weighed competing evidence from the TSB and the experience of the US National Transportation Safety Board, where no such effect had been found.[39]

Regarding the privacy interests of the pilots, the judge stated that the pilots' privacy interest in this case was not comparable to cases that protect personal and private information in the workplace. The judge noted that what the pilots were doing and saying occurred in the context of a highly regulated environment intimately involved with public safety.[40]

In his judgment, the judge balanced relevance and reliability against the asserted privilege and held the following:[41]

> The contents of the CVR are relevant and reliable. The conversation recorded does not contain private or scandalous material.
>
> This litigation is important and substantial both in personal, and in monetary, terms. It is important that the process of determining the claims is fair to all parties and provides the best opportunity for the court to fulfil its function in trial. The public interest is served in this way.
>
> Section 7(1)(d) of the Class Proceedings Act provides that in certifying an action it is, among other things, important to achieving a fair and efficient resolution of the dispute. Behaviour modification is an objective of a class action. This too provides a public interest rationale for transparency in the litigation process.
>
> The flight crew's Discovery evidence showed gaps in their ability to provide relevant and material facts about their conduct at material times in the flight. This information is important to having a complete understanding of the crew's awareness and response to factors that were significant to the decision to land the aircraft in the conditions existing at that time.
>
> Notwithstanding the able arguments to the contrary, I am not convinced that the release of the CVR under the very stringent conditions proposed would interfere with

> aviation safety, damage relations between pilots and their employers, or would impede investigation of aviation accidents.

In this decision, the Canadian court, in applying the public interest versus the protected privileged CVR, ordered the release of the CVR transcript to the litigating parties.

3.3.3 USA

3.3.3.1 In re Air Crash Near Clarence Ctr., N.Y., 09-md-2085 (W.D.N.Y. Oct. 19, 2010)

On 12 February 2009, Colgan Air, Inc., Bombardier DHC-8-400, operating as Continental Connection flight 3407, from Newark to Buffalo, experienced a loss of control on an instrument approach to Buffalo-Niagara International Airport, Buffalo, New York, and crashed about five nautical miles northeast of the airport in Clarence Centre, New York. All 49 people on board Flight 3407, and one person on the ground, were killed. The NTSB conducted the investigation into the accident, and the final report was published on 2 February 2010. The probable cause was stated to be

> the captain's inappropriate response to the activation of the stick shaker, which led to an aerodynamic stall from which the airplane did not recover. Contributing to the accident were (1) the flight crew's failure to monitor airspeed in relation to the rising position of the low-speed cue, (2) the flight crew's failure to adhere to sterile cockpit procedures, (3) the captain's failure to effectively manage the flight, and (4) Colgan Air's inadequate procedures for airspeed selection and management during approaches in icing conditions.[42]

In the litigation after the accident, the plaintiffs filed a motion to compel the production of the audio recording of the cockpit voice recorder (CVR), arguing that it was necessary for a fair trial. Defendants, Colgan Air, Inc. (Colgan), the operator of the code-share flight with Continental, and Pinnacle Airlines Corp., the parent company of Colgan, opposed the production of the audio recording. In contrast, defendants Aerospace Corp. and Bombardier, Inc. joined in the plaintiffs' motion. Defendant Continental Airlines, Inc. did not take a position on the motion. [43] The plaintiffs argued that the written transcript of the CVR was incomplete and inaccurate, and that it contained evidence regarding the fear, pain, and suffering before the impact, the pilots' attentiveness and situational awareness, and the cockpit atmosphere, which made it necessary to be released. The Bombardier defendants submitted that the recording had evidence central to two of their defenses, namely, the misuse of the aircraft and the negligence by the captain and first officer. Colgan argued that sounds from the cabin could not be heard on the CVR, and that the written transcript was sufficient to convey the information relevant to the case. It further argued that producing the CVR audio recording would be unfairly prejudicial because "it invades the privacy right of the flight crew and their families" and "sensationalize[s] the allegations of pilot error."[44]

The District Court in Re Air Crash Near Clarence Ctr. granted the plaintiffs' motion on 19 October 2010. The Court entered an Order to compel production of the CVR audio recording from Continental Connection Flight 3407 and further ordered that the CVR recording be produced with a Protective Order.[45]

The Court stated:

> Pursuant to the parties' joint submission and the provisions of 49 U.S.C. § 1154(a)(4)(A)(i)(ii), which require entry of a protective order prohibiting dissemination of the CVR recording to any person not required access to it for the judicial proceedings in which it is produced, it hereby is ordered as follows: IT HEREBY IS ORDERED, that the following previously downloaded CVR Recording files, which were provided to the Court on two CD's for in-camera review (hereinafter collectively referred to as "CVR Recording"), shall be produced in accordance with the provisions of this Protective Order: FURTHER, that one copy of the CVR Recording will be provided to each of the following: a) Plaintiffs' Liaison Counsel (who shall be responsible for copying and dissemination of copies to Plaintiffs' counsel); b) Counsel for the Defendant, Colgan Air, Inc. c) Counsel for the Defendant, Pinnacle Airlines Corp.; d) Counsel for Bombardier Aerospace Corporation and Bombardier, Inc.; and e) Counsel for Defendant, Continental Airlines, Inc. f) Counsel for Defendant, FlightSafety International, Inc.[46]

The Court also stressed that the CVR recording produced, and any copies or excerpts thereof, were to be used only in that proceeding.[47] Reaching this conclusion, the Court followed the federal regulation 49 U.S.C. § 1154 (a)(3) which covers the discovery of a CVR audio recording and permits discovery if, after an *in camera* review, the court decides (1) that the available written transcript does not provide the moving party with sufficient information for the party to receive a fair trial, and (2) discovery is necessary for the moving party to receive a fair trial.[48] In addition, aiming to balance the privacy of the crew with the need for a complete and fair investigation, the statute makes it clear that an order to produce the CVR audio recording may occur only under the terms of a protective order limiting its use to the judicial proceeding and also prohibits the dissemination of the recording to any person that does not require access to it.

Conducting an "*in camera*" review, the court agreed that the written transcript of the recording was incomplete and inaccurate, expressly noting that there were "several minor transcription errors, out-of-sequence notations, and editorial insertions that were not readily audible on the recording." The court also determined that the plaintiffs' experts should be permitted to evaluate the reasoning of the NTSB committee that interpreted the audio recording and decided on how to classify words, sounds, and noises, including the designations of "unintelligible" and "non-pertinent" words. In addition, the court held that disclosure was necessary so that the tone of voice, pitch, volume, inflection, and the ambient noise and other sounds relevant to the operation of the aircraft could be accurately reflected. Deciding that all these factors may be relevant to the crew members' state of mind, emotional condition, and situational awareness, the court concluded that "fairness dictates that the parties be permitted to examine the raw recording." The court also stated that the CVR "is often the only piece of neutral evidence in an air crash case, and noted that as the NTSB had already completed its investigation, there was little concern with regards to protecting the integrity of the investigation and that concerns for the crews privacy rights and the possibility of unfairly prejudicing the jury pool, the court would issue a protective order to control the distribution of the audio recording. [49]

3.3.3.2 US Airways Flight 1702

On 13 March 2014, US Airways Flight 1702 took off from Philadelphia International Airport, Pennsylvania, scheduled to fly to Fort Lauderdale/Hollywood International Airport, Fort Lauderdale, Florida, under day visual meteorological conditions. The Airbus A320 aircraft experienced substantial damage after the captain rejected the take-off after rotation on runway 27L at Philadelphia International Airport. The aircraft came to rest on the edge of the runway, and the crew and passengers evacuated via the emergency slides. There were 149 passengers and 5 crew members on board. Two passengers reported minor injuries from the evacuation.[50]

The NTSB investigated the accident and stated that the probable cause of the accident was

> the captain's decision to reject the take-off after the airplane had rotated. Contributing to the accident was the flight crew's failure to follow standard operating procedures by not verifying that the airplane's flight management computer was properly configured for take-off, and the captain's failure to perform the correct action in response to the electronic centralized aircraft monitoring alert.[51]

In accordance with Part 121 of the U.S Federal Aviation Regulations,[52] Flight 1702 was required to have a cockpit voice recorder (CVR) which states that the CVR must be "operating continuously from the use of the checklist before the flight to completion of the final checklist at the end of the flight," and continuously record on a solid-state drive for a two-hour loop.[53] The aircraft's CVR was undamaged, and data was successfully downloaded. The 2-hour, 4-minute recording contained good quality audio information on three of the channels, while channel 4, which was recording the cockpit area microphone (CAM), was unusable. The CVR's full transcript was prepared for the accident flight and was included in the CVR Group Chairman's Factual Report.[54] The entire flight from the aircraft starting its engine and push from the gate, as well as the approximately 38 minutes of the crash sequence, was recorded, including the communications in the cockpit and the tower, pilot utterances, and mechanical sounds, such as wheels hitting runway markers, engine noises, and a tail strike.[55]

As part of its investigation, the NTSB prepared a partial transcript of the CVR recording containing important information. It revealed that the first officer made an essential error when he placed the wrong runway into the flight computer and that the captain did not detect this until the aircraft was on the runway for takeoff. The partial transcript was made publicly available. As it was only a partial transcription of the CVR recording, important information was not included. There were over forty unintelligible notations, numerous instances of so-called "questionable insertions," five instances of specifically labeled "unintelligible voice(s)," and several non-specified "expletives."[56] The reconstruction of the accident revealed that "at speeds well below V1, the aircraft was displaying an electronic centralized aircraft management (ECAM) warning, a level-two caution chime, a Master Caution warning, and a repeating aural instruction to 'retard thrust'."[57] The substance and tone of the deleted expletives were therefore important evidence for determining the intent of the captain in choosing to proceed with a takeoff roll at that particular moment. [58]

Several passengers sued for compensation in various jurisdictions, and they filed motions to gain access to the CVR audio from the flight. Many plaintiffs accepted the airline's proposal not to contest liability. They waived their claims for punitive damages, and therefore, the issue of releasing the CVR audio was not dealt with. However, two passengers rejected the airline's proposal, and they requested access to the CVR audio, which provided new information legally justifying their claims of punitive damages. The airline opposed the plaintiffs' request, and the trial court denied the plaintiffs' first request to obtain the CVR audio and refused to release the audio. [59] The pilots and the airline had access to the full CVR audio. When the pilots were deposed, they provided potentially exculpatory evidence that could not be challenged by the plaintiffs' lawyers who did not have access to the CVR audio. The pilots claimed to have had a conversation that allegedly occurred in the cockpit, but it was not included in the NTSB-prepared CVR transcript.[60]

The plaintiffs filed a second motion to have the CVR audio released, and the lower court in Berthiaume reversed its previous decision, ordering that a full-length, unedited, and unmixed copy of the CVR audio recordings from Flight 1702 be released.[61] The unedited and complete audio recordings revealed that the pilots had not accurately stated what they had said at the critical moments when the decision to proceed with an obviously dangerous takeoff roll was made. In addition, the alleged conversation that they submitted had taken place was completely absent from the audio recording. This would not have come to light if the release of the audio transcript had not been ordered.

In America, federal statute provides special protections for CVR audio in the form of 49 U.S.C. § 1154, which was initially enacted in 1990. One of the aims of providing this protection was to protect the NTSB against premature public conclusions and speculations on what caused the accident. Plaintiffs often requested access to CVR audio, often causing delays in the investigation. Privacy, fear of sensationalism, and other reasons for protection should be balanced with the essential fact that all parties receive a fair trial.

In accordance with 49 U.S.C. § 1154

> a court may allow discovery by a party of a cockpit . . . recorder recording if, after an in camera review of the recording, the court decides that – (A) the parts of the transcript made available to the public under section 1114(c) or 1114(d) of this title . . . do not provide the party with sufficient information for the party to receive a fair trial; and (B)

> discovery of the cockpit . . . recorder recording is necessary to provide the party with sufficient information for the party to receive a fair trial.[62]

In addition, it is important to note that if a judge does allow the discovery and orders the release of the CVR audio, a protective order limiting the use of the CVR audio to the judicial proceeding and prohibiting dissemination to the public must also be issued.[63]

The following are some of the reasons outlined why the NTSB-prepared CVR transcript may not be sufficient to enable a fair trial for the parties involved in an aviation accident or serious incident.

> The NTSB is making determinations about what is and what is not relevant in the CVR audio to achieve its goal of determining the probable cause of an air crash. What might not be relevant to the NTSB's determination of probable cause might be relevant in the legal determination of culpability;
>
> The NTSB has the discretion to omit dissenting interpretations of CVR audio transcription from the NTSB-prepared transcript made available on the aviation docket;
>
> The flight crew is customarily permitted an opportunity to listen and review the CVR recording and resulting transcript, and then recommend additions or changes. The NTSB has the discretion to omit from the CVR report that changes or comments from the crew were made;
>
> The written transcript of a recording, by its nature, is almost always incomplete and may be inaccurate;
>
> Inherent in creating the written transcript are collective determinations and classifications of words, sounds, noises that cannot be accurately reduced to a transcript. For example, a transcript often contains numerous characterizations of noises, designations of "non-pertinent" words, notations of "expletives," and words that the NTSB committee could not decipher ("unintelligible"). Each determination involves subjective judgment by the NTSB committee that includes none of a victim's own selected experts; A "better-trained ear" might discover errors or omissions not apparent on the transcript;
>
> The written transcript does not and cannot reflect tone of voice, pitch, volume, or inflexion, nor does it necessarily accurately reflect ambient and other noises pertinent to the aircraft's operation; The written transcript cannot reflect the true situational environment in the cockpit. The tone of voice, pitch, and inflection of statements made by crew members, all of which may be relevant to their state of mind, emotional condition, and situational awareness, are absent on a printed page;
>
> The CVR audio is one of the few neutral pieces of evidence available to plaintiffs to support their claims; The CVR audio is often the best and most reliable tool available for reconstructing what occurred; and The CVR audio may be used to impeach surviving crew members or controllers whose recollection of the events or delivery of the words can be self-serving.[64]

An examination of cases reveals that § 1154 is applied inconsistently, highlighting the challenges that litigants and judges face in such cases. In re Air Crash Near Kirksville, after the court held an in camera review of the CVR audio, without providing any reasoning, it stated that "Plaintiffs have not met their burden of establishing that discovery of the cockpit recorder recording is necessary to provide sufficient information for Plaintiffs to receive a fair trial."[65] However, in *Berthiaume v US Airways, Inc.*,[66] following the US Airways Flight 1702, the court first denied the plaintiffs' first request to obtain the CVR audio without providing a reason for its decision. The pilots and the airline had access to the full CVR audio; however, when the pilots provided their depositions, the plaintiffs' lawyers did not hear the CVR audio.

3.3.4 France – AF 447

Air France Flight 447, an Airbus 330, took off from Rio de Janeiro at 7:00 p.m. on 1 June 2009, carrying 216 passengers and 12 crew members bound for Paris. The aircraft began to face heavy turbulence when it was over the Atlantic Ocean off northern Brazil. Inconsistent airspeed indications and miscommunication led to the pilots inadvertently stalling the aircraft. After several unsuccessful attempts to recover the aircraft from the stall, it impacted the Atlantic Ocean at 02:14 UTC, killing everyone on board. On 26 April 2011, nearly two years after the accident, the flight data recorder chassis without the crash-survivable memory unit was located. On 1 May, the memory unit was found and retrieved, and on 2 May 2011, a remotely operated vehicle retrieved the CVR from the ocean floor.[67]

The two recorders were then shipped to Cayenne from 7 to 11 May and were then flown on a scheduled flight to Paris, where they arrived on the morning of 12 May. The readout of the recorder commenced on 13 May, and all 1,300 parameters from the FDR were available by 14 May. On 15 May 2011, all the data from both the flight data recorder and the cockpit voice recorder had been downloaded. Readout of the entire 2 hours of the CVR recording was performed. After the first analytical work on the recorders, the BEA published a note describing the factual series of events that led to the accident and presented some new findings. A third interim report was published on 29 July 2011.[68] On 5 July 2012, the final report was released, confirming the findings of the preliminary reports with additional details and recommendations to improve safety.

In October 2011, a transcript of the CVR was leaked and published in the book *Erreurs de Pilotage* (*Pilot Errors*) by Jean Pierre Otelli.[69] The last 2 minutes of the flight, as captured by the cockpit voice recorder reveals that the aircraft dropped 38,000 feet in just 3 minutes and 30 seconds, and this was reported in the book to be the panic-stricken conversations of the confused pilots, highlighting their role in stalling the aircraft while the flight computer was under alternate law at high altitude.[70] Both the BEA, which was conducting the official ICAO Annex 13 investigation, and Air France condemned the disclosure of the CVR transcript. The BEA stated, "Any attempt at interpretation at this stage is partial and, as a result, can only fan the flames of the controversies of the last few months, which is harmful to all concerned." It said that the disclosure showed a lack of respect for the crew members who had died in the accident and that it was a violation of European regulations. The BEA, in a press release, stated that:

> The BEA strongly condemns the disclosure of this transcription, which is a violation of Article 14 of the European Regulation of 20 October 2010 that came into effect on 2 December 2010. This transcription mentions personal conversations between the crew members that have no bearing on the event, which shows a lack of respect for the memory of the late crew members. The BEA safety investigation has not yet been completed and any attempt at interpretation at this stage is partial and, as a result, can only fan the flames of the controversies of the last few months, which is harmful to all concerned. [71]

Air France said that it was sensationalized and unverifiable information and that it "impairs the memory of the crew and passengers who lost their lives."[72] In addition to this disclosure, on 6 December 2011, a magazine, *Popular Mechanics*, published an English translation of the controversially leaked CVR and the transcript of the sensitive data highlighting the "simple but persistent" human error as the most direct cause of the accident and the failure to follow proper crew resource management procedures as a contributory factor.[73]

The BEA subsequently released its final report, and the official CVR transcript did not include groups of words that were deemed to have no bearing on the flight. A criminal investigation for manslaughter commenced on 5 June 2009 under the supervision of Investigating Magistrate Sylvie Zimmerman from the Paris High Court, leading to both Air France and Airbus being charged with involuntary manslaughter. Air France was accused of insufficiently training the pilots who became disoriented by the weather. Airbus was accused of underestimating the gravity of a defective speed monitoring probe on the A330, which was later replaced on all the A330 aircraft.

During the trial, the families of the deceased asked the judge to grant their motion requesting that the audio of the cockpit voice recorder, with the last 4 minutes of the flight before it crashed into the Atlantic, be entered as evidence. They argued that, even though it would be very difficult to hear, it was "absolutely necessary" to establish exactly what happened. The lawyers for both sides received a transcript of the recording, but no one heard it. They did not oppose the release of the recording in the trial, provided it was played behind closed doors. The judge agreed, and the recording was played for the court and the parties involved, but not for the public or the press.[74]

Many jurisdictions that afford privilege to the CVR/FDR and their contents to both promote safety and protect the privacy of flight crews also have legislation that allows a court to order the disclosure of such crucial evidence to establish the causes of an aviation accident in litigation in certain circumstances.

3.4 UPDATES TO RELEVANT LEGISLATIVE ENACTMENTS

3.4.1 ICAO Annex 13

Annex 13 has been updated numerous times since its first edition in 1951, and the 13th edition, effective as of July 2024, is currently in force. A brief overview of some of the amendments and improved provisions regarding the non-disclosure of records and the coordination between investigators in charge and judicial authorities will be provided.

The 4th edition of 1976 included provisions related to the use of flight recorders and privileged status to be granted to certain investigation records; the 5th edition of 1979 included provisions related to the coordination between investigator-in-charge and judicial authorities; the 6th edition of 1981 included provisions related to the strengthening of the specification regarding disclosure of records; the 7th edition of 1988 included a new attachment regarding disclosure of records; the 8th edition of 1994 included new specifications concerning the separation of any judicial or administrative proceedings to apportion blame or liability from an accident investigation; strengthening of the specifications concerning the use and read-out of the flight recorders; strengthening of the specifications concerning autopsy examinations and coordination with the judicial authorities; strengthening of the specifications concerning disclosure of records and deletion of the related attachment.

The 9th, 10th, and 11th editions contained additional provisions enhancing the protection of records obtained during an accident investigation and their non-disclosure, as well as further provisions focusing on the coordination between the investigators in charge and the judicial authorities. It can be said that these improvements were essential, particularly in light of the numerous cases in which aviation professionals faced criminal or civil litigation following aviation accidents.

3.4.1.1 9th Edition – 2001

The 9th edition of 2001 includes new provisions on voluntary incident reporting systems and a non-punitive environment, provisions related to the use of flight recorders, and the privileged status to be granted to certain investigation records. It also provides provisions for the non-disclosure of recordings and transcripts from air traffic control units, as well as legal guidance for protecting information from safety data collection and processing systems.

Chapter 5 deals with the Investigation and the Responsibility for instituting and conducting the Investigation. The following relevant provisions are highlighted to illustrate ICAO's attempt to enhance and emphasize the independence and role of accident investigation bodies, and to limit the intermingling of safety and criminal investigations conducted after an aviation accident.

"General *5.4 The accident investigation authority shall have independence in the conduct of the investigation and have unrestricted authority over its conduct, consistent with the provisions of this Annex. The investigation shall include:*

a) *the gathering, recording and analysis of all available information on that accident or incident;*
b) *if appropriate, the issuance of safety recommendations;*
c) *if possible, the determination of the causes; and d) the completion of the final report.*

When possible, the scene of the accident shall be visited, the wreckage examined and statements taken from witnesses.

5.4.1 Recommendation – *Any judicial or administrative proceedings to apportion blame or liability should be separate from any investigation conducted under the provisions of this Annex.*

Coordination – Judicial authorities

5.10 The State conducting the investigation shall recognize the need for coordination between the investigator-in-charge and the judicial authorities. Particular attention shall be given to evidence which requires prompt recording and analysis for the investigation to be successful, such as the examination and identification of victims and read-outs of flight recorder recordings.

Note 1. The responsibility of the State of Occurrence for such coordination is set out in 5.1.

Note 2. Possible conflicts between investigating and judicial authorities regarding the custody of flight recorders and their recordings may be resolved by an official of the judicial authority carrying the recordings to the place of read-out, thus maintaining custody.

Non-disclosure of records

5.12 The State conducting the investigation of an accident or incident shall not make the following records available for purposes other than accident or incident investigation, unless the appropriate authority for the administration of justice in that State determines that their disclosure outweighs the adverse domestic and international impact such action may have on that or any future investigations:

a) all statements taken from persons by the investigation authorities in the course of their investigation;

b) all communications between persons having been involved in the operation of the aircraft;-

c) medical or private information regarding persons involved in the accident or incident;

d) cockpit voice recordings and transcripts from such recordings; and

e) opinions expressed in the analysis of information, including flight recorder information.

5.12.1 These records shall be included in the final report or its appendices only when pertinent to the analysis of the accident or incident. Parts of the records not relevant to the analysis shall not be disclosed.

Note. Information contained in the records listed above, which includes information given voluntarily by persons interviewed during the investigation of an accident or incident, could be utilized inappropriately for subsequent disciplinary, civil, administrative and criminal proceedings. If such information is distributed, it may, in the future, no longer be openly disclosed to investigators. Lack of access to such information would impede the investigation process and seriously affect flight safety.

Note 2. Attachment E contains legal guidance for the protection of information from safety data collection and processing systems."

3.4.1.2 10th edition – 2010

Further enhancements were made in the 10th edition of 2010 which includes, inter alia, the following pertinent amendments: "strengthening of provision concerning the separation of investigation from any judicial or administrative proceedings to apportion blame or liability; new provision to ensure that administrative or judicial investigations do not impede investigations; widening the specification concerning the disclosure of records to address cockpit airborne image recordings and their transcripts; new provision to avoid disclosure of the names of the persons involved in accidents and incidents; new specification regarding the release of information and progress of the investigation; revised provision concerning the need to make the Final Report publicly available; revised specifications in the Appendix concerning the use of 'causes" and/or 'contributing factors.'"

It is also important to note that the following editorial practices were made in the writing of the specifications, namely, the operative verb "shall" was used for Standards and the operative verb "should" for Recommended Practices.[75] To indicate at a glance the status of each statement, the following practice has been adhered to: Standards have been printed in light face roman; Recommended Practices have been printed in light face italics, the status being indicated by the prefix Recommendation; Notes have been printed in light face italics, the status being indicated by the prefix Note.

It is important to stress the enhanced provisions included in the 10th edition, some of which are indicated in bold letters above.

Chapter 5 states:

"5.4 The accident investigation authority shall have independence in the conduct of the investigation and have unrestricted authority over its conduct, consistent with the provisions of this Annex. The investigation shall normally include:

a) the gathering, recording and analysis of all relevant information on that accident or incident;

b) if appropriate, the issuance of safety recommendations;

c) if possible, the determination of the causes and/or contributing factors; and

d) the completion of the final report.

Where feasible, the scene of the accident shall be visited, the wreckage examined and statements taken from witnesses. **The extent of the investigation and the procedure to be followed in carrying out such an investigation shall be determined by the accident investigation authority, depending on the lessons it expects to draw from the investigation for the improvement of safety**.

5.4.1 Any investigation conducted in accordance with the provisions of this Annex shall be separate from any judicial or administrative proceedings to apportion blame or liability. **[The word "Recommendation" has been deleted.]**

Note. Separation can be achieved by the investigation being conducted by State accident investigation authority experts, and any judicial or administrative proceedings being conducted by other appropriate experts. Coordination, as per 5.10, between the two processes would likely be required at the accident site and in the gathering of factual information, with due consideration to the provisions in 5.12.

5.4.2 Recommendation – The accident investigation authority should develop documented policies and procedures detailing its accident investigation duties. These should include: organization and planning; investigation; and reporting.

5.4.3 Recommendation – A State should ensure that any investigations conducted under the provisions of this Annex have unrestricted access to all evidential material without delay and are not impeded by administrative or judicial investigations or proceedings.

Note. The intent of this recommendation may be achieved through legislation, protocols or agreements between the accident investigation authorities and the judicial authorities.

Coordination – Judicial authorities

5.10 The State conducting the investigation shall recognize the need for coordination between the investigator-in-charge and the judicial authorities. Particular attention shall be given to evidence which requires prompt recording and analysis for the investigation to be successful, such as the examination and identification of victims and read-outs of flight recorder recordings.

Note 1. The responsibility of the State of Occurrence for such coordination is set out in 5.1.

Note 2. Possible conflicts between investigating and judicial authorities regarding the custody of flight recorders and their recordings may be resolved by an official of the judicial authority carrying the recordings to the place of read-out, thus maintaining custody.

Note 3. Possible conflicts between investigating and judicial authorities regarding the custody of the wreckage may be resolved by an official of the judicial authority accompanying the wreckage to the place of examination and being present at such examination when a modification of the condition of the wreckage is required, thus maintaining custody.

Non-disclosure of records

5.12 The State conducting the investigation of an accident or incident shall not make the following records available for purposes other than accident or incident investigation, unless the appropriate authority for the administration of justice in that State determines that their disclosure outweighs the adverse domestic and international impact such action may have on that or any future investigations:

a) *all statements taken from persons by the investigation authorities in the course of their investigation;*
b) *all communications between persons having been involved in the operation of the aircraft;*
c) *medical or private information regarding persons involved in the accident or incident;*
d) *cockpit voice recordings and transcripts from such recordings;*
e) *recordings and transcriptions of recordings from air traffic control units;*
f) *cockpit airborne image recordings and any part or transcripts from such recordings; and*

g) *opinions expressed in the analysis of information, including flight recorder information.*

5.12.1 These records shall be included in the final report or its appendices only when pertinent to the analysis of the accident or incident. Parts of the records not relevant to the analysis shall not be disclosed.

Note 1. Information contained in the records listed above, which includes information given voluntarily by persons interviewed during the investigation of an accident or incident, could be utilized inappropriately for subsequent disciplinary, civil, administrative and criminal proceedings. If such information is distributed, it may, in the future, no longer be openly disclosed to investigators. Lack of access to such information would impede the investigation process and seriously affect flight safety.

Note 2. Attachment E contains legal guidance for the protection of information from safety data collection and processing systems.

5.12.2 The names of the persons involved in the accident or incident shall not be disclosed to the public by the accident investigation authority."

At 5.4, the 9th edition merely states, "When possible, the scene of the accident shall be visited, the wreckage examined, and statements taken from witnesses." In contrast, the 10th edition has extended that point by adding, "The extent of the investigation and the procedure to be followed in carrying out such an investigation shall be determined by the accident investigation authority, depending on the lessons it expects to draw from the investigation for the improvement of safety," after the first sentence.

The 10th edition includes a new provision and a Note at 5.4.1, which refers to additional investigations that may take place after an accident and stresses that all investigations shall remain separate. It states:

"Any investigation conducted in accordance with the provisions of this Annex shall be separate from any judicial or administrative proceedings to apportion blame or liability."

The notes states:

> Note. Separation can be achieved by the investigation being conducted by State accident investigation authority experts, and any judicial or administrative proceedings being conducted by other appropriate experts. Coordination, as per 5.10, between the two processes would likely be required at the accident site and in the gathering of factual information, with due consideration to the provisions in 5.12.

Two recommendations are included as well as a Note.

> 5.4.2 **Recommendation.—** The accident investigation authority should develop documented policies and procedures detailing its accident investigation duties. These should include: organization and planning; investigation; and reporting.
>
> 5.4.3 **Recommendation.—** A State should ensure that any investigations conducted under the provisions of this Annex have unrestricted access to all evidential material

> without delay and are not impeded by administrative or judicial investigations or proceedings.
> Note. The intent of this recommendation may be achieved through legislation, protocols or agreements between the accident investigation authorities and the judicial authorities.

With regard to provisions related to 5.10 and the **coordination with judicial authorities**, the same wording is used as that in the 9th edition, but the 10th edition includes a third note which states:

> Note 3. Possible conflicts between investigating and judicial authorities regarding the custody of the wreckage may be resolved by an official of the judicial authority accompanying the wreckage to the place of examination and being present at such examination when a modification of the condition of the wreckage is required, thus maintaining custody.

The general philosophy that the technical investigators have unrestricted and timely access to all evidential material and that any other investigation or proceeding should not in any way hinder their investigation is stressed and expanded on in the 10th edition.

Provisions related to "Non-disclosure of records" include the exact same wording as that in the 9th edition, however, at 5.12 an additional two records are included in the list of records not be disclosed, namely, the "*recordings and transcriptions of recordings from air traffic control units*[76]*; and cockpit airborne image recordings and any part or transcripts from such recordings*[77]*;*

(i) 5.12.1 includes a second note stating *"Note 2. Attachment E contains legal guidance for the protection of information from safety data collection and processing systems."*
(ii) 5.12.2 is added, stating that *"The names of the persons involved in the accident or incident shall not be disclosed to the public by the accident investigation authority."*

3.4.1.2.1 Attachment E: Legal Guidance for the Protection of Information From Safety Data Collection and Processing Systems

Following the ICAO 35th Assembly, which noted that inconsistencies of domestic laws and regulations may result in many States not adequately protecting the use of safety information from inappropriate use, Attachment E was introduced. Emphasizing that the protection of safety information from inappropriate use is essential to ensure its continued availability, and that using such information for other than safety-related purposes may impede the availability of such information in the future with an adverse effect on safety, ICAO produced legal guidance for the protection of information from safety data collection and processing systems (SDCPS) in Attachment E to the 10th edition of Annex. The guidance is aimed at assisting States to enact national laws and regulations to protect information gathered from SDCPS, while allowing for the proper administration of justice. The objective is to prevent the inappropriate use of information collected solely for the purpose of improving aviation safety.

Principles for Protection of Safety Information:

The guidance in Attachment E to ICAO Annex 13[78] takes the form of a series of principles that could be adapted or modified to meet the particular needs of the State enacting laws and regulations to protect safety information.

Attachment E provides clarification that safety information refers to information contained in SDCPS established for the sole purpose of improving aviation safety and qualified for protection under specified conditions. Operational personnel refer to personnel involved in aviation operations who are in a position to report safety information to SDCPS, including, but not limited to, flight crews, air traffic controllers, aeronautical station operators, maintenance technicians, cabin crews, flight dispatchers, and apron personnel. Inappropriate use refers to the use of safety information for purposes different from the purposes for which it was collected, namely, use of the information for disciplinary, civil, administrative, and criminal proceedings against operational personnel, and/or disclosure of the information to the public.

SDCPS refers to processing and reporting systems, databases, schemes for the exchange of information, and recorded information and includes records pertaining to accident and incident investigations, mandatory incident reporting systems, voluntary incident reporting systems, as described in Annex 13, and self-disclosure reporting systems described in Annex 6 including automatic data capture systems and manual data capture systems.

It also has a note that information on safety data collection and processing systems can be found in the ICAO Safety Management Manual (Doc 9859).

Attachment E emphasizes that the sole purpose of protecting safety information from inappropriate use is to ensure its continued availability so that proper and timely preventive actions can be taken and aviation safety improved. It also states that it is not the purpose of protecting safety information to interfere with the proper administration of justice. It highlights that protecting qualified safety information under specific conditions is part of the safety responsibilities of every State. In light of that, it stipulates that national laws and regulations protecting safety information should ensure that a balance is struck between the need for the protection of safety information to improve aviation safety and the need for the proper administration of justice, and that safety information should be protected from inappropriate use.

The specific conditions for affording safety information protection from inappropriate use should include, but not be limited to: "that the collection of information was for explicit safety purposes and the disclosure of the information would inhibit its continued availability." In addition, the protection should be specific for each SDCPS, based upon the nature of the safety information it contains, and a formal procedure should be established to protect qualified safety information, in accordance with specified conditions.

It specifies that safety information should not be used for any other purpose for which it was collected and that the use of safety information in disciplinary, civil, administrative, and criminal proceedings should be carried out only under suitable safeguards provided by national law.

It also outlines the circumstances under which national laws and regulations can provide exceptions to the protection of safety information, which are as follows:

> a. There is evidence that the occurrence was caused by an act considered, in accordance with the law, to be conduct with intent to cause damage, or conduct with knowledge that damage would probably result, equivalent to reckless conduct, gross negligence or willful misconduct;
> b. An appropriate authority considers that circumstances reasonably indicate that the occurrence may have been caused by conduct with intent to cause damage, or conduct with knowledge that damage would probably result, equivalent to reckless conduct, gross negligence or willful misconduct;
> c. A review by an appropriate authority determines that the release of the safety information is necessary for the proper administration of justice, and that its release outweighs the adverse domestic and international impact such release may have on the future availability of safety information.

Regarding the public disclosure of such information, the Attachment provides that, subject to the principles of protection and exception outlined, any person seeking disclosure of safety information should justify its release. Formal criteria for disclosure of safety information should be established and should include, but not necessarily be limited to, the following:

> Disclosure of the safety information is necessary to correct conditions that compromise safety and/or to change policies and regulations; Disclosure of the safety information does not inhibit its future availability in order to improve safety; Disclosure of relevant personal information included in the safety information complies with applicable privacy laws; Disclosure of the safety information is made in a de-identified, summarized or aggregate form.

It also provides that each SDCPS should have a designated custodian of safety information and that it is the custodians' responsibility to apply all possible protection regarding the disclosure of the information, unless the custodian has the consent of the originator of the information for disclosure, or is satisfied that the release of the safety information is in accordance with the principles of exception.

Protection of Recorded Information:

Dealing specifically with cockpit voice recorders, it states that taking into account the above principles of protection, national laws and regulations should consider ambient workplace recordings required by legislation to be privileged protected information, namely, information deserving enhanced protection. It also states that

> National laws and regulations should provide specific measures of protection to such recordings as to their confidentiality and access by the public. Such specific measures of protection of workplace recordings required by legislation may include the issuance of orders of non-public disclosure.

3.4.1.3 11th edition – 2016

In 2016, the 11th edition came into force, providing, inter alia, a new definition for the accident investigation authority; a standard on the establishment of an independent accident investigation authority; a new provision on cooperation between investigation authorities; enhanced protection of investigation records in 5.12; and a new Appendix on the protection of investigation records.

The General provisions of 5.4 in Chapter 5 are identical to the 10th edition; however, the following amendments were made.

A Note was added to 5.4.2: Recommendation: "*Note: Guidance related to policies and procedures for investigation is provided in the* Manual on Accident and Incident Investigation Policies and Procedures (Doc 9962)." In addition, the wording of 5.4.3 has been modified; 5.4.4 has been included, and the Note has been expanded as follows:

> 5.4.3 Recommendation – *A State should ensure that any investigation conducted under the provisions of this Annex have unrestricted access to all evidential material without delay.*
> 5.4.4 Recommendation – *A State should ensure cooperation between the accident investigation authority and judicial authorities so that an investigation is not impeded by administrative and judicial investigations.*
> *Note: Cooperation may be achieved by legislation, protocols, agreements or other arrangements, and may cover the following subjects: access to the site of the accident; preservation of and access to evidence; initial and ongoing debriefings of the status of each process; exchange of information; appropriate use of safety information; and resolution of conflicts.*

With regard to the protection of accident investigation records, the enhanced provisions and differences with the previous 2010, 10th edition, highlighted in bold, are as follows:

5.12 The State conducting the investigation of an accident or incident shall not make the following records available for purposes other than accident or incident investigation, unless the competent authority designated by that State ***determines, in accordance with national laws and subject to Appendix 2 and 5.12.5, that their disclosure or use outweighs the likely adverse domestic and international impact such action may have on that or any future investigations:***

a) *cockpit voice recordings and airborne image recordings and any transcripts from such recordings; and*
b) *records in the custody or control of the accident investigation authority being:*
   1) *all statements taken from persons by the accident investigation authority in the course of their investigation;*
   2) *all communications between persons having been involved in the operation of the aircraft;*

3) *medical or private information regarding persons involved in the accident or incident;*
4) *recordings and transcripts of recordings from air traffic control units;*
5) *analysis of and opinions about information, including flight recorder information, made by the accident investigation authority and accredited representatives in relation to the accident or incident; and*
6) *the draft Final Report of an accident or incident investigation.*

5.12.1 Recommendation – States should determine whether any other records obtained or generated by the accident investigation authority, as a part of an accident or incident investigation, need to be protected in the same way as the records listed in 5.12.

5.12.2 The records listed in 5.12 shall be included in the Final Report or its appendices only when pertinent to the analysis of the accident or incident. Parts of the records not relevant to the analysis shall not be disclosed.

Note. The records listed in 5.12 include information relating to an accident or incident. The disclosure or use of such information for purposes where the disclosure or use is not necessary in the interest of safety may mean that, in the future, the information will no longer be openly disclosed to investigators. Lack of access to such information would impede the investigation process and seriously affect aviation safety.

5.12.3 The names of the persons involved in the accident or incident shall not be disclosed to the public by the accident investigation authority.

5.12.4 States shall ensure that requests for records in the custody or control of the accident investigation authority are directed to the original source of the information, where available.

5.12.4.1 Recommendation – The accident investigation authority should retain, where possible, only copies of records obtained in the course of an investigation.

5.12.5 States shall take measures to ensure that audio content of cockpit voice recordings as well as image and audio content of airborne image recordings are not disclosed to the public.

It should be noted that this can be achieved if there are national laws in place to ensure that the public does not obtain access to the CVR recordings and transcripts. In addition, where such data is being disclosed, there should be safeguards, such as protective orders, closed proceedings, or in-camera reviews in place.

5.12.6 States issuing or receiving a draft Final Report shall take measures to ensure that it is not disclosed to the public.

Note. Appendix 2 contains additional provisions on the protection of accident and incident investigation records. These provisions appear separately for convenience but form part of the SARPs.

Appendix 2: Protection of Accident and Incident Investigation Records has improved provisions with regard to the protection of safety data and records. The introduction has a note that states that the disclosure or use of the records listed in Chapter 5, 5.12, in criminal, civil, administrative or disciplinary proceedings, or their public disclosure, can have negative consequences for the individuals and organizations involved in accidents and incidents, which may likely cause them or others to be reluctant to cooperate with accident investigation authorities in the future. It specifies that the provisions specified in this Appendix are intended to assist States in developing national laws, regulations, and policies to protect accident and incident investigation records appropriately, and assist the competent authority in making the "balancing test" determination. The balancing test outlined in the Appendix refers to the determination by the competent authority, in accordance with 5.12, of the impact the disclosure or use of accident and incident investigation records may have on current or future investigations; and record(s) refers to those listed in 5.12. It also has a note that provisions on the use and protection of safety information and related sources other than accident and incident investigation records are included in Annex 19, Safety Management.

The Appendix contains the following important provision: The protections in Section 5.12 and the Appendix, as provided by States, shall be afforded to the entire recording of the cockpit voice recorder and airborne image recorder, as well as any transcripts from such recordings. These protections shall apply from the time an accident or incident occurs and continue after the publication of the Final Report. In addition, the protection provided shall also apply to the other records listed in Section 5.12. Such protection shall apply from the time they come into the custody or control of the accident investigation authority and continue after the publication of the Final Report. It is therefore clearly provided that the protection afforded to CVRs and any transcripts shall apply from the time an accident or incident occurs and continue after the publication of the final report and that the protection of other records listed in 5.12 b) shall apply from the time they come into the custody or control of the accident investigation authority and continue after the publication of the final report.

With regard to the non-disclosure of audio or image recordings to the public:

> 2.3 States shall take action to achieve the non-disclosure of audio content of cockpit voice recordings as well as image and audio content of airborne image recordings to the public, as per 5.12.5, such as:
>
> a) prevention of disclosure through the adoption of national laws, regulations and policies; or
>
> b) adoption of authoritative safeguards such as protective orders, closed proceedings or in-camera review; or
>
> c) prevention of disclosure of recordings through technical means, such as encrypting or overwriting, before returning the cockpit voice recorders or airborne image recorders to the owners.
>
> Note. Ambient workplace recordings, such as cockpit voice recordings and airborne image recordings, required by SARPs contained in the Annexes to the Chicago Convention may be perceived as constituting an invasion of the privacy of operational personnel if disclosed or used for purposes other than those for which the recordings were made.

In cases where there is a request for disclosure of a record, the balancing test to be applied is explained as follows:

4.1 Where the request is for a record to be disclosed or used in a criminal, civil, administrative or disciplinary proceeding, the competent authority shall be satisfied that a material fact in question in the proceedings cannot be determined without that record, before administering the balancing test.

Note. A material fact in question is a legal term used to refer to a fact that is significant or essential to the matter at hand, that one party alleges and that the other controverts, and is to be determined by the competent authority administering the balancing test.

4.2 When administering the balancing test, the competent authority shall take into consideration factors such as:

a) the purpose for which the record was created or generated;

b) the requester's intended use of that record;

c) whether the rights or interests of a person or organization will be adversely affected by the disclosure or use of that record;

d) whether the person or organization to whom that record relates has consented to make that record available;

e) whether suitable safeguards are in place to limit the further disclosure or use of that record;

f) whether that record has been or can be de-identified, summarized or aggregated;

g) whether there is an urgent need to access that record to prevent a serious risk to health or life;

h) whether that record is of a sensitive or restrictive nature; and

i) whether that record reasonably indicates that the accident or incident may have been caused by an act or omission considered, in accordance with national laws and regulations, to be gross negligence, wilful misconduct, or done with criminal intent.

Note 1. The administration of the balancing test can be done once for a certain category of records and the result incorporated into national laws and regulations.

Note 2. The competent authority may need to administer a balancing test for determining whether to permit the disclosure of a record, and a separate balancing test for determining whether to permit the use of a record.

Note 3. Guidance material on the balancing test can be found in the Manual on Protection of Safety Information.

It requires each State to have a competent authority or competent authorities appropriate to the task of administering the balancing test. Noting that different competent authorities may be designated for various circumstances, it gives the example that the competent authority to apply the balancing test in criminal or civil proceedings may be a judicial authority, and that another competent authority for applying the balancing test in cases where the purpose of the request for disclosure is for public accessibility. It stipulates that the competent authority should record the reasons for its decision when administering the balancing test and that the reasons should be made available and referred to as necessary for subsequent decisions.

The final report is addressed in Section 6, which recommends that, to limit the use of the Final Report for purposes other than preventing accidents and incidents, States consider establishing a separate investigation for those purposes. They should also distinguish between the parts of the final report to allow the use of factual information while preventing the use of analysis, conclusions, and safety recommendations for assigning blame or liability. Additionally, they could implement rules and procedures to prevent the Final Report from being used as evidence in legal proceedings to allocate blame or liability. The note states that, according to Chapter 6, 6.5, in order to prevent future accidents, Final Reports are publicly available and not protected under 5.12. However, using parts of the Final Report – especially the analysis, conclusions, and safety recommendations – as evidence in national courts to assign blame or determine liability conflicts with the investigation's original purpose.

It is crucial to stress the necessity for states to have national laws limiting the use of final reports for purposes other than accident prevention and establishing an independent investigation to identify potential blameworthy parties to apportion blame without inappropriate use of protected information gathered from SDCPS.

The Appendix also includes a recommendation that, in the interest of safety and in accordance with Annex 13, States should consider that accident investigation personnel should not be compelled to give an opinion on matters of blame or liability in civil, criminal, administrative, or disciplinary proceedings.

The international standards and procedures outlined in Annex 13 are complemented by ICAO Doc 9756, Manual of Aircraft Accident and Incident Investigation, ICAO Doc 9156, Accident/Incident Reporting Manual, and numerous other manuals. In addition to Annex 13, the 2015 second edition of the Manual on Protection of Safety Information, Part 1,[79] aims to provide guidance on the protection of accident and incident investigation records and is mainly for the benefit of the accident investigation authorities, regulators, judicial authorities, service providers, and other involved stakeholders.

The manual also reiterates that the purpose of an investigation into an aircraft accident or incident conducted under ICAO Annex 13 is to prevent accidents and incidents, that it is not the purpose of an investigation to apportion blame or liability, and any judicial or administrative proceedings to apportion blame or liability shall be separate from the Annex 13 safety investigation. It states that there should be clear, appropriate legislation safeguarding the rights of the investigators to have complete and unhampered access to the accident site and all related evidence, and to ensure that the technical investigation is kept separate from any criminal or administrative proceedings. The safeguards provided by Annex 13 regarding documents and other information obtained during the technical safety investigation are included. The following records stipulated in Annex 13, Chapter 5, shall not be released unless the competent authority has decided that the benefits of disclosure outweigh the adverse domestic and international impact this may have on future investigations.

a) all statements taken from persons by the investigation authorities in the course of their investigation;
b) all communications between persons having been involved in the operation of the aircraft;
c) medical or private information regarding persons involved in the accident or incident;
d) cockpit voice recordings and transcripts from such recordings;
e) recordings and transcriptions of recordings from air traffic units;

f) cockpit airborne image recordings and any part or transcripts from such recordings; and
g) opinions expressed in the analysis of information, including flight recorder information.

On 18 March 2024, Amendment 19 to the International Standards and Recommended Practices, Aircraft Accident and Incident Investigation (Annex 13 to the Convention on International Civil Aviation) was adopted by the Council at the fifth meeting of the ICAO 231st Session. With regard to Annex 13 and the investigation of aviation accidents and serious incidents, the amendments relate to, inter alia, assisting the safety investigation authorities of the Contracting States in their investigations of Remotely Piloted Aircraft. In addition, Amendment 19 also recognizes the expectations of the public and the media to be informed. It therefore includes new investigation provisions, making available without delay information and data from recorders installed on aircraft and requiring investigators to provide timely and more frequent factual information during safety investigations. Amendment 19 reflects the fact that the use of modern technologies allows for shortening the consultation period for draft final reports, thus expediting the publication of the final report. Finally, Amendment 19 introduces a preference that final reports be sent in electronic format to ICAO for uploading into the ICAO central database, thereby improving access and data analysis. Crucially, the Council also decided to enhance current search and rescue (SAR) SARPs to expedite response times, facilitate assistance from other States during operations, reduce risks to personnel at accident sites, and provide better information to rescue coordination centers.[80]

3.4.1.4 12th edition – 2020

The July 2020 12th edition largely adopted a range of amendments to Annex 13 based on the work of the ICAO Accident Investigation Panel (AIGP) and became applicable on 5 November 2020. Specifically, the proposed amendments relate to the definition of Accredited Representative; notification and dissemination of Final Reports; timely investigation of accidents and serious incidents; release of the final report; facilitation of the entry for investigators; rights and entitlement of an expert; safety recommendations; serious incidents; and delegation of investigations.[81]

Regarding the protection of accident and incident investigation records, 5.12 is the same as the previous edition; however, there is a change in 5.12.5, which provides that States shall take measures to ensure that audio content of cockpit voice recordings, as well as image and audio content of airborne image recordings, are not disclosed to the public.

A significant amendment proposed is with regard to serious incidents, where, instead of relying on a prescriptive list of potential serious incidents, it is intended to apply a risk-based analysis approach based on a simplified version of the Aviation Risk Management Solutions (ARMS) event risk classification (ERC) matrix.

Chapter 1 defines the term "serious incident" at

1. As an incident involving circumstances indicating that there was a high probability of an accident and associated with the operation of an aircraft which, in the case of a manned aircraft, takes place between the time any person boards the aircraft with the intention of flight until such time as all such persons have disembarked, or in the case of an unmanned aircraft, takes place between the time the aircraft is ready to move with the purpose of flight until such time as it comes to rest at the end of the flight and the primary propulsion system is shut down.

2. There may be a high probability of an accident if there are few or no safety defences remaining to prevent the incident from progressing to an accident. To determine this, an event risk-based analysis (that takes into account the most credible scenario had the incident escalated and the effectiveness of the remaining defences between the incident and the potential accident) can be performed as follows: a) consider whether there is a credible scenario by which this incident could have escalated to an accident; and b) assess the remaining defences between the incident and the potential accident as: — effective, if several defences remained and needed to coincidently fail; or — limited, if few or no defences remained, or when the accident was only avoided due to providence.

2.1 Consider both the number and robustness of the remaining defences between the incident and the potential accident. Ignore defences that failed, and consider only those that worked and any subsequent defences still in place.

Note 1. The most credible scenario refers to the realistic assessment of injury and/or damage resulting from the potential accident.

Note 2. Defences include crew, their training and procedures, ATC, alerts (within and outside the aircraft), aircraft systems and redundancies, structural design of the aircraft and aerodrome infrastructure.

3.4.1.5 13th edition – 2024

In July 2024, the 13th edition of Annex 13 was issued. Effective 28 November 2024, this edition supersedes all previous editions. Key differences focused on enhancing the efficiency and effectiveness of aircraft accident and incident investigations, enhancing safety improvements, and streamlining reporting processes.

This edition includes the following additional 5.4.5 and 5.4.6 points to 5.12:

5.4.5 Recommendation.— For accidents or incidents that draw heightened public attention, the accident investigation authority should publicly release relevant factual information within the early days of the investigation.

Note. The provision of factual information in the early days of the investigation is intended to address the substantial public interest in the accident or incident and to help ensure that the information in the public domain is as accurate as possible.

Guidance on accidents and incidents, that draw heightened public attention, and various formats and methods for the provision of information is contained in the Manual of Aircraft Accident and Incident Investigation (Doc 9756), Part II – Procedures and Checklists.

5.4.6 Recommendation.— For accidents or incidents that draw heightened public attention, the accident investigation authority should publish a written Preliminary Report within thirty days of the accident or incident, containing established factual information and indicating the progress of the investigation.

Note 1. Guidance on the purpose, format, and content of the written Preliminary Report is contained in the Manual of Aircraft Accident and Incident Investigation (Doc 9756), Part IV – Reporting.

Note 2. The Recommendation in 5.4.6 does not intend to preclude the State conducting the investigation from consulting States participating in the investigation before publishing the written Preliminary Report.

Note 3. A list of examples of accidents and incidents that draw heightened public attention is contained in the Manual of Aircraft Accident and Incident Investigation (Doc 9756), Part IV – Reporting.

The latest edition includes the additional provision regarding information on accidents and incidents. Provision 5.14 provides that States that have any data available from a flight recorder of an aircraft involved in an accident or incident shall, without delay, provide the State conducting the investigation with all such data available. It also states that they shall not divulge such data without the express consent of the State conducting the investigation. Additionally, 5.15 stipulates that any State, facilities, or services that have been, or would generally have been used by an aircraft prior to an accident or an incident, which have information pertinent to the investigation, shall provide such information to the State conducting the investigation.

Amendments include changes to the responsibility of the State conducting the investigation and the consultation period, highlighted in bold below. The previous edition provided for receiving comments within sixty days of the date of the transmittal letter, whereas the 13th edition states that the consultation period is thirty days. Note 1 has remained the same; however, 6.3 included states that:

> 6.3 The usual consultation period shall be thirty days from the date of the transmittal correspondence. The consultation period shall be extended to sixty days by the State conducting the investigation if it is notified of the need for additional time by the State invited to 12comment. If the State conducting the investigation receives comments **within the consultation period**, it shall either amend the draft Final Report to include the substance of the comments received or, if desired by the State that provided comments, append the comments to the Final Report. If the State conducting the investigation receives no comments within **the consultation period**, it shall issue the Final Report in accordance with 6.4, unless further extension of that period has been agreed by the States concerned.

The requirements for the international dissemination of the final report were amended to include Notes 2, 3, through 6.7. When States conducting an investigation into an accident or incident have released a Final Report, a copy of the report shall be sent to ICAO. Note 1 states that whenever practicable, the final report sent to ICAO is to be in one of ICAO's working languages. Added to that are Notes 2 and 3, which provide that the final reports are recorded in an ICAO central database, the e-Library of final reports, which is publicly available, and that the copy of the report sent is preferably prepared in an electronic format to facilitate its upload onto the e-Library of Final Reports.

3.4.2 European Level – EU Directive 94/56 and Regulation 996/2010

The 1994 Directive 94/56, which established the fundamental principles for investigating civil aviation accidents and incidents, has been repealed and replaced by EU Regulation 996/2010, which came into force on 2 December 2010. This regulation aimed to enhance the efficiency and independence of accident investigations and strengthen the rights of victims.[82]

The Regulation aims to improve aviation safety by ensuring a high level of efficiency, expediency, and quality of European civil aviation safety investigations. It provides for rules concerning the timely availability of information relating to all persons as well as dangerous goods on board an aircraft involved in an accident.

The significant advancement regarding just culture is illustrated by the Regulation, which notes that the civil aviation system should equally promote a non-punitive environment, facilitating the spontaneous reporting of occurrences and thereby advancing the principle of just culture. It states that the information provided by a person in the context of a safety investigation should not be used against that person, in full respect of constitutional principles and national law.

With regard to the protection of sensitive safety information, Article 14 of the Regulation establishes the following list of records that shall not be made available or used for purposes other than safety investigation: the identity of persons who have given evidence; opinions and notes of investigators; draft reports; FDR data; cockpit voice and image recordings, and their transcripts; written or electronic recordings and transcriptions of recordings from air traffic control units; and occurrence reports filed under Regulation 376/2014. It also lists the records that shall not be made available or used for purposes other than the safety investigation, or to improve safety, namely, all communications between persons having been involved in the operation of the aircraft; written or electronic recordings and transcriptions of recordings from air traffic control units, including reports and results made for internal purposes; covering letters for the transmission of safety recommendations from the safety investigation authority to the addressee, where so requested by the safety investigation authority issuing the recommendation; and occurrence reports filed under Directive 2003/42/EC. In addition, flight data recorder recordings shall not be made available or used for purposes other than those for the safety investigation, airworthiness, or maintenance purposes, except when such records are de-identified or disclosed under secure procedures.

However, it is recognized that the administration of justice or the competent authority in an EU Member State may decide on the disclosure of records in accordance with national law. Member States are invited to limit the cases in which such a decision of disclosure may be taken.

Referring to the coordination between the safety and judicial investigations, the Regulation provides in Article 12:

> When a judicial investigation is also instituted, the investigator-in-charge shall be notified thereof. In such a case, the investigator-in-charge shall ensure traceability and retain custody of flight recorders and any physical evidence. The judicial authority may

> appoint an official from that authority to accompany the flight recorders or physical evidence to the place of the read-out or treatment. Where examination or analysis of such physical evidence may modify, alter or destroy it, prior agreement from the judicial authorities will be required, without prejudice to national law. Where such agreement is not obtained according to the advance arrangements referred to in paragraph 3 within a reasonable time and not later than 2 weeks following the request, it shall not prevent the investigator-in-charge from conducting the examination or analysis. Where the judicial authority is entitled to seize any evidence, the investigator-in-charge shall have immediate and unlimited access to and use of such evidence.[83]

Article 15 of the Regulation stipulates that the anonymity of those involved in an accident or incident shall be protected; information deemed relevant to the prevention of accidents and incidents shall be communicated to aircraft (and equipment) manufacturers, maintenance organizations, aircraft operators, and training organizations; European Aviation Safety Agency (EASA) and national CAAs receive relevant factual information obtained during the safety investigation, except information referred to in Article 14(1); victims and their relatives or their associations or the public are appropriately informed without compromising the objectives of the safety investigation.[84]

Other key provisions include, inter alia, the following: A safety recommendation shall in no case create a presumption of blame or liability for an accident, serious incident or incident.[85] The required civil aviation accident emergency plan at the national level shall also cover assistance to the victims of civil aviation accidents and their relatives.[86]

Regulation 996/2010 has been amended by Regulation (EU) No 376/2014 of 3 April 2014, Regulation (EU) 2018/1139 of 4 July 2018[87], and Regulation (EU) 2024/1230 of 24 April 2024.[88]

Of importance to the points being discussed is Regulation (EU) No 376/2014 of 3 April 2014.[89] The Regulation aims to improve aviation safety by ensuring that relevant safety information relating to civil aviation is reported, collected, stored, integrated in a European database, protected, exchanged, disseminated, and analyzed. It lays down rules on: the reporting of occurrences that endanger or that, if not corrected or addressed, would endanger an aircraft, its occupants, any other person, equipment, or installation affecting aircraft operations (mandatory reporting); and the reporting of other relevant safety-related information in that context (voluntary reporting); analysis and follow-up action in respect of reported occurrences and other safety-related information; the protection of aviation professionals; appropriate use of collected safety information; the integration of information into the European Central Repository; and the dissemination of anonymized information to interested parties to provide such parties with the information they need to improve aviation safety.

The Regulation seeks to ensure that front-line aviation professionals and other persons working or involved in aviation report occurrences that pose a significant risk to aviation safety, so that appropriate safety measures can be taken based on the information collected. A "just culture" is prescribed, which encourages individuals to report occurrences without exempting them from their normal responsibilities.

The purpose of the Regulation is to increase the willingness to report by requiring Member States, among others, to exempt reporters of and persons mentioned in occurrence reports from civil or administrative sanctions, under certain conditions. The Regulation defines an occurrence as "any safety-related event which endangers or which, if not corrected or addressed, could endanger an aircraft, its occupants or any other person and includes in particular an accident or serious incident." The Regulation stipulates an obligation for specific categories of natural persons to report an occurrence. It provides that non-designated persons may voluntarily report details of occurrences and other safety-related information not covered by the mandatory reporting requirement.

It refers to a just culture, defined as "a culture in which front-line operators or other persons are not punished for actions, omissions or decisions taken by them that are commensurate with their experience and training, but in which gross negligence, willful violations and destructive acts are not tolerated."[90] It states that the civil aviation system should promote a "safety culture," facilitating the spontaneous reporting of occurrences to advance a just culture. It affirms that a just culture is an essential element of a broader safety culture, which is the basis of a robust safety management system.

It notes that all Member State organizations shall adopt internal rules describing how "just culture" principles, in particular the principle of having access to tools enabling all staff members to report such events, with guaranteed protection, are guaranteed and implemented within that organization. It goes further and provides that, in the context of developing a "just culture" environment, Member States should keep the option of extending the prohibition on using occurrence reports as evidence against reporters in administrative and disciplinary proceedings to civil or criminal proceedings.[91] Aiming to foster a just culture, the handling of the report should be in a way that the reporter and other persons mentioned in the reports are protected from prejudice or prosecution and that their confidentiality is safeguarded.

It is essential to note that the Regulation stipulates that Member States will not initiate civil or administrative proceedings in respect of unpremeditated or inadvertent infringements of the law that come to their attention solely because they have been reported mandatorily or voluntarily in accordance with the Regulation. This protection does not apply where there has been "willful misconduct" or "a manifest, severe and serious disregard of an obvious risk and profound failure of professional responsibility to take such care as is evidently required in the circumstances, causing foreseeable damage to a person or property, or which seriously compromises the level of aviation safety," hereinafter referred to in short as intent or gross negligence.

The number of cases where courts in different jurisdictions have accepted the accident investigation report as evidence against aviation professionals facing criminal prosecution, as well as the use of confidential safety data and other information obtained during investigations or through confidential and reporting systems, is a significant concern for the aviation industry. It also raises serious questions about whether the principles of conducting safety accident investigations are being undermined.

The debate regarding the admissibility of the accident investigation report, data from the DFDR and CVR, and other aviation-sensitive data, for the practical and balanced administration of justice, remains current, and it remains to be seen what impact the latest Annex 13 amendments will have on the precedents set during the last 15 years.

The events surrounding the circumstances of the Air India Flight 171 accident will once again raise the question of implementing the recommendation by the Hellenic Air Accident Investigation and Aviation Safety Board (AAIASB) after the 2005 Helios accident, that "EASA/JAA and ICAO to study the feasibility of requiring the installation of crash-protected image recorders in the flight deck of commercial aircraft."[92] This development, which has been resisted for many years by pilots around the world, but which is often raised, may be considered necessary to provide additional information and insight into the circumstances of complex accidents, such as that of AI 171.

Despite the increased protection of aviation-sensitive data provided by Appendix 2 of Annex 13 regarding mandatory recording that includes image recorders, it will be interesting to see how future courts will approach the issue of the admissibility of such image recorders. The legal implications regarding the admissibility of such video footage following an aviation accident are highly controversial despite the safety and judicial benefits that it may have.

3.5 CONCLUSION

The protections afforded by Annex 13 are positive steps in the right direction, elevating the protection of sensitive aviation data and upholding just culture principles. At the same time, it provides a pathway for judicial authorities to obtain access to such data when deemed necessary by applying the balancing test.

The privileges and protection afforded by Annex 13 safeguard a just culture and strengthen the accident investigation process, and promote the ability to learn from past accidents and improve safety standards while providing a balanced approach for the administration of justice and access to data when that is required.

NOTES

1. ICAO. 1994. *Aircraft Accident Investigation: Annex 13 to the Convention of International Civil Aviation*. Montreal: ICAO.
2. ICAO. 1987. *Accident/Incident Reporting Manual. Doc 9156*. Montreal: ICAO.
3. European Council, EU Directive 94/56/EC, *Establishing the Fundamental Principles Governing the Investigation of Civil Aviation accidents and Incidents*, 1994.
4. Regulation (EU) No. 996/2010 of 20 October 2010 on the investigation and prevention of accidents and incidents in civil aviation and repealing Directive 94/56/EC, which came into force on 2 December 2010 (OJ 2010 L295/35). Available at https://eur-lex.europa.eu/legal-content/EN/TXT/PDF/?uri=CELEX:32010R0996&from=en.

5. ICAO. 2000. *Manual of Aircraft Accident Investigation. Doc 9756.* Montreal: ICAO. Now, Part I-2nd ed, 2015; Part II Procedures and Checklist, 2024; Part III Investigations-2nd ed, 2024; Part IV-3rd ed, 2020.
6. ICAO Civil Aviation Aircraft Accident and Incident Investigation, Annex 13 to the Convention on International.
7. Directive 94/56/EC of November 1994 establishing the fundamental principles governing the investigation of civil aviation accidents and incidents (OJ 1994 L319/14). Available at https://eur-lex.europa.eu/legal-content/EN/TXT/PDF/?uri=CELEX:31994L0056&from=EN.
8. Regulation (EU) No. 996/2010 of 20 October 2010 on the investigation and prevention of accidents and incidents in civil aviation and repealing Directive 94/56/EC which came into force on 2 December 2010 (OJ 2010 L295/35). Available at https://eur-lex.europa.eu/legal-content/EN/TXT/PDF/?uri=CELEX:32010R0996&from=en.
9. *Rogers v Hoyle* (EWHC/QB, 2013).
10. AAIB Bulletin 2011, para 21.
11. *Rogers & Rogers v Hoyle* (EWHC/QB, 2013), para 21.
12. Ibid., para 118.
13. Hoyle v Rogers & Anors, 2014 at para 29.
14. Kavanagh, G., and Waters, M., Landmark English court of appeal decision upholds admissibility of accident investigation reports in civil proceedings, HFW Aviation Briefings, March 2014. Available at http://www.hfw.com/Landmark-English-Court-of-Appeal-decision-accident-investigation-reports-March-2014.
15. *The Chief Constable of Sussex Police v The Secretary of State for Transport [2016] EWHC 2280 (QB).*
16. Ibid, para 40.
17. Ibid., para 1–4.
18. Ibid., para 35–38.
19. Opinion of Lord Jones in the cause Frank Mulholland QC, The Lord Advocate For An order in terms of regulation 18 of The Civil Aviation (Investigation of Air Accidents and Incidents) Regulations 1996, 2015 SLT 450.
20. *The Chief Constable of Sussex Police v The Secretary of State for Transport [2016] EWHC 2280 (QB),* para 28.
21. Ibid., Sing J at para 41–45.
22. Ibid., Sing J at para 46–50.
23. Ibid., Sing J at para 51–54.
24. Ibid., Sing J at 55–56.
25. *The Queen v Her Majesty's Senior Coroner for Norfolk [2016] EWHC 2279 (Admin).*
26. Ibid., para 5–9.
27. Ibid., para 4.
28. Ibid., para 13.
29. Ibid., para 55.
30. Ibid., para 53.
31. The Transportation Safety Board of Canada, Aviation Investigation Report A11P0149 Loss of Control and Collision with Ground Northern Thunderbird Air Inc. Beechcraft King Air 100, C-Gxrx Vancouver International Airport Richmond, British Columbia 27 October 201. Available at https://www.tsb.gc.ca/eng/rapports-reports/aviation/2011/A11P0149/a11p0149.html.
32. *Cohen et al v Northern Thunderbird Air Inc,* 2017 BCSC 315.
33. Martins, C., and MacDonald, A., "Claim for privilege over contents of cockpit voice recorder denied," WeirFoulds LLP, 29 March 2017. Available at https://www.lexology.com/library/detail.aspx?g=0994e3dc-157b-420f-a421-d7594cf03b12.

34. Ibid.
35. Ibid.
36. Transportation Safety Board of Canada, Aviation Investigation Report A15h0002 18 May 2017, Collision with terrain, Air Canada, Airbus Industrie A320-211, C-FTJP, Halifax/Stanfield International Airport, Halifax, Nova Scotia, 29 March 2015. Available at www.bst.gc.ca/sites/default/files/rapports-reports/aviation/A15H0002/eng/a15h0002.pdf.
37. Campbell, F., "Court orders TSB to hand over cockpit recording from 2015 crash at Halifax airport," The Guardian, 21 November. Available at https://www.theguardian.pe.ca/news/canada/court-orders-tsb-to-hand-over-cockpit-recording-from-2015-crash-at-halifax-airport-378861/.
38. *Canada (Transportation Safety Board) v. Carroll-Byrne*, 2021 NSCA 34, Nova Scotia Court of Appeal, Docket CA 495035, 16 April 2021. Available at https://decisia.lexum.com/nsc/nsca/en/item/495674/index.do.
39. Ibid., para 76.
40. Ibid., para 83.
41. Ibid., paras 64–68.
42. NTSB, Accident Report National Transportation Safety Board, NTSB/AAR-10/01 PB2010-910401. Available at https://asn.flightsafety.org/reports/2009/20090212_DH8D_N200WQ.pdf.
43. Nemsick, J.R., "Court orders production of audio recording of cockpit voice recorder," Holland & Knight Newsletter, December 2010. Available at https://www.hklaw.com/en/insights/publications/2010/12/court-orders-production-of-audio-recording-of-cock.
44. Ibid.
45. In Re: Air crash near clarence center, New York, on 12 February 2009, Protective Order 09-Md-2085. Available at https://cases.justia.com/federal/district-courts/new-york/nywdce/1:2009cv00174/72735/138/0.pdf.
46. Ibid.
47. Ibid.
48. 49 U.S.C. § 1154 (a)(3).
49. Nemsick, J.R., op cit.
50. NTSB, Accident Number DCA14MA081, at page 4, 14 November 2016. Available at https://asn.flightsafety.org/reports/2014/20140313_A320_N113UW.pdf.
51. Ibid., at page 3.
52. 14 C.F.R. §§ 91.609, 121.359 (2018).
53. 14 C.F.R. § 121.35 (2018).
54. NTSB, Accident Number DCA14MA081, op cit., at page 19.
55. Rapoport, D.E. and Sims, M.S., "Cockpit voice recorder audio evidence is centrally important in civil litigation and discoverable under 49 U.S.C. § 1154: The flight 1702 example," Issues in Aviation Law and Policy, Vol. 18:2, 2019. Available at https://rapoportlaw.com/wp-content/uploads/2023/01/Cockpit-Voice-Recorder-Audio-Evidence-is-Centrally-Important-in-Civil-Litigation-and-Discoverable-under-49-USC-1154-The-Flight.pdf.
56. See Plaintiff's Memorandum of Law in Support of their Motion to Compel Production of Cockpit Voice Recorder (CVR) Recording, Berthiaume v. US Airways, Inc., Common Pleas Ct., Phila. County (Jan. Term 2016, No. 00659). cited in Rapoport, D.E., op cit.
57. See Plaintiffs' Response to Defendants' Motion for Summary Judgment on Punitive Damages, Berthiuame, No. 00659, cited in Rapoport, D.E., op cit.
58. Rapoport, D.E. and Sims, M.S., op cit.
59. Ibid.
60. Plaintiffs' Renewed Motion to Compel Production of CVR, Berthiaume, No. 00659.

61. Order, Berthiaume, No. 00659 (Common Pleas Ct., Phila. County, September 29, 2017).
62. 49 U.S.C. § 1154(a)(3) (2018).
63. 49 U.S.C. § 1154(a)(4) (2018).
64. Ibid.
65. Kirksville, 2006 U.S. Dist. Lexis 32976, at 5–6.
66. No. 00659 (Common Pleas Ct., Phila. County, Jan. Term 2016).
67. BEA, Final report on the accident on 1st June 2009 to the Airbus A330-203 registered F-GZCP operated by Air France flight AF 447 Rio de Janeiro – Paris (PDF), (France) (5 July 2012), translated by BEA from French, Le Bourget: BEA Bureau of Enquiry and Analysis for Civil Aviation Safety, from the original on 11 July 2012. Available at https://web.archive.org/web/20120711071354/http://www.bea.aero/docspa/2009/f-cp090601.en/pdf/f-cp090601.en.pdf.
68. Ibid.
69. Otelli, Jean-Pierre (2011). Erreurs de pilotage: Tome 5 [Pilot Error: Volume 5] (in French). Levallois-Perret: Altipresse. ISBN 979-10-90465-03-9. OCLC 780308849.
70. Gilbert, D., "AF447 pilot: 'Damn it, we're going to crash,'" CNN, 14 October 2011. Available at https://edition.cnn.com/2011/10/14/world/americas/af447-transcript/.
71. Charette, R.N., "Air France flight 447's final minutes reconstructed," 12 December 2011. Available at https://spectrum.ieee.org/air-france-flight-447s-final-minutes-reconstructed.
72. Ibid.
73. Hylton, W.S., "What happened to air France flight 447?." The New York Times Magazine, 4 May 2011. Available at https://www.nytimes.com/2011/05/08/magazine/mag-08Plane-t.html.
74. Rfi, "Black box recording of deadly Rio-Paris flight to be played in court," 13 October 2022, modified, 13 October 2022. Available at https://www.rfi.fr/en/france/20221013-black-box-recording-of-deadly-rio-paris-flight-to-be-played-in-court.
75. Annex 10, Foreword, Editorial Practices, 10th edition, 18 November 2010 at page xii.
76. Annex 13, 10th edition, 5.12. (e).
77. Annex 13, 10th edition, 5.12. (f).
78. ICAO Annex 13, Attachment E: Legal Guidance for the Protection of Information From Safety Data Collection and Processing Systems. Available at www.icao.int/Meetings/AMC/MA/Directors%20General%20of%20Civil%20Aviation%20Conference%20on%20a%20Global%20Strategy%20for%20Aviation%20Safety%20(DGCA-06)/Annex13attE_en.pdf.
79. Manual on Protection of Safety Information, Doc 9756 AN/965, Part I Organization and Planning, 2nd edition 2015. Available at https://skybrary.aero/sites/default/files/bookshelf/3282.pdf.
80. ICAO, "ICAO Council adopts new international aviation Standards and Recommended Practices for remotely piloted aircraft systems," 5 April 2024. Available at https://www.icao.int/Newsroom/Pages/ICAO-Council-adopts-new-international-aviation-Standards-and-Recommended-Practices-for-remotely-piloted-aircraft-systems.aspx.
81. APAC-AIG/6–WP/5 Agenda Item 2: Update on ICAO AIG-related requirements and activities Proposed Amendments to Annex 13. Available at www.icao.int/APAC/Meetings/2018%20APACAIG6%20%20Workshop/APAC-AIG6%20WP-05%20AI_2%20-%20[Australia]%20Proposed%20amendment%20to%20Annex%2013.pdf.
82. Ibid., Assistance to the victims of air accidents and their relatives.
83. Ibid., Article 12 Coordination of investigations.
84. Ibid., Communication of Information.
85. Ibid., Article 17.3 Safety Recommendations.
86. Article 21- Article 21 Assistance to the victims of air accidents and their relatives.

87. Regulation (EU) 2018/1139 of 4 July 2018 on common rules in the field of civil aviation and establishing a European Union Aviation Safety Agency.
88. Regulation (EU) 2024/1230 of 24 April 2024 amends Regulations 80/2009, 996/2010, and 65/2014 as regards certain reporting requirements in the fields of road transport and aviation.
89. Regulation (EU) No 376/2014 of 3 April 2014 on the reporting, analysis and follow-up of occurrences in civil aviation, amending Regulation (EU) No 996/2010 and repealing Directive 2003/42/EC and Regulations (EC) No 1321/2007 and (EC) No 1330/2007.
90. Ibid., Article 2, Definitions at 12.
91. Ibid., para 44.
92. AAIASB, Helios 737 Flight 522 Accident Investigation Report, Recommendation 4.2.2.4.

4 Knowing and Doing

4.1 INTRODUCTION

There are many cases where aviation professionals have faced criminal prosecution after an aviation accident or serious incident, and it is essential for individual aviation professionals, including CEOs, senior managers, pilots, ATCs, and engineers, as well as airlines, manufacturers, and aviation organizations, as legal entities, to be aware of potential legal consequences and criminal proceedings against them following accidents or serious incidents.

Three serious incidents involving near midair collisions that occurred in Switzerland and the subsequent criminal proceedings against the air traffic controllers involved, along with the recent midair collision between an American Airlines passenger jet and a military helicopter on 25 January, 2025, at Reagan Washington National Airport, highlight different approaches to holding individual aviation professionals liable and assigning accountability in jurisdictions with different legal systems. The detailed overview and analysis of the Boeing 737 MAX-8 Lion Air Flight 610 and Ethiopian Airlines Flight 302 accidents, the Alaska Airlines Flight 1282 incident on 5 January 2024, and the Air France Flight 447 accident, as well as the subsequent civil and criminal lawsuits against individuals, airlines, and the corporate entities Boeing and Airbus, illustrate the criminalization of aviation professionals and organizations.

4.2 AIR TRAFFIC CONTROLLERS – CASES

4.2.1 Swiss International Airlines Flight SWR132 and Swiss International Airlines SWR202W Near Collision, Zurich Airport (15 March 2011)

On 15 March 2011, Swiss International Airlines Airbus A320 flight SWR 1326 received clearance to taxi to the take-off position on runway 16. While taxiing to the take-off position, the air traffic control officer at the aerodrome control cleared the aircraft for take-off. The crew acknowledged this clearance and initiated their take-off roll. At approximately the same time, another Airbus A320, Swiss International Airlines SWR 202W, which was waiting in the take-off position on runway 28, received clearance for take-off. The crew acknowledged this clearance and immediately initiated their take-off roll. During the take-off roll, the crew of SWR 202W noticed SWR 1326, which was converging from the right on runway 16, and immediately initiated an aborted take-off.

 DOI: 10.1201/9781003724872-4

The Swiss Transportation Safety Investigation Board investigated the incident. The final report was published on 2 May 2012,[1] and the serious incident was

> attributable to the fact that the air traffic control officer concerned gave take-off clearance to an aircraft on runway 28 although another aircraft on runway 16, to which he had given take-off clearance shortly before, was still on its take-off roll. The result was that an inadvertent convergence of these aircraft occurred, involving a high risk of collision.
>
> The following factors significantly contributed to the genesis of the serious incident:
>
> - At a time with a very high volume of traffic at Zurich airport, survey flights were being carried out, which increased the complexity of operation for air traffic control.
> - The air traffic control officer concerned was engaged on tasks which did not have a high priority at this time.
> - The aerodrome control centre work concept allowed only inadequate mutual support in the case of a high volume of traffic and in general did not feature any monitoring for early detection and correction of errors.
> - The air traffic control's collision warning system was inappropriate for resolving the impending conflict.

The genesis of the serious incident was favoured by the complex operation on two intersecting runways which is subject to a small error tolerance in the event of a high volume of traffic.[2]

Twenty days after the SAIB report was published, the cantonal prosecutor (Winterthur/ Unterland, Airport Branch) commenced the investigation into possible negligence hindering public transport. The prosecution alleged that the controller who had cleared the two aircraft to take off from two crossing runways had negligently disrupted public transport and endangered people. He was subsequently charged under Article 237 of the Criminal Code, which penalizes anyone who willfully or negligently endangers public transport, including air transport, and thereby "causes danger to the life and limb of other people." Anyone found guilty could face imprisonment or a fine.

On 7 December 2016, the Bulach District Court ruled that the collision risk had been insufficiently high and acquitted the controller. The prosecution appealed the judgment, and on 4 December 2018, the High Court of the Canton of Zurich[3] found the ATC guilty and sentenced him to 90 days of 210 Swiss Francs fine on probation for two years.[4] The High Court ruled that the controller's conduct resulted in a severe and real collision risk (not a hypothetical one) which endangered the passengers and crew of both aircraft, amounting to negligence. The controller was found guilty and given a monetary penalty. The defense appealed to the Supreme Court against the conviction.

The ATC argued that he was denied the right to a fair trial, in particular his rights of defense, as he alleged that the lower court based its conviction on a hypothetical fact described in the indictment, which claimed that the existence of a concrete danger to life and limb would have existed if the launch of SWR 202W had only been aborted on the ATC's order two seconds after the effective abort. He further argued that only the effective and two hypothetical variants, i.e., the take-off roll of aircraft SWR 202W initiated five seconds earlier or the failure of the aborted take-off, should be assessed, and that further, according to the expert, there was no concrete danger in any of the situations. A further basis for his appeal was his allegation that the lower court, contrary to the presumption of innocence, did not take into account various pieces of evidence.

The Federal Supreme Court emphasized that it was up to the court to determine whether the danger that occurred was sufficient to fulfill the elements of the offense pursuant to Article 237 of the Criminal Code and, if so, whether the danger was due to negligence. [5] On 29 October 2019, four months after the conviction, the Supreme Court upheld the appeal and acquitted the ATC.[6] The Court stated that Article 237 of the Criminal Code requires an actual risk and not a potential or hypothetical risk, and that the court should look at what actually happened, not what could have happened. The court held that, as such, no actual collision risk existed and the controller was not guilty under Article 237 of the Criminal Code.[7] The court referred the case back to the lower court for a new order of costs and held that no costs were to be charged in the Federal Supreme Court proceedings, and the Canton of Zurich must pay the complainant compensation.[8]

4.2.2 Darwin Airways Saab 2000 Flight DWT 124/ Sportcruiser Incident, Zurich (22 August 2012)

On 22 August 2012, a Darwin Airline Saab 2000 scheduled to fly from Zurich, Switzerland, to Genoa, Italy, was departing while a private Sportcruiser aircraft that was engaged in flight training was on final approach. The ATC who was employed by Skyguide had cleared the Saab 2000 to take off from Runway 28 while the Sportcruiser was on short final approach to perform a touch-and-go landing on Crossing Runway 16. To resolve the potentially critical situation, the pilots of the Sportcruiser turned away at low altitude, and the two aircraft converged to a lateral distance of 205 m and an altitude distance of 75 feet.[9]

Only the crew of the Saab submitted a report, which triggered the investigation into the occurrence. The crew of the Sportcruiser stated that they were not in a position to assess the risk adequately and therefore did not file a safety report. The tower controller stated that the tower assessed the situation as being non-critical and did not submit a report, contrary to their duty and obligation to do so.

On 11 September 2012, the Swiss BFU opened an investigation into the event, describing it as a close encounter between a VFR aircraft intending to do a touch-and-go on RWY 16 and an IFR aircraft departing from RWY 28. The final report, released on 24 September 2014, states that the minimum separation between the aircraft was reduced to 205m laterally and 75 feet vertically and that the probable causes were the air traffic controller giving a take-off clearance on runway 28 to a commercial aircraft while a light aircraft was on its approach to runway 16, and the incorrect assessment of the situation by the air traffic controller (which was determined to be a direct causal factor). The following factors were identified as systemic factors which contributed to the serious incident: the inadequate risk assessment by air traffic control; a complex training flight was taking place at a time when the volume of traffic was increasing and at medium complexity; visual approaches were rarely carried out on runway 16; and the Traffic Alert and Collision System (TCAS) fitted in the commercial aircraft did not provide any information to the crew on the ground about other aircraft which restricted their situational awareness. The action by the ATC, instructing the light aircraft, which was in landing configuration and close to the ground, to perform a tight 360° turn to resolve the conflict, and the misinterpreted motivation to provide service on the part of air traffic control were identified as risk factors.[10]

The air traffic controller on duty was criminally charged with negligent disruption of public transport within the meaning of Article 237 of the Criminal Code, which states that:[11]

> (1) Any person who wilfully obstructs, disrupts or endangers public traffic, in particular traffic on the roads, on water or in the air and as a result knowingly causes danger to the life and limb of other people is liable to a custodial sentence not exceeding three years or to a monetary penalty. If the offender thus knowingly endangers the life and limb of a large number of people, a custodial sentence of from one to ten years may be imposed. (2) If the person concerned acts through negligence, the penalty is a custodial sentence not exceeding three years or a monetary penalty.
> (2) If the person concerned acts through negligence, the penalty is a custodial sentence not exceeding three years or a monetary penalty.

It should be noted that at the court hearing, a key point in dispute was whether the collision risk had been real or merely hypothetical, with the prosecution and defense offering differing views on this issue. In March 2019, the Bulach District Court found the ATC guilty. The prosecution asked for a prison sentence to be suspended pending a probation period; however, the court imposed a monetary penalty. The defense appealed the judgment.

Criticizing the court's decision, Skyguide stated that Switzerland is one of the few states that has chosen to depart from international standards and recommendations, including the Annexes to ICAO, with regard to using safety reports to commence judicial proceedings. IFATCA and European Cockpit Association (ECA) stated that the 1942 penal code binds the Swiss court system in these cases in a way that is contrary to aviation safety. They called for a review of the regulations to ensure consistency with other States and international standards, and to incorporate the principles of just culture into their legal system.[12]

In November 2017, Darwin Airline filed for insolvency, and a day later, the Swiss Federal Office of Civil Aviation revoked Darwin Airline's operating certificate due to financial reasons.[13]

Eight and a half years later, on 19 February 2021, the Superior Court of the Canton of Zurich acquitted the ATC. The court reversed the first instance ruling of the District Court of Bülach, stating that the ATC had not acted negligently or wilfully.[14]

4.2.3 Ryanair, Boeing B737 Flight FR058 and TAP Air Portugal A319, Unintentional Convergence, Napf, Lucerne (12 April 2013)

On 12 April 2013, a Ryanair Boeing 737 and a TAP Air Portugal A319 unintentionally infringed the prescribed minimum separation in the upper Swiss airspace around Toggenburg. Due to expected turbulence, the crew of the Ryanair 3595 requested a climb from flight level 360 to 380 without providing their call sign with their request. The air traffic controller did not inquire who was making the request and mistakenly gave permission to the pilot of another Ryanair aircraft RYR 6DW, in the same sector, to climb to flight level 380, who ignored the clearance. The crew of the first Ryanair aircraft, who had made the request but had not received clearance, then responded with their own call sign, RYR 3595, and initiated the climb. Neither the controller nor the crew of RYR 6DW responded. The RYR 3995 aircraft came as close as 0.8 nautical miles horizontally and 650 feet vertically to an Air Portugal Airbus A319, which was cruising on a crossing track at flight level 370. The TCAS commanded RYR 3595 to descend and TAP Portugal A319 to climb. Both crews immediately followed their TCAS commands, and the conflict was avoided. No one was injured, and there was no damage to property.

The occurrence was investigated by the Swiss Accident Investigation Board (SAIB)[15] and the final report was published on 9 October 2014.[16] The final report states that the serious incident is:

> attributable to the fact that the crew of a commercial aircraft initiated a climb without clearance, which lead to a dangerous convergence with another commercial aircraft. The following factors were identified as the cause of the serious incident:
>
> The crew initiated the climb on the basis of a clearance which had been issued to another commercial flight belonging to the same aircraft operator.
>
> The air traffic controller did not realize that the clearance issued was not read back by the crew for which it had been intended. The following was identified as a contributing factor to the serious incident:
>
> A request by a flight crew for clearance to a higher flight level without specification of their radio callsign;
>
> The issue of altitude clearance by air traffic control without verification of the crew which had made the request;
>
> Absent reaction of another crew to whom the clearance was addressed to; Insufficient attention was given to the prevailing weather conditions when the decision to combine sectors was made.[17]

On 8 December 2014, the Federal Prosecutor commenced an investigation, and initially examined the actions of the pilot of RYR 3595. On 22 December 2016, the investigation was extended to include the ATC involved. They were both charged with negligent traffic disruption. The pilot was found guilty and sentenced on 4 April 2017 with a penalty order.[18]

The Federal Criminal Court upheld the ATC's conviction of endangering the lives of the passengers and crew of both aircraft under Article 237 of the Criminal Code in its ruling of 30 May 2018. It sentenced him to a conditional penalty of 60 daily penalty units of 300 Swiss Francs for a probationary period of two years for the negligent disruption of public transport in accordance with Art. 237 para. 2 of the Swiss Criminal Code.[19] The captain of the Ryanair B737 RYR 3959 was found guilty in separate proceedings.

The ATC filed a petition in the Federal Supreme Court to be acquitted of the charges of negligent disruption of public transport and argued, inter alia, that:[20]

(i) The lower court failed to establish the actual risk of collision. It mistakenly relied on the analysis of the Swiss Accident Investigation Board (SAIB) instead of allowing his request for evidence and obtaining an expert opinion to clarify the real risk. He also argued that an expert opinion should have explained when the Traffic Collision Avoidance System triggers an evasive action.

(ii) The lower court used the definition of a serious incident, which is stipulated in EU Regulation 996/2010[21] Art 2 (16) as being "an incident involving circumstances indicating that there was a high probability of an accident and is associated with the operation of an aircraft" and that even though an evasive action is a serious incident, this does not automatically mean a concrete endangering according to Swiss law.

It is essential to note that, unbeknown to the ATC, the lower court provided the following list of questions to the SAIB, namely.[22]

(a) What was the opinion of the SIAB regarding Eurocontrol's Evaluation of 9 September 2018, which qualified the incident as ICAO Category B, and particularly with regards to the Risk Analysis Tool?

(b) Did the evaluation of Eurocontrol result in any changes, additions or corrections to the SAIB report No 2211, and if so, to what extent?

(c) What was the opinion of the SAIB regarding the document "Risk Assessment of Incidents and ATM Specific Occurrences"?

(d) Did the "Risk Assessment" result in changes, additions or corrections to the SAIB Report No. 2211, and if so, to what extent?

(c) What was the response of the SAIB to the Memo of Skyguide (Air Navigation service provider of Switzerland) of 27 March 2018?

(f) Did this Memo result in any changes, additions or corrections to the SAIB Report No. 2211, and if so, to what extent?"

Only after the lower courts delivered their verdict did the ATC become aware that the SAIB provided answers to the list of questions.

The ATC also alleged that a violation of Article 237(2) of the Criminal Code, which requires a concrete endangerment of life and limb, was not proven, and argued that even though the safety distance between the two aircraft was not observed, there was no specific risk to the passengers and crews. A third argument put forward in his appeal was that he did not breach his duty of care within the meaning of Article 12(3) of the Criminal Code.

The Federal Supreme Court stated that the specific facts of the case would ultimately determine whether there was a specific risk in the legal sense. The court rejected the argument by the defense that at no time had there ever been a concrete danger, as the trajectories of the two aircraft had not crossed, even without evasive maneuvers. The court stated that external factors influencing air traffic must always be taken into account and that the minimum vertical and horizontal distances must be observed. The Federal Supreme Court held that the fact that the prescribed safety distance between the two aircraft had been greatly undercut, and as a result, an evasive maneuver was necessary, was a clear indication of a concrete hazard.[23]

Rejecting all the arguments, the Federal Supreme Court dismissed the appeal on 27 June 2019 and confirmed the ATC's guilty verdict for the negligent disruption of public transport (Article 237 of the Penal Code). He was sentenced to 60 days of 300 Swiss Francs on probation for 2 years (18,000 francs), the cost of the lower court proceedings in the amount of 900 francs for the prosecutor, 2,000 for the court case, and 3,000 for the cost of the proceeding in the Supreme Federal Court.[24]

4.2.4 Discussion

The Federal Supreme Court in the Ryanair ruling could have far-reaching consequences for the safety culture and just culture in aviation. As far as we know, this is the first legally binding criminal conviction of an air traffic controller in Switzerland. Both ATCs and pilots have criticized the Supreme Court's decision as well as the earlier convictions handed down by lower Swiss courts for operational incidents that did not result in any injury or damage.

It should be noted that when the lower court assessed the actual risk of collision, it relied solely on the analysis of the Swiss Transportation Safety Investigation Board (STSB) and did not have this question clarified by an expert considering criminal procedural law. The Federal Criminal Court's approach to establishing the facts by referring to the STSB's report is contrary to the philosophy and purpose of conducting an accident investigation. Guilt, liability, and blameworthiness do not fall within the ambit of a safety investigation and should not be determined in criminal proceedings based only on the findings of the final accident investigation report. This practice undoubtedly undermines the sole purpose of conducting the safety investigation and can impede safety.

In all three cases, the court concluded that a real collision risk had existed, which led to a "danger to the life and limb of other people" within the meaning of Article 237 of the Criminal Code. Even though the Supreme Court case law does not provide clear guidelines as to what exactly is required to reach that conclusion, there must be an actual collision risk and not a potential or hypothetical risk. Hence, only residual risk after avoiding action can be considered.[25] It is unclear why the mere occurrence of a significant loss of required separation and TCAS commands alone would justify the conclusion that an actual collision risk existed. In addition to the question of what constitutes a significant loss of separation, the horizontal and vertical distances between two aircraft at a given time do not conclusively create a collision risk. A proper risk assessment depends on the actual and predicted 3D trajectories of the conflicting aircraft over time, and an actual collision risk exists only if the trajectories would possibly intersect. No such finding was made in this case. Furthermore, the issuance of TCAS commands does not necessarily indicate a high collision risk. Modern TCAS equipment communicates between the conflicting aircraft and will, if specific requirements are met, issue a Resolution Advisory (RA) commanding one aircraft to climb and the other to descend. Pilots are trained to immediately comply with any such TCAS RA, which would almost always resolve the conflict. As such, the crews of both RYR 3595 and TAP 706 rapidly followed their TCAS commands and resolved the conflict. Given these factors, a realistic assessment should have determined that the actual collision risk remained within reasonable limits. As the pilots in all three cases executed avoidance action, the potential danger was quickly resolved, and therefore, a realistic assessment should conclude that the residual risk thereafter was within reasonable bounds and that there was no "danger to the life and limb of other people" as defined in Article 237 of the Criminal Code.[26]

It is important to note that in the Ryanair and TAP incident, the air traffic control safety nets, the TCAS, recognized the convergence of the two aircraft and the system, working as it was supposed to, assisted in preventing a potential midair accident. It is also essential to note that, in this case, the air traffic controller and one of the pilots involved filed an Air Safety Report and reported the incident openly and honestly. This resulted in both an internal and external investigation,[27] and, contrary to the principles of just culture, the ATC was subjected to judicial proceedings.

The decision of the Supreme Court does not align with the concept of just culture, which establishes that aviation professionals should not be punished for actions, omissions, or decisions taken by them that are commensurate with their experience and training, but it does not tolerate gross negligence, willful violations, or destructive acts.[28] Apart from gross negligence, egregious conduct or intent, the emphasis should be on aviation safety and not on punishing those identified in an accident investigation report for their slight errors which do not amount to gross negligence or other unacceptable behavior in the case of a technically corrected, if at all likely, existing hazard without any personal injury or damage to property. The Supreme Court's ruling will discourage aviation professionals from reporting mistakes without fearing disciplinary consequences unless they were willful violations or grossly negligent, and will discourage them from treating errors as opportunities for learning and enhancing aviation safety, setting back aviation safety and the implementation of a just culture.[29]

It can be said that the Federal Supreme Court's decision turns a specific dangerous offense, such as Art. 237 of the Swiss Criminal Code, into an abstract one.[30]

In addition, the only potential criminal conduct examined was that of the ATC. Skyguide's role and any possible responsibility for the negligent actions of ATCs, if any, were not considered.

4.2.5 Midair Collision PSA Airlines Bombardier CRJ700 Airplane and Sikorsky UH-60 Military Helicopter, Raegan Airport, Washington D.C., USA (29 January 2025)

On 29 January 2025, approximately 2048 eastern standard time (EST), a Sikorsky UH-60L, operated by the U.S. Army under the callsign PAT25, and an MHI (Mitsubishi Heavy Industries) RJ Aviation (formerly Bombardier) CL-600-2C10 (CRJ700), N709PS, operated by PSA Airlines as flight 5342, collided in flight approximately 0.5 miles southeast of Ronald Reagan Washington National Airport (DCA), Arlington, Virginia, and impacted the Potomac River in southwest Washington, District of Columbia. All 60 passengers and the 4 crew members on board the airplane and the 3 crew members aboard the helicopter were killed. Both aircrafts were destroyed.[31]

The NTSB commenced the investigation and invited qualified parties, including PSA Airlines, GE Aerospace, Sikorsky, the FAA, the U.S. Army, National Air Traffic Controllers Association, Air Line Pilots Association, Association of Flight Attendants, International Association of Machinists and Aerospace Workers, Collins Aerospace, and the Metropolitan Washington Airports Authority, to participate in the investigation. The Transportation Safety Board of Canada provided an accredited representative and Transport Canada and technical advisors.

According to earlier FAA reports, the military helicopter deviated from its flight path and flew above its mandated altitude. Additionally, the staffing configuration was not appropriate for the time of day and volume of traffic, as one air traffic controller handled the duties of two people, with the supervisor merging two positions and allowing one controller to leave early. The same controller was directing helicopters and instructing arriving and departing planes. About 30 seconds before this crash, air traffic control was in communication with the military helicopter. In two separate communications, it is reported that air traffic control asked the helicopter if it had the plane in sight; however, these communications allegedly went unanswered. The plane's radio transponder stopped working about 2,400 feet short of the runway, directly above the Potomac River.[32]

At a news conference after the preliminary report was released, the NTSB's Chairwoman, Jennifer Homendy, described the flight patterns around Reagan airport as "an intolerable risk" due to helicopters and commercial planes operating in close proximity in the busy airspace over the U.S. capital and urged the FAA to implement several "urgent safety recommendations." She also stated that the NTSB investigators identified that between 2021 and 2024, there was at least one "close call" each month between a commercial plane operating at DCA and a helicopter, and that there were 15,214 near-miss events where aircraft were within one nautical mile of colliding, with a vertical separation of less than 400 feet. There were also 85 cases where two aircraft were separated by less than 1,500 feet, with a vertical separation of less than 200 feet.[33]

In May 2025, air traffic controllers had to instruct two passenger aircraft, Delta Flight 1671 and Republic Flight 5825, to perform go-arounds and abort landing at Reagan Airport due to a Black Hawk helicopter inbound to the Pentagon Army

Heliport. The NTSB and FAA are investigating the serious incident. The closest proximity of the first aircraft, Delta Flight 1671, to the helicopter was 0.89 miles and 400 feet. The second flight, Republic 5825, came within 0.4 miles and 200 feet of the helicopter. [34]

The midair crash of an American Airlines regional passenger jet and a U.S. Army Black Hawk helicopter raises significant legal and regulatory concerns. Relatives of the deceased will undoubtedly look into potential fault and liability of parties and will examine inter alia, the crew's actions and the airline's training and maintenance programs, the U.S. military and the helicopter's flight path, the crew and air traffic control actions and their communications, as well as the aircraft manufacturers, government oversight, and military operations. Undoubtedly, the midair collision was not the result of a single failure or decision, but rather the culmination of multiple failures that could arise from operational decisions, inadequate equipment, maintenance, personnel errors, manufacturing defects, and other systemic failures.

The family of one of the passengers on board American Airlines filed personal injury and wrongful death claims totaling $250 million against the FAA and the Army, alleging negligence on their behalf. The government has six months to settle or deny the claims, and the family then has two years to file the lawsuits in federal court. Their lawyer is also investigating potential claims of willful neglect by the agencies overseeing the environment around National Airport, and the U.S. military, given the "congestion of commercial aircraft and the helicopters that went ignored in the airspace near Reagan National Airport." Letters were sent to American Airlines, its regional carrier PSA, Sikorsky Aircraft, and Collins Aerospace to preserve all evidence in the midair crash.[35] Relatives of the other passengers are also expected to file claims.

Three cases in Switzerland where ATCs were charged and criminally prosecuted for negligent disruption of public transport and endangering the lives of passengers and crew after the three near midair collisions in which there were no injuries to passengers or crew, and no deaths were discussed. In stark contrast, the midair collision between the American Airlines passenger jet and the military helicopter in the USA with 67 deaths, and the developments in the aftermath, with no criminal investigation (as there was no indication of terrorism or any other criminal activity), highlight the very different approaches to holding individual aviation professionals liable and apportioning accountability in jurisdictions with different legal systems.

The diverging approaches and differences are further emphasized by our discussion of the Lion Air and Ethiopian Airlines Boeing 737 MAX 8 accidents, the Alaska Airlines incident, and the Air France 447 accident.

4.3 BOEING 737 MAX

4.3.1 Boeing 737 MAX 8 – Lion Air Flight 610 & Ethiopian Airlines Flight 302

Lion Air Flight 610 was a scheduled domestic passenger flight from Soekarno–Hatta International Airport, Tangerang, to Depati Amir Airport, Pangkal Pinang, in Indonesia. On 29 October 2018, the Boeing 737 MAX 8 operating the route, carrying 181 passengers and eight crew members, crashed into the Java Sea 13 minutes after take-off, killing all 189 people on board. It was the first significant accident and hull loss of a 737 MAX, a recently introduced aircraft at that time. The flight crew had communicated with air traffic control and indicated that they were having flight control and altitude issues before the aircraft disappeared from the radar. It was the deadliest accident involving the Boeing 737 family since the 737 was introduced in 1967. One diver also died during recovery operations.

The final report of the investigation released by Indonesia's National Transportation Safety Committee (NTSC) on 25 October 2019 describes a series of failures ranging from poor communication to bad design to inadequate flying skills. The final report criticized Boeing's design and the FAA's certification process for the Maneuvering Characteristics Augmentation System (MCAS). It said that the issues were compounded by maintenance issues and lapses by Lion Air's repair crews and its pilots. The report identified that a new software function in the flight control system, the Maneuvering Characteristics Augmentation System (MCAS), caused the aircraft to tilt downward continually. Normally, pilots can quickly and manually override such automated systems by taking hold of the central control column; however, in this aircraft, the crew would have had to follow a specific sequence of steps to retake control of the plane's "angle of attack." The NTSC final report states,

> The MCAS was a new feature introduced on the Boeing 737-8 (MAX) to enhance pitch characteristics with flaps up during manual flight in elevated angles of attack. The investigation considered that the design and certification of this feature were inadequate. The aircraft flight manual and flight crew training did not include information about MCAS.[36]

The final report also made several recommendations, to which Boeing responded that it would address. It said that they would be taking "actions to enhance the safety of the 737 MAX to prevent the flight control conditions that occurred in this accident from ever happening again."[37] In the aftermath, Boeing issued updates on the emergency procedures related to the changes in the flight-stabilizing MCAS feature. The US Federal Aviation Administration (FAA) and Boeing issued warnings and training advisories to all Boeing 737 MAX series operators, reminding pilots to follow the runaway stabilizer checklist to prevent the MCAS from causing similar problems. In addition, Boeing said that a software update would be made available to update MCAS's behavior.

Approximately four and a half months after the Lion Air crash and amid continued scrutiny of the 737 MAX, another MAX 8 crashed.

On 10 March 2019, Ethiopian Airlines Flight 302, a scheduled international passenger flight from Addis Ababa to Jomo Kenyatta International Airport, Nairobi, Kenya, crashed into a field six minutes after taking off from Addis Ababa, Ethiopia. All 157 passengers and crew on board died, and the airplane was destroyed.

The Ethiopian Accident Investigation Bureau conducted the investigation, and it focused on the activation of the MCAS as the probable cause of the accident. The preliminary report issued on 4 April highlighted similarities to the Lion Air accident. It stated that Ethiopian Air Flight 302 pilots tried to follow Boeing instructions for an MCAS malfunction, but they could not level the nose manually due to the aircraft's high speed.

Hours later, Boeing CEO Dennis Muilenburg issued a statement. It started with

> We at Boeing are sorry for the lives lost in the recent 737 MAX accidents. These tragedies continue to weigh heavily on our hearts and minds, and we extend our sympathies to the loved ones of the passengers and crew on board Lion Air Flight 610 and Ethiopian Airlines Flight 302. All of us feel the immense gravity of these events across our company and recognize the devastation of the families and friends of the loved ones who perished.

He then went on to admit that it was a software error that led to the accidents by saying "with the release of the preliminary report of the Ethiopian Airlines Flight 302 accident investigation, it's apparent that in both flights the Maneuvering Characteristics Augmentation System, known as MCAS, activated in response to erroneous angle of attack information."[38]

The final report states,

Repetitive and uncommanded airplane-nose-down inputs from the MCAS due to erroneous AOA input, and its unrecoverable activation system which made the airplane dive with the rate of -33,000 ft/min close to the ground was the most probable cause of the accident.[39]

Several contributory factors focusing on the design of MCAS, the design and certification of the 737 MAX, and Boeing's training and operational material were also listed.

In March 2017, the FAA certified the 737 MAX 8 and, eleven months later, approved the 737 MAX 9. In May 2017, Malindo Air, a Malaysian subsidiary of Indonesian budget airline Lion Air, was the first airline to receive a 737 MAX. The aircraft made its first commercial flight on May 22 from Malaysia's capital, Kuala Lumpur, to Singapore. By the end of September 2018, Boeing had received orders for nearly 5,000 MAX jets.[40] However, in March 2019, within days of the second accident, the FAA and regulators worldwide ordered the grounding of all 737 MAX jets. The FAA initially maintained that the aircraft was airworthy and waited until three days after the accident to ground the aircraft, by which time evidence had emerged of similarities to the Lion Air crash. Ethiopian investigators concluded that the flight crew had tried to follow the procedures to override the automated stabilization system, which forced the plane into a dive, but they were unsuccessful. Boeing was under intense pressure to explain the problems associated with the MCAS system. It continued to produce the 737 MAX even as it was out of service, aiming for a software fix to the MCAS that would satisfy regulators. However, due to several setbacks, the intended timeline was revised many times, resulting in a significant decrease in Boeing's stock.

It was later revealed that Boeing concealed essential information and that their test pilots and senior pilots involved in the MAX's development had not received detailed briefings about how fast or steep the MCAS automated system could push down a plane's nose. Nor were they informed that the system relied on a single sensor instead of two to verify the accuracy of incoming data about the angle of the aircraft's nose. Boeing then released internal messages that revealed how a top technical pilot working on the MAX had complained about the system's erratic behavior in 2016, and that he had obtained permission from the FAA to remove any mention of the MCAS from the MAX pilot manual. Neither he nor Boeing had revealed to the FAA that they were overhauling the system. "I basically lied to the regulators (unknowingly)," the test pilot wrote in one of the messages made public by Boeing.[41]

In May 2019, Boeing disclosed a safety alert to warn pilots about bad readings from a key sensor on the MAX, but it did not notify airlines or the FAA about the problem until after the Lion Air accident.[42]

Boeing's CEO, Dennis Muilenburg, was ousted as CEO on 23 December 2019, and on 13 January 2020, David Calhoun, the chairman of Boeing's board, took over as CEO. Once the FAA announced in November 2020 that it had approved a flight-control software update and other changes by Boeing, the 737 MAX resumed commercial flights in the U.S. at the end of December 2020. Eventually, other regulators, including those in Canada, Europe, Australia, and India, followed the FAA in lifting bans on the 737 MAX. China was among the last countries to do so, and it permitted the planes to operate in early 2024. The Boeing 737 MAX was grounded worldwide between March 2019 and December 2020 and again in 2024.[43]

In response to the accidents, Congress passed the Aircraft Certification, Safety, and Accountability Act, which was enacted into law on 27 December 2020, adopting several reforms to the FAA's aircraft certification system and processes.[44] The Senate Committee on Commerce, Science, and Transportation (Senate Committee) played a leading role in drafting this bipartisan legislation, which made clear that a course correction on safety oversight was required in light of the 737 MAX tragedies. In January 2023, the Senate Committee sent a letter to the U.S. Department of Transportation stating that, in 2023, Congress would be considering the reauthorization of the FAA and that an essential part of the review would be evaluating the FAA's compliance with the requirements of the Act. The letter requested that the Department of Transportation Office of the Inspector General (OIG) conduct an independent review of the FAA's compliance with congressionally mandated aviation safety reforms in two phases. Firstly, it should review the FAA's compliance with requirements relating directly to ongoing certification activities relating to the 737 MAX, and this should specifically include a review of the FAA's compliance with the following sections of the Act, sections 106 (Limitation on Delegation), 107 (Oversight of Organization Designation Authorization Unit Members), 110 (Appeals of Certification Decisions), and 116 (Flight Crew Alerting). It also stated that concerning section 110 compliance, the OIG should review any action the FAA had taken to provide transparency regarding communications between Boeing and FAA senior executives. The second phase should evaluate FAA's compliance with other sections of the Act the Committee considered to be highly important for the long-term improvement of the FAA's system, but particularly the FAA's compliance with Sections 102 (Safety Management Systems), 105 (Disclosure of Safety

Critical Information), 115 (System Safety Assessments and Other Requirements), 117 (Changed Product Rule), 121 (Implementation of Recommendations), and 122 (Oversight of FAA Compliance Program). In making this request, the letter noted that the Committee recognized that the Act imposed requirements on the FAA that considerably modified its relationship with the industry by requiring more rigorous oversight and regulation than what the FAA had previously provided. It noted that the OIG's evaluation should focus above all on whether the FAA was appropriately responding to the aviation safety reforms mandated by Congress.[45]

4.3.1.1 Senate Hearings

On 29 October 2019, one year to the day after the first of the two accidents, Boeing's CEO, Dennis Muilenburg, testified before a Congressional Committee. He apologized to the family members of the 346 people who died in the two crashes. For close to nine hours over two days of congressional hearings, he was asked questions on Boeing's role in the 737 MAX accidents in Indonesia and Ethiopia. Some of the victims' family members attended the hearings. The often-intense examination by both Democrats and Republicans focused on Boeing's "flying coffins" and "a pattern of deliberate concealment" regarding the MCAS anti-stall system. Muilenburg admitted to mistakes in the design and development of the plane, as well as the company's handling of the aftermath. He said that he would have made a different decision about the actions Boeing took after the Lion Air accident had he known more about the issue.[46]

Questions revolved around whether Boeing downplayed safety concerns, hid design flaws from regulators, and tried to cover up its mistakes and missteps. Three critical facts emerged from the two-day hearing and the testimony provided. Firstly, Boeing knew MCAS had a problematic single point of failure two years before the MAX 737 aircraft had been approved to fly, and three years before the Lion Air accident. It appeared that a significant error in the design of the new flight control system was relying on information from just a single Angle of Attack (AoA) sensor[47] for MCAS to activate. If the AoA sensed the aircraft was pitched up too high, MCAS would automatically and repeatedly force the nose of the plane down. This is what happened in both the Lion Air and Ethiopian Airlines accidents, except that the sensor was wrong. Indonesian investigators found that a Lion Air maintenance crew had installed a new, faulty AoA sensor the day before the accident flight, and that they had failed to recalibrate and test it. Experts testified that relying on just one sensor for a safety-critical system is not standard practice in aviation engineering, and doing so was unusual and unprecedented. The Senate Committee released a redacted email during the hearing, which highlighted the fact that in 2015, Boeing was aware that this could be problematic. One of the engineers had also voiced his concerns about relying on just one sensor to trigger the system, writing in an email, "Are we vulnerable to single AOA sensor failures with the MCAS implementation or is there some checking that occurs?"[48] Boeing, however, decided to continue with the single-sensor design, with no backup to prevent MCAS from forcing the plane into a nosedive. When Boeing's chief engineer was asked if he had received the email and if he had responded to it, he replied that he had only recently become aware of it. He went a step further and also said that the email in no way was indicative of a Boeing culture to prioritize profits above safety. He said, "I think it highlights our engineers do raise questions, in an open culture. They question things." He was then cut off from speaking further by the Chair of the Senate Committee.[49]

Secondly, Boeing was aware that its assumptions about how pilots would respond to the MCAS could be wrong. The MCAS was developed based on the assumption that if the system activated erroneously, pilots would recognize that in four seconds, and that they would also know how to cut off the system. They had never made the pilots aware that the system existed. Boeing had convinced the FAA that the system was running only in the background, and therefore, it was not necessary to include that in the training and flight deck manuals. Pilots have subsequently said, "We were the backup system? How can we be backup if we don't know something's going to take over our plane?" Boeing had known that some pilots would require 10 seconds or more to establish what was happening. A document dated 11 June 2018 was produced showing that Boeing employees had raised concerns about the amount of time it would take for pilots to react to a potential MCAS failure. The document, called a "coordination sheet," suggested some pilots would take more than four seconds to react, and stated that a slow reaction time scenario (greater than) 10 seconds would be catastrophic.[50]

Thirdly, it emerged that after the Lion Air crash, Boeing knew of internal MCAS concerns but refused to ground the MAX planes. In his testimony, Muilenburg admitted that after the first crash and before the second, he knew about internal messages between Boeing technical pilots from 2016 that discussed "egregious" problems with the MCAS system. He stated that he had not thoroughly read the messages, as he had given them to the company's lawyers, and that he had only recently become fully aware of their content. Republican Ted Cruz replied,

> You're the CEO, the buck stops with you. How did your team not put in front of you, run in with their hair on fire, saying, "We've got a real problem here?" How did that not happen and what does that say about the culture at Boeing? How did you not, in February, set out a nine-alarm fire to say, "We need to figure out exactly what happened?"[51]

Other Committee members also pushed the question of why Boeing did not ground the plane after the first crash in Indonesia, when the company knew that the MCAS system played a significant role in causing the accident. Muilenburg said, "Senator, I think about that the decision over and over, every day. If we knew everything back then that we know now, we would have made a different decision."[52]

In September 2000, after an 18-month investigation, the Chair of the Senate Committee and the Chair of the Subcommittee on Aviation released the Committee's final report on the Boeing 737 MAX. The report outlined the serious flaws and missteps in the design, development, and certification of the aircraft, which entered commercial service in 2017. The Chair of the House Committee said that

> We are making this report public to put a spotlight not only on the broken safety culture at Boeing but also the gaps in the regulatory system at the FAA that allowed this fatally-flawed plane into service. Critically, our report gives Congress a roadmap on the steps we must take to reinforce aviation safety and regulatory transparency, increase Federal oversight, and improve corporate accountability to help ensure the story of the Boeing 737 MAX is never, ever repeated.[53]

The report states that

> "The MAX crashes were not the result of a singular failure, technical mistake, or mismanaged event." "They were the horrific culmination of a series of faulty technical assumptions by Boeing's engineers, a lack of transparency on the part of Boeing's management, and grossly insufficient oversight by the FAA."[54]

The report refers to the company's rushed production and cost-cutting measures as contributing to safety failures and states that the FAA had given too much oversight to Boeing itself during the certification process. In particular, the report contained the following five central themes and more than six dozen investigative findings:

> Production pressures that jeopardized the safety of the flying public. There was tremendous financial pressure on Boeing and the 737 MAX program to compete with Airbus' new A320neo aircraft. Among other things, this pressure resulted in extensive efforts to cut costs, maintain the 737 MAX program schedule, and avoid slowing the 737 MAX production line.
>
> Faulty Design and Performance Assumptions. Boeing made fundamentally faulty assumptions about critical technologies on the 737 MAX, most notably with MCAS, the software designed to automatically push the airplane's nose down in certain conditions. Boeing also expected that pilots, who were largely unaware that MCAS existed, would be able to mitigate any potential malfunction.
>
> Culture of Concealment. Boeing withheld crucial information from the FAA, its customers, and 737 MAX pilots, including internal test data that revealed it took a Boeing test pilot more than 10 seconds to diagnose and respond to uncommanded MCAS activation in a flight simulator, a condition the pilot described as "catastrophic." Federal guidelines assume pilots will respond to this condition within four seconds.
>
> Conflicted Representation. The FAA's current oversight structure with respect to Boeing creates inherent conflicts of interest that have jeopardized the safety of the flying public. The report documents multiple instances in which Boeing employees who have been authorized to perform work on behalf of the FAA failed to alert the FAA to potential safety and/or certification issues.
>
> Boeing's Influence Over the FAA's Oversight Structure. Multiple career FAA officials have documented examples where FAA management overruled a determination of the FAA's own technical experts at the behest of Boeing. These examples are consistent with results of a recent draft FAA employee "safety culture" survey that showed many FAA employees believed its senior leaders are more concerned with helping industry achieve its goals and are not held accountable for safety-related decisions.[55]

4.3.2 Legal Proceedings

4.3.2.1 Civil Litigation

In September 2022, the Securities and Exchange Commission charged The Boeing Company and its former CEO, Dennis Muilenburg, with making materially misleading public statements following the 2018 and 2019 accidents by saying, one month after the Lion Air accident that the 737 MAX was "as safe as any airplane that has ever flown the skies" even though the company had determined MCAS posed a safety risk in need of repair.[56] It said that

> Boeing and Muilenburg put profits over people by misleading investors about the safety of the 737 MAX all in an effort to rehabilitate Boeing's image following two tragic accidents that resulted in the loss of 346 lives and incalculable grief to so many families.[ ] But public companies and their executives must provide accurate and complete information when they make disclosures to investors, no matter the circumstances. When they don't, we will hold them accountable, as we did here.[57]

The Commission found that both parties had negligently violated the anti-fraud provisions of federal securities laws.

Without admitting or denying the findings, the parties consented to cease-and-desist orders, and Boeing agreed to pay a $200 million fine, while Muilenburg agreed to pay $1 million to settle the charges.[58]

After both the Lion Air and the Ethiopian Airlines fatal accidents, relatives of the deceased passengers and crew filed civil complaints against Boeing for inter alia, wrongful death and negligence, seeking compensation. Some of the many cases include the following.

In September 2018, the family of the Indian pilot of the Lion Air flight sued Boeing, demanding a trial for wrongful death.[59] In December 2018, relatives of the Indonesian co-pilot of the Lion Air flight filed a wrongful death lawsuit against Boeing in Chicago. The legal proceedings claim that:

> The Boeing aircraft's sensors improperly caused the plane's automatic anti-stall system to lower the nose of the plane and cause it to dive steeply and crash; The aircraft's anti-stall system and flight control systems failed to timely respond to pilot control of the aircraft; and that the aircraft's manual did not have proper instructions, policies and procedures for taking over the aircraft when these systems malfunctioned.[60]

The first wrongful death lawsuit following the Ethiopian Airlines accident was filed in the United States District Court for the Northern District of Illinois. At the end of May 2019, District Judge Jorge L. Alonso ordered all Ethiopian Airlines cases in the U.S. federal court in Illinois to be consolidated into one proceeding for issues and discovery purposes. By March 2019, approximately 29 wrongful death lawsuits were filed in the state and federal courts in Chicago by the relatives of those who perished in the Lion Air crash. The cases filed in state court were transferred to the federal court in Chicago, where they were assigned, along with the cases originally filed in federal court, to District Court Judge Thomas M. Durkin for coordinated proceedings.[61]

On 4 April 2019, a lawsuit on behalf of the first American citizen to claim compensation was filed by the family of a 24-year-old passenger who died in the Ethiopian Airlines accident. The civil case was filed in the federal district court in Chicago against Boeing, based in Chicago, Rosemount Aerospace, Inc. of Delaware, which manufactured the allegedly defective part, and Ethiopian Airlines. The complaint alleges negligence as well as breach of warranty, strict liability, failure to warn, and civil conspiracy, and states that "Blinded by its greed, Boeing haphazardly rushed the 737 MAX 8 to market, with the knowledge and tacit approval of the United States Federal Aviation Administration (FAA)." It goes on to state "Boeing's decision to put profits over safety" ..... "and the regulators that enabled it, must be held accountable for their reckless actions."[62] An additional, separate claim was filed against the FAA.[63] On 5 April 2019, the second wrongful death lawsuit after the Ethiopian Airlines crash was filed in the United States District Court for the Northern District of Illinois. On 10 April, the third wrongful death lawsuit was filed in the same court.[64]

On the same day, Boeing's shareholders filed a lawsuit in Chicago, arguing that Boeing had misled them by hiding what was known about the 737-MAX aircraft's dangerous design to generate profits and drive stock prices higher. According to the shareholder lawsuit, Boeing "effectively put profitability and growth ahead of airplane safety and honesty" by rushing the 737 MAX to market to compete with Airbus, while leaving out "extra" or "optional" features designed to prevent the loss of control that occurred in the Ethiopian Airlines and Lion Air crashes.

By June 2019, numerous court hearings had taken place in the Chicago Federal Court related to both the Lion Air and Ethiopian Airlines accidents. In July 2019, a lawsuit was filed against Boeing, specifically seeking punitive damages for violations of the Illinois Consumer Fraud and Deceptive Business Practices Act, alleging fraud, deception, and misrepresentations made by Boeing in order to rush the 737 MAX 8 to market. The lawsuit further alleged that Boeing chose to advance a corporate culture "that emphasized development speed and profits over safety, knowing that the proliferation of such corporate culture would drive enormous corporate profits but significantly increase the risk of an aviation disaster resulting in catastrophic loss of life."[65]

In 2019, Southwest Airlines Pilot Association (SWAPA) filed a lawsuit in the Dallas County District Court against Boeing, accusing it of misrepresenting and omitting facts about the safety of the 737 MAX to pilots. The complaint states that the pilots' 2016 Collective Bargaining Agreement (CBA) with Southwest specifically stated that pilots would fly the newer model, and that as a result of the defective 737 MAX, Southwest, as the largest operator of that model, had lost millions of dollars after the plane was grounded and pilots' flight schedules were decreased. The suit states, "Had SWAPA known the truth about the 737 MAX aircraft in 2016, it never would have approved the inclusion of the 737 MAX aircraft as a term in its CBA and agreed to operate the aircraft for Southwest."[66] The Boeing Company was sued for $100 million in lost income as a result of the grounding of the 737 MAX aircraft and the cancellation of over 30,000 flights since the FAA grounded the aircraft. It also accuses Boeing of rushing the redesigned 737 to market, prioritizing the company's profits over safety and sound design and engineering practices, saying that "Boeing ... withheld critical information from regulators and deliberately misled its customers, pilots and the public about "the true scope of the design changes to the 737 MAX."[67] The Texas Supreme Court first refused to hear the dispute in May 2024, but later agreed to review it.[68] On 10 January 2025, the Texas Supreme Court agreed to hear their lawsuit against Boeing over the airline's use of the global aircraft manufacturer's defective 737 MAX and to determine whether federal transportation labor relations laws preclude the Southwest Airlines Pilots Association from suing Boeing over lost wages stemming from the 737 grounding in 2019.[69] In its opinion delivered on 20 June 2025, the Supreme Court held that the pilots, represented by the Southwest Airlines Pilots Association, could proceed with their lawsuit against Boeing over allegations that the aircraft manufacturer misled them about the safety of the 737 MAX aircraft. The judge affirmed the Court of Appeals' judgment, which remanded the case to the trial court for further proceedings on the claims submitted by SWAPA on its behalf.[70]

According to a June 2023 court document, relatives of 115 victims filed civil complaints against Boeing. The civil trials centered on compensatory damages, with no evidence regarding any liability of Boeing being presented. As of 22 October 2024, thirty cases were still pending on behalf of 29 deceased passengers. In December 2024, Boeing reached a last-minute settlement with the family of one of the passengers who was on board Ethiopian Airlines. The out-of-court settlement was reached days before the trial was to commence in Chicago, averting a federal civil trial. The suit initially involved six plaintiffs, five of whom had previously settled the case. The remaining case, which was settled, involved an Indian-born woman who was in her second year of medical school. Boeing "accepted responsibility for the MAX accidents publicly and in civil litigation because the design of the MCAS...contributed to these events."[71]

Many of the civil lawsuits filed by the relatives claimed compensation, which included compensation for the suffering and terror that their relatives may have experienced just before the plane crashed. Their lawyers argued that there is "no dispute that passengers and crew members were conscious and fully aware that the plane was plummeting before it actually crashed at nearly 600 mph," and that the passengers "undeniably suffered horrific emotional distress, pain and suffering, and physical impact/injury while they endured extreme G-forces, braced for impact, knew the airplane was malfunctioning, and ultimately plummeted nose-down to the ground at terrifying speed."[72]

In November 2021, Boeing said, "the 737 MAX had an unsafe condition, and that it will not attempt to blame anyone else." It reached a settlement agreement, agreeing to acknowledge liability for compensatory damages in lawsuits filed by families of the 157 people killed in the 2019 Ethiopian Airlines crash. It further stated that it was "committed to ensuring that all families who lost loved ones in the accidents are fully and fairly compensated for their loss."[73] As a result of the agreement, the claimants would not seek punitive damages, and Boeing would not contest the lawsuits filed in Illinois. All the planned depositions with former and senior Boeing executives were canceled. However, in February 2023, Boeing argued that compensation should not include pre-impact pain and suffering before the plane crashed. They submitted that, while they did not dispute that passengers suffered during the flight, any speculative pain sustained in the milliseconds before the impact was not relevant to determining damages as they would have been unaware that they were injured before they died. They relied on a medical expert who submitted that the crash took place at a speed faster than the human brain could process pain. They claimed that "undisputed evidence shows that death was instantaneous, and any speculation about what the passengers might have felt as the plane made an impact is unfounded."[74] They argued that, as the applicable law was Illinois law, damages could only be paid for the victims' "conscious pain and suffering," assuming that there was provable evidence that suffering had occurred. The judge rejected Boeing's motion to rule out pre-impact pain and suffering damages and held that pain and suffering could be considered when determining compensation for the victims' relatives. He said that

> there is sufficient evidence to support a reasonable inference that these passengers experienced pre-impact fright and terror, and that experience is part of the process or manner of death and that a jury could reasonably infer from the evidence that the passengers 'perceived that they were going to crash, horrifically, to their certain death.'[75]

Families of the victims of the Lion Air crash disclosed that shortly after the accident, they were pressured to sign an agreement preventing them from taking legal action against Boeing or Lion Air. They said that they were persuaded that, for them to get the initial mandatory compensation that they were entitled to under international legal instruments, they had to first sign a document which, in effect, took away their right to sue for additional compensation. It was reported that approximately 50 families signed the agreement.[76]

In a sad twist for some of the relatives of those who died in the Lion Air accident, their lawyer, a well-known Los Angeles attorney, was found to have misappropriated approximately $2 million in client funds received as compensation. In the court hearing for contempt, the judge labeled his conduct as "unconscionable" and referred the case to the U.S. attorney's office for criminal investigation. Evidence was presented that he no longer had the money in his possession as it had been spent on maintaining his costly and luxurious lifestyle, and that he only had about $15,000 in his operating accounts. His lawyers expressed concern about his mental state. A trustee was appointed to oversee any remaining assets that he or his firm had.[77] In a rare move, another US law firm undertook to compensate those families who should have received the funds from the lawyer who was disbarred for misappropriating their funds.[78]

4.3.2.2 Criminal Proceedings

In January 2021, the U.S. Department of Justice (DOJ) filed a criminal charge in the Northern District of Texas, charging Boeing with one count of conspiracy to defraud the United States by circumventing proper federal oversight of its aircraft design.

The charge was related to a conspiracy to defraud the FAA in connection with the FAA's evaluation of Boeing's 737 MAX aircraft. Boeing then entered into a deferred prosecution agreement (DPA) with the Department of Justice to resolve the criminal charge. In accordance with the agreement, in exchange for deferring prosecution for three years, Boeing agreed to pay a total monetary amount of over $2.5 billion, composed of a criminal financial penalty of $243.6 million and compensation payments to Boeing's 737 MAX airline customers of $1.77 billion. In addition, a $500 million crash-victim beneficiaries fund would be established to compensate the relatives and legal beneficiaries of the 346 passengers who perished in the Boeing 737 MAX Lion Air Flight 610 and Ethiopian Airlines Flight 302 accidents.[79] The plea agreement includes Boeing pleading guilty, a fine, three years of probation, and independent safety audits. In an online meeting, the disappointed family members and their lawyers labeled the plea agreement "a sweetheart deal." They said that the offer was deceptive, generous, and not in the public interest, that it does not acknowledge that Boeing's crime resulted in the death of 346 people, and that it allows Boeing to hide their misdeeds from the public.[80]

In October 2021, the only individual who was prosecuted was the former Boeing 737 MAX Chief Technical Pilot, who was indicted for allegedly deceiving the FAA Aircraft Evaluation Group in connection with its evaluation of Boeing's 737 MAX aircraft and scheming to defraud the airline's customers for Boeing's financial gain. It was alleged that he deceived the FAA Aircraft Evaluation Group (AEG) during the agency's evaluation and certification of Boeing's 737 MAX aircraft by provided the agency with materially false, inaccurate, and incomplete information about a new part of the flight controls for the Boeing 737 MAX, the MCAS, and that, as a result of his alleged deception, a key document published by the FAA AEG and the aircraft manuals and pilot-training materials did not make any reference to MCAS. He was charged with two counts of fraud involving aircraft parts in interstate commerce and four counts of wire fraud, each carrying a maximum sentence of 20 years imprisonment.[81] The DOJ stated that the indictment highlighted the fact that anyone who contemplated criminally impeding a regulator's function would be prosecuted and held accountable. The FBI also said that "The FBI will continue to hold individuals like [the technical pilot] accountable for their fraudulent acts which undermine public safety."[82]

The FAA required only brief computer-based training for pilots instead of more extensive practice in simulators that could have cost Boeing up to $1 million per aircraft. The wire fraud charges were based on communications that the technical pilot had with the FAA and with two big Boeing customers, Southwest Airlines and American Airlines. His defense lawyers argued that Boeing engineers did not tell him about changes to the MCAS flight software, and that he was a scapegoat for Boeing and FAA officials attempting to avoid accountability. The technical pilot did not testify. There was only one witness called by the defense, a current Boeing pilot, who testified for approximately one hour. Prosecutors submitted internal messages with colleagues, and relying on one in particular in which he stated that he had unknowingly misled regulators, his lawyers argued that this message was a complaint about a flight simulator, and not the MCAS. A witness for the prosecution, an

FAA official who worked with him, testified that he lied to her that MCAS would never activate during normal airline use, only in certain high-speed situations that pilots would never encounter. His defense team argued that Boeing engineers did not tell him that the scope of the system had been expanded, and that he told the FAA official what he knew at that time. On 23 March 2022, after a trial lasting less than three days and jury deliberation of under two hours, the federal jury found him not guilty, and he was acquitted of all charges.[83]

4.3.3 Crime Victims

In October 2022, the United States District Court for the Northern District of Texas held that over a dozen family members and representatives of the deceased had satisfactorily established that they were directly and proximately harmed by Boeing's conspiracy to defraud the United States and held that the deceased were crime victims under the Crime Victims' Rights Act (CVRA). The Texas federal judge, Justice Reed O'Connor, ruled that the Justice Department violated the rights of relatives of the victims of the two accidents by not consulting them before approving the deal with Boeing. The families requested that the judge nullify the settlement agreement and lift Boeing's immunity from prosecution. In February, the same judge held that, despite "Boeing's egregious criminal conduct," federal law did not give him the power to overturn the settlement.[84] He also refused to impose an independent monitor, stating that there was no factual record to justify that Boeing presented an "ongoing threat to public safety."[85]

In the U.S., there are two federal statutes outlining the federal government's responsibilities toward crime victims and the specific rights afforded to them. The Victim's Rights and Restitution Act (VRRA)[86] describes the services the federal government is required to provide to victims of federal crime. The Crime Victims' Rights Act (CVRA)[87] places an explicit duty on federal courts to ensure that victims are afforded those rights. The CVRA defines a crime victim as a person against whom the federal offense is committed, or, if that person is killed or incapacitated, that person's family member or other lawful representative, and grants the following rights to crime victims.

(1) The right to be reasonably protected from the accused.
(2) The right to reasonable, accurate, and timely notice of any public court proceeding, or any parole proceeding, involving the crime or of any release or escape of the accused.
(3) The right not to be excluded from any such public court proceeding, unless the court, after receiving clear and convincing evidence, determines that testimony by the victim would be materially altered if the victim heard other testimony at that proceeding.
(4) The right to be reasonably heard at any public proceeding in the district court involving release, plea, sentencing, or any parole proceeding.
(5) The reasonable right to confer with the attorney for the Government in the case.

(6) The right to full and timely restitution as provided in law.
(7) The right to proceedings free from unreasonable delay.
(8) The right to be treated with fairness and with respect for the victim's dignity and privacy.
(9) The right to be informed in a timely manner of any plea bargain or deferred prosecution agreement.
(10) The right to be informed of the rights under this section and the services described in section 503(c) of the Victims' Rights and Restitution Act of 1990, and provided contact information for the Office of the Victims' Rights Ombudsman of the Department of Justice.

4.3.4 Boeing 737 MAX 9 – Alaska Airlines Flight 1282

On 5 January 2024, Alaska Airlines Flight 1282, a Boeing 737 MAX 9, returned to Portland International Airport, Portland, Oregon, shortly after takeoff when the Boeing aircraft suffered a rapid decompression after the left mid-exit door plug departed. The aircraft landed without further incident, and the 6 crew members and 171 passengers disembarked at the gate. Seven passengers and one flight attendant received minor injuries.

The NTSB examined the aircraft structure, flight deck, cabin interior, cabin safety systems, and pressurization system. In its preliminary report of 7 February 2024, it states that the accident Mid-Exit Door (MED) plug was manufactured by Spirit AeroSystems, Malaysia, on 24 March 2023 and was received at Spirit AeroSystems Wichita on 10 May 2023. The plug was then installed and rigged on the fuselage and shipped to Boeing on 20 August 2023. The fuselage arrived at the Boeing Renton, Washington, facility on 31 August 2023. The report provides the following specific details of the MED plug, which is primarily constructed of aluminum and installed in the fuselage using two upper guide fittings and two lower hinge fittings. The two upper guide fittings are located on the upper sides of the plug and engage with two upper guide rollers fixed to the upper sides of the fuselage opening. Two lower hinge guide fittings are fixed to the lower section of the plug and engage with the two lower hinge fittings attached to the bottom of the fuselage opening at the lower hinge bracket assemblies. Once the plug is in place, it is secured from moving vertically by a total of four bolts. A bolt is installed through each upper guide fitting and each lower hinge guide fitting. Once these bolts are installed, they are secured using castle nuts and cotter pins. The outboard motion of the plug is prevented by twelve stop fittings (six along each forward and aft edge) installed on the fuselage door frame structure. The door plug is only intended to be opened for maintenance and inspection, which requires removing the vertical movement arrestor bolts and upper guide track bolts. The strap assemblies below the second stop pad from the top restrict the plug from opening further than 15 degrees, which is suitable for maintenance and inspection purposes.[88] The NTSB report states that the MED plug, which was recovered in the backyard of a private residence, was mostly intact with some damage from the event and appeared to be manufactured in accordance with the engineering drawings. It notes that two vertical movement arrestor bolts, two upper guide track bolts, forward lower hinge guide fitting, and forward lift assist spring were missing and have not been recovered.[89] The NTSB announced that a hearing would be held on 6 and 7 August 2024 regarding its investigation.[90]

Hours after the accident, Alaska Airlines took precautionary measures. They grounded 65 of its B737 MAX 9 fleet to inspect the MED plugs and said that another 18 had just undergone a maintenance inspection and were ready to return to service. A day later, on 6 January, the FAA issued an Emergency Airworthiness Directive (EAD) grounding all Boeing 737 MAX 9 aircraft with a mid-cabin door plug installed and requiring them to undergo specific inspections before returning the aircraft to service. Following the directive, Alaska Airlines grounded the entire MAX 9 fleet.[91] Other airlines, such as United Airlines, Turkish Airlines, and Lion Air, also grounded their fleets.[92] United Airlines and Alaska Airlines are the only two US carriers that fly the Boeing 737 MAX 9. During the inspection, United Airlines reported that loose bolts and other installation issues were identified in the door plug.[93] Alaska Airlines also stated that its inspections had revealed loose bolts on many of its aircraft.[94]

On 21 January, the FAA published a Safety Alert for Operators of airplanes with the same MED plug as the accident airplane, but on the Boeing 737-900ER. The alert recommended that operators inspect, as soon as possible, the four locations where the retaining hardware secures the door to the airframe. Boeing issued multiple multi-operator messages, which included, inter alia, revised instructions for inspecting 737-9 aircraft with the MED plugs.[95] A preliminary statement from the NTSB said it was possible that the bolts that were to keep the door plug panel in place were never installed, and that prior to the incident, the aircraft had been restricted from flying overseas due to repeated pressurization warnings.

On 9 January, Boeing CEO Dave Calhoun made the first public acknowledgment of errors. In a meeting with Boeing staff, he admitted to mistakes made by Boeing and stated,

> We're going to approach this, No. 1, acknowledging our mistake. We are going to approach it with 100 per cent, complete transparency, every step of the way. We're going to work with the NTSB, who is investigating the accident itself, to find out what the root cause is.

He also said that he was shaken "to the bone" by the incident and vowed that incidents like the midair panel blowout can "never happen again."[96]

On 15 January 2024, Boeing's President and CEO, in a message to employees, announced some immediate actions that the company would take to enhance quality assurance and controls in the 737 production. He stated that in response to the Alaska Airlines Flight 1282 accident, Boeing was working with the five affected airlines to inspect their 737-9 fleet, and that in conjunction with working on getting the FAA approval to unground the fleet, they were also closely examining their quality practices in their factories and across their production system. He went on to say that in recent years, Boeing had strengthened its Quality Management System, but that it was clear there was still work to be done. The immediate actions announced included additional quality inspections, team sessions on quality, an enhanced Boeing review of Spirit AeroSystems' work, airline oversight inspections, and an independent assessment by an outside party on Boeing's quality management system. He went on to clarify that these actions were independent of the FAA's investigation and their focus on increasing their oversight of the 737-9 production. He stressed that Boeing would cooperate fully and transparently as it worked with the FAA and the NTSB to restore trust with the FAA and its customers.[97]

4.3.4.1 Senate Hearings

On 6 March 2024, the Chair of the NTSB appeared before the Senate Committee on Commerce, Science, and Transportation to provide the Committee with an update on the progress of their investigation into the Alaska Airlines incident of 5 January. At that hearing, the Committee inquired whether the NTSB had received timely access to the necessary documents, information, and witnesses. The Committee requested a written response by 13 March at the latest, specifying whether Boeing had provided documentation on the work to open, reinstall, and close the door plug, along with a list of the 25 door crew employees.

In the letter dated 13 March 2024, the NTSB Chair specified that the aircraft in question underwent rivet repairs at Boeing's Renton, Washington, facility in September 2023 before being delivered to Alaska Airlines. It also stated that the door plug that failed during the incident flight was opened to allow the rivet repair work to be performed. It also noted that it was still unknown who had worked on the specific door plug involved in the incident. When investigators requested security video footage to obtain this information, they were informed that the video footage had been overwritten. The letter states that not having that information would impede the NTSB's investigation.[98]

The letter provided a detailed and analytical timeframe of their requests to Boeing for relevant documents, names, and other pertinent information as follows:

> NTSB investigators first requested documents that would have contained this information from Boeing on January 9, 2024. Shortly thereafter, we identified the door crew manager and were advised that he was out on medical leave. We requested status updates on February 15, 2024, and February 22, 2024, after which we were advised by his attorney that he would not be able to provide a statement or interview to NTSB due to medical issues.
>
> On February 2, 2024, Boeing gave NTSB names of individuals who may provide insight regarding the work performed to open, reinstall, and close the door plug in September 2023. The team continued its investigative work. Needing to prepare for interviews in Renton beginning March 3, and still unaware of who completed the door plug work, NTSB investigators requested from Boeing the names of all employees who reported to the door crew manager in September 2023. The intent of this request was to help inform our efforts to uncover who may have been involved with, and who may have information on, the opening, reinstallation, and closure of the door plug on the accident aircraft. This request was made via email on March 2. That list was provided to NTSB following the hearing on March 6 at 2:00 p.m. EST. However, this list did not identify which personnel conducted the door plug work. After NTSB received this list,

> I called Boeing Chief Executive Officer David Calhoun and asked for the names of the people who performed the work. He stated he was unable to provide that information and maintained that Boeing has no records of the work being performed.[99]

It is essential to note that the letter emphasized two key points. Firstly, that the purpose of the NTSB investigation is not punitive in nature. The names of the employees who worked on the door plug were sought so that information and lessons could be learned about Boeing's quality-assurance processes and safety culture, and to prevent a recurrence of similar events. Secondly, it expressed concern that focusing on the names of individual front-line workers would negatively impact the investigation and discourage employees from providing the NTSB with relevant information. The NTSB would therefore utilize its authority to protect the identities of the door crew and other front-line employees who come forward with any relevant information.[100] In addition, the NTSB letter sent to Boeing enclosed a reminder of the regulatory restrictions to which Boeing had agreed as a party to the NTSB investigation.

The NTSB Chair replied as follows to various questions from the Committee members regarding timely access to pertinent information and documentation:

> We have been informed that they have a procedure to maintain documents on when work is performed, including when door plugs are open, closed or removed. We have not been able to verify that. And without that information that raises concerns about quality assurance, quality management, safety management systems within Boeing. We have gone through emails, we've gone through texts, we've looked at pictures to begin to get a picture of the date in mid-September, the two dates in mid-September that we believe the work occurred. We haven't received that information directly from Boeing. We also believe we know what shift it occurred on. But we still know there is one team, one team that deals with the doors of 25 people. Why we don't have those names today, two months later, is really disappointing.[101]

After the testimony given by the NTSB Chair, J. Homendy, the Chair of the Committee, S. Sen. Maria Cantwell, sent a letter to the CEO of Boeing asking for their "full and immediate" cooperation, and gave Boeing 48 hours to provide the NTSB with the specific information requested. The letter stated:

> Today's National Transportation Safety Board (NTSB) hearing before the U.S. Senate Committee on Commerce, Science and Transportation brought to light the NTSB's frustrations with getting access to information related to the Alaska Airlines 1282 investigation. It has been two months since this accident happened. Specifically, NTSB Chair Homendy confirmed that Boeing and its suppliers still have not provided documentation of the door plug removal and reinstallation or the names of the 25 persons assigned to the team that performs this work. The NTSB needs prompt access to this information. Please provide this investigative information to the NTSB within the next 48 hours so they can conduct their investigation. If complying with this demand is not possible for some reason, please provide me with a thorough explanation of why not within the same time period. We are additionally asking the FAA for information about what FAA Aviation Safety Inspectors were in place to safeguard against quality assurance problems.[102]

Boeing responded in writing, stating that they had conducted an extensive search but could not find a record of the work done on the 737 MAX final assembly line in Renton to open and reinstall the panel that blew out on 5 January on Alaska Airlines Flight 1282. Consequently, their working hypothesis was that no records were available as the documents required by their processes were not created when the door plug was opened.[103] Boeing provided the following statement to the NTSB:

> We have deep respect for the NTSB and the critical role they play in aviation safety. Since the first moments following the Alaska Airlines Flight 1282 accident, we have worked proactively and transparently to fully support the NTSB's investigation. Our team works tirelessly with the NTSB team to respond comprehensively to all NTSB information requests and bring information to them that would be relevant to their investigation. Early in the investigation, we provided the NTSB with names of Boeing employees, including door specialists, who we believed would have relevant information. We have now provided the full list of individuals on the 737 door team, in response to a recent request. With respect to documentation, if the door plug removal was undocumented there would be no documentation to share. We will continue to cooperate fully and transparently with the NTSB's investigation.[104]

4.3.4.2 FAA Oversight

The events of Alaska Airlines Flight 1282 raised questions regarding Boeing's quality control and the FAAs oversight of Boeing. On 11 January, the Chair of the Senate Commerce, Science, and Transportation Committee sent a letter to FAA Administrator Michael Whitaker, requesting documents and information related to their safety oversight of both Boeing and Spirit AeroSystems.

In her letter, the Chair referred to a previous request made in January 2023 that the FAA initiate a Special Technical Audit of eleven areas related to Boeing's production systems and notes that the former Acting Administrator responded in April 2023 that *"such an audit was not needed as the agency has [already] implemented tools to complete audits [of Boeing] for the bulk of this information at regular intervals." FAA's reply pointed to the Quality System Audit (QSA) program, which evaluates manufacturers' production systems to ensure compliance with FAA regulations.*"[105]

Specifically, she states:

> In short, it appears that FAA's oversight processes have not been effective in ensuring that Boeing produces airplanes that are in condition for safe operation, as required by law and by FAA regulations. In reviewing FAA orders on how oversight processes are to be conducted, it appears that there may be ways for manufacturers to avoid audit accountability.[106]

The FAA was asked to provide the Committee with documentation of its safety audits of Boeing and Spirit AeroSystems over the last two years. She submitted several questions regarding the FAA's oversight of the manufacturers' quality-control processes, requested copies of any follow-up reports, letters of investigation, or other documents provided to Boeing or Spirit AeroSystems, and asked for a written response to her letter by 25 January. The letter states:

> To help the Committee determine whether FAA's oversight processes are effective, please provide us with copies of notification letters from the last 24 months for all Quality Systems Audits of Boeing and for all Supplier Control Audits of Spirit AeroSystems. Also, please provide us with copies of any reports relating to these audits and any letters of investigation or other documents provided to Boeing or Spirit AeroSystems following the audits. Specifically regarding Spirit AeroSystems, please provide the Committee with an explanation of FAA's oversight of Spirit's production system and of FAA's oversight of Boeing's supplier control system as it relates to Spirit. Please identify what, if any, improvements in oversight by FAA that you intend to implement to ensure that Spirit's future performance meets all FAA regulatory requirements.
>
> In reviewing FAA orders on how oversight processes are to be conducted, it appears that there may be ways for manufacturers to avoid audit accountability. For example, FAA Order 8120.23A requires that, before performing a Quality System Audit, the Agency must provide 50 days advance notice. This generous notice period clears the way for manufacturers to correct noncompliant conditions prior to the audit, ensuring that non-compliant conditions are rarely if ever detected during an audit. In effect, manufacturers must only get their house in order once an audit is announced.
>
> While the order directs FAA audit teams to determine whether the manufacturer has various documented procedures, it is not clear from the order to what depth the audit teams review manufacturers' performance to determine whether they comply with their own internal requirements. For example, the order requires auditors to "[p] erform, as necessary, a combination of document and product reviews to determine if the quality system element meets applicable requirements," leaving the depth of the reviews to the audit team's discretion. How is the FAA ensuring that documented procedures are being routinely and uniformly followed?[107]

During Alaska Airlines' inspection, and after United Airlines stated that loose bolts and other installation issues in the door plug were identified,[108] the FAA issued a statement recommending that all operators of the Boeing 737 MAX 9 conduct a visual inspection of mid-exit door plugs to ensure the door is properly secured.[109] On 24 January, the FAA approved a new inspection process that allowed all grounded 737 MAX 9 aircraft to return to service after the inspection had been successfully completed and stated that the FAA would not agree to any Boeing request to expand the production of both the MAX 8 and MAX 9 aircraft until they were satisfied that quality-control concerns had been addressed.[110]

The following timeline of the FAA's actions after the Alaska Airlines incident also raises several important issues.[111] After grounding the Boeing 737-9 aircraft on 17 January, the FAA increased its oversight of Boeing and investigated its manufacturing practices and production lines, including those of its subcontractor, Spirit AeroSystems, bolstering its oversight of Boeing. The FAA stated that all the 737-9 MAX aircraft with door plugs would remain grounded until the FAA approves an inspection and maintenance process that satisfies all FAA safety requirements. The inspection and examination of the maintenance process were deemed necessary before deciding to return the Boeing 737-9 MAXs to service. In addition, on 28 February, the FAA informed Boeing that it had to develop a comprehensive action plan to address its systemic quality-control issues to meet the FAA's safety standards. The FAA stated: "Boeing must commit to real and profound improvements. Making foundational change will require a sustained effort from Boeing's leadership, and we are going to hold them accountable every step of the way, with mutually understood milestones and expectations." [112]

Boeing was given 90 days to provide the FAA with a comprehensive action plan that would include the results of the production-line audit, the findings from the expert review panel, and the steps that Boeing would take to improve its Safety Management System (SMS) program. Boeing had committed in 2019 to integrate its SMS program with a Quality Management System (QMS) to ensure the same level of oversight is applied to Boeing's suppliers and to create a measurable, systemic shift in manufacturing quality control. The expert panel was required by the Aircraft Certification, Safety, and Accountability Act of 2020. In addition to the panel's conclusion that Boeing must examine every aspect of its quality-control process and ensure that it focuses on safety, it also concluded that Boeing's safety culture was still lacking, despite improvements in recent years.

The Expert Panel reviewed over 4,000 pages of Boeing documents and seven surveys. It conducted more than 250 interviews and meetings with Boeing employees across six company locations, identifying 27 findings and making 53 recommendations. A summary of their work is as follows:[113]

The Expert Panel observed a disconnect between Boeing's senior management and other members of the organization on safety culture. Interviewees, including ODA Unit Members (UM), also questioned whether Boeing's safety reporting systems would function in a way that ensures open communication and non-retaliation. The Expert Panel also observed inadequate and confusing implementation of the five components of a positive safety culture (Reporting Culture, Just Culture, Flexible Culture, Learning Culture, and Informed Culture).The Expert Panel found Boeing's SMS procedures reflect the International Civil Aviation Organization (ICAO) and the FAA SMS frameworks. However, the Boeing SMS procedures are not structured in a way that ensures all employees understand their role in the company's SMS. The procedures and training are complex and in a constant state of change, creating employee confusion especially among different work sites and employee groups. The Expert Panel also found a lack of awareness of safety-related metrics at all levels of the organization; employees had difficulty distinguishing the differences among various measuring methods, their purpose, and outcomes.Boeing's restructuring of the management of the ODA unit decreased opportunities for interference and retaliation against UMs, and provides effective organizational messaging regarding independence of UMs. However, the restructuring, while better, still allows opportunities for retaliation to occur, particularly with regards to salary and furlough ranking. This influences the ability of UMs to execute their delegated functions effectively. The Expert Panel also found additional issues at Boeing that affect aviation safety, which include inadequate human factors consideration commensurate to its importance to aviation safety and lack of pilot input in aircraft design and operation.The report gave Boeing six months to review the recommendations and develop an action plan that includes a milestone-based approach that would comprehensively address each of the recommendations.

In February 2024, the head of the Boeing 737 MAX program was replaced as part of the company's increased focus on quality and safety standards. The new appointee took on the roles of vice president and general manager for Boeing's 737 program and the Renton, Washington, factory that produces the planes. Other changes included the creation of a new position by the company's commercial division, senior vice president for BCA Quality, which would concentrate on quality control and assurance.[114]

In the aftermath of the Alaska Airlines incident and the NTSB's preliminary report stating that it appeared that four bolts designed to keep the 737-9's MED plug in place were not installed after the plug was opened in Boeing's factory, Boeing acknowledged that it was accountable and stated:

> Shortly after the January 5 accident, Boeing undertook a major effort—including consultation with experts, airline customers, and stakeholders2—to identify additional short- and long-term improvements in seven specific areas: (i) fully implementing the Company's Safety Management System (SMS) across the production system; (ii) simplifying and enhancing processes and procedures; (iii) reducing incoming defects from suppliers; (iv) improving employee training; (v) ensuring total production system compliance; (vi) strengthening Boeing's culture of safety and quality through engagement and communication; and (vii) simplifying installation and build plans.[115]

Boeing's Executive Summary provided specific details and outlined key areas to be addressed. These included, inter alia, enhancement training for new manufacturing and quality employees; an additional 300-plus hours of coursework across multiple skills for new mechanics and inspectors; deployed workplace coaches and peer mentors onto the factory floor to provide oversight and support for mechanics and inspectors; and enhanced training for existing manufacturing and quality employees to ensure continuous proficiency with safety, quality, and compliance requirements. In addition, the following 6 Key Performance Indicators (KPIs) focusing on safety and production health were identified as part of Boeings Safety & Quality Plan: employee proficiency, a notice of escape, supplier shortages, rework hours per airplane, travelers at the factory, and ticketing performance measures. Each KPI included defined criteria triggering corrective action and SMS risk monitoring. Regarding the Aircraft Certification, Safety, and Accountability Act (ACSAA), the company developed detailed plans and deliverables for each recommendation from the FAA's Expert Review Panel, focusing on enhancing Boeing's safety culture, SMS, QMS, Organization Designation Authorization, human factors, and pilot input.[116]

4.3.5 Legal Proceedings

4.3.5.1 Civil Litigation

The Boeing 737 MAX 9 door plug incident was another black mark on the 737-MAX series aircraft. It drew attention once again to Boeing's responsibility and accountability and raised many legal and ethical issues.

Days after the incident, many civil lawsuits seeking compensation were filed by the passengers who suffered physical and mental injuries. In Oregon, a lawsuit was filed on behalf of three passengers who were sitting two rows diagonally behind a 15-year-old whose shirt was sucked off when the side panel detached and left a hole that resulted in the depressurization of the cabin and oxygen masks being deployed before the aircraft returned to Portland airport for an emergency landing. They claimed both compensatory damages for severe mental, emotional, and psychological injuries, including post-traumatic stress, and physical injuries, as well as punitive damages in the amount of $1 billion. The lawsuit seeks to hold Boeing accountable for its alleged negligence, which jeopardized the lives of the 174 passengers and six crew members who were on board the flight. The substantial punitive damages are sought on the grounds that the incident could have been prevented, and that the defects in manufacturing the aircraft impacted numerous other aircraft and threatened the lives of passengers on all the Boeing 737 MAX 9.[117] Alaska Airlines offered all passengers counseling sessions and a refund. Within 24 hours, the airline gave each passenger $1,500 cash as an immediate gesture of care to cover any incidental expenses.[118]

On 11 January, a product liability class-action lawsuit was filed against Boeing in Washington Superior Court for King County. The lawsuit claimed that Boeing allegedly manufactured a defective 737 MAX 9 aircraft and permitted it to fly knowing that it was not adequately secured. It further alleges that Boeing knowingly and publicly admitted that the left side door "plug" was not properly secured to the fuselage, either during manufacture or while the aircraft was being built by Boeing and/or its subcontractor, Spirit AeroSystems; and that Boeing delivered the 737-MAX 9 aircraft to Alaska Airlines without properly securing the left door plug to the airframe and that the other bolts or seals required to secure the door were potentially defective. The claim was for product liability and construction defects. The plaintiffs claimed both special and general damages for compensation for their injuries, which included a concussion, soft tissue injuries, breathing problems, and emotional distress, as well as attorney fees and costs and pre-and post-judgment interest.[119]

Another lawsuit seeking damages against Boeing was filed in Washington on behalf of six passengers. It alleged that the B737 MAX 9 door plugs were defective in their construction and that Boeing delivered the aircraft to Alaska Airlines without properly securing the plug to the airframe. Alaska Airlines is not named as a defendant in the lawsuit. The passengers claimed that many oxygen masks did not seem to work, as no oxygen flowed despite pulling on the tubes, and that they suffered injuries, including bleeding ears, as well as emotional trauma.[120]

Spirit AeroSystems, the manufacturer of the door plug that was blown out in midair, faced a class-action lawsuit that was filed prior to this incident, alleging that

Spirit AeroSystems had experienced "sustained quality failures" in its products. The suit was filed in Federal Court on behalf of investors in Spirit AeroSystems, which was initially a manufacturing unit of Boeing until it was sold to an investment firm in 2005. The plaintiffs allege manufacturing problems, including a complaint from one Spirit employee who sent an email to one of the company's executives alleging an "excessive amount of defects" and claiming that the "quality failures were so severe and persistent that Boeing even placed Spirit on probation for multiple years." The complaint also alleged that Spirit experienced two specific manufacturing problems, namely that Spirit had "mis-drilled holes on the 737 MAX aft pressure bulkhead," which is at the rear of the plane, and a problem involving a "defect relating to the tail fin fittings on certain 737 MAX aircraft," an issue that Boeing raised in April 2023. They also allege that the company's problems were widespread and included the routine presence of foreign object debris in Spirit products, missing fasteners, peeling paint, and poor skin quality, and that these constant quality failures were partially due to the company's culture, which prioritized production numbers and short-term financial gains over product quality. The company stated that it strongly disagreed with the allegations and that it would defend itself when the matter went to trial.[121]

4.3.5.2 Criminal Proceedings

The U.S. Department of Justice has opened a criminal investigation into the incident. In parallel, the DOJ also conducted a review of Boeing's compliance with the previous settlement agreement reached after the 737 MAX 8 accidents in 2018 and 2019, which killed 346 people.

As a reminder, the previous agreement was regarding the Department of Justice (DOJ) criminal charges of fraud and misleading the FAA with regard to the MCAS. Boeing and the DOJ reached a settlement agreement to defer prosecution on condition that Boeing strengthen its compliance program, include more stringent compliance reporting requirements, and pay $2.5 billion in compensation as part of the settlement agreement. The Alaska Airlines incident fell within that review, as it occurred in the period subject to the deferred prosecution agreement. As a result, the DOJ had to decide whether Boeing's actions in the Alaska Airlines Flight 1282 incident violated the settlement agreement. If so, Boeing could be faced with criminal prosecution on the original count of fraud if it were found at fault for violating the 2021 agreement. Additionally, the three-year probationary agreement, which required keeping the DOJ updated on compliance improvements, could have been extended.[122]

After the January Alaska Airlines incident, on 14 May 2024, the DOJ stated in a court filing that the Government had determined that Boeing breached its obligations by failing to "design, implement, and enforce a compliance and ethics program to prevent and detect violations of the U.S. fraud laws throughout its operations."[123] It determined that it violated the 2021 agreement which granted the company immunity from a criminal charge of conspiracy to commit fraud resulting from the two 737 MAX-8 accidents in exchange for its commitment to overhaul its compliance system and pay a fine of $2.5 billion. It recommended that criminal charges be brought against Boeing.

On the same day, Boeing replied, stating,

> We believe that we have honored the terms of that agreement, and look forward to the opportunity to respond to the Department on this issue. As we do so, we will engage with the Department with the utmost transparency, as we have throughout the entire term of the agreement, including in response to their questions following the Alaska Airlines 1282 accident.[124]

Boeing was given until 13 June to respond, and the Justice Department said that a decision on whether to prosecute Boeing would be made by 7 July. Families of the victims and their lawyers felt the DOJ had made the right decision and that this was an important step toward holding Boeing accountable for the deaths of the 346 people who died in the two MAX accidents, and urged the Justice Department to go ahead and prosecute Boeing.

It is essential to highlight that at no point did the DOJ consider filing any criminal charges against any Boeing executive to hold them criminally accountable for any of their actions or omissions. The only individual who was prosecuted was the Boeing 737 MAX Chief Technical Pilot at the time of the accidents, who was indicted and then acquitted in March 2022.

The specific criminal charges that could have been filed against Boeing have not been specified; however, it has been speculated that the charges would extend beyond the original 2021 fraud conspiracy charge. Criminal charges against Boeing could possibly have resulted in tougher oversight and very costly penalties, which would have undoubtedly further damaged Boeing's reputation and increased its financial pressure. Boeing reported operating losses amounting to $31.9 billion from the commencement of the 20-month grounding of the 737 MAX after the second fatal accident in 2019. In addition, it could have potentially lost its investment grade credit rating for the first time in its history and faced business restrictions, potentially jeopardizing Boeing's status as a federal contractor if found guilty of a crime.[125] This would be extremely damaging to Boeing, considering it derives significant revenue from U.S. government contracts. In 2023, 37% of its revenue came from US government contracts.[126] A further possibility, and the most likely scenario, was that instead of prosecuting Boeing, the DOJ would extend the 2021 settlement for another year or propose a new settlement with stricter terms. These could include additional oversight and monitoring of the company's operations and compliance by a third party, possibly a federal monitor, financial penalties, and also requiring Boeing to admit its wrongdoing and plead guilty.[127]

Families of the victims and their representatives were against a settlement and asked the DOJ to proceed with "aggressive criminal prosecution" and to impose a fine of approximately $25 billion. They believed that "Because Boeing's crime is the deadliest corporate crime in U.S. history, a maximum fine of more than $24 billion is legally justified and clearly appropriate." They also asked that the DOJ initiate criminal proceedings against individual corporate officials, including the CEO at the time of the two accidents.[128]

In June 2024, after the Alaska Airlines MAX 9 incident, the whistleblower reports and the response by the U.S. Justice Department that determined Boeing breached the 2021 deferred prosecution agreement, family members of those who were killed in the two 737 MAX 8 accidents in 2018 and 2019 filed a court petition asking U.S. District Judge Reed O'Connor to name a corporate monitor to examine Boeing's safety and compliance procedures. In February 2023, the same judge refused to impose an independent monitor, stating that there was no factual record to justify that Boeing presented an "ongoing threat to public safety." The Justice Department also objected to imposing an independent monitor, saying that it "would be duplicative to DOJ oversight and counterproductive to the processes that are operative now."[129]

On 7 July 2024, Boeing reported that it agreed to plead guilty to a criminal charge of fraud resulting from the two MAX 737 accidents. The plea deal, which had to receive the approval of a federal judge to take effect, includes Boeing agreeing to pay an additional $243.6 million fine, an additional $455 million into a crash victims' fund to be divided evenly per victim of the two fatal 737 MAX crashes, undergo three years of safety compliance monitoring by an independent monitor, and invest approximately $455 million over the next three years to improve and enhance its compliance and safety programs. The agreement also included a provision that Boeing's board of directors meet with the families of the victims.

It should be noted that the agreement only covers the wrongdoings of Boeing, the company, stemming from the 2018 Lion Air and 2019 Ethiopian Airlines accidents; it does not include any possible wrongdoing related to the Alaska Airlines incident and does not grant immunity to any former or current individual Boeing officials.[130]

The Justice Department was to submit the written plea agreement to a U.S. District Court in Texas by July 19th, where Judge Reed O'Connor, who has been overseeing the case from the beginning and who criticized what he called "Boeing's egregious criminal conduct," could either accept or reject the plea. If the judge rejects the agreement, this would lead to another round of negotiations between the Justice Department and Boeing. The plea agreement announced does not address what effect, if any, a guilty plea would have on the eligibility of Boeing to do business with the federal government if found guilty of a crime.

In a previous matter in 2006, when Boeing paid a $615 million fine to settle criminal and civil charges related to the company using information stolen from a rival to win a space-launch contract, the Air Force stated that due to "compelling national interest," Boeing would be permitted to continue competing for contracts.[131] This is an essential factor that will have drastic consequences for both the Boeing Company and the U.S. government, and many critics have expressed concern regarding the impact that a potential ban on a major U.S. defense contractor may have. As a Connecticut Democrat stated during a Senate hearing on Boeing's broken safety culture, "We want Boeing to succeed. Boeing needs to succeed for the sake of the jobs it provides, for the sake of local economies it supports, for the sake of the American traveling public, for the sake of our military."[132] As federal agencies can provide waivers to companies convicted of felonies to keep them eligible for government contracts, it is expected that this would also be done in this particular case.

On 31 July, relatives of the deceased asked the judge to reject the agreement and proceed to trial within seventy days, stating that the plea agreement was too lenient, the fine was too small, and it did not apportion accountability to Boeing. One of the lawyers representing the family members provided evidence, which included redacted information, allegedly giving additional evidence of Boeing's wrongdoing, which was filed under seal as part of civil lawsuits against Boeing. Another lawyer who said that the DOJ favored Boeing because it is a major government contractor stated, "To actually charge Boeing and its senior management with the actual crimes committed, including the homicide of 346 passengers, would make any explanation of ongoing business dealings difficult and uncomfortable, particularly in an election year," Boeing and the Justice Department had 14 days to respond to the families' filings.[133]

It should be note, that, defending the plea deal, the DOJ stated that even if the matter did go to trial, they would still try Boeing on the charge of conspiracy and not the more serious crimes of manslaughter or death resulting from fraud involving aircraft parts, as they did not have enough evidence to prosecute Boeing for the more serious crimes. The DOJ said that "The agreement is a strong and significant resolution that holds Boeing accountable and serves the public interest. It holds Boeing to account for the most serious, readily provable offense."[134]

In an important development, on 6 December 2024, Justice Reed O'Connor rejected the July plea agreement for Boeing to plead guilty to one count of criminal fraud, face independent monitoring, and pay a $243m fine. The judge cited the company and the U.S. government's diversity, equity, and inclusion (DEI) policies and said that the agreement undermined the court and that diversity requirements for hiring the monitor were "contradictory." He further stated that the proposed agreement did not require Boeing to comply with the monitor's recommendations. It also gave the company a say in selecting the monitor, as, in accordance with the agreement, the DOJ was to choose six candidates to serve as monitors, and Boeing had the option to strike one of them. In his decision, Judge O'Connor said the government's previous years of overseeing the firm had "failed" and that it was in the public interest that the court had to "step in" to ensure a fair outcome. He said,

> In a case of this magnitude, it is in the utmost interest of justice that the public is confident this monitor selection is done based solely on competency. The parties' DEI [diversity, equity and inclusion] efforts only serve to undermine this confidence in the government and Boeing's ethics and anti-fraud efforts.

Boeing and the Department of Justice were given 30 days to develop a new plan in response to the ruling.[135] Judges do not typically reject or overturn plea agreements reached by the parties over issues that the parties have not disputed. The agreement would have resulted in Boeing being found guilty of conspiring to defraud the U.S. FAA regarding problematic software that affected the flight control systems of the 737 MAX. The judge had said that the agreement marginalizes the court in the selection and oversight of the independent monitor, forbids imposing a probation condition requiring Boeing to comply with the monitor's anti-fraud recommendations. He went on to say that the deal, labeled as a "sweetheart deal" that failed to adequately hold Boeing accountable for the deaths of the passengers and crew on board both the Boeing 737 MAX aircraft and did not prevent future recurrence of such accidents, had been rejected by the families from the outset.[136] As a result, Boeing and the DOJ could appeal the judge's rejection of the plea deal or present another renegotiated agreement for the court to approve. The parties agreed to present a new plea agreement to the court by 4 January 2025.

On 3 January 2025, Boeing and the Department of Justice informed the court that they had not yet reached a revised plea agreement and requested an extension. In their request, they acknowledged the possible impact of the DOJ policy under the new administration. They said they

> will endeavor to update the court before [February 16], but also recognize that the upcoming change in department leadership, and the need to brief incoming officials, may necessitate additional time for the parties to determine whether they can reach a revised proposed plea agreement.[137]

The parties were granted an extension until February 16 to renegotiate the terms of the plea agreement and submit an updated proposal. The proposal would include revisions that address the reasons the court rejected the initial agreement, including concerns about the process of selecting the compliance monitor, particularly regarding race and ethnicity. An important factor is that the extension allows the DOJ under the new administration to participate in the final negotiations of the revised plea agreement.[138]

In an unparalleled development, the DOJ decided to grant Boeing a non-prosecution agreement on 23 May 2025 and to drop the criminal charges against Boeing. In a court filing, the Justice Department said Boeing would admit to "conspiracy to obstruct and impede" an investigation by the US FAA. As part of the agreement, Boeing would agree to pay more than $1.1 billion in fines, including $444.5 million for an accident victims' fund and over $240 million as an additional criminal fine. It would also continue making improvements to its anti-fraud compliance and ethics program and strengthen its compliance, safety, and quality programs.[139] The DOJ stated in the documents filed that the agreement was "a fair and just resolution that serves the public." It said the agreement guarantees further accountability and substantial benefits from Boeing immediately, and avoids the uncertainty and litigation risk presented by proceeding to trial. The DOJ noted that it had discussed the terms of the agreement in a meeting with relatives of the deceased, some of whom were said to support the agreement while others were against it. Those who disagreed argued that this gave a message to other companies not to worry about making their products safe, and that "even if you kill them, just pay a small fine and move on."[140] One of the lawyers representing families of the victims, who is a former federal judge and now a law professor, stated that "This kind of non-prosecution deal is unprecedented and obviously wrong for the deadliest corporate crime in U.S. history."[141]

On 6 November 2025, the court granted the request from the DOJ to dismiss the criminal case against Boeing. Judge Reed O'Connor stated that he "disagreed" that dropping the charge was in the public interest, but said his concerns did not give him sufficient reason to deny the proposal." The DOJ defended its agreement, saying "Rather than allow for protracted litigation, this agreement provides finality for the victims and requires Boeing to act now. We are confident that this resolution is the most just outcome." On 14 November, relatives of some of the victims of the two crashes filed an appeal in the 5th Circuit Court, asking the Appeals Court to reverse the decision to dismiss the criminal case.[142]

On 12 November 2025, in the first civil trial brought by the family of a United Nations consultant who died in the Ethiopian Airlines crash, a federal court ordered Boeing to pay $28.45 million, plus 26% interest, amounting to $35.85 million, which includes $10 million for the pain and suffering and emotional distress experienced before the crash.[143]

4.3.6 Whistleblowers

After the two MAX 737 accidents, numerous investigations into the circumstances leading to and following the two crashes led to safety reforms in the form of the Aircraft Certification, Safety, and Accountability Act, enacted into law on 27 December 2020. The Senate Committee on Commerce, Science, and Transportation's investigation and aviation safety work was informed by whistleblowers, frontline Federal Aviation Administration officials, and aviation industry engineers. As part of the investigation of the design and certification of the 737 MAX, and oversight of the Federal Aviation Administration's implementation of the Act, the Aviation Safety Whistleblower Report was released in December 2021.[144]

The report states that seven individuals, all of whom agreed to be identified in the report, had a wealth of experience in the U.S. aircraft certification ecosystem. They had technical expertise from the FAA, engineering experience at Boeing and General Electric, and knowledge of aviation production, management, safety, and compliance processes. They also engaged with the Committee and provided insight into overseeing the law's implementation. They contacted the Committee to convey their experiences and recommendations regarding the aircraft safety and certification environment at the FAA and within the industry, and provided information that indicated systemic problems continued to exist, including understaffed FAA offices charged with certification oversight responsibility for manufacturers and the continued risk of undue pressure under the FAA's system of delegated authority. Specific issues highlighted included

> undue pressure on the line engineers and production staff, line engineers with technical expertise ignored, Boeing oversight office in Seattle lack enough safety engineers, FAA certification processes do not require compliance with latest airworthiness standards, FAA's strong oversight eroded under the ODA program, FAA and industry struggle with technical engineering capacity necessary for complex aircraft systems.

The recommendations made included

> strengthen the FAAs direct oversight of the ODA program, take measures to address undue pressure at Boeing ODA, ensure sufficient FAA technical and engineering capacity for safety oversight, require that manufacturers adopt formal safety management systems with root cause analysis followed by corrective action, measure and improve FAA safety culture for frontline staff, and mandate integrated aircraft safety analysis of designs.[145]

Amid the problems that Boeing was facing with the Alaska Airlines incident and the door plugs on its MAX 737, and the speculation surrounding the safety culture of the company, a whistleblower who was in the middle of litigation against Boeing was found dead in his car on the day that he was supposed to continue his deposition against Boeing. On 9 March 2024, Mr. John Barnett, who had worked at Boeing for 32 years before retiring in 2017, was found dead in his car in a hotel parking lot. At the time of his death, he was in Charleston, South Carolina, where he was giving testimony against Boeing, accusing it of repeatedly ignoring several safety-related concerns. The Charleston County coroner confirmed his death, saying that the 62-year-old man had died from what appeared to be a "self-inflicted" wound.

From 2010, he was the quality manager at the North Charleston factory, which builds the 787 Dreamliner, until he retired, citing work-related stress as the reason. During his time at the factory, he raised several concerns related to Boeing's actions and filed an administrative complaint with the Occupational Safety and Health Administration. In 2017, he complained to the FAA that he had raised concerns regarding oxygen systems on the 787 Dreamliner and the tracking of components. He alleged that Boeing was not addressing quality and safety issues and that he was being punished for raising the complaint.[146]

He told the FAA that he had uncovered serious problems related to the oxygen systems on the 787 Dreamliner, claiming that tests on emergency oxygen systems due to be fitted on the aircraft had a failure rate of 25%, which, in effect, could result in one in four oxygen masks not working correctly when deployed in an emergency. He stated that he raised these concerns to Boeing, but that no remedial action was taken. Boeing denied these allegations and indicated that it was taking measures, and as a result, the FAA stated that it could not verify the concerns raised. Boeing did, however, acknowledge that it had identified several oxygen bottles received from the supplier that were not deploying properly. It said that they had removed those specific bottles and that no defective bottles were placed on airplanes. He also alleged that workers had failed to follow procedures intended to track components through the factory, thus allowing defective components to go missing, and that, in some cases, substandard parts were even removed from scrap bins and fitted onto new aircraft that were being built to prevent delays on the production line. With regard to the tracking components, a review by the FAA upheld Mr. Barnett's concerns and confirmed that the location of at least 53 "non-conforming" parts in the factory was unknown and considered lost, and that Boeing was asked to take remedial action. In 2019, he publicly stated that the pressure to get new aircraft built meant the assembly process was rushed and that safety was compromised. Before he resigned, he filed an administrative complaint with the Occupational Safety and Health Administration under the FAA's Whistleblower Protection Program. The agency said it had no reasonable cause to believe Boeing violated whistleblower laws, and in 2021, it closed the complaint in favor of Boeing after a four-year investigation.[147] In 2021, he filed a lawsuit against Boeing, alleging several safety concerns and violations, including stray titanium shavings falling into electrical wiring, defective oxygen tanks, and managers urging him to cut corners. He claimed that under-pressure workers even fitted substandard parts from scrap bins to aircraft on the production line to save time, and that this was done, at least on one occasion, with the knowledge of a senior manager, and that Boeing South Carolina was strictly driven by schedule and cost. In his legal action against Boeing, he also accused the company of defaming him and damaging his reputation, which ultimately led to his early retirement. Replying to this allegation, Boeing stated that he voluntarily resigned and that, as a company, it provides employees with several ways to raise concerns and complaints with processes in place to protect them, and that the concerns and complaints are thoroughly investigated and resolved.[148]

The week before his death, he gave a formal deposition, which included being questioned by Boeing's lawyers, followed by a cross-examination by his lawyers. The day of his death, the third day of deposition, he was expected to continue with his testimony, but he failed to appear in court and was found dead in the car park of his hotel. His lawyers called for strengthening whistleblower laws that apply to aerospace employees and to ensure a more expeditious manner to resolve concerns raised by whistleblowers. The trial of his case against Boeing would be continued under his estate.[149] In March 2025, Mr. Barnett's family filed a wrongful death suit against Boeing, accusing the company of driving him to his death after he suffered repeated retaliation, a hostile work environment, and bullying, which caused his post-traumatic stress disorder, anxiety, panic attacks, and depression, all of which led to his suicide. In May 2025, a settlement was reached, dismissing the lawsuit pending completion of the settlement within 60 days. No details of the settlement were provided.[150]

The second Boeing whistleblower, Mr. Joshua Dean, died at the age of 45 after a short, sudden illness.[151] The former quality auditor at Spirit AeroSystems filed a complaint with the Federal Aviation Administration, alleging "serious and gross misconduct by senior quality management of the 737-production line" at Spirit. He started working at Spirit in 2019 as a mechanical engineer but lost his job the following year due to COVID-19 layoffs. He returned to Spirit in May 2021 as a quality auditor. In October 2022, he reported finding a serious manufacturing defect. He alleged that the mechanics had improperly drilled holes in the aft pressure bulkhead of the MAX and that the management had ignored the concerns raised. He also said that because his focus was on those safety concerns, he missed a different manufacturing defect, which was identified by another auditor who found cracks in approximately 40% of the "dagger fittings" – the fittings that attach the vertical tail fin to the tail. In April 2023, Boeing paused deliveries of the MAX aircraft at the Renton plant when it was notified by Spirit of a production defect related to the installation of two fittings made by Spirit, which were not attached correctly to the fuselage before the aircraft was sent to Boeing. When this was discovered, he was fired for allegedly failing to conduct inspections that were his responsibility, resulting in faulty tail fin fittings being shipped to Boeing. Boeing stated that the problem could date back to 2019 and that this issue would likely affect a significant number of undelivered 737 MAX aircraft. The FAA said that, based on the data presented by Boeing, it had confirmed Boeing's assessment that there was no immediate safety concern and that all affected aircraft would be reviewed before delivery.

Mr. Dean also identified errors related to misaligned and improperly drilled holes in the MAX's aft pressure bulkhead break rings, which secure the dome-shaped end cap at the back of the passenger cabin to the fuselage skin and are crucial for maintaining safe air pressure during flight. Upon discovering this, he filed a safety complaint with the FAA, claiming that Spirit had used him as a scapegoat and that the company had lied to the FAA about the defects in the aft pressure bulkhead. The FAA responded with a letter stating it had investigated the safety issues he raised. The letter indicated, although not explicitly, that safety concerns had been addressed, stating, "The investigation determined that your allegations were appropriately addressed under an FAA-approved safety program. However, due to the privacy provisions of those programs, specific details cannot be released."[152] Soon after, he filed a whistleblower complaint with the Department of Labor, accusing senior Spirit AeroSystems Quality Managers of gross misconduct and claiming that his contract was terminated in retaliation for raising safety concerns. At the time of his death, the case was still pending. The claims Mr. Dean made were also presented during his deposition in the December lawsuit filed by Spirit investors, who alleged that Spirit management withheld information about quality defects, failed to address known issues, and harmed shareholders by decreasing Spirit's stock value. The FAA was investigating the circumstances surrounding Mr. Dean's allegations against Spirit.

After the January 2024 Alaska Airlines incident and the FAA's investigation report that the aircraft involved appeared to have left a Boeing factory without the bolts required to secure the panel in place, Boeing entered negotiations to acquire Spirit AeroSystems for approximately $35 per share, in an attempt to stabilize a crucial part of the supply chain for the MAX aircraft. A major obstacle that had to be overcome was the fact that Spirit also supplies parts to Boeing's biggest competitor, Airbus (EADSY). In light of the financial investment required to improve production quality and the FAA's action to limit the company's ability to increase production of the 737 MAX, Boeing proposed in June 2024 to fund the acquisition primarily through stock. The negotiations focused on Boeing paying over $4 billion for two-thirds of Spirit's business, which supplies Boeing with parts. It is reported that Boeing and Airbus have largely succeeded in dividing Spirit's programs into work that Boeing will take back and segments of Spirit that Airbus will buy, which make their parts and account for about one-fifth of Spirit's revenue.[153]

Testifying at a Capitol Hill hearing, another Boeing whistleblower and a former Spirit colleague of Mr. Dean confirmed some of the allegations he had made. Mr. Sam Salehpour, an engineer at Boeing, told an investigative subcommittee of the Senate Homeland Security and Governmental Affairs Committee that there was no safety culture at Boeing and that if Boeing did not address the lack of safety protocols, many people could die.[154] He wrote to the Federal Aviation Administration on

19 January 2024, two weeks after the Alaska Airlines incident. The FAA confirmed that the allegations were being investigated. Mr. Salehpour stated that problems arose during the production of the Dreamliner after changes were made to how large sections of the fuselage were assembled and the tiny gaps found at the joins of the 787 fuselage sections, which arrived at Boeing from different manufacturers. When Boeing discovered these gaps in 2020, deliveries of the Dreamliner were delayed for nearly two years. The problem was later resolved, and the FAA approved the resumption of the 787 deliveries. In April 2024, he stated that since 2012, excessive force had been used to push fuselage sections together to make it appear as though the gaps didn't exist, and that this practice continued even after deliveries of the Dreamliner were halted in 2020. He claimed that his concerns were ignored and that he had then been transferred out of the 787 program to the 777 program. While working on the 777 program, he allegedly also observed misalignment problems being fixed by applying an unmeasured and unlimited amount of force and by people jumping on the parts to fit the misaligned holes and align the parts together. He indicated that this issue involved over 400 777 and 1,000 787 aircraft. He was interviewed about his claims regarding the 787 production on 5 April 2024.

The chairman of the US Senate Permanent Subcommittee on Investigations stated that the allegations would be investigated, and he was called to appear before the Subcommittee's hearing in April 2024. The Subcommittee notified Boeing of the claims made regarding "alarming and dangerous manufacturing deficiencies that are creating potentially catastrophic safety risks." It requested Boeing's immediate cooperation with the Subcommittee's review of the allegations and of Boeing's safety culture. The Subcommittee also wrote a letter to the FAA requesting information regarding the whistleblower's allegations and Boeing's safety standards and quality control.[155]

Details of another whistleblower, Mr. Sam Mohawk, a Quality Assurance Inspector at Boeing's Renton plant, who claimed that Boeing was cutting corners by losing track of parts that had been labeled as "non-conforming" or inadequate, were released by the Chairman of the Subcommittee on Investigations on 18 June 2024. He alleged that some parts, which should have been disposed of, were mislabeled or repaired and that the parts may have been used in newly built aircraft. He said that as many as 400 faulty 737 MAX aircraft parts may have been lost and deleted from a cataloging system. He claimed that his supervisors had told him to hide this evidence from the FAA and that he had been retaliated against. These claims were released hours before Boeing's CEO, David Calhoun, was due to give testimony in front of the Senate Subcommittee to answer questions related to Boeing's "broken safety culture."[156]

The detailed description of the whistleblowers' reports and the impact it had on them as individuals illustrates the moral, ethical, professional, and legal dilemmas faced by aviation professionals who become aware of critical safety-related issues and make the difficult decision to report their findings and potential safety risks to senior managers. Whistleblowers often face tremendous pressure at work for speaking out, become ostracized, and on many occasions, they lose their jobs. This has a significant impact on their personal life and psychological well-being. This directly contrasts with the positive reporting culture that is the foundation of the safety management system and the principles of just culture.

The organizational and safety culture in dealing with whistleblowers and those who report critical safety information and raise safety concerns against senior managers' decisions is a vital factor that illustrates an organization's commitment to an open, transparent safety reporting culture, and that safety is a core value of that organization. The whistleblower protection under the current safety management system and just culture principles needs to be reviewed at the ICAO level, and guidance must be provided in the next revision of the ICAO SMS Manual 9859.

The organizations and senior managers that do not support and adequately address safety-critical risks raised by whistleblowers expose themselves and the organization to ethical dilemmas, severe legal and financial consequences, and irreparable reputational damage.

4.4 AIR FRANCE 447

On 31 May 2009, Air France Flight 447, an A330, took off from Rio de Janeiro Galeão Airport, Brazil, for Paris Charles de Gaulle, France, with 216 passengers, 9 cabin crew, and 3 pilots on board. At around 2 h 02, the Captain left the cockpit. At around 2 h 08, the crew made a course change of 12 degrees to the left to avoid returns detected by the weather radar. At 2 h 10 min 05, likely following the obstruction of the Pitot probes by ice crystals, the speed indications were incorrect, and some automatic systems disconnected. The two copilots did not control the aircraft's flight path. They were rejoined 1 minute 30 later by the captain, while the aircraft was in a stall situation that lasted until the aircraft impacted with the sea at 2 h 14 min 28 on 1 June 2009, killing all 228 persons on board.[157]

The technical investigation into the accident was conducted by the French Bureau d'Enquêtes et d'Analyses pour la Sécurité de l'Aviation Civile (BEA), assisted by accredited representatives from Brazil, the United States, the United Kingdom, Germany, and Senegal. The BEA released the first intermediate report on 2 July 2009 and the third one on 29 July 2011. The final report, released on 5 June 2012, confirmed the findings of the preliminary reports and made several recommendations. It concluded that:

> The accident resulted from the following succession of events:
>
> - Temporary inconsistency between the measured speeds, likely as a result of the obstruction of the pitot tubes by ice crystals, caused autopilot disconnection and [flight control mode] reconfiguration to "alternate law (ALT)."
> - The crew made inappropriate control inputs that destabilized the flight path.
> - The crew failed to follow appropriate procedure for loss of displayed airspeed information.
> - The crew were late in identifying and correcting the deviation from the flight path.
> - The crew lacked understanding of the approach to stall.

- The crew failed to recognize the aircraft had stalled, and consequently did not make inputs that would have made recovering from the stall possible.[158]

A press release by the BEA on 5 June 2009 states, "The BEA reminds those concerned that in such circumstances, it is advisable to avoid all hasty interpretations and speculation based on partial or non-validated information."[159]

The wreckage of AF 447 was found on 2 April 2011, 22 months after it disappeared. The protected module of the flight data recorder (FDR) was located and identified on 1 May 2011. A day later, the CVR was located, and it was raised on board the Ile de Sein cable vessel on 3 May. The flight recorders were transported to the BEA by air on 12 May. Recovery of parts of the aircraft continued until the underwater search and recovery operation for the wreckage of AF 447 ended on 16 June 2011.[160]

In October 2011, a transcript of the CVR was leaked and published in the book "Erreurs de Pilotage" (Pilot Errors) by Jean Pierre Otelli. The book contained the transcript of the last two minutes of the flight captured by the cockpit voice recorder, which revealed the conversation between the pilots who were panicked and confused. It highlighted the copilot's role in stalling the aircraft while the flight computer was under alternate law at high altitude, as well as the crew's failure to adhere to principles of crew resource management. The co-pilot is heard saying, "Climb, climb, climb," to which the pilot replies, "But I've been pulling back on the stick for a while now." The aircraft's warning system repeating the word "Stall!" is heard. The captain then says, "Watch out, you are pulling up," and the co-pilot replies, "Am I pulling up?" Three seconds before impact, one of the crew is heard exclaiming, "Damn it, we're going to crash, this can't be true!"[161]

Strongly condemning the disclosure of parts of the CVR transcript, the BEA stressed that it was a violation of European regulations and disrespectful to the crew members who had died in the accident. It also emphasized that "Any attempt at interpretation at this stage is partial and, as a result, can only fan the flames of the controversies of the last few months, which is harmful to all concerned." Air France said that this "sensationalized and unverifiable information impairs the memory of the crew and passengers who lost their lives."[162]

4.4.1 Legal Proceedings

4.4.1.1 Civil Litigation

Passengers from 32 nationalities died in the crash, and their relatives filed civil claims seeking compensation for their loss in many different jurisdictions. In accordance with the 1999 Montreal Convention, Air France is liable to compensate the deceased's relatives for all recoverable damages suffered up to $155,000, and recoverable damages sustained more than $155,000, unless Air France can prove that it was not in any way negligent or otherwise at fault. In addition, an advance payment of $25,000 to cover each family's immediate economic needs had to be given within 15 days of identifying the claimants, which is then credited against the airline's final compensation amount to each of the relatives. Many civil lawsuits claiming compensation were filed in U.S. courts by relatives, as it allows relatives to claim for "care, comfort, or society," unlike many other countries that limit compensation. Relatives could initiate civil proceedings against Air France in the US, provided that the US was the passenger's ultimate destination, or the passenger's ticket was issued in the US, or the passenger's principal and permanent residence was in the United States.[163]

In the US, many wrongful death suits were filed against Airbus and Air France, which were later consolidated to be heard before a federal judge sitting in San Francisco. In October 2010, based on the forum non conveniens law, the judge dismissed the cases, saying that they should be heard in France and not the US. In his ruling, he noted that as the criminal case was being heard in France, the French court had access to evidence gathered during the investigation, and thus it was more appropriate that the cases be heard there.[164]

In March 2010, a court in Rio de Janeiro ordered Air France to pay $1.16 million as compensation for the death of a passenger, a 41-year-old woman who was Rio's attorney general. Axa, Air France's insurance company, said that it would appeal the amount of damages granted.[165] In December 2010, the court awarded compensatory damages of $727,000 (€540,000) to the parents and grandparents of a 31-year-old Brazilian woman who died in the accident together with her husband and parents-in-law. Her mother was also awarded $3,000 a month.[166]

4.4.1.2 Criminal Investigation

A parallel criminal investigation was initiated on 5 June 2009. In March 2011, preliminary manslaughter charges were filed against both Airbus and Air France. The French prosecutors alleged that both Air France and Airbus should be prosecuted for negligence and face manslaughter charges. They alleged that both organizations were aware of the technical problems with the pitot tubes but failed to inform and train pilots on how to resolve the issues.

In July 2019, prosecutors recommended that Airbus should not be prosecuted and that the case should be dropped due to lack of evidence, but that Air France should be charged with manslaughter and negligence on the grounds that they did not provide the pilots with sufficient information and training on the procedures to follow in such a situation, especially after a number of incidents of the same kind had occurred in the months before the accident occurred.[167] In September 2019, French judges also dropped the charges against Air France, saying that "this accident is clearly explained by a combination of elements which had never occurred, and which therefore highlighted dangers which could not have been perceived before." The investigations "did not lead to characterizing a culpable failure by Airbus or Air France in connection (...) with the piloting errors (...) at the origin of the accident."[168]

However, in January 2021, the Paris public prosecutor requested that Air France and Airbus stand trial on charges of manslaughter. An Appeals Court hearing was held in March 2021 to decide on the matter. The prosecutor alleges there were "blameworthy infringements" by Air France, particularly with regard to crew training, and that Airbus underestimated the risks posed by ice on the pitot sensors.[169] On 12 May 2021, the Paris Court of Appeal reversed the 2019 court's decision not to pursue criminal proceedings against either company and ruled that both Air France and Airbus should be prosecuted for involuntary manslaughter as a result of the Air France Flight AF447 accident.[170]

The trial focused on the defective pitot tubes (used to measure the flight speed of aircraft) and how a malfunction with the tubes, which became blocked with ice crystals during a mid-Atlantic storm, caused alarms to sound in the cockpit of the Airbus A330 and the autopilot system to switch off. Technical experts provided evidence that, after the instrument failure, the pilots put the aircraft into a climb that caused the aircraft to lose upward lift from the air moving under its wings, thus losing altitude. Both companies maintained that they were not guilty and that pilot error was the main cause of the accident. The relatives of the deceased argued that both Airbus and Air France knew of the problems with the pitot tubes before the accident and that they had not trained the pilots to deal with such a high-altitude emergency. The court held that Airbus had committed "four acts of imprudence or negligence," including not replacing specific models of the pitot tubes that seemed to freeze more often on its A330-A340 fleet, and "withholding information" from flight operators. The court said Air France had committed two "acts of imprudence" in the way it disseminated an information note on the faulty tubes to its pilots. The court held that, despite those acts and omissions by Airbus and Air France, there was no causal link between those failures and the accident to show that an offense had been committed.[171]

The company's lawyers said that the court's decision was a "difficult decision from a human point of view, but technically and legally justified." The relative's representative said, "We expected an impartial judgment; this was not the case. We are disgusted. […] All that remains of these 14 years of waiting is despair, dismay, and anger." One of the lawyers added, "We are told: 'responsible but not guilty'. And it is true that we were waiting for the word 'guilty'"[172]

In April 2023, the Paris Appeals Court's public prosecutor said that an appeal would be lodged to allow "the full potential of the legal appeals procedure" to take its course.[173]

On 29 September 2025, sixteen years after the accident, the French Appeals Court commenced the appeals trial proceedings. If convicted, the two companies would have faced the maximum fine of €225,000 for corporate manslaughter and significant reputational damage.To prove manslaughter, the prosecutors had to establish negligence as well as how any negligence caused the disaster. It should be emphasized that the court in 2013 held that both companies had been negligent, but it did not establish a causal connection between the negligence and the crash.

The eight weeks trial ended on 26 November 2025. The trial focused on earlier problems with the pitot tube as well as the alleged weaknesses in data-sharing and training that prosecutors argued had indirectly caused the crash. Air France and the prosecutors argued that the pilots were not to blame. Air France rejected the claims that the crew was poorly trained in dealing with stalls or emergencies at high altitude. Airbus focused on the final accident report which questioned the crew's response to the loss of data and failure to follow procedures. It is expected that judges will take months to reach a verdict and that any verdict will be appealed further.[174]

4.5 CONCLUSION

Our discussion of the AF 447 and the Boeing 737 MAX accidents highlights complex judicial developments following aviation accidents, the legal ramifications that organizations and post-holders could be faced with when failing to effectively exercise their duties, responsibilities, and accountabilities, and failing to mitigate known risks in accordance with the severity and probability of risks that are known or should have been mitigated. It also highlights the differences in subsequent legal proceedings and outcomes, as well as the divergence in how different jurisdictions approach accountability in the aftermath of an aviation accident.

NOTES

1. Swiss Accident Investigation Board, Final Report no. 2136 of the Swiss Accident Investigation Board SAIB, 6 March 2012. Available at https://www.sust.admin.ch/inhalte/AV-berichte/2136_e.pdf.
2. Ibid., p. 7.
3. Obergericht des Kantons Zürich SB170072-O/U/hb.
4. Baumgartner, M., "Latest developments in Switzerland: The delicate balance – Safety versus justice interest," The Aviation & Space Journal (n.1/2020 ISSN 2281-9134). Jan–March 2020. Available at www.aviationspacejournal.com/.
5. Baumgartner, M., op cit.
6. Federal Supreme Court, Bundesgericht Judgment 6B_332/2019.
7. Frankhauser, A., "Supreme Court acquits air traffic controller," Proton Legal LLC, International Law Office. 8 January 2020. Available at https://www.internationallawoffice.com/Newsletters/Aviation/Switzerland/Proton-Legal-LLC/Supreme-Court-acquits-air-traffic-controller?utm_source=ILO+Newsletter&utm_medium=email&utm_content=Newsletter+2020-01-08&utm_campaign=Aviation+Newsletter and see Judgment 6B_332/2019.
8. Baumgartner, M., op cit.
9. Ibid.
10. Hradecky, S., "Incident: Darwin SAAB 2000 at Zurich on Aug 22nd 2012, close encounter with touch and go on crossing runway," 9 September 2012, updated 24 September 2014. Available at http://avherald.com/h?article=455b97eb.
11. Frankhauser, A., op cit.
12. Eurocockpit, "Two air traffic controllers in Switzerland convicted," 14 December 2008. Available at https://www.eurocockpit.be/news/two-air-traffic-controllers-switzerland-convicted.
13. Polek, G., "Switzerland's Darwin airline ceases operations," 28 November 2017. Available at https://www.ainonline.com/aviation-news/air-transport/2017-11-28/switzerlands-darwin-airline-ceases-operations.
14. Skyguide, "Criminal proceedings on the incident of 22 August 2012 – Superior Court of Zurich acquits air traffic controller," 20 February 2021. Available at https://www.skyguide.ch/en/events-media-board/news/#p106936-106937-106938.
15. The Swiss Accident Investigation Board (SAIB) has been renamed and is now called the Swiss Transportation Safety Investigation Board (STSB).

16. SAIB, Final Report no. 2211 of the Swiss Accident Investigation Board SAIB concerning the serious incident (Airprox) involving the Boeing B737-800 aircraft, EI-ENK operated by Ryanair under flight number RYR 3595, 9 October 2014. Available at https://www.sust.admin.ch/inhalte/AV-berichte/2211_e.pdf.
17. SAIB, Final Report no. 2211, p. 6.
18. Baumgartner, M., op cit.
19. Judgment SK.2018.1.
20. Ibid.
21. Regulation (EU) No 996/2010 of the European Parliament and of the Council of 20 October 2010 on the investigation and prevention of accidents and incidents in civil aviation and repealing Directive 94/56/EC. Available at https://eur-lex.europa.eu/LexUriServ/LexUriServ.do?uri=OJ:L:2010:295:0035:0050:EN:PDF.
22. Baumgartner, M., op cit.
23. Batschwaroff, B., et al., "Conviction of air traffic controller," 17 July 2019. Available at https://www.vischer.com/en/knowledge/blog/conviction-of-air-traffic-controller-38592/#page=1.
24. Ibid.
25. Fankhauser, A., "Supreme Court upholds air traffic controller conviction," bellpark-legal, 14 August 2019. Available at https://www.lexology.com/library/detail.aspx?g=4023baa2-cca3-4404-802b-ac41b46a474d.
26. Ibid.
27. Skyguide, "Federal Court rejects appeal by air traffic controller – Conviction legally binding," 4 July 2019. Available at https://www.skyguide.ch/en/events-media-board/news/#p95885-95887-95888.
28. See also EU Regulation 376/2014, which Switzerland adopted by virtue of the EU-Swiss Air Transport Agreement.
29. Fankhauser, A., op cit.
30. Batschwaroff, B., et al., "Conviction of air traffic controller," 17 July 2019. Available at https://www.vischer.com/en/knowledge/blog/conviction-of-air-traffic-controller-38592/#page=1.
31. NTSB, Aviation Investigation Preliminary Report, Accident Number: DCA25MA108DCA25MA108. Available at https://www.ntsb.gov/investigations/Pages/DCA25MA108.aspx.
32. King Law, "Washington DC plane crash lawsuit – June 2025 update," 2025. Available at https://www.robertkinglawfirm.com/washington-dc-plane-crash-lawsuit/.
33. Lewis, R., "'There's a serious safety issue,' investigators say following DCA midair collision," NPR, 12 March 2025. Available at https://www.npr.org/2025/03/11/nx-s1-5324543/ntsb-dca-mid-air-collision-american-black-hawk.
34. Muntean, P., "Army halts some helicopter flights to Pentagon following 2 aborted landings at Reagan National Airport," 5 May 2025. Available at https://edition.cnn.com/2025/05/02/us/ntsb-investigation-dca-aborted-landings.
35. Fields, A., "DC plane crash victim's family files claims against FAA, Army," The Hill, 19 February 2025. Available at https://thehill.com/business/5151368-faa-aviation-accident-lawsuit/.
36. National Transportation Safety Committee, Final KNKT.18.10.35.04, Aircraft Accident Investigation Report, p. 20, 25 October 2019. Available at https://knkt.go.id/Repo/Files/Laporan/Penerbangan/2018/KNKT.18.10.33.04-Final-Report.pdf.
37. BBC, "Boeing 737 Max Lion Air crash caused by series of failures," 25 October 2019. Available at https://www.bbc.com/news/business-50177788.

38. Boeing, “Boeing CEO Dennis Muilenburg addresses the Ethiopian Airlines Flight 302 preliminary report,” 4 April 2019. Available at https://boeing.mediaroom.com/2019-04-04-Boeing-CEO-Dennis-Muilenburg-Addresses-the-Ethiopian-Airlines-Flight-302-Preliminary-Report.
39. Ethiopia Ministry of Transport and Logistics Aircraft Accident Investigation Bureau, Aircraft Accident Investigation Report B737 - MAX 8, ET-AVJ, 23 December 2022. Available at https://bea.aero/fileadmin/user_upload/ET_302__B737-8MAX_ACCIDENT_FINAL_REPORT.pdf.
40. The Associated Press, “Key events in the troubled history of the Boeing 737 Max,” 8 July 2024. Available at https://apnews.com/article/boeing-plea-737-max-crashes-b34daa014406657e720bec4a990dccf6.
41. Klee, M., “A complete timeline of the Boeing 737 Max disaster,” 18 May 2024. Available at https://www.rollingstone.com/culture/culture-features/boeing-737-max-disasters-timeline-1235007089/.
42. The Associated Press, op. cit.
43. Ibid.
44. H. R. 8408, In the Senate of the United States, 18 November 2020. Available at https://www.congress.gov/bill/116th-congress/house-bill/8408/text.
45. US Committee of Commerce, Science and Transportation, Letter by Maria Cantwell, Chair US Committee of Commerce, Science and Transportation, 3 January 2023. Available at 2023 BEFORE 01_03_23_Letter to DOT OIG re ACSAA Implementation (final).
46. Klee, M., op. cit.
47. AoA sensors are small vanes on the nose of the plane that measure the pitch of the aircraft as it moves into the headwind.
48. Schaper, D., “3 takeaways from 2 days of tense Boeing congressional hearings,” 2 November 2019. Available at https://www.npr.org/2019/11/02/775553377/3-takeaways-from-2-days-of-tense-boeing-congressional-hearings.
49. Ibid.
50. Ibid.
51. Ibid.
52. Ibid.
53. House Committee on Transportation and Infrastructure, “After 18-month investigation, Chairs DeFazio and Larsen release final committee report on Boeing 737 MAX,” 16 September 2000. Available at https://democrats-transportation.house.gov/news/press-releases/after-18-month-investigation-chairs-defazio-and-larsen-release-final-committee-report-on-boeing-737-max.
54. Schaper, D., “Congressional inquiry faults Boeing and FAA failures for deadly 737 Max plane crashes,” 16 September 2020. Available at https://www.npr.org/2020/09/16/913426448/congressional-inquiry-faults-boeing-and-faa-failures-for-deadly-737-max-plane-cr.
55. House Committee on Transportation and Infrastructure, op cit.
56. Associated Press, “Key events in the troubled history of the Boeing 737 Max,” 8 July 2024. Available at https://apnews.com/article/boeing-plea-737-max-crashes-b34daa014406657e720bec4a990dccf6.
57. Securities and Exchange Commission, “Boeing to pay $200 million to settle SEC charges that it misled investors about the 737 MAX,” 22 September 2022. Available at https://www.sec.gov/newsroom/press-releases/2022-170.
58. Ibid.

59. Anurag Kotoky, A., "Mother of dead Indian pilot criticises Boeing, US FAA for 'rushing' 737 Max return," The Print, 19 November 2020. Available at https://theprint.in/world/mother-of-dead-indian-pilot-criticises-boeing-us-faa-for-rushing-737-max-return/547930/.
60. Eric Levenson, E., "Family of pilot in fatal Lion Air crash sues Boeing for allegedly making a defective plane," CNN, 28 December 2018. Available at https://edition.cnn.com/2018/12/28/world/lion-air-crash-boeing-lawsuit/index.html.
61. Rapoport Weisberg & Sims, "Boeing 737 Max 8 lawsuits timeline," 7 January 2021. Available at https://rapoportlaw.com/boeing-737-max-8-lawsuits/.
62. Cotchett, Pitre & McCarthy, "CPM files wrongful death lawsuit and FAA claim on behalf of young American woman killed in Boeing 737 MAX 8 crash in Ethiopia," 2019. Available at https://www.cpmlegal.com/news-Wrongful-Death-Lawsuit-and-FAA-Claim-Filed-on-Behalf-of-Young-American-Woman-Killed-in-Boeing-737-MAX-8-Crash-in-Ethiopia.
63. Ibid.
64. Rapoport Weisberg & Sims, "Boeing 737 Max 8 lawsuits timeline," 7 January 2021. Available at https://rapoportlaw.com/boeing-737-max-8-lawsuits/.
65. Ibid.
66. Osibamowo, T., "In reversal, Texas high court will hear Southwest Airlines pilots' suit over Boeing 737 Max crashes," Kera News, 10 January 2025. Available at https://www.keranews.org/transportation/2025-01-10/texas-supreme-court-southwest-airlines-pilots-union-lawsuit-over-boeing-737-max-fatal-crashes.
67. Goodwyn, W., op cit.
68. Pesquera, A., "About face: Court takes up Boeing suit it had rejected," 10 January 2025. Available at https://www.law.com/texaslawyer/2025/01/10/about-face-court-takes-up-boeing-suit-it-had-rejected.
69. Osibamowo, T., op cit.
70. Supreme Court of Texas, No. 22-0631. Available at The Boeing Company, Petitioner, v. Southwest Airlines Pilots Association (SWAPA) on behalf of itself and its members. Available at https://cases.justia.com/texas/supreme-court/2025-22-0631.pdf?ts=1750428088.
71. France 24, "Boeing reaches settlement to avert civil trial over 2019 MAX crash," New Wires, 11 December 2024. Available at https://www.france24.com/en/americas/20241112-boeing-civil-trial.
72. Bakirci, N., "Boeing may have to pay for victims' 'pain and suffering' in Ethiopian airlines crash lawsuit," last updated 12 July 2023. Available at https://www.findlaw.com/legalblogs/consumer-protection/boeing-to-pay-for-victims-pain-and-suffering-in-ethiopian-airlines-crash-lawsuit/.
73. Ibid.
74. Ibid.
75. Ibid.
76. BBC, "Families cheated of Boeing crash compensation," 12 July 2019. Available at https://www.bbc.com/news/world-asia-48953892.
77. Hamilton, M., and Ryan, H., "Judge freezes assets of famed L.A. lawyer Tom Girardi, citing millions unpaid to clients," by Matt Los Angeles Times, 14 December 2020. Available at https://www.latimes.com/california/story/2020-12-14/judge-freezes-assets-lawyer-tom-girardi-cites-millions-unpaid-to-clients.
78. Llewellyn, A., "Lion Air victims get payout after Boeing settlement cash vanishes," AL Jazeera News, 11 August 2022. Available at https://www.aljazeera.com/economy/2022/8/11/lion-air-victims-compensated-after-lawyer-accused-of-stealing-settlement.

79. U.S. Department of Justice, Press Release, "Boeing charged with 737 Max fraud conspiracy and agrees to pay over $2.5 billion," 7 January 2021. Available at https://libguides.union.edu/c.php?g=1110124&p=8108257.
80. Koenig, D., "US wants Boeing to plead guilty to fraud over fatal crashes, lawyers say," Associated Press, 2 July 2024. Available at https://apnews.com/article/boeing-criminal-charges-plea-deal-86117543504039112fde0ac6bdbf75a.
81. U.S. Department of Justice, "Former Boeing 737 MAX chief technical pilot indicted for fraud thursday," Press Release, 14 October 2021. Available at https://www.justice.gov/opa/pr/former-boeing-737-max-chief-technical-pilot-indicted-fraud.
82. Ibid.
83. Koenig, D., "Former Boeing test pilot found not guilty of deceiving FAA," 24 March 2022. Available at https://apnews.com/article/business-texas-fort-worth-federal-aviation-administration-boeing-co-db0e14a239e43406d34d7dde99022089.
84. Klee, M., "A complete timeline of the Boeing 737 Max disaster," 18 May 2024. Available at https://www.rollingstone.com/culture/culture-features/boeing-737-max-disasters-timeline-1235007089/.
85. Ibid.
86. Victims' Rights and Restitution Act, 34 U.S.C. § 20141.
87. Crime Victims' Rights Act, 18 U.S.C. § 3771.
88. NTSB Accident Investigation Preliminary Report of DCA24MA063, p. 6. Available at https://www.ntsb.gov/investigations/Documents/DCA24MA063%20Preliminary%20report.pdf.
89. Ibid., p. 9 and 10.
90. NTSB, "NTSB schedules investigative hearing on Boeing 737-9 MAX door plug blowout," 12 March 2024. Available at https://www.ntsb.gov/news/press-releases/Pages/NR20240312.aspx.
91. Alaska Airlines Boeing 737-9 avoided potentially "tragic" incident due to empty seats near panel blowout, says safety board, 7 January 2024. Available at https://www.abc.net.au/news/2024-01-08/alaska-airline-blow-out-avoided-tragedy/103292076.
92. Tarigan, E.Y., "Indonesia temporarily grounds Boeing 737-9 Max jetliners after Alaska Airlines incident," AP News, 9 January 2024. Available at https://apnews.com/article/indonesia-boeing-7379-max-lion-airb66848a36da9a472e8c0b437b9fb7b42.
93. Aratani, L., and Cho, K.K., "United finds loose bolts on Boeing jets grounded after blowout incident," Washington Port, January 2024. Available at https://www.washingtonpost.com/business/2024/01/08/boeing-737-max-inspections-begin/.
94. Costello, T., and Wile, R., "Alaska Airlines CEO: We found 'many' loose bolts on our Max 9 planes following near-disaster," NBC News, 24 January 2024. Available at https://www.nbcnews.com/business/business-news/alaska-airlines-found-more-loose-bolts-boeing-737-max-9-ceo-says-rcna135316.
95. NTSB Accident Investigation Preliminary Report of DCA24MA063, p. 18. Available at https://www.ntsb.gov/investigations/Documents/DCA24MA063%20Preliminary%20report.pdf.
96. Deal, S., "Boeing announces immediate actions to strengthen quality," Boeing, 15 January 2024. Available at https://www.boeing.com/737-9-updates/jan-15-2024-boeing-announces-immediate-actions-to-strengthen-quality.
97. Ibid.
98. NTSB Office of the Chair Letter to Chair of Congress Committee on Commerce, Science, and Transportation, 13 March 2024. Available at https://www.ntsb.gov/news/Documents/Letter%20to%20Senate%20Committee%20on%20Commerce,%20Science%20&%20Transportation%20on%20Boeing%20737-9%20MAX%20Door%20Plug%20Blowout.pdf.

99. Ibid.
100. Ibid.
101. US Senate Committee on Commerce, Science and Transportation, "Cantwell to Boeing: Where are the documents?," Press Releases, 6 March 2024. Available at https://www.commerce.senate.gov/2024/3/cantwell-to-boeing-where-are-the-documents.
102. See letter at https://www.commerce.senate.gov/services/files/992C15CC-520E-4A4E-934F-4FE882F4447D.
103. Gates D., "Boeing admits it can't find records on the Alaska Airlines door plug work," Seattle Times, 8 March 2024. Available at https://www.seattletimes.com/business/boeing-aerospace/ntsb-boeing-employees-who-installed-max-door-plug-still-unidentified/.
104. Boeing Updates, "Boeing statement on providing information for the NTSB investigation," 6 March 2024. Available at https://www.boeing.com/737-9-updates#updates.
105. Committee on Commerce, Science & Transportation, "Cantwell gives FAA 2 weeks to provide answers on its Boeing production line oversight," Press Release, 11 January 2024. Available at https://www.commerce.senate.gov/2024/1/cantwell-gives-faa-2-weeks-to-provide-answers-on-its-boeing-production-line-oversight.
106. Ibid.
107. Ibid.
108. Aratani, L., and Cho, K.K., "United finds loose bolts on Boeing jets grounded after blowout incident," Washington Port, January 2024. Available at https://www.washingtonpost.com/business/2024/01/08/boeing-737-max-inspections-begin/.
109. McMichael, C., "FAA recommends airlines inspect door plugs on another Boeing model," 22 January 2024. Available at https://abcnews.go.com/US/faa-recommends-airlines-inspect-door-plugs-boeing-model/story?id=106063.
110. Koenig, D., "FAA approves inspection process that could clear the way for grounded Boeing planes to fly again," 25 January 2024. Available at https://apnews.com/article/boeing-ceo-congress-senate-hearing-calhoun-cantwell-f83248428fc32b968a5b9192b79d88ff.
111. FAA, "Updates on Boeing 737-9 MAX aircraft." Available at https://www.faa.gov/newsroom/updates-boeing-737-9-max-aircraft.
112. Ibid.
113. Section 103 Organization Designation Authorizations (ODA) for Transport Airplanes Expert Panel Review Report Final Report, pgs 4–5. Available at https://www.faa.gov/newsroom/Sec103_ExpertPanelReview_Report_Final.pdf.
114. Gardner, L., "Head of troubled Boeing 737 MAX program leaves company," 21 February 2024. Available at https://www.politico.com/news/2024/02/21/head-of-troubled-boeing-737-max-program-leaves-company-00142478.
115. Boeing, "Strengthening safety and quality," 2024. Available at https://www.boeing.com/strengthening-safety-and-quality#acsaa.
116. Boeing, "Boeing executive summary," 2024. Available at https://www.boeing.com/content/dam/boeing/boeingdotcom/safety/Safety-and-Quality-Plan_Executive%20Summary-5-30-2024.pdf.
117. Johnson, J.W., "Passengers Sue Boeing and Alaska airlines after panel blows out," 23 February 2024. Available at https://www.prlog.org/13008469-passengers-sue-boeing-and-alaska-airlines-after-panel-blows-out.html.
118. Takahama, E., "Alaska airlines paid $1,500 to flight 1282 passengers. That won't stop the lawsuits," Seattle News, 12 January 2024. Available at https://www.seattletimes.com/business/boeing-aerospace/alaska-airlines-paid-1500-to-flight-1282-passengers-that-wont-stop-the-lawsuits/.
119. Brennan, R., "Boeing hit with products liability class action over Alaska airlines plane losing door 'Plug' mid-flight," 16 January 2024. Available at https://www.law.com/2024/01/16/boeing-hit-with-product-liability-class-action-over-alaska-airlines-plane-losing-door-plug-mid-flight/.

120. Genovese, D., "Alaska Airlines passengers sue Boeing for 'waking nightmare'," Fox Business, 14 January 2024. Available at https://www.foxbusiness.com/lifestyle/alaska-airlines-passengers-sue-boeing-for-waking-nightmare.
121. Picchi, A., "Boeing supplier that made Alaska Airlines door plug was warned of 'defects' with other parts, lawsuit claims," CBS News, 10 January 2024. Available at https://www.cbsnews.com/news/boeing-loose-bolts-alaska-airlines-united-airlines-spirit-aerosystems-door-plug/.
122. Johnson, G., "The DOJ has opened a criminal investigation into the Alaska Airlines 737 blowout, a report says," AP News, 10 March 2024. Available at https://apnews.com/article/boeing-ntsb-door-plug-emergency-landing-2d23408a25eff999579c88071836dbec.
123. See U.S. Department of Justice, Case 4:21-cr-00005-O Document 199 Filed 05/14/24 ID 3686, 14 May 2024. Available at https://storage.courtlistener.com/recap/gov.uscourts.txnd.342880/gov.uscourts.txnd.342880.199.0.pdf.
124. Shepardson, D., and Spector, M., "US says Boeing breached 2021 737 MAX criminal prosecution deal," Reuters, 15 May 2024. Available at https://www.reuters.com/business/aerospace-defense/us-says-boeing-breached-2021-deferred-prosecution-737-max-agreement-2024-05-14/.
125. Isidore C., and Pere, E., "Prosecutors urge Justice Department to file criminal charges against Boeing over 737 Max," CNN, 24 June 2024. Available at https://edition.cnn.com/2024/06/24/business/boeing-DOJ-criminal-faa-737-max/index.html.
126. Prentice, C., et al., "US prosecutors recommend Justice Dept. criminally charge Boeing," Reuters, 24 June 2024. Available at https://www.reuters.com/legal/us-prosecutors-recommend-DOJ-criminally-charge-boeing-deadline-looms-2024-06-23/.
127. Ibid.
128. Giorno, T., "Boeing crash victims' families push DOJ to fine company $24 billion for deadliest corporate crime in US history," The Hill, 19 June 2024. Available at https://thehill.com/business/4730056-boeing-crash-families-urge-criminal-prosecution/.
129. Shepardson, D., and Spector, M., "Boeing 737 MAX crash victim families ask judge to name corporate," Reuters, 25 June 2024. Available at https://www.reuters.com/business/aerospace-defense/boeing-737-max-crash-victim-families-ask-judge-name-corporate-monitor-2024-06-24/.
130. Shepardson, D., "US judge questions DOJ decision to drop Boeing independent monitor," 3 September 2025. Available at https://www.reuters.com/sustainability/boards-policy-regulation/us-judge-questions-doj-decision-drop-boeing-independent-monitor-2025-09-03/.
131. Koenig, D., and Richer, A.D., "Sweetheart deal': Families of 737 Max crash victims not satisfied by Boeing guilty plea," Associated Press, 8 July 2024. Available at https://www.csmonitor.com/USA/2024/0708/boeing-guilty-plea-737-Max-crashes.
132. Ibid.
133. Koenig, D., "Lawyers for families of passengers killed in 737 Max crashes ask court to block Boeing plea deal," AP News, 1 August 2024. Available at https://apnews.com/article/boeing-fraud-plea-deal-victims-justice-department-0cd99f8e7fd4e8e98621a91b8eb2e102#.
134. Koenig, D., "The Justice Department is defending a plea deal it struck with Boeing over planes that crashed and killed 346 people," AP, 15 August 2024. Available at https://abcnews.go.com/US/wireStory/justice-department-defends-boeing-plea-deal-criticism-737-112847445#:~:text=Boeing%20agreed%20last%20month%20to,on%20probation%20for%20three%20years.
135. "US judge blocks Boeing's guilty plea in 737 MAX crashes case over fears diversity policies would drive 'racial considerations'," ABC News, 6 December 2024. Available at https://www.abc.net.au/news/2024-12-06/us-judge-rejects-boeing-guilty-plea-deal-over-diversity-policies/104692412.

136. Reuters, "US judge rejects Boeing plea deal in fatal 737 MAX crashes," 5 December 2024. Available at https://www.voanews.com/a/us-judge-rejects-boeing-s-plea-deal-in-a-conspiracy-case-stemming-from-fatal-plane-crashes-/7888754.html.
137. Bauer, A., and Rocco, M., "The court's rejection of the Boeing-DOJ plea agreement: Strategic implications of DEI policies," 9 January 2025. Available at https://ssrga.com/bauer_suite/the-courts-rejection-of-the-boeing-DOJ-plea-agreement-strategic-implications-of-dei-policies/.
138. Versprille, A., and Mekelburg, M., "Boeing, DOJ in talks to revise plea deal for 737 Max crashes," Bloomberg, 3 January 2025. Available at https://www.bnnbloomberg.ca/business/2025/01/03/boeing-DOJ-in-talks-to-revise-plea-deal-over-737-max-crashes/.
139. Rose, J., "DOJ confirms it has a deal with Boeing to drop prosecution over deadly 737 Max crashes," NPR, 23 May 2025. Available at https://www.npr.org/2025/05/23/nx-s1-5409364/boeing-justic-department-737-max-plane-crashes-charges-deal.
140. Jamali, L., "Boeing to avoid prosecution in US Justice Department deal over crashes," BBC, 24 May 2025. Available at https://www.bbc.com/news/articles/c14kg0lj8k6o.
141. Ibid.
142. Shepardson, D., "Crash victims' families appeal US judge's decision to dismiss Boeing criminal case," 14 November 2025. Available at https://www.reuters.com/world/families-appeal-judges-decision-dismiss-boeing-criminal-case-2025-11-13/
143. Ibid.
144. U.S. Senate Committee on Commerce, Science, and Transportation Chair, Maria Cantwell, Aviation Safety Whistleblower Report, Executive Summary, December 202. Available at https://www.commerce.senate.gov/services/files/48E3E2DE-6DFC-4602-BADF-8926F551B670.
145. Ibid.
146. Leggett, T., "Boeing whistleblower John Barnett found dead in US," BBC, 11 March 2024. Available at https://www.bbc.com/news/business-68534703.
147. Strassman, M., and Kaplan, M., "Family of Boeing whistleblower John Barnett speaks out following his death," CBS, 28 March 2024. Available at https://www.cbsnews.com/news/john-barnett-boeing-whistleblower-family-interview/.
148. Ibid.
149. Ibid.
150. Phillips, P., "Settlement reached in lawsuit filed against Boeing in whistleblower death," 13 May 2025. Available at https://www.live5news.com/2025/05/13/settlement-reached-lawsuit-filed-against-boeing-whistleblower-death/.
151. Gates, D., and Rosenblatt, L., "Whistleblower Josh Dean of Boeing supplier Spirit AeroSystems has died," Seattle Times, 1 May 2024. Available at https://www.seattletimes.com/business/whistleblower-josh-dean-of-boeing-supplier-spirit-aerosystems-has-died/.
152. Ibid.
153. Miller, H., "Boeing, spirit aerosystems deal shines light on this steady aerospace climber," Investor's Business Daily, 25 June 2024. Available at https://www.investors.com/news/boeing-stock-spirit-aerosystems-deal-ftai-aviation/.
154. France, A., "'No safety culture': Hundreds could die if Boeing fails to address jet safety, alleges whistleblower," The Standard, 17 April 2024. Available at https://www.standard.co.uk/news/world/boeing-safety-whistleblower-sam-salehpour-737-max-plane-door-b1152178.html.
155. Ibid.
156. Molyneaux, I., "New Boeing whistleblower claims released as CEO prepares to give testimony," Aerotime, 18 June 2024. Available at https://www.aerotime.aero/articles/boeing-whistleblower-sam-mohawk-richard-blumenthal.

157. BEA, "Final report on the accident on 1st June 2009 to the Airbus A330-203 registered F-GZCP operated by Air France flight AF 447 Rio de Janeiro – Paris," July 2012. Available at https://asn.flightsafety.org/wikibase/321502.
158. Ibid., p. 200.
159. BEA, Press release, Flight AF 447, A330-203, registered F-GZCP, 5 June 2009. Available at https://archive.ph/20120724172013/http://www.bea.aero/anglaise/actualite/pressrelease20090605.html#selection-311.0-327.26.
160. Ibid.
161. Gilbert, D., "AF447 pilot: 'Damn it, we're going to crash,'" CNN, 5 July 2012. Available at https://edition.cnn.com/2011/10/14/world/americas/af447-transcript.
162. Ibid.
163. Danko, M., "Compensating the families of Air France Flight 447," 5 June 2009. Available at https://www.aviationlawmonitor.com/2009/06/claims-and-defenses/compensating-the-families-of-air-france-flight-447/.
164. Danko, M., "US court tosses out all Air France flight 447 cases," 7 October 2010. Available at https://www.aviationlawmonitor.com/2010/10/lawsuits-1/us-court-tosses-out-all-air-france-flight-447-cases/.
165. France24, "Air France insurer Axa to appeal Brazilian compensation ruling," 12 March 2010. Available at https://www.france24.com/en/20100312-air-france-insurer-axa-appeal-brazilian-compensation-ruling.
166. France24, "Brazil court orders Air France to compensate family of Rio-Paris air crash victim," 28 December 2010. Available at https://www.france24.com/en/20101228-air-france-pay-700000-dollars-family-rio-paris-crash-victim-flight-447-clarkson-seba.
167. Charpentreau, C., AF447: Air France sent back to court, case dismissed for Airbus, 22 July 2019. Available at https://www.aerotime.aero/clement.charpentreau/23726-af447-air-france-sent-back-to-court-case-dismissed-for-airbus.
168. Le Figaro, "Rio-Paris crash: the public prosecutor's office requests a trial for Air France and Airbus," 27 January 2021. Available at https://www.lefigaro.fr/societes/crash-du-rio-paris-le-parquet-general-demande-un-proces-pour-air-france-et-airbus-20210127.
169. Boucey, B., and Vidalon, D., "2021 Trial Air France and airbus," Reuters, Paris 27 January 2021. Available at https://www.yahoo.com/news/air-france-airbus-face-paris-154554095.html.
170. France24, "Air France and Airbus to face trial over 2009 Rio-Paris crash, French court says," 12 May 2021. Available at https://www.france24.com/en/france/20210512-air-france-and-airbus-to-face-trial-over-2009-rio-paris-crash-french-court-says.
171. France24, "Airbus, Air France acquitted of manslaughter charges in trial over 2009 Rio-Paris crash," 17 April 2023. Available at https://www.france24.com/en/france/20230417-french-court-acquits-air-france-airbus-over-2009-rio-paris-crash.
172. Ibid.
173. RFI, "Prosecutor to appeal acquittal of Airbus, Air France in Rio-Paris crash case" 28 April 2023. Available at https://www.rfi.fr/en/france/20230428-french-prosecutor-to-appeal-acquittal-of-airbus-air-france-in-rio-paris-crash.
174. Hepher T., "Air France, Airbus dispute pilot roles in Rio-Paris crash," 27 November 2025. Available at https://www.reuters.com/business/aerospace-defense/french-appeals-trial-over-2009-rio-paris-crash-reaches-climax-2025-11-27/

5 Contrasting Legal Systems

5.1 INTRODUCTION

The cornerstone of successful accident investigations and safety reporting programs is the free exchange of information and admission of unintentional mistakes or omissions attributed to human factors, which are now threatened as a result of the increasing criminalization of aviation personnel. Traditionally, aviation accidents were considered to be the result of human error and/or technological failures. Earlier litigation focused more on compensation and the courts awarding damages, and thus, criminal law applied only to a limited extent. As a result of the tremendous technological advancements and growth of the industry, society considers aviation accidents as organizational or systemic failures and therefore demands accountability and blameworthiness. For many decades, the judicial authorities took a back step toward aviation accidents and the aviation industry in general, allowing this important industry to develop unhindered and to enhance aviation safety without the added pressure of facing criminal proceedings. This is not to say that there were no cases in which the judicial authorities took a harsh approach toward individuals following an aviation accident and prosecuted them. As a result of the changes in society's perception toward aviation accidents, the impact that an aviation accident has on society, the increased media attention given to an aviation accident stemming from the tremendous emotional pain and suffering as well as political, economic and industrial implications that may arise, the focus seems to have shifted to identifying those responsible for the accident and to apportion blameworthiness. Consequently, the judicial authorities are more pressed to fulfill this social demand for justice, and not surprisingly, the judicial authorities feel the need to more actively investigate aviation accidents to answer the increasing demands for accountability.

The judicial investigation, conducted in parallel to the safety investigation in countries with a civil or other legal system, is punitive in nature. It is aimed at identifying those responsible for the accident, determining fault, and apportioning blame. The judicial authorities focus on the most likely parties whose acts and omissions have contributed to the accident. They then gather facts and evidence to build their case and to secure a conviction in a court of law. In contrast, the technical investigation is non-punitive and focuses on enhancing safety by making safety recommendations of corrective measures to eliminate the possibility of similar accidents and serious incidents from recurring. The accident scenario and sequence of events leading up to the accident are derived from the facts collected to determine the cause and contributing factors that led to the accident without apportioning blame or liability.

DOI: 10.1201/9781003724872-5

There is a significant divergence in the methodology and approach of these two separate but parallel investigations, depending on the legal system in each jurisdiction. Understanding the key differences between the French and American legal systems is essential to fully grasp the contrasting judicial approaches to investigating potential criminal conduct and assigning responsibility following an aviation accident. This is evident when examining the steps taken by the French judiciary after the Concorde Flight 4590, Air Inter Flight 148, and Air France 447 accidents discussed in Chapter 3, as well as the actions of the U.S. Department of Justice following the two Boeing 737 MAX 8 accidents and the Alaska Airlines MAX 9 serious incident.

5.2 COUNTRIES WITH A CIVIL LEGAL SYSTEM: FRANCE

French criminal law is codified in the Penal Code and the Code of Criminal Procedure, which outline the types of criminal offenses, penalties, and the procedures for prosecution and trial. The complex criminal justice system is further complicated by the involvement of investigative judges in serious cases, often leading to a lengthy and complicated process. Once the investigative judges complete their investigation, prosecutors decide whether to direct the case to an alternative to prosecution, send it to the investigating judge for further investigation, dismiss it, or prosecute. If they choose prosecution, they determine the offenses and which trial procedures, such as a guilty plea or rapid trial, to invoke. The case file is then passed on to the court, which usually consists of three judges, except in serious cases that also have a jury.[1]

The French legal system is a civil law system that differs in many ways from the common law legal system in countries like England and Wales, the US, and Australia. The criminal process is inquisitorial, where, in cases except for minor offenses, an investigative judge plays a role in conducting investigations and preparing the case for trial once it has been decided to proceed. The case then moves to a different judge, who then hears the case. In common law countries, the system is accusatorial or adversarial, where the prosecution and defense each present their case before an impartial judge who has not participated in investigating the case, and acts as an independent referee.

Investigative authorities, therefore, have broader powers than those in America. In France, there is a clear separation between prosecutorial, investigative, and adjudicative functions. The French judiciary has two branches. The standing judiciary has the role of a prosecutor and is comprised of public prosecutors who are subordinate to the Minister of Justice and the executive. The sitting judiciary is made up of the investigating magistrate and the trial judge who represent the investigative and adjudicative functions.[2]

Another important difference is that in France, law enforcement authorities have more extensive powers than in America with regard to the gathering and use of criminal evidence. Under French law, most evidence considered in an investigation can be used in the criminal prosecution, and this protection is an integral part of the system because the trial judge makes an independent review of evidence. In America, on the other hand, the criminal system reviews evidence to ensure rights are protected at the prosecution phase, which can result in some evidence being inadmissible or excluded during the trial. In France, the protection is provided through an organ represented by the magistrature, whereas America implements protections that restrict the use of evidence in criminal prosecutions.[3]

The French criminal process involves three main phases, corresponding to the three functions outlined above: prosecutorial, investigative, and adjudicative. The prosecution phase is conducted by the prosecutor, followed by an investigation phase directed by the investigating magistrate, and then the trial is ruled over by the trial judge.

The aviation sector was previously governed by the French Code of Civil Aviation prior to 2010. It is now regulated under Section 6 of the French Code of Transport, which covers all modes of transportation. In October 2023, Decree No. n°2023-1008 repealed most regulatory provisions that previously remained in the French Code of Civil Aviation, and these have now been incorporated into the Code of Transport. Safety is regulated on an international level by the ICAO and its Annexes, and on a European level by EASA and European legislation. The various departments of the Civil Aviation Authority, the Dirección General de Aeronáutica Civil (DGAC), including the Organization for Civil Aviation Security and the Safety Oversight Directorate, enforce air safety regulations. The Minister for Transport has the authority to conduct safety inspections of aircraft, equipment, organizations, and their employees. French safety rules are contained in Article L6341-1 and the subsequent Articles of the French Code of Transport. In accordance with the French Code of Transport,[4] any regulated actor must report any event that affects the safety of air operations or is likely to do so to the aviation authorities. Failure to do so may result in imprisonment for one year and a fine of €15,000.[5]

With regards to investigating aviation accidents and serious incidents, Regulation (EU) 996/2010 (amended by Regulation (EU) 376/2014 and Regulation (EU) 2018/1139) is also applicable. Following ICAO Annex 13 and EU and local law, the Bureau of Enquiry and Analysis for Civil Aviation Safety (BEA) has the responsibility to conduct official safety investigations of civil aircraft accidents and serious incidents in France. A parallel criminal investigation into aviation accidents resulting in bodily injuries or death is conducted by the Air Transport Gendarmerie (GTA), under the supervision of the investigating judge. Court-appointed experts can assist in determining the cause of the accident.

The BEA leads the technical investigation to determine the causes of the accident, with the sole purpose of enhancing safety and preventing recurrences. The reports of the BEA are made public and can be found on their website. In contrast, when a judge orders a criminal investigation, the report issued by the expert is not public and cannot be disclosed. The criminal file is not made public. Only the judge and the parties to the criminal proceedings have access to the criminal file, and they must respect the secrecy of criminal investigations.

In France, the legal system provides that the wreckage and documents remain under the control of the judicial authority. It should be highlighted once again that France has notified ICAO and filed a difference between its national regulations and the ICAO Annex 13 International Standards and Recommended Practices, as follows:

> In France, in accordance with Recommendation 5.4.1, an investigation separate from any investigation conducted under the provisions of this Annex is conducted when the judicial authority deems that there is a possible criminal offence. The law, in conformity with Standard 5.10, does establish the relationship between the two investigations and allows the investigator-in charge unhampered access to the wreckage and all relevant documents so as to be able to perform the necessary examinations and work without delay. However, it does not grant him/her total control over the wreckage and documents, the latter of which generally remain under the control of the judicial authority (Supplement to Annex 13 2003).[6]

The CVR and FDR are therefore placed under seal by the judicial authorities and handed to the BEA to be read out under its control. In accordance with EU law, from 2014 onwards, agreements have been put in place or amended to ensure coordination between safety and judicial investigations.

The BEA, therefore, conducts the safety investigation in parallel with the judicial investigation conducted by GTA to establish criminal responsibilities. In addition to the GTA that ensures safety and security in airport areas, it also has judicial police powers to investigate aviation accidents that occur in France and abroad when the accident involves the death of French passengers.

Unlike other countries with a common law system, such as the USA, there is no discovery process, and French law does not oblige the parties to disclose documents as everyone is assumed to cooperate in establishing the truth. If a party refuses to disclose a document covered by business secrecy, the court must determine whether the refusal is legitimate. In criminal matters, search warrants can be issued.[7]

According to Article 121-2 of the French Criminal Code, an airline, as a separate legal entity, can be held criminally responsible for an aviation accident if it can be proved that the accident was a result of the airline's negligence, endangerment, or a breach of any safety rule. In cases where the public prosecutor initiates criminal proceedings against an air carrier and passengers or their representatives have already claimed compensation in civil courts, the civil claims for damages will be suspended. In addition, it is possible to make a civil claim for damages arising from circumstances that result in a criminal trial, and the criminal court has jurisdiction to rule on a civil action for damages resulting from a criminal offense.[8]

5.3 COUNTRIES WITH A COMMON LAW LEGAL SYSTEM

Common law countries such as Australia, the UK, and the USA prioritize technical investigation unless a crime, like a terrorist act, is suspected. In contrast, civil law countries that have adopted the Napoleonic Code allow for a parallel investigation by the judiciary, which has greater powers than technical investigators regarding access to wreckage and sensitive aviation data obtained from the CVR and FDR.

5.3.1 USA

In America, the investigation conducted by the National Transportation Safety Board normally takes the primary role, unless it is suspected that a crime has been committed. Cases discussed in our first book where the judicial authorities suspected criminal activity and commenced their own investigation include Trans World Airlines B 747 Flight 800, Alaska Airlines MD-83 Flight 261, Emery DC-8 Cargo flight, and USAir Boeing 737 Flight 5050.

5.4 CRIMINAL INVESTIGATION AND JUDICIAL ACTION: CASE STUDIES

There are key differences in the legal philosophies, approaches to precedent, and overall structures of the French and the U.S. legal systems. However, these differences and the distinct powers of the executive, legislative, and judicial branches become more acute when one considers their distinct approaches to dealing with potential criminal conduct and accountability in the aftermath of an aviation accident.

The following analysis of the legal recourse and ramifications in the US, which has a common law legal system, and in France, based on civil law, highlights several interesting facts and differences in the philosophy of prosecuting individuals in the aftermath of serious aviation accidents in countries with different legal systems.

5.4.1 Civil Law: France

In addition to the Air France 447 case previously discussed, the following two notable cases of prosecuted aviation professionals, including senior and middle managers, draw attention to criminal prosecutions after an aviation accident.

5.4.2 Concorde Flight 4590

On 25 July 2000, the first fatal accident involving the Concorde occurred, shortly after Concorde 203, F-BTSC departed from Paris, scheduled to fly to New York. Less than two minutes after take-off, the left main landing gear was destroyed after having run over a strip of metal lost by a Continental Airlines DC-10 aircraft, which departed five minutes earlier. The tire exploded, and a piece of rubber was thrown against the underside of the left wing, rupturing a part of tank 5. A severe fire broke out under the left wing, and engines 1 and 2 suffered a loss of thrust. The aircraft crashed into a hotel in Gonesse and burst into flames. All 109 people on board were killed, in addition to four people in the hotel.

Parallel to the judicial investigation, the official technical investigation was conducted by the BEA. Throughout the investigation, the judicial authorities maintained control over the wreckage site and seized maintenance records and other documents, as well as the CVR and FDR. As a result of the parallel investigations and the priority that the judicial investigations have over the wreckage and documents, the UK AAIB, as an accredited representative, expressed significant concerns regarding the fact that the judicial investigation withheld specific evidence and that their involvement hindered the investigation.

In the final report, comments made by the UK accredited representative expressing their concerns regarding the manner in which the French judicial authorities affected the technical investigation were appended. They stated that the BEA and the AAIB cooperated during the investigation but the French judicial authorities, inter alia, did not allow the AAIB investigators to examine all the items of the wreckage or to participate in the component examinations of the strip of metal that burst the tire and the part of the tank five lower skin that was found on the runway, only briefly allowed them to participate in the examination of most of the flight deck controls and instruments and did not allow them to be systematically involved in the examination of evidence. They were also not allowed full access to all relevant evidence in a timely manner. In particular, the judicial authorities severely restricted their access to the accident site, withheld photographic evidence of the runway surface for six weeks – a delay that proved valuable in understanding the events on the runway – and hindered the prompt examination of evidence, resulting in significant delays in safety actions.[9]

It should be noted that since 2014, in accordance with EU law, agreements have been established or amended in France to ensure coordination between judicial and safety investigations, allowing access to the same data and evidence without restrictions while remaining independent and separate. See, for example, the Advance Arrangement Relating to Air Safety Investigations. The purpose of this Advance Arrangement is to clarify the relationship between the safety investigation authority and the judicial authority with regard to accidents or serious incidents within the scope of Regulation (EU) No 996/2010. In particular, the arrangement covers "the access to the site of the accident; preservation of and access to evidence; initial and ongoing debriefings of the status of each process; exchange of information; appropriate use of safety information; resolution of conflicts. It acts as a framework for establishing specific protocols that may be agreed between the Director of the BEA and the magistrate concerned during the two investigations and that may prove nec essary for the coordination of the investigations and the division of responsibilities and costs concerning processes of common interest."[10]

The final report of the BEA attributed the accident to the high-speed passage of a tire over a part that had been lost by an aircraft that had taken off five minutes earlier, and the subsequent destruction of the tire. The tire debris then pierced the No. 5 fuel tank within the left wing, the fuel stream caught fire, the debris and some unburned fuel entered the engine intakes, resulting in loss of engine power.

Following the judicial inquiry into the accident, in March 2008, charges of manslaughter were filed against Continental Airlines, accusing it of negligently allowing its staff to use banned titanium strips for aircraft repairs. A Continental mechanic who fitted the titanium strip that fell onto the runway before the doomed Concorde flight, a Continental maintenance official, a former Concorde chief engineer of Aerospatiale accused of not taking action to strengthen the fuel tanks, the former head of the Concorde program accused of underestimating the gravity of previous tyre and fuel tank incidents and failing to demand design changes, as well as the former senior official at the French civil aviation directorate accused of underestimating the gravity of previous tyre and fuel tank incidents and failing to demand design changes, were charged.

In September 2006, the highest court in France rejected a request to dismiss the charges and decided that the trial would commence. The trial began in February 2010 in the Paris suburb of Pontoise. In November 2012, a French appeals court overturned the involuntary manslaughter charges against Continental Airlines, which had merged with United Airlines two years earlier, ruling that it had no criminal wrongdoing in the accident. The appellate court also overturned the conviction of a Continental mechanic accused of wrongly using titanium to construct a replacement part known as a wear strip for the DC-10 and of improperly attaching the strip to the aircraft, leading to it falling onto the runway. The ruling did not dispute the lower court's finding that linked the metal strip from the Continental aircraft to the chain of events causing the accident and the deaths of all 109 passengers and crew aboard, as well as the four people on the ground, but stated that the criminal manslaughter charge was unjustified. The French accident investigators concluded that a small strip of metal that had fallen off the Continental DC-10 had punctured a tire of the Concorde as it took off. The tire disintegrated in seconds, sending rubber debris into the fuel tanks, leading to the chain of events that caused the crash.

In addition, the court also upheld a lower court's order from 2010, which required the company to pay civil damages of €1 million (approximately $1.3 million) to Air France, compensating the French carrier for damage to its image. Air France was not a defendant in the case, but it joined as a civil party claiming that it should be compensated for the damages that it had paid to the relatives of the deceased. This case is an important precedent-setting case, as it is the first in France where a court held that someone can be held responsible in civil law for an accident without also incurring criminal responsibility.[11] This was the first decision in France of this importance where a court has held that someone can have civil responsibility for an accident without also being criminally responsible.

5.4.3 Air Inter Flight 148

On 20 January 1992, Air Inter Flight 148, an A320 domestic flight that departed from Lyon Airport, France, scheduled to land at Strasbourg Airport, France, with 90 passengers and six crew on board, crashed into the Vosges Mountains while on approach for landing on a VOR/DME approach.[12] Eighty-seven people were killed and nine were injured. The French BEA investigated the accident and determined that "While various factors contributed to the crash of Flight 148, the BEA concluded that the accident occurred because the pilots inadvertently left the autopilot set in the Vertical Speed mode, instead of the Flight Path Angle mode, when they entered a '3.3' descent angle. As a result, the autopilot interpreted this as a command to descend at the rapid rate of 3,300 feet per minute."[13] It should be noted that the aircraft was not equipped with a GPWS[14] as it was not a requirement for French aircraft at that time.

A criminal investigation was conducted, leading to charges against six individuals for manslaughter, related to their alleged errors that may have impacted the safety of the A320 aircraft. They include: the engineering chief of Airbus, who was indicted over the design of the A320 cockpit and the aircraft's potentially faulty DME navigation system; the head of DGAC technical control and its director general, who participated in the decision not to require this device on French aircraft and failed to ensure the aircraft was equipped with a GPWS that would have warned pilots they were near the ground, which is now internationally mandated; the chief executive of Air Inter (the domestic subsidiary of Air France, now merged with Dutch carrier KLM); and the airline operations director at the time of the accident, who was charged because both of the A320 pilots had relatively little experience with fly-by-wire aircraft. All pleaded not guilty.

It took 14 years for the case to go to court, and on 7 November 2006, the court found the air traffic controller had committed "errors" and that the Airbus technical director had been negligent; however, it held that there was no definite causal link between the accident and the six defendants. All six were acquitted. Airbus and Air France were held liable to pay damages.[15]

These cases clearly illustrate how it is routine in the French legal system to criminally investigate aviation accidents and charge aviation professionals for their acts or omissions that caused or contributed to the accident. Aviation professionals are often formally charged many years after the accident, after lengthy investigations, and the defendants have to wait, generally, over a decade for the court process and appeals to take place. The cases often result in an acquittal, emphasizing the prosecutor's difficulty in proving the direct causal link between the defendants' alleged acts and omissions and the accident. In addition, the decision by the public prosecutor to appeal the decision to acquit Airbus and Air France of the manslaughter charges after the Air France 447 accident illustrates the extent to which the French judicial authorities are prepared to go to fulfill their legal and social responsibilities in bringing those they consider to be responsible for a crime to justice and apportion accountability in the aftermath of an aviation accident.

Considering the delay between the accident and the appeal court decision, which often reverses criminal sanctions imposed by a lower court, and the fact that punishing aviation professionals after an aviation accident for unintentional consequences, albeit serious ones, does not deter future criminal conduct, one has to consider what benefits criminalizing unintentional acts or omissions bring to aviation safety, particularly in light of the adverse effects that criminalization has on safety reporting and on enhancing aviation safety.

To illustrate other criminal charges that can arise from aviation business activities unrelated to aviation accidents in France, the following case against Airbus is discussed.

5.4.4 Other Airbus Criminal Prosecution

In January 2020, in the largest global foreign bribery resolution to date, Airbus agreed to pay global fines of €3.6bn, reaching a settlement with the United Kingdom,

United States, and French authorities stemming from charges related to using bribery to use third-party business partners around the world to bribe government officials as well as non-governmental airline executives to obtain and retain business, including contracts to sell aircraft.

In the UK, Airbus concluded a deferred prosecution agreement (DPA) with the Serious Fraud Office (SFO), agreeing to pay a total of €991m. In France, the French CJIP cited corruption of foreign officials, fraud, and money laundering in the sale of jets and satellites, and Airbus agreed to pay almost €2.08bn and more than US$525m in the US.

The investigation began in the UK by the Serious Fraud Office (SFO) in 2016 and in 2017. The SFO entered into a joint investigation agreement with France's Parquet National Financier (PNF), the national prosecutorial office dedicated to financial matters.[16] The UK's Serious Fraud Office charged Airbus with five counts of failure to prevent bribery across five jurisdictions between 2011 and 2015. The judge stated that the payment agreed in the deferred prosecution of €991 million highlighted the gravity of the organization's conduct as well as its cooperation and reform program established under its new leadership.[17]

As part of the coordinated investigation between the UK's SFO and the French PNF, France led the investigation into bribery schemes in certain jurisdictions in the Middle East, Asia, and South America. In accordance with its Convention judiciaire d'intérêt public (CJIP), the French Public Prosecutor can offer organizations a judicial criminal settlement agreement instead of prosecuting them criminally. The CJIP and Airbus agreement to pay over €2 billion is reported to be the tenth largest ever imposed, with the amount amounting to twice the combined value of the last five agreements reached.[18]

In the USA, the DOJ charged Airbus with conspiracy to violate the anti-bribery provision of the Foreign Corrupt Practices Act (FCPA) and conspiracy to violate the AECA and its implementing regulations, the International Traffic in Arms Regulations (ITAR). The FCPA charge arose out of Airbus's scheme to offer and pay bribes to foreign officials, including Chinese officials, to obtain and retain business, including contracts to sell aircraft. The AECA charged Airbus for its "willful failure to disclose political contributions, commissions or fees to the U.S. government, as required under the ITAR, in connection with the sale or export of defense articles and defense services to the Armed Forces of a foreign country or international organization."[19] As part of the deferred prosecution agreement with the department, Airbus agreed to continue to cooperate with the department in any ongoing investigations and prosecutions relating to the conduct, including that of individuals, and to enhance its compliance program.[20]

5.4.5 Common Law: US

In the USA, the decision to prosecute an individual or a corporation is made by the Department of Justice (DOJ), and prosecutors have substantial discretion in determining when, whom, how, and even whether to prosecute for violations of federal criminal law. It is possible for the courts to review the exercise of that discretion, but this will occur only in rare instances and mainly to protect the defendant or potential defendant's constitutional rights.[21] In accordance with the guidelines governing the decision to prosecute, prosecutors must weigh all the factors typically considered in the sound exercise of prosecutorial judgment. It should ensure that the general purposes of the criminal law, namely, to punish appropriately and deter further criminal conduct, protect the public from dangerous and fraudulent conduct, rehabilitate, and compensate victims, are adequately met, while taking into account the special nature of the corporation. The following additional factors are to be assessed in the case of corporations:[22]

1. the nature and seriousness of the offense, including the risk of harm to the public, and applicable policies and priorities, if any, governing the prosecution of corporations for particular categories of crime;
2. the pervasiveness of wrongdoing within the corporation, including the complicity in, or the condoning of, the wrongdoing by individuals in corporate management;
3. the corporation's history of misconduct, including prior criminal, civil, and regulatory enforcement actions against it, both domestically and internationally;
4. the corporation's willingness to cooperate, including as to potential wrongdoing by its current and former employees, directors, officers, and agents, as well as other individuals and entities that engaged in the misconduct under investigation;
5. the adequacy and effectiveness of the corporation's compliance program at the time of the offense, as well as at the time of a charging decision;
6. the corporation's timely and voluntary self-disclosure of wrongdoing;
7. the corporation's remedial actions, including, but not limited to, any efforts to implement an adequate and effective corporate compliance program or to improve an existing one, to replace responsible management, to discipline or terminate wrongdoers, to execute financial compensation measures that punish wrongdoing, or to pay restitution;
8. collateral consequences, including whether there is disproportionate harm to shareholders, pension holders, employees, and others not proven personally culpable, as well as impact on the public arising from the prosecution;
9. the adequacy of remedies such as civil or regulatory enforcement actions, domestically or internationally, including remedies resulting from the corporation's cooperation with relevant government agencies;
10. the adequacy of the prosecution of individuals responsible for the corporation's misconduct; and
11. the interests of any victims, including what steps the corporation has taken to identify potential victims, or other persons or entities who were significantly, even if indirectly, harmed by the criminal conduct, and what steps the corporation has taken to mitigate such harm

Prosecuting a corporation may result in a criminal trial; however, in most cases, one of the alternative options is preferred, and the matter is not taken to trial. Alternatives include the corporation pleading guilty, entering into a deferred prosecution agreement, signing a non-prosecution agreement, and waiving prosecution in favor of civil penalties or civil or regulatory sanctions that may be available. The severity of misconduct, as well as the sanctions, will be considered when contemplating alternatives to prosecution.

A deferred prosecution agreement generally rests upon the filing of a formal charging document by the government, and the agreement is then filed with the appropriate court. In contrast, a non-prosecution agreement does not involve the filing of formal charges, and the parties maintain the agreement.[23] Whether a plea agreement, a deferred prosecution agreement, or a non-prosecution agreement is entered into, it should, to the greatest extent possible, include an agreed-upon statement of facts outlining the criminal conduct that forms the basis for the agreement, and a statement of relevant considerations that explains the Department's reasons for entering into the agreement. Relevant considerations may, include inter alia, the corporation's voluntary self-disclosure or any self-reporting to the Department, cooperation with the Department's investigation, and remedial efforts or lack thereof; the basis for and extent of cooperation credit, if any, that the corporation is receiving; the seriousness and pervasiveness of the criminal conduct; the corporation's history of misconduct; the state of the corporation's compliance program at the time of the underlying criminal conduct and at the time of the resolution; the reasons for imposing an independent compliance monitor or any other compliance undertaking, if applicable; other relevant factors; and any other key considerations related to the DOJ's decision.[24]

The DOJ further elaborates on these factors, emphasizing that the nature and severity of the crime, along with the potential harm to the public, are primary considerations. For conduct involving national and multinational corporations, it is essential to take into account any relevant federal, economic, tax, and criminal law enforcement policies. When evaluating widespread misconduct within a company, the most important factor is the behavior and role of management, as they shape the company's corporate culture and whether criminal conduct is discouraged or tacitly approved. Since a corporation can only act through natural persons and is responsible for the actions of individuals attributable to it, it may be appropriate to charge a corporation for even minor misconduct when the misconduct was widespread and committed by many employees, all employees in a particular role, or was condoned by senior management. However, imposing liability on a corporation, especially one with a strong compliance program, under a strict respondeat superior theory for a single isolated act of a rogue employee may not be appropriate. Prosecutors should also review the company's history of misconduct, including any past criminal, civil, and regulatory enforcement actions and resolutions, domestically or internationally. A non-exhaustive list of factors to be considered when assessing a corporation's history of misconduct includes:[25]

1. The amount of time that has elapsed since the prior criminal, civil, or regulatory action or resolution concluded, the duration of the conduct underlying the prior resolution, and whether the conduct at issue in the current investigation occurred before, at the same time, or after the conduct underlying the prior resolution;
2. Whether a prior action or resolution was criminal, civil, or regulatory, and whether it involved U.S. federal or state authorities or foreign authorities;
3. The seriousness and pervasiveness of the conduct underlying the prior action or resolution, and the role, if any, of senior management in that conduct;
4. Whether the conduct underlying the prior action or resolution was similar in nature to the conduct currently under investigation (including similar conduct prosecuted under different statutes), involved the same personnel, or shared the same root cause as the conduct currently under investigation;
5. The form and terms of a prior resolution, including any factual admissions made by the corporation;
6. Whether, during the conduct that is the subject of the current investigation, the corporation was serving a term of probation or was subject to supervision, monitorship, or other obligation imposed by prior resolutions;
7. Whether the conduct at issue in the prior and current matters reflects broader weaknesses in the corporation's compliance culture or practices;
8. Whether the prior action or resolution involved a corporate entity related to the corporation and the relationship between the related entity and the corporation, including whether the entities have common management or share compliance resources;
9. Whether the corporation under investigation operates in a highly regulated industry, and, if so, whether the corporation's history of regulatory actions is comparable to that of similarly situated companies in the industry; and
10. Whether the corporation voluntarily self-disclosed the conduct giving rise to the current matter or prior action(s) or resolution(s).

Cooperation is a mitigating factor. Failure to cooperate by a corporation is not taken as evidence of misconduct, unless the lack of cooperation involves criminal misconduct or demonstrates a consciousness of guilt, such as, for example, enticing perjury, making false statements, or refusing to comply with lawful discovery requests. Failure to cooperate does not automatically result in the filing of charges. Producing evidence relevant to assessing individual culpability should be prioritized. If the company is unable to identify all relevant individuals or provide complete factual information despite its good faith efforts to cooperate fully, the organization may still be eligible for cooperation credit. Where a company genuinely cannot gain access to specific evidence or is legally prohibited from disclosing it to the government, the company has the burden to explain the restrictions it is facing to the prosecutor.

In assessing a corporation's cooperation during a criminal investigation, prosecutors should consider the non-exhaustive factors listed, including inter alia: Timely disclosure of all relevant facts including those obtained during any internal company investigation, the identification of all individuals involved in or responsible for the misconduct at issue, regardless of their position, status, or seniority and all relevant facts relating to the misconduct and the involvement by those individuals; Proactive cooperation; Timely voluntary preservation, collection, and disclosure of relevant documents and information relating to their provenance; De-confliction of witness interviews and other investigative steps that a corporation takes as part of any internal investigation to prevent the company's investigation from conflicting or interfering with the DOJ's investigation; and, Where appropriate and possible, making corporate officers and employees possessing relevant information available for interviews by the Department.[26]

Compliance programs are established by corporate management to prevent and detect misconduct and to ensure that corporate activities are conducted in accordance with applicable criminal and civil laws, regulations, and rules. The existence of a compliance program is not sufficient to justify not charging a corporation for criminal misconduct undertaken by its officers, directors, employees, or agents. In some cases, the nature of the crime may warrant prosecution even if the organization does have a compliance program. The DOJ goes on to state that the adequacy of a corporation's compliance program, including its corporate culture, can significantly impact any resolution. Prosecutors, therefore, evaluate a corporate compliance program as a factor in determining, inter alia, whether to charge the corporation, the terms of a corporate resolution, and the need for an independent compliance monitor. Prosecutors should evaluate the corporation's commitment to fostering a strong culture of compliance at all levels of the company, as well as the adequacy and effectiveness of the corporation's compliance program, both at the time of the offense and at the time of a charging decision.[27]

Corporations are encouraged, as part of their compliance programs, to conduct internal investigations and to self-disclose discovered misconduct to the appropriate authorities. A voluntary self-disclosure in this case would occur only when a company discloses misconduct to the Department promptly and voluntarily, namely, where it has no preexisting obligation to do so. Voluntary self-disclosure policies should not include any aggravating factors if a corporation has met the requirements of the applicable policy, fully cooperated, and has remediated the criminal conduct in a timely and appropriate manner. In such cases, the DOJ will not impose an independent compliance monitor on a cooperating company that meets the requirements of the applicable voluntary self-disclosure policy and, at the time of resolution, demonstrates that it has implemented and tested an effective compliance program. The DOJ presumes not to prosecute a corporation that has voluntarily self-disclosed, fully cooperated, and promptly and properly fixed misconduct found through due diligence conducted just before or after a legitimate, good-faith acquisition of another corporation.[28]

Prosecutors also consider the collateral consequences of a corporate criminal conviction, including whether the likely punishment is appropriate given the nature and seriousness of the crime. For corporations, prosecutors may consider the potential substantial consequences to the corporation's employees, investors, pensioners, and customers, many of whom may have played no role in the criminal conduct, were unaware of it, were unable to prevent it, or were victimized by it. In addition, another factor considered is the potential for non-penal sanctions that may accompany a criminal charge, such as suspension or debarment from eligibility for government contracts or federally funded programs.[29]

When considering whether to enter into a deferred prosecution or non-prosecution agreement, the prosecutors should consider the interests of any victims or other individuals or entities who were significantly, even if indirectly, harmed by the criminal conduct.

According to the Crime Victims' Rights Act and the Attorney General Guidelines for Victim and Witness Assistance, prosecutors shall make best efforts to obtain the victim's views in advance of and about major case decisions such as voluntary dismissals, plea negotiations, non-prosecution agreements, deferred prosecution agreements, pretrial diversion agreements, plea agreements, agreements in favor of the release of the accused pending judicial proceedings, sentencing recommendations, and restitution. In addition, prosecutors should make best efforts to provide information and assistance to individuals or entities who may not fall within the statutory definition of a victim, but who were nevertheless significantly, even if indirectly, harmed by the criminal conduct, within available resources and to the extent reasonable, feasible, and appropriate. This includes consultation with prosecutors prior to entry into a non-prosecution agreement, deferred prosecution agreement, pretrial diversion agreement, or plea agreement, as well as any agreement that would require an offender to pay restitution or other compensation to, or for the benefit of, the significantly harmed persons or entities.[30]

When the prosecutor decides to prosecute the corporation, the organization should be charged with the most serious, readily provable offense(s) consistent with the nature of the defendant's misconduct and that is likely to result in a sustainable conviction.

Prosecutors may enter into plea agreements with corporations for the same reasons and under the same constraints applicable to plea agreements with natural persons. When negotiating plea agreements with corporations, prosecutors should generally seek a plea to an appropriate offense. The terms of the plea agreement should include provisions that ensure punishment, deterrence, rehabilitation, and compliance with the agreement in the corporate context. In other words, a corporation should, inter alia, generally be required to plead guilty to the most serious and readily provable offense charged. Any negotiated departures or variances from the advisory Sentencing Guidelines must be justifiable and must be disclosed to the sentencing court. It is crucial that a corporation be aware that pleading guilty to criminal charges is an admission of guilt and not merely a resolution of a problem that will allow it to return to normal operations. A corporate plea agreement should also include provisions recognizing the separate legal identity of the corporation and ensuring that the principles of punishment, deterrence, and rehabilitation are met. For a corporation, punishment and deterrence are generally in the form of substantial fines, mandatory restitution, and institution of appropriate compliance measures, including, if necessary, continued judicial oversight or the use of special masters or corporate monitors. In addition, where the company is a government contractor, permanent or temporary debarment may be appropriate. Another factor that a prosecutor should consider in determining whether to enter into a plea agreement is whether the corporation is seeking immunity for its employees and officers or whether the corporation is willing to cooperate in the investigation of culpable individuals. As rehabilitation entails no future wrongdoing, the organization may be required to implement a compliance program or to reform an existing one as a condition of probation. When the company agrees to cooperate as part of a plea agreement, the corporation will be requested to disclose relevant factual information and documents, make employees and agents available for debriefing, file appropriate certified financial statements, agree to governmental or third-party audits, and take any other required steps to ensure the full scope of the corporate wrongdoing is disclosed.[31]

Prosecutors should carefully assess the need for the imposition of a monitor on a case-by-case basis, without applying any presumption for or against such imposition by considering the potential benefits that employing a monitor may have for the corporation and the public, and whether the costs of a monitor and its impact on the company's operations substantially outweigh the potential benefits of a monitor. Some of the factors prosecutors consider are:[32]

1. Whether the corporation voluntarily self-disclosed the underlying misconduct in a manner that satisfies the particular DOJ component's voluntary self-disclosure policy;
2. Whether, at the time of the resolution and after a thorough risk assessment, the corporation has implemented an effective compliance program and sufficient internal controls to detect and prevent similar misconduct in the future;
3. Whether, at the time of the resolution, the corporation has adequately tested its compliance program and internal controls to demonstrate that they would likely detect and prevent similar misconduct in the future;
4. Whether the underlying criminal conduct was long-lasting or pervasive across the business organization or was approved, facilitated, or ignored by senior management, executives, or directors (including by means of a corporate culture that tolerated risky behavior or misconduct, or did not encourage open discussion and reporting of possible risks and concerns);
5. Whether the underlying criminal conduct involved the exploitation of an inadequate compliance program or system of internal controls;
6. Whether the underlying criminal conduct involved active participation of compliance personnel or the failure of compliance personnel to appropriately escalate or respond to red flags;
7. Whether the corporation took adequate investigative or remedial measures to address the underlying criminal conduct, including, where appropriate, the termination of business relationships and practices that contributed to the criminal conduct, and discipline or termination of personnel involved, including with respect to those with supervisory, management, or oversight responsibilities for the misconduct;

8. Whether, at the time of the resolution, the corporation's risk profile has substantially changed, such that the risk of recurrence of the misconduct is minimal or nonexistent;
9. Whether the corporation faces any unique risks or compliance challenges, including with respect to the particular region or business sector in which the corporation operates or the nature of the corporation's customers; and
10. Whether and the extent to which the corporation is subject to oversight from industry regulators or is receiving a monitor from another domestic or foreign enforcement authority or regulator.

The DOJ highlights that a monitor should be imposed where there is a demonstrated need for, and a clear benefit to be derived from, a monitorship, such as, for example, where a corporation's compliance program and controls are untested, ineffective, inadequately resourced, or not fully implemented at the time of a resolution. Any agreement imposing a monitorship, including a deferred prosecution agreement, a non-prosecution agreement, or a guilty plea, should include details outlining the reasons for requiring a monitor. The monitor's mandate and scope of authority should be clearly specified, along with well-defined duties and responsibilities.[33]

Since 2000, the U.S. Department of Justice has prosecuted numerous companies for a range of criminal activities, including fraud, bribery, environmental crimes, occupational safety violations, antitrust violations, and money laundering, with only a few of these cases resulting in the prosecution of individuals involved in the criminal acts.[34] The year 2000 had the highest number of federal prosecutions of corporations over the last 25 years, with 304 prosecutions, followed by a steady decrease to 90 prosecutions in 2021. From 2021, when President Biden took office, the numbers have started increasing to 99 prosecutions in 2022 and 113 in 2023. In 2022, 81.4% of the organizations prosecuted employed fewer than 50 workers, and 7.0% employed 1,000 employees or more. In 2023, approximately 76% had fewer than 50 employees, and about 12% had 1,000 employees or more. This seems to be a common tendency as it is reported that approximately 70% of the 4,946 corporations the DOJ prosecuted between 1992 and 2021 were small businesses having less than 50 employees, with only about 6% employing 1,000 or more people.[35]

Federal practice and the priorities of the Department of Justice change under a new presidential administration. In 2015, the DOJ announced its focus on individual accountability in corporate prosecution cases and adopted the so-called Yates Memorandum. In 2017 and 2018, several changes made by the DOJ were designed to reduce the impact of criminal prosecutions. The revisions included stepping away from the Yates Memorandum, which focused on individual prosecutions, statements discouraging the use of corporate monitors, and policies aimed at limiting the piling on of corporate fines. In 2021, the Biden Administration announced further changes to the guidelines for prosecuting organizations. This included, inter alia, restoring the Yates Memorandum guidance that to be eligible for cooperation credit, a company must provide non-privileged information about all individuals involved in misconduct, clarifying that a corporate monitor may be appropriate, and that a company's entire criminal, civil, and regulatory record should be relevant. The DOJ issued policies aimed at providing incentives for corporations to voluntarily self-report, fully cooperate, and implement remedial actions. In 2017, the DOJ stated that where an enforcement action was warranted, despite voluntary self-disclosure, for actions such as pervasive misconduct, executive management involvement, or substantial resulting profits, any company that takes such steps would not be prosecuted. It is also committed to recommending that any applicable fine be reduced by 50% and that, if the company had an effective compliance program, a monitor would not be appointed. In 2018, the DOJ clarified that this policy would be nonbinding for all criminal cases.

DOJ policies issued in February 2017, April 2019, and June 2020 encouraged companies to develop more robust compliance programs. The policies aimed to provide enhanced transparency regarding the DOJ's expectations and evaluation of compliance programs, and to offer corporations an incentive and opportunity to improve their programs. The evaluation of such programs was an important factor in the DOJ's decision whether to prosecute a business organization, and the amount, if any, of any monetary penalty to be imposed. In the June 2020 update to its guidance, "Evaluation of Corporate Compliance Programs," the DOJ strongly encouraged prosecutors to assess the efficacy of compliance regimes by considering whether companies have identified and directed their resources to the highest risk areas, tested the effectiveness of their systems by timely and effectively monitoring relevant data sources, and continuously revised and improved their systems in light of "lessons learned."[36]

Clearly, prosecution guidelines and the priorities of the DOJ with respect to prosecuting corporations and holding them accountable for criminal acts and misdeeds are variable and often change with each presidential administration's focus and approach toward prosecuting corporations.

5.4.5.1 Boeing

The legal recourse and ramifications for Boeing as a legal entity, following the Boeing 737 MAX accidents and the Alaska Airlines Flight 1282 incident, have elicited considerable criticism and highlighted several concerns that primarily revolve around two key issues. The first is the political will prevalent at that time in holding large corporations guilty based on the notion that some corporations are "Too Big to Jail," and the plea agreements reached when prosecuting large corporations.

5.4.5.1.1 Prosecuting Large Corporations

Individuals committing criminal acts are prosecuted and, if found guilty, face the consequences and corresponding punishments attributed to their criminal conduct in accordance with the applicable law by the relevant courts having jurisdiction to do so. However, when one considers the prosecution and punishment of corporations, significant differences emerge.

From 2000, several companies were prosecuted for their criminal conduct, including fraud, bribery, environmental crime, occupational safety violations, antitrust, and money laundering by the Department of Justice. Between 2001 and 2014, only 34% of the 306 cases in which federal prosecutors reached negotiated plea agreements with corporate wrongdoers involved individuals prosecuted, resulting in a total of 414 individuals prosecuted. Even though corporate plea agreements have increased since 2001, there is no major increase in the total number of individuals given prison sentences. Additionally, defendants who plead guilty to or are convicted of corporate crimes receive prison sentences less frequently and serve less time in jail than defendants involved in non-corporate crimes. This has resulted in the notion that the law allows, and the government permits, senior managers to pay a fine by using shareholder assets to avoid criminal prosecution and/or prison sentences by means of reaching plea agreements.[37]

In November 2012, BP Exploration and Production Inc. (BP) agreed to plead guilty to felony manslaughter, environmental crimes, and obstruction of Congress after the 2010 Deepwater Horizon disaster that killed 11 people and caused the most significant environmental disaster in U.S. history. The charges, which include 11 counts of felony manslaughter, one count of felony obstruction of Congress, and violations of the Clean Water Act and the Migratory Bird Treaty Act, were filed against BP in the U.S. District Court for the Eastern District of Louisiana. BP reached a plea agreement with the DOJ, where it agreed to plead guilty to the charges and pay a record $4 billion in criminal fines and penalties for its conduct. The guilty plea agreement also included BP agreeing to retain a process safety and risk management monitor, an independent auditor to oversee BP's process safety, risk management, and drilling equipment maintenance with respect to deepwater drilling in the Gulf of Mexico, and to retain an ethics monitor to improve BP's code of conduct.[38]

The Attorney General at that time said,

> The $4 billion in penalties and fines is the single largest criminal resolution in the history of the United States and constitutes a major achievement toward fulfilling a promise that the Justice Department made nearly two years ago to respond to the consequences of this epic environmental disaster and seek justice on behalf of its victims.

"The explosion of the rig was a disaster that resulted from BP's culture of privileging profit over prudence." "We hope that BP's acknowledgment of its misconduct – through its agreement to plead guilty to 11 counts of felony manslaughter brings some measure of justice to the family members of the people who died onboard the rig."[39]

In addition to the criminal charges filed against BP, two of the most senior-ranking BP supervisors onboard the Deepwater Horizon on 20 April 2010 were each criminally charged with 11 felony counts of seaman's manslaughter, 11 felony counts of involuntary manslaughter, and one violation of the Clean Water Act resulting from their alleged negligent and grossly negligent conduct. Penalties include a maximum of 10 years imprisonment on each seaman's manslaughter count, up to eight years on each involuntary manslaughter count, and up to one year in prison on the Clean Water Act count. A third individual, a former BP executive who served as a Deputy Incident Commander and BP's second-highest ranking representative, was charged with obstruction of Congress and making false statements to law enforcement officials. The maximum penalty is five years imprisonment on each count.[40] The seaman's manslaughter charges were dropped in March 2015,[41] and in December, federal prosecutors dropped the involuntary manslaughter charges.[42] One of the most senior officials pled guilty to the one remaining charge, a Clean Water Act misdemeanor, and the other went to trial and was acquitted of this misdemeanor.[43]

In another high-profile case, Volkswagen AG (VW) was charged with three felony counts, namely: "(i) conspiracy to defraud the United States, engage in wire fraud, and violate the Clean Air Act; (ii) obstruction of justice; and (iii) importation of merchandise by means of false statements." In January 2017, VW agreed to a plea agreement to resolve the criminal charges. In the Federal U.S. District Court of the Eastern District of Michigan, VW pleaded guilty, first, to participating in a conspiracy to defraud the US and the company's U.S. customers and to violate the Clean Air Act by lying and misleading customers about whether certain VW, Audi, and Porsche diesel vehicles complied with U.S. emissions standards, using cheating software to circumvent the U.S. testing process, and concealing material facts about its cheating from U.S. regulators. Secondly, it pleaded guilty to obstruction of justice for destroying documents related to the scheme and, thirdly, to importing these cars into the United States with false statements regarding the vehicles' compliance with emissions limits.[44] In addition, six current and former senior VW executives were also charged with wire fraud for their roles in the scheme, alleging that they had engaged in a 10-year conspiracy to cheat U.S. emissions tests and then cover up the excess emissions even when regulators questioned irregularities.[45] VW agreed to pay a $2.8 billion criminal fine for its scheme to sell approximately 590,000 diesel vehicles in the U.S. by using a defeat device to cheat on mandatory emissions tests, and lying and obstructing justice to further the scheme. It also agreed to resolve the separate civil environmental, customs, and financial claims against the company by paying $1.5 billion in civil penalties.[46]

A further issue to consider is whether the practice of corporations paying a fine for their criminal actions is an adequate and effective deterrent to criminal conduct and whether the government and prosecutors should do more to hold large corporations accountable for crimes they have committed. One suggestion provided by Professor Brandon L. Garrett is for Congress to provide additional investigative resources so that federal prosecutors can more aptly deal with large companies. For example, in the 1980s, Congress passed legislation providing tens of millions of dollars to investigate and prosecute banking crimes, and also extended the statute of limitations for bank fraud, providing prosecutors with additional time to investigate and bring charges. When the former executives of Enron were prosecuted, the defense of Kenneth Lay cost $25 million, and that of Jeffrey Skilling cost $70 million. Prof. Garrett further submits that judges should have a stronger role in evaluating whether internal compliance measures, agreed upon in a plea agreement, are effective in practice, and that large corporations should be required to issue an apology for their conduct.[47]

5.4.5.1.2 Too Big To Go To Jail (TBTJ)

Even though several large corporations, including AIG, Google, Halliburton, HSBC, JPMorgan, KPMG, Merrill Lynch, and Pfizer, have been prosecuted, there is a notion that some companies are "too big to jail." The "Too Big to Jail" (TBTGJ) notion focuses on what happens when criminal charges are brought against a major company in the United States. In most cases, when a corporation is considered too economically essential to collapse, plea agreements are agreed to, which, in effect, allow the corporation to avoid the consequences of a criminal conviction. This term was commonly used after the financial crisis to describe the fear that the biggest banks were so critical to the American and global economy that the government had no choice but to prevent them from totally collapsing. In the book "Too Big to Jail: How Prosecutors Compromise with Corporations," law professor Brandon L. Garrett examines this notion with respect to large corporations, including banks, pharmaceutical companies, oil and gas companies, and consulting companies. Notably, he also argues that the concern "extends to whether officers and employees are held accountable; they can literally be put in jail."[48]

Garrett also argues that current-day prosecutors are transforming their approach to take legal action against corporate wrongdoers as they are more readily agreeing to deferred prosecution agreements, which often allow many corporations to avoid a conviction but usually require hefty fines and the imposition of an independent monitor to assist in improving and reforming the organization's corporate culture and governance. Many such plea agreements include the requirement of having independent monitors to supervise compliance and have a short timeframe, often two years, within which to conduct the monitoring and implement the change. More importantly, in most cases, there is no judge tasked with reviewing the monitor's progress or checking the corporation's compliance with the monitor's reforms.[49]

When an organization is deemed to be TBTJ, the government acknowledges that the defendant company's potential failure is so politically unjustifiable that prosecutors must reduce the severity of the punishment for the organization's criminal conduct. Since the 2008 financial crisis, organizations have regularly settled serious criminal charges with plea agreements that protect their profitability. In addition, their executives and senior managers also avoid accountability for allegedly fraudulent conduct. For example, in March 2013, there were Senate Judiciary Committee hearings on the DOJ's deferred prosecution agreement with the global bank HSBC for facilitating money laundering by Mexican drug cartels and other similar organizations. The agreement, which resulted in the bank being fined $1.92 billion, with no individuals prosecuted, drew much criticism.[50] The then Attorney General acknowledged that the threat of economic distress constrains DOJ prosecutors investigating the crimes of global banks. He said,

> I am concerned that the size of some of these institutions becomes so large that it does become difficult for us to prosecute them when we are hit with indications that if we do prosecute—if we do bring a criminal charge—it will have a negative impact on the national economy, perhaps even the world economy. I think that is a function of the fact that some of these institutions have become too large . . . . I think it has an inhibiting influence, impact on our ability to bring resolutions that I think would be more appropriate.[51]

5.4.5.2 Boeing Inc.

Boeing goes back to 1910 when, on 10 March, William Boeing bought a shipyard on the Duwamish River in Seattle. The facility later became his first airplane factory.[52] Today, Boeing has a strong international presence and is now one of the largest and most important companies in the United States and one of the world's two leading manufacturers of large commercial jets. Boeing is organized into three business units: Commercial Airplanes; Defense, Space & Security; and Global Services. It employs over 170,000 people across the United States and in more than 65 countries. It develops, manufactures, and services commercial airplanes, defense products, and space systems for customers in more than 150 countries.[53] Boeing's revenue (net income obtained from the amount of money received from customers in exchange for the sales of goods or services minus costs and expenses), for the quarter ending 30 September 2024, saw a decrease of 1.46% year-over-year to reach $17.840B. Its annual revenue (rounded up) for the twelve months ending 30 September 2024 was $73B. In 2023 its annual revenue was $78B. In 2022 it was $66.6B and in 2021 it was $62B. In 2020, it was $58B, with $76.5B in 2019 and $101B in 2018.[54]

Commercial aircraft manufactured by Boeing include the 737, 767, 777, and 787, as well as the Boeing Business Jet range. New aircraft development and manufacture include the 737 MAX and the 777X. Approximately half the world's aircraft fleet is Boeing aircraft, with over 10,000 commercial jets in service worldwide, and about 90% of global cargo is carried onboard Boeing planes. Regarding Defense, Space & Security, its broad portfolio includes the KC-46 aerial refueling aircraft, based on the Boeing 767 commercial airplane; the AH-64 Apache helicopter; the 702 family of satellites; the CST-100 Starliner spacecraft; and the autonomous Echo Voyager. As part of Boeing's Global Services, it provides aftermarket support for mixed fleets worldwide. It delivers innovative and comprehensive service solutions for commercial, defense, and space customers, regardless of the equipment's original manufacturer.

Boeing is ranked among the top five US defense contractors and has a substantial involvement in government contracting. Its involvement in defense, space, and security highlights the company's importance to national interests. Some of Boeing's 2024 contracts include a $6.9 billion contract with the U.S. Air Force to manufacture and deliver small diameter bombs to the U.S., Japan, Bulgaria, and Ukraine military; a potential $7.48 billion contract from the Air Force for Joint Direct Attack Munitions, spares, repair, and technical support services; and Boeing's joint venture with Lockheed Martin for a potential $1.1 billion contract with the U.S. Space Force.[55] In December 2024, Boeing secured a $450 million contract to incorporate the production of command and control capabilities for the F-15 Japan Super Interceptor Program. The contract is expected to be completed by February 2030.[56]

The overview of Boeing as a separate legal entity highlights the company's growth, the financial impact of the two 737 MAX-8 accidents, which caused a sharp drop in revenue from 2018 to 2019, and its steady recovery thereafter. In addition, the company's importance to the US and global economy is evident. A glimpse at the scale, amount, and time span of some of its existing and potential contracts reveals the domino effect that would occur if such a company were to collapse. Having said that, however, the authors do not consider that such companies, termed Too Big To Jail (TBTJ), should not go to trial to face accountability for criminal crimes that can be proved and attributed to them in accordance with the prevailing law. We believe that this would better serve justice and the society's need for accountability, and also foster better trust in the judicial process.

The investigations by the U.S. Department of Justice into the two 737 MAX accidents resulted in Boeing being charged with one count of conspiracy to defraud regulators. The subsequent plea agreement, reached in 2021, required Boeing to avoid prosecution on the criminal fraud conspiracy charge if it paid a $2.5 billion settlement fine and underwent a three-year probation period, which included a compliance and ethics program. Days before the three-year probation period was to expire, the events of the Alaska Airlines incident led to the Department of Justice reopening the case. The DOJ had to decide whether to accept the imposition of a fine, which would, on the one hand, have a crippling effect on one of America's largest employers, resulting in extreme financial disruption and job loss, and on the other, provide justice for the deceased and their relatives. In the end, another agreement was reached and, in July 2024, Boeing agreed to plead guilty to the original charge, pay an additional $243.6 million penalty, and submit to independent monitoring for three years.

A criminal conviction could potentially jeopardize Boeing's status as a federal contractor. However, any potential impact, if any, of the guilty plea between Boeing and the U.S. government appears to be minimal, as evidenced by the various multi-billion-dollar long-term contracts and existing agreements. In 2006, the Air Force cited "compelling national interest" when it decided to let Boeing continue competing for contracts after it had paid a US$615 million fine to settle criminal and civil charges, including that it used information stolen from a competitor to win a space-launch contract.[57] It seems, therefore, that some corporations are too big to fail because the government is far too reliant on them.[58]

Considering the scale, size, and revenue of Boeing, the amount of the fine imposed in both the plea agreements raises questions about why the DOJ did not impose steeper penalties. Perhaps the increased competition Boeing is facing from rival manufacturers was considered. The Chinese state-backed manufacturer Comac is producing the C919 passenger jet, which started commercial flights in May 2023, and is a potential rival to the 737 Max and Airbus A320 Neo fleets.[59]

Despite the fines imposed and Boeing's guilty plea, the bigger questions are whether the DOJ should have taken action against individual executives and whether it has done enough to apportion accountability to the guilty parties and deter future wrongdoing. It is essential that justice is not only said to be done but must also be seen to be done. No one is above the law, and the public should have confidence in the legal system, knowing that parties who have committed a crime, whether large corporations or individual executives, should be held legally liable and accountable for their criminal conduct.[60]

An interesting development is that in December 2024, Judge O'Connor rejected Boeing's agreement to plead guilty to fraud. This could, in effect, result in appealing the judge's rejection of the plea deal or submitting another renegotiated agreement to the court for approval. Boeing and the DOJ have been given 30 days to notify the court of how they plan to proceed. Under the agreement, the DOJ would choose six candidates to serve as a monitor, and Boeing had the option to strike one of them. The judge, in his ruling, states that he was concerned that Boeing would decide which one to strike "in a discriminatory manner and with racial considerations." He referred to Boeing's policies, which commit to goals such as adequate representation of Black people in company leadership, and criticized the diversity, equity and inclusion (DEI) policies at Boeing and the Justice Department as "against the public interest." He said that "The parties' DEI efforts only serve to undermine this confidence in the government and Boeing's anti-fraud efforts," and "In a case of this magnitude, it is in the utmost interest of justice that the public is confident this monitor selection is done based solely on competency."[61]

CONCLUSION: COMPARISON OF THE FRENCH AND THE U.S. LEGAL SYSTEM

There are notable key differences in the legal systems of France and the USA and in the legal philosophies of both countries, which have an impact on how laws are created, interpreted, and applied.[62] As French legal philosophy has its roots in Roman law and is influenced by the Napoleonic Code, it emphasizes codified laws. The civil law tradition places a stronger emphasis on statutes as the primary source of law. The USA legal philosophy stems from a common law system based on case law and the doctrine of judicial precedent (stare decisis), where previously established points of law must be applied to future cases with materially the same facts. This provides a system where laws are consistently applied and allows for the predictable application of the law. In France, previous court decisions have only persuasive authority and do not bind lower courts; therefore, judges have more flexibility in interpreting laws. In France, as in the UK and other parliamentary systems, there is less separation between the executive and legislative branches than in countries like the USA.[63]

Regarding aviation accidents, a notable difference, as mentioned earlier, is that a criminal investigation is automatically launched after an aviation accident, often resulting in criminal charges. In contrast, in the USA, it is very rare for aviation professionals to be charged with manslaughter or for aviation organizations to face corporate manslaughter charges. The powers that judicial authorities have when conducting investigations in France are wider, as they generally have control of the accident wreckage and pertinent evidence. French courts have the jurisdiction to hear aviation accident cases even if there is only one plaintiff, defendant, or a defendant's insurer who is a French citizen. In addition, under French law, any person who has been harmed by an offense can file a complaint asking the criminal prosecutor to investigate the offense. If, within three months there is no investigation or if the prosecutor does not commence an investigation, that person can then file a complaint with civil action, which overrides a filing without follow-up or a lack of response from the public prosecutor, and allows the victim of an offense to refer the matter to an investigating judge to open a judicial investigation to establish whether or not an offense exists and to determine the wrongdoers. This procedure allows the victim to get compensatory damages from the defendant(s) if they are found guilty by the criminal courts. In France, judges can appoint an expert to gather evidence from any local or international third party and provide a report before charges are filed. Judges are also assisted by the "special aviation police," namely the Gendarmerie des Transports Aériens, who have the power to apprehend witnesses and search premises.[64] In the USA, the NTSB investigator in charge appoints parties who are specialized in their area of expertise, which always includes an FAA representative, to assist. No legal personnel or judiciary are involved, unless the Attorney General, in consultation with the NTSB Chairperson, determines that an intentional criminal act is involved. Only factual portions of the final NTSB report can be admitted into a court of law; the final report in its entirety should not be introduced as evidence in litigation.

NOTES

1. Hodgson, J. and Soubise, L. "Prosecution in France," Oxford Academic, November 2016. Available at https://academic.oup.com/edited-volume/41333/chapter/352363260.
2. Vergnolle, S., "Understanding the French criminal justice system as a tool for reforming international legal cooperation and cross-border data requests," November 2016. Available at https://hal.science/hal-03605105v1/document.
3. Ibid.
4. Article L6223-1and Article L6232-10 of the French Code of Transport.
5. Laville de la Plaigne, G., and Samaille, "Aviation laws and regulations-France, M., Clyde & Co, LLP. ICLG, 7 March 2025." Available at https://iclg.com/practice-areas/aviation-laws-and-regulations/france.
6. Supplement to Annex 13, Aircraft Accident and Incident Investigation, Ninth Edition, 2003. Available at: ICAO Available http://www.ntsb.gov/Events/symp_rec/proceedings/May_4/SessionIII/Pres_frostell/index.htm.
7. Cadain, A., "Aviation liability in France," Kennedys, 3 December 2019. Available at https://www.lexology.com/library/detail.aspx?g=ee94cc52-2bd0-45fd-991b-7f7199ded81b.
8. Article 3 and Article 2 of the Code of Criminal Procedure, cited in Cadain, A., "Aviation liability in France," Kennedys, 3 December 2019. Available at https://www.lexology.com/library/detail.aspx?g=ee94cc52-2bd0-45fd 991b-7f7199ded81b.
9. *BEA Final Report.* 2004 Translation f-sc000725a, Comments from the UK Accredited Representative. Available at http://www.bea-fr.org/docspa/2000/f-sc000725a/pdf/f-sc000725a.pdf [accessed: 28 October 2005].
10. FR-MoU-SIA-Justice-FR, Accord Prealable Relatif Aux Enquettes De Securite Aerienne of 16 September 2014. Available http://www.icao.int/sites/default/files/safety/airnavigation/AIG/Protocols/FR-MoU-SIA-Justice-FR.pdf.
11. Clark, N., "French court overturns convictions in Concorde crash," The New York Time, 29 November 2012. Available at http://www.nytimes.com/2012/11/30/business/global/french-court-overturns-conviction-in-concorde-crash.html?_r=0.
12. VOR/DME is a non-precision approach where the pilot-in-command is in charge of the descent.
13. BEA, Report number: BEA F-ED920120, "Official report into the accident on 20 January 1992 near Mont Sainte-Odile (Bas-Rhin) of the AIRBUS A320 registered F-GGED operated by Air Inter," 26 November 1993. Available https://asn.flightsafety.org/reports/1992/19920120_A320_F-GGED.pdf.

14. GPWS – Ground Proximity Warning System.
15. Reilhac, G., "Airbus and Air France held liable for 1992 crash," 10 August 2007. Available at https://www.reuters.com/article/world/airbus-and-air-france-held-liable-for-1992-crash-idUSL07766914/.
16. Aziz Rahman, A., "Airbus, international cooperation and the rise of Deferred Prosecution Agreements," International Bar Association. Available at https://www.ibanet.org/article/4835DC62-76DB-46EF-A7ED-E78FA02F4826.
17. Blanco, M., et al., "Airbus' sky high settlement – Focus on global reach and collaboration in anti-corruption prosecutions," Norton Rose Fulbright, 13 February 2020. Available at https://www.nortonrosefulbright.com/en-id/knowledge/publications/5a4118df/airbus-skyhigh-settlement-focus-on-global-reach-and-collaboration-in-anti-corruption-prosecutions.
18. Ibid.
19. US Department of Justice, "Airbus agrees to pay over $3.9 billion in global penalties to resolve foreign bribery and ITAR case," 31 January 2020, updated 6 February 2025. Available at https://www.justice.gov/archives/opa/pr/airbus-agrees-pay-over-39-billion-global-penalties-resolve-foreign-bribery-and-itar-case.
20. Ibid.
21. Ibid.
22. Department of Justice, Justice Manual, Title 9: Criminal, 9-28.200 – General Considerations of Corporate Liability, updated March 2023. Available at https://www.justice.gov/jm/jm-9-28000-principles-federal-prosecution-business-organizations.
23. Op cit., Doyle, C.
24. Department of Justice, Justice Manual, Title 9: Criminal, 9-28.200 – General Considerations of Corporate Liability.
25. Ibid., Department of Justice, Justice Manual, Title 9: Criminal, 9-28. 9-28.600 - The Corporation's History of Misconduct.
26. Ibid., Department of Justice, Justice Manual, Title 9: Criminal, 9-28.700 - The Value of Cooperation.
27. Ibid., Department of Justice, Justice Manual, Title 9: Criminal, 9-28.800 - Corporate Compliance Programs.
28. Ibid., Department of Justice, Justice Manual, Title 9: Criminal, 9-28.900 - Voluntary Self-Disclosures.
29. Ibid., Department of Justice, Justice Manual, Title 9: Criminal, 9-28.1100 - Collateral Consequences.
30. Ibid., Department of Justice, Justice Manual, Title 9: Criminal, 9-28.1400 - Interests of the Victims and Others Significantly Harmed.
31. Ibid., Department of Justice, Justice Manual, Title 9: Criminal 9-28.1600 - Plea Agreements with Corporations.
32. Ibid., Department of Justice, Justice Manual, Title 9: Criminal 9-28.1700 - Use of Independent Compliance Monitors in Corporate Resolutions.
33. Ibid.
34. Garrett, B.L., *The Corporate Criminal as Scapegoat*, 101 Va. L. Rev. 1789, 1802 (2015).
35. Corbett, J., "Corporate prosecutions up under Biden, says watchdog, but not nearly enough," 25 March 2024. Available at https://www.commondreams.org/news/corporate-prosecution.
36. Ibid.
37. Werle, N., "Prosecuting corporate crime when firms are too big to jail: Investigation, deterrence, and judicial review," Yale Law Journal, 2019. Available at www.yalelawjournal.org/pdf/Werle_6rys3t3n.pdf.

38. US Department of Justice, "BP exploration and production inc. Agrees to plead guilty to felony manslaughter, environmental crimes and obstruction of congress surrounding deepwater horizon incident," 15 November 2012, Updated 8 October 2014. Available at https://www.justice.gov/opa/pr/bp-exploration-and-production-inc-agrees-plead-guilty-felony-manslaughter-environmental#:~:text=(BP)%20has%20agreed%20to%20plead,environmental%20disaster%20in%20U.S.%20history%2C.
39. Ibid.
40. Ibid.
41. Captain, C., "Manslaughter charges dropped for two BP employees," 1 March 2015. Available at https://forum.gcaptain.com/t/manslaughter-charges-dropped-for-two-bp-employees/14397.
42. Pavlo, W., "Two years after ruling, BP engineer still carries burden of prosecution," 8 January 2018, updated 14 April 2022. Available at https://www.forbes.com/sites/walterpavlo/2018/01/08/two-years-after-ruling-bp-engineer-still-carries-burden-of prosecution/#:~:text=Vidrine%20would%20eventually%20plead%20guilty,to%20trial%20and%20was%20acquitted.
43. Ibid.
44. US Department of Justice, "Volkswagen AG pleads guilty in connection with conspiracy to cheat U.S. emissions tests," 10 March 2017. Available at https://www.justice.gov/opa/pr/volkswagen-ag-pleads-guilty-connection-conspiracy-cheat-us-emissions-tests.
45. Shepardson, D., "U.S. indicts six as Volkswagen agrees to $4.3 billion diesel settlement," Reuters, 12 January 2017. Available at https://www.reuters.com/article/business/us-indicts-six-as-volkswagen-agrees-to-43-billion-diesel-settlement-idUSKBN14V1T0/.
46. US Department of Justice, "Volkswagen AG agrees to plead guilty and pay $4.3 billion in criminal and civil penalties; six Volkswagen executives and employees are indicted in connection with conspiracy to cheat U.S. emissions tests," 11 January 2017. Available at https://www.justice.gov/opa/pr/volkswagen-ag-agrees-plead-guilty-and-pay-43-billion-criminal-and-civil-penalties-six.
47. Eisen, L.B., "Too big to jail: How prosecutors compromise with corporations," 18 December 2014. Available at https://www.brennancenter.org/our-work/analysis-opinion/too-big-jail-how-prosecutors-compromise-corporations.
48. Ibid.
49. Ibid.
50. Werle, N., "Prosecuting corporate crime when firms are too big to jail: Investigation, deterrence, and judicial review," Yale Law Journal, 2019. Available at www.yalelawjournal.org/pdf/Werle_6rys3t3n.pdf.
51. Ibid.
52. Boeing, "Boeing's chronology," 2024. Available at www.boeing.com/content/dam/boeing/boeingdotcom/history/pdf/Boeing-Chronology.pdf.
53. Boeing, "Boeing in brief," 2024. Available at https://www.boeing.com/company/general-info#overview.
54. BA Microtrends, "Boeing revenue 2010–2024," BA, 2024. Available at https://www.macrotrends.net/stocks/charts/BA/boeing/revenue#google_vignette.
55. Myatt, S., "Top 10 US government contractors 2024," 8 October 2024. Available at https://executivebiz.com/articles/top-10-government-contractors-2024/.
56. Zacks Equity Research, "Boeing clinches a $450M contract to support the F-15 JSI program," 12 December 2024. Available at https://www.nasdaq.com/articles/boeing-clinches-450m-contract-support-f-15-jsi-program.

57. Koenig, D., and Richer, A.D., "Boeing to plead guilty to criminal fraud charge over 737 Max crashes," The Associated Press, 8 July 2024. Available at https://globalnews.ca/news/10610077/boeing-guilty-plea-737-max-crashes-fraud/#:%7E:text=The%20Air%20Force%20cited%20%E2%80%9Ccompelling,win%20a%20space%2Dlaunch%20contract.
58. Bhardwaj, A., "Boeing's fraud case shows that some businesses are still too big to fail," 10 July 2024. Available at https://theconversation.com/boeings-fraud-case-shows-that-some-businesses-are-still-too-big-to-fail-234328.
59. Sherman, N., and Leggett, T., "What's the right punishment for 'too big to fail' Boeing?" BBC, 8 July 2024. Available at https://www.bbc.com/news/articles/c6p2jegl4r9o.
60. Bhardwaj, A., op. cit.
61. IRF, "US judge rejects Boeing 737 MAX accord over diversity policies," 5 December 2024. Available at https://www.rfi.fr/en/international-news/20241205-us-judge-rejects-boeing-737-max-accord-over-diversity-policies.
62. France Tax Law, "Introduction to the French legal system: Understanding the basics," 12 March 2024. Available at https://www.francetaxlaw.com/news/introduction-to-the-french-legal-system/.
63. Ibid.
64. Solomon, E.D., and Relles, D.L., "Criminalization of air disasters: What goal, if any," Journal of Air Law and Commerce, Volume 76, Issue 3 Article 1. Available at https://core.ac.uk.

6 The State of Play

6.1 INTRODUCTION

Financial, technical, and human resources, as well as the limitations of the technical investigation, may pose constraints that can adversely affect the outcome of the technical, safety aviation accident investigation conducted in accordance with Annex 13. This may be more evident in smaller countries having limited resources and the technical and financial ability to undertake a large-scale, complex air accident investigation. This difficulty is evident within the EU, where small EU Member States with limited experience in aviation accidents and limited technical, financial, and human resources to conduct a major accident investigation have collaboration agreements with other Accident Investigation Branches in the form of memoranda of cooperation for mutual assistance to overcome some of the difficulties. In addition to potential internal limitations of some accident investigation bodies conducting complex investigations, other factors, such as external pressures, the media, public demand for justice, financial interests, and political influence, may be exerted in some form or another during the technical investigations.

In the preceding chapters, we discussed the complexities and inconsistencies regarding the protection and admissibility of safety data, such as the CVR transcripts, flight data recorder information, and the final accident investigation report as evidence in court. Additionally, our analysis of the legal approach to criminalizing aviation professionals and organizations following aviation accidents in different jurisdictions reveals several significant differences in how aviation professionals and corporations involved in aviation accidents are prosecuted and held criminally accountable. This highlights the need for a forum with a uniform set of rules and procedures specifically designed to address the complexities of aviation accidents and serious incidents, ensuring that trials of aviation professionals are conducted more fairly, equally, with greater certainty and predictability.

In our first book, we suggested the establishment of a Central European Accident Investigation Body as well as the following alternatives, which were

> considered at a theoretical level only and [ ] offered more as suggestions rather than formal recommendations:

1. Smaller Member States may choose to have a close collaboration with a specific Accident Investigation Body of a larger Member State. This will be different from the Memoranda of Understanding that Accident Investigation Bodies have with other Bodies, which call for assistance in the investigation of a serious accident or incident. This collaboration will be in the form of each small Member State that wishes to partner up with an Accident

DOI: 10.1201/9781003724872-6

Investigation Body of a larger Member State that will provide training, equipment, resources, and participation in accident investigation. The advantages of this proposal compared to the original are that it requires no centralized authority, is cheaper and quicker to organize, but lacks an organic element that would give voice to smaller organizations.

2. As another option to having a Central European Accident Investigation Branch, it may be more feasible to have several regional Accident Investigation Bodies comprised of a number of neighboring States.
3. A third and midway option is for small countries to have a more proactive, sustainable, and efficient Accident Investigation Body. This would lead to a collaboration of equals in setting up an agency which would have sufficient membership and resources to effectively investigate member state accidents and would not require dependence upon large country investigation bodies. The advantage is thus the mutual benefit that will accrue to these countries whilst retaining a degree of autonomy over their national aviation domains. This suggestion potentially overcomes mega European political issues of location and so on, as it would not compete with, but complement the existing arrangements.
4. A further option may be establishing a European Accident Investigation Branch, which will not fall within the structure of the European Union, similar to the European Space Agency (ESA). Membership in this Body may be optional for European member States, but may include non-EU member States such as Switzerland. This will ensure that all States will maintain their national Accident Investigation Bodies whilst being able to provide support and expertise. This will ensure close ties between the European Accident Investigation Bodies.[1]

The centralization of accident investigations within the EU but also in other parts of the world could enhance the role of the accident investigation bodies from a reactive role in investigating accidents or serious occurrences to a more proactive and predictive role by expanding its function to safety data analysis investigations, grouping similar accidents or occurrences in the same region that provide a wider understanding of root causes and contributory factors and, most importantly, safety research.

The IATA Operational Safety Audit (IOSA) Risk-Based Approach (RBI) maturity assessment requirements for training, fatigue, and SMS-related ISARPs encourage operators to conduct research in those areas. We suggest that accident investigation bodies could play a significant role in forming partnerships to make research more accessible to operators, as data could be shared in an environment of mutual trust with the sole objective of enhancing aviation safety.

6.2 A EUROPEAN ACCIDENT INVESTIGATION BRANCH

With the implementation of a common regulatory framework within the EU (EU OPS -1) and the establishment of the European Aviation Safety Agency (EASA) which oversees the harmonization and implementation of these regulations and the EU Directive 2003/42 on occurrence reporting in civil aviation, the next step would be the establishment of a European Accident Investigation Body which will investigate major aviation accidents and serious incidents within the EU. The Ethiopian

Airplane Accident Investigation Bureau (EAIB) will ensure the uniform application of procedures and methodologies within an organization that has technical, financial, and human resources to advance the investigation of accidents across the EU. This independent, centralized investigation body will be detached from local media and political influences, conducting investigations without being influenced by external factors or interference. It will also be better able to absorb the pressures exercised by manufacturers and other bodies that may attempt to influence the investigation. This body will also be able to create highly sophisticated laboratories and testing facilities equipped to perform technical analyses, without relying on the manufacturers for such analyses.

There is no doubt that a meticulous and detailed investigation enhances aviation safety by identifying active and latent failures, human errors, human factors, design defects, operational and other procedures, and makes appropriate recommendations for corrective measures. A European Accident Investigation Branch, where all interested parties, within their respective disciplines, contribute their expertise and knowledge in an open and cooperative manner, will establish a transparent framework that allows for an independent and objective investigation into the causes of the accident.

In January 2011, the European Network of Civil Aviation Safety Investigation Authorities (ENCASIA) was established following the entry into force of Regulation (EU) No 996/2010 on the investigation and prevention of accidents and incidents in civil aviation. The Regulation aims to improve aviation safety by ensuring a high level of efficiency, expediency, and quality of European civil aviation safety investigations, with the sole objective of preventing future accidents and incidents without apportioning blame or liability. The Regulation states that the coordination between investigation authorities should be recognized and strengthened in a European context by building on their existing cooperation, and that this could be achieved through the European Network of Civil Aviation Safety Investigation Authorities (the Network), with clearly defined roles and tasks. It also clarifies that the objectives of the Regulation may be better attained through cooperation with third countries, which could participate as observers.[2]

ENCASIA is a network of civil aviation accident investigation authorities to further improve the quality of investigations conducted by air safety investigation authorities of the Member States and to strengthen their independence. It is a forum to encourage high standards in investigation, exchange information, and share best practices, facilitating safety improvements, and supporting and harmonizing safety investigations. It organizes training activities and programs to develop the skills of investigators further. It is composed of the Heads of the civil aviation safety investigation authorities in each of the 27 Member States and, in the case of a multi-modal authority, the Head of its Aviation Branch. ENCASIA builds upon the existing cooperation between the authorities and the investigation resources available in the Member States, allowing each Member State to conduct independent investigations and contribute to the prevention of accidents through their activities.[3]

Countries with a civil legal system are more likely to prosecute aviation professionals after aviation accidents than countries with a common law legal system, which seem more reluctant to do so. Cases discussed in this book, including inter alia the Air France 447 accident and the two Boeing 737 MAX accidents, further highlight this point. In addition, the extent of persons charged and the web of defendants prosecuted is widened to include CEOs, senior managers, as well as the aviation organizations as separate legal entities. Furthermore, our analysis of court proceedings and the judiciary's approach in some cases highlights the connection between the safety management system, hazard identification, risk assessment process, and the organizations and individuals' assigned duties, responsibilities, accountability, and potential blameworthiness.

Since the accident investigation report could be used by prosecuting authorities and courts across different legal systems within the European Union, and considering the complexities and growing list of possible defendants, a central accident investigation body would be better positioned to prepare a report aligned with the latest Annex 13 guidelines and EU requirements. This approach helps ensure a more balanced and fair administration of justice.

6.3 EUROPEAN AVIATION TRIBUNAL/COURT

6.3.1 Review of Suggestions

In our first book, we argued that the inconsistencies in how various countries around the world approach the issue of criminalization of pilots, ATCs, and other aviation professionals raise serious doubts as to whether justice is being provided equally. Drawing attention to the fact that a pilot having an accident in, for example, France, Greece, Italy, and other jurisdictions that do not have a common law legal system will be prosecuted for his acts or omissions leading up to the accident, whereas a pilot who performs the same actions/omissions in another EU Member State may not be faced with prosecution, we suggested the need for the establishment of a European Aviation Tribunal to review the evidence and decide whether there has been willful misconduct or willful negligence before proceeding with the prosecution in the relevant national courts. However, if this independent judicial review determines that there is no evidence to support willful misconduct, then no prosecution should take place. This will ensure that aviation personnel who engage in willful misconduct or willful negligence will be prosecuted and that those who lack the mens rea required for a crime may freely and truthfully provide pertinent information without the fear of prosecution, thus enhancing safety.

In an effort to ensure that all aviation professionals are treated equally, a European Tribunal that reviews evidence collected from technical and judicial investigations to determine whether to initiate criminal prosecutions in relevant national courts could provide the necessary forum to achieve this goal. This body should consist of judges with experience and expertise in aviation and should operate with transparency, fairness, and impartiality. A European Aviation Tribunal would examine the evidence and decide whether there has been willful misconduct or willful negligence. If such misconduct is found, prosecution should proceed in the appropriate national courts. However, if this independent judicial review concludes that there is no evidence of willful misconduct, then no prosecution should occur. This approach ensures that aviation personnel who engage in willful misconduct or negligence are prosecuted, while those lacking the mens rea required for a crime can provide relevant information freely and honestly without fear of prosecution, thereby enhancing safety. This proposal offers an alternative that allows national courts to retain their independence and sovereignty, ensuring equality and significantly reducing external influences that may adversely affect accident investigations and their outcomes.

As an alternative to the Aviation Tribunal, we suggested that *"The establishment of a European Aviation court would have a common legal basis to commence a criminal prosecution, dealing specifically with aviation matters and having the specialized knowledge and experience in such matters."*[4]

A European Aviation Court would deal with the prosecution of aviation professionals. This would result in a uniform set of rules creating uniformity, certainty, and predictability. The European Aviation Court could serve as a central forum for the criminal prosecution of aviation personnel. Specific rules of procedure and evidence could be established to function similarly to those of the European Court of Human Rights.

The following section discusses some recent developments.

6.4 RECENT DEVELOPMENTS

6.4.1 Regional Accident and Incident Investigation Organization (RAIOs)

At the 2008 Accident Investigation and Prevention Divisional Meeting, recommendations were adopted regarding regional cooperation in accident and incident investigations.[5] Recommendation 6/2 specifically urged ICAO to develop guidance material for States on how to establish and manage a regional accident and incident investigation system. As such, the first edition of the Manual on Regional Accident and Incident Investigation Organization (Doc 9946) was developed.

During the 39th ICAO Assembly in 2016, aiming to strengthen global aviation safety and the role of regional bodies, the Cooperative Platform of RAIOs was formed based on resolutions promoting the strengthening of RAIOs and facilitating their interaction. The Assembly recommended that States cooperate in the investigation of aircraft accidents, particularly where the investigation requires highly specialized experts and facilities, and that in so doing, States and regional accident and incident investigation organizations, where possible, inter alia, when requested to do so, provide expert assistance and facilities for the investigation of major aircraft accidents, and give States that seek investigation experience the opportunity to attend investigations of aircraft accidents, to develop and enhance investigation expertise. It goes on to encourage States to consider, as necessary, the ICAO Manual on Regional Accident and Incident Investigation Organization (Doc 9946), which provides guidance on establishing and managing a regional accident and incident investigation system within a region or sub-region.

The 2015 second edition of the Manual of Aircraft Accident and Incident Investigation states at 2.1.7.,

> ICAO encourages States to foster regional accident and incident investigation organizations and regional aviation safety groups. Regional arrangements may include aircraft accident and incident investigation matters, such as the delegation of investigations or parts thereof, or enlisting the mutual assistance and cooperation of States in an investigation.[6]

The Manual provides guidance on establishing and managing a regional accident and incident investigation organization, and also outlines the duties and responsibilities of States, individually and/or collectively, with respect to establishing and managing a regional accident and incident investigation system.

Cooperation need not result in States giving up their sovereignty. There are also many advantages of having a Regional Accident and Incident Investigation Organization, which include, inter alia, conducting a more efficient and effective investigation to enhance aviation safety, sharing and gaining both expertise and training, better use of available resources, being more cost and time effective, and eliminating the duplication of work. Appendix 1 of the Manual includes a Model Agreement for the Establishment and Management of an RAIO. Any agreement establishing RAIO must be registered with ICAO, as per Art. 83 of the Convention. The establishment of an RAIO must define organizational and operational procedures, as well as the policies of the RAIO agreed upon by Member States, and regulations, as per ICAO SARPs, for conducting investigations. Additionally, it must establish a mechanism for amending its rules and procedures consistent with amendments to Annex 13.

Examples of RAIOs include the following. The ARCM (Regional Accident Investigation Committee - South America), which focuses on aviation accident investigation in South America; BAGAIA (Regional Aviation Safety Authority - African region), responsible for accident investigation within the African region; ENCASIA (European Accident and Incident Investigation Committee), focusing on accident investigation in the European region; GRIAA (Central American Regional Investigation Organization) responsible for accident investigation in the Central American region, and IAC (Interstate Aviation Committee), which is a Russian organization investigating accidents and incidents in the Commonwealth of Independent States region.

A development over the past decade or so is that the aviation industry is increasingly resorting to international arbitration to settle aviation-related disputes and the establishment of the aviation-specific arbitration organizations and institutions, such as the International Aviation Arbitration Center (IAAC), which was formed in June 2014, and the Hague Court of Arbitration for Aviation (HCAA), launched in July 2022.

6.4.2 The Shanghai International Aviation Court of Arbitration (SIACA)

The Shanghai International Aviation Court of Arbitration was established in June 2014 to deal with international aviation disputes. As the world's first arbitration service platform focusing on the aviation field, SIACA was supported by the Shanghai International Economic and Trade Arbitration Commission, the International Air Transport Association (IATA), and the China Air Transport Association. SIACA launched the world's first Aviation Arbitration Rules to assist the aviation industry, and in 2023, it introduced the "List of Arbitrators for Aviation Disputes 2023." Disputes revolve around the establishment, change, or termination of civil and commercial relationships connected to the aviation industry, including manufacturing, sale, and other transactions of aircraft and aircraft components, air transportation, airport services, supply of aviation fuel and materials, aviation intermediary services, aviation finance, and aviation facilities and other contractual disputes directly related to aviation manufacturing and air transportation.[7] On its tenth anniversary a report was published highlighting some of the more important cases it dealt with which include disputes related to

> civil aviation airworthiness technology development services, ownership agreements for drone design rights, procurement of aircraft materials and equipment for large passenger aircraft, cross-border procurement of aviation production equipment, production contracts for concept aircraft, international ground handling service agreements, airline catering service contracts, disputes over apron rental services, and equity investment development disputes.[8]

Some of the noteworthy characteristics of the SHIAC are that it focuses on expanding the panel of experts and recruits more experts on emerging aviation issues and developments in the aviation industry, such as from the fields of general aviation, unmanned aerial vehicles, internet plus aviation, construction and operation of aviation facilities, and aviation environmental protection, and focuses on training and providing awareness. The SHAIC uses Ad Hoc Arbitration Service Guidance to implement ad hoc arbitration rules, such as the IATA arbitration rules. In effect, this means that SHIAC can appoint arbitrators and administer procedures, as authorized by the disputing parties or the tribunal, in cases applying the IATA arbitration rules.[9]

6.4.3 The Hague Court of Arbitration for Aviation (HCAA)

In July 2022, the Hague Court of Arbitration for Aviation was established. It is a non-profit, independent, and specialized court of arbitration and center for mediation created for the global aviation industry, located in The Hague, Netherlands. It is a private Dutch non-government organization that serves the global aviation industry by providing and promoting specialized arbitration and other forms of alternative dispute resolution services tailored to the specific dispute resolution needs of the aviation industry. Made up of an international group of attorneys, technical experts, and other professionals experienced in aviation and arbitration, specialized within the legal, commercial, technical, and cultural aspects of commercial and private aviation, it provides a forum to address the complex challenges faced by the aviation industry, which requires prompt, efficient, and effective means to resolve disputes. It is administered by the Netherlands Arbitration Institute, one of the world's oldest arbitral institutions, and operates in accordance with the HCAA's Arbitration Rules and Mediation Rules. Experienced arbitration and aviation experts serve as impartial experts in aviation-related disputes, providing crucial expert knowledge in this complex, intricate, and heavily regulated industry. This distinguishing characteristic sets HCAA apart from other arbitration organizations resolving aviation disputes.[10]

Some of the advantages of the HCAA include, inter alia, the following:

(i) Established for the aviation industry. The HCAA was created to center on the aviation industry, including airlines, airports, aircraft manufacturers, leasing companies, financial institutions, MRO service providers, and its procedures are structured to address technical, regulatory, and commercial difficulties efficiently and promptly.

(ii) Industry Experts. Its arbitrators and mediators consist of a panel of specialists with extensive experience and knowledge in aviation matters, ensuring they fully understand the complexities of the aviation industry and, as a result, make more informed and effective decisions. The parties involved in the dispute can choose their co-arbitrators from a list of qualified, experienced, and knowledgeable professionals in the aviation industry, complemented by a tribunal chair who is a senior, experienced arbitrator.

(iii) Efficiency. Experts with specialized industry experience and knowledge ensure that decisions can be made quickly, thereby reducing the time, resources, and costs typically incurred in prolonged arbitration or mediation proceedings. The HCAA Arbitration Rules, with the updated rules effective since 14 February 2023, provide for expedited proceedings, aiming to deliver a final and binding award within six months after the initial case management conference. Additionally, the costs are lower compared to other arbitration organizations. Expenses range from EUR 660 for disputes valued below EUR 25,000 to a flat fee of EUR 75,000 for disputes exceeding EUR 250 million, with a sliding scale of fees for disputes valued between EUR 25,000 and EUR 250 million.[11]

(iv) Avoiding litigation. Going to arbitration or mediation instead of filing court proceedings has the advantages of offering confidentiality, specialization, efficiency, and the mitigation of reputation damage. The HCAA provides for a final and binding award that can be enforced in over 170 countries, based on the framework of the New York Convention on the Recognition and Enforcement of Foreign Arbitral Awards.[12]

(v) The HCAA is conducted in accordance with the HCAA Rules, specifically drafted to resolve aviation disputes. Under the Rules, electronic communications are permitted. Article 3 states that communications and submissions are to be provided electronically, thus conforming to the global nature of aviation and the move toward electronic communication. Another critical

> point is that the Rules empower a tribunal to make interim and emergency measures. This can protect a party in arbitration by maintaining the status quo until the dispute has been resolved. A claimant in a dispute involving the leasing of an aircraft, for example, may seek an order preventing the lessor from seizing the plane until the merits of the dispute are determined.[13]

As outlined above, our suggestion of establishing a forum dedicated to dealing with complex aviation legal challenges in a uniform, consistent, and just manner by a group of aviation-legal experts has materialized mainly with the creation of the HCAA and the many advantages and features which differ from national criminal courts and other organizations or centers offering alternative dispute resolution to parties. Even though the HCAA does not focus on whether aviation professionals involved in aviation incidents or accidents with potential criminal consequences should be prosecuted, it is a significant step in the right direction.

6.4.4 Aviation Expertise Centre of the PPS – the Netherlands

In the Netherlands, civil aviation cases related to aviation safety involving a possible criminal offense are dealt with by the Public Prosecution Service (PPS) in North Holland. This includes cases of inter alia, drones flying without the necessary permission, trespassing on airport property, and pilots flying under the influence of alcohol. All such cases are referred to the Aviation Expertise Centre of OM Noord-Holland, which is handled by the national coordinating aviation officer of the Public Prosecutor's Office, a position that has existed since 1984. In 2006, the Board of Procurators General set out the investigation and prosecution procedure to be followed in aviation cases involving criminal law. These procedures initially focused on parties in commercial air transport and then expanded to include general aviation. However, as a result of the rapidly developing aviation industry, in January 2024, the PPS established the Aviation Expertise Centre to provide aviation experts with the necessary support in such cases. The Centre also aspires to gain insight into the different approaches member states take in dealing with such cases, and to exchange best practices and experiences. In March 2024, the new Aviation Expertise Centre of the PPS was officially launched and deals with possible criminal cases concerning incidents in which the safety of civil aviation is or may be impacted, and focuses on unwanted drone flights, strengthening the approach to unruly passengers, and setting up a European network of prosecutors to handle aviation cases.[14] A specific objective of the PPS Aviation Expertise Centre is to establish a network of European prosecutors who are or may be responsible for handling aviation cases, and it invites prosecutors to apply to the Aviation Expertise Centre.

The principles of a just culture, in which people are not punished for behavior appropriate to their training and experience, but in which deliberate violations and gross negligence are not tolerated, undoubtedly enhance safety. Within the European Union, Regulation 376/2014 outlines rules to promote a Just Culture. Even though this Regulation does not have a direct impact on each member state's national criminal laws, all member states are encouraged to incorporate Just Culture principles into their national criminal laws as well. The Netherlands, and the PPS is one of the member states that does so with the Instruction for Criminal Investigation and Prosecution of Civil Aviation Occurrences with regard to criminal investigation and prosecution in the event of the reporting of occurrences in civil aviation, based on Directive 2003/42/EC, aiming to contribute to improving aviation safety by ensuring that all safety-relevant information is reported, collated, stored, protected, and disseminated. The Instruction for Criminal Investigation and Prosecution of Civil Aviation Occurrences contains rules for the criminal investigation and prosecution of criminal offenses in the event of a civil aviation occurrence and came into force on 1 March 2020. [15] The PPS stresses that just culture is in the public interest, and to this end, the Aviation Expertise Centre publishes its decisions on its website, aiming to provide awareness and insight into how Just Culture works in criminal cases.[16] In addition, the Aviation Expertise Centre is working closely with EUROCONTROL, which has set up a Just Culture Task Force in 2009, to which both authors have been members since its inception, to organize specific courses for judges, prosecutors, and aviation professionals every six months in collaboration with the International Federation of Air Traffic Controllers' Associations (IFATCA) and the European Cockpit Association (ECA). The courses focus on training aviation professionals to potentially provide expert assistance to judges and prosecutors in accordance with Just Culture principles, while simultaneously respecting their independence and objectivity.[17]

Examples of some of the cases heard by the PPS include, inter alia, the following: prosecuting a pilot in 2021 for violating the rules of the air traffic circuit at Hilversum airport, which could have endangered another aircraft already flying in the same circuit. The judge of the district court in Haarlem referred to the arrogant attitude of the pilot after the violation and sentenced him to a higher than usual penalty because of his attitude;[18] cases of unruly passenger behavior such a when a passenger on board a flight from Buenos Aires to Amsterdam in November 2023 who used violence against three passengers was charged and convicted for his unruly behavior; another passenger who did not obey the captain's instructions and the safety procedures was sentenced to two weeks imprisonment with a probation of two years; Several drone cases including that of a man who flew a drone without a license above a prison in Heerhugowaard, at night, with a mobile telephone intended for a prisoner attached to the drone. He was convicted and sentenced to 60 hours of community service for flying a drone where it was not allowed and 20 hours for flying it out of daylight hours; and, in several cases, passengers who smoked on board the aircraft were given monetary fines.[19] In 2022, the prosecution officer heard a case that occurred in December 2021, where a captain of a passenger aircraft refused to cooperate with a blood alcohol test, an offense punishable under Article 11.6(6) of the Aviation Act. The prosecution officer demanded a fine of €7,000 and a 59-week flight disqualification. The judge sentenced him to a €5,000 fine and disqualified him from flying for 59 weeks, of which 28 weeks were conditional.[20]

It is important to note that a primary aim of establishing a prosecutor expert course which was developed from the initiative of the JC Task Force is to prepare safety experts to assist national prosecutors in aviation cases to decide whether or not to commence criminal proceedings against the aviation professionals involved in the safety incidents or accidents and to create a list of experts with specific training in this area which can be made available to judicial authorities. This would, as we have outlined in our first book, create better coordination between the safety and judicial authorities and adhere to the legal principle and philosophy of ICAO Annex 13 that the safety investigation should not be used in a court of law or as criminal evidence in cases where aviation professionals are being prosecuted subsequent to accidents or incidents. It also provides a uniform framework of principles and guidelines, which would be uniformly and more fairly applied in cases where aviation professionals are prosecuted. This would not jeopardize the independence of the national prosecutor. Consistently applying the principles of a just culture policy where criminal charges are filed only in cases of "gross negligence" and "willful misconduct" and where omissions, actions, or decisions of a reasonable person are not prosecuted would adhere to the principles of a just culture.

6.5 CONCLUSION

The complexities surrounding the admissibility of the accident investigation report and different judicial systems will remain some of the most significant challenges in addressing the criminalization of aviation accidents. The latest edition of Annex 13 offers a positive development by providing clarity and greater certainty regarding the role and importance of accident investigation reports, while also establishing a pathway for courts to access these reports and related investigation data. The role and importance of accident investigation bodies need to be strengthened, and the creation of a European Accident Investigation Body, along with regional bodies, can play a new role in improving aviation safety through enhanced safety data analysis, investigations, and research.

The inconsistencies in how different countries around the world approach the criminalization of aviation professionals and organizations have been highlighted in the previous chapters, raising serious doubts about whether justice is being applied fairly. For example, a pilot involved in an accident in a country with a civil law or similar legal system may be prosecuted for their acts or omissions leading up to the accident, whereas a pilot performing the same actions or omissions in a country with a common law legal system may not face prosecution. Our suggestion to establish an Aviation Tribunal or Aviation Court, at the European, regional, or international level, is emphasized again.

NOTES

1. Michaelides-Mateou, S., and Mateou, A., "Flying in the face of criminalization: The safety implications of prosecuting aviation professionals for accidents," Ashgate, 2010, Chapter 6 pages 151–152.
2. Regulation (Eu) No 996/2010 of The European Parliament and of The Council of 20 October 2010 on the investigation and prevention of accidents and incidents in civil aviation and repealing Directive 94/56/EC, para 17 and 19.
3. European Commission, Mobility and Transport, ENCASIA. Available at https://transport.ec.europa.eu/transport-modes/air/encasia_en.

4. Michaelides-Mateou, S., and Mateou, A., "Flying in the face of criminalization: The safety implications of prosecuting aviation professionals for accidents," Ashgate, 2010, pg. 136.
5. Accident Investigation and Prevention (AIG) Divisional Meeting (2008) (AIG/08) held in Montréal from 13 to 18 October 2008, Recommendations 6/1, 6/2, 6/3, and 6/4.
6. ICAO, Manual of Aircraft Accident and Incident Investigation, Doc 9946, Second Edition, 2015. Available at https://skybrary.aero/sites/default/files/bookshelf/3282.pdf.
7. "Shanghai International Aviation Court of Arbitration (SIACA) air silk road investment and trade dispute resolution center leading aviation cases," 2025 Reports. Available at https://jusmundi.com/en/document/publication/en-preface-siaca-leading-cases.
8. Ibid.
9. Shanghai International Arbitration Center, "Shanghai International Aviation Court of Arbitration: Take-off in aviation arbitration," 29 May 2018. Available at https://globalarbitrationreview.com/review/the-asia-pacific-arbitration-review/2019/article/shanghai-international-aviation-court-of-arbitration-take-in-aviation-arbitration.
10. Hague CAA, "The Hague court of arbitration for aviation," Available at https://www.haguecaa.org/.
11. Eversheds Sutherland, "Launch of the Hague court of arbitration for aviation: Prepare for take-off," 12 February 2024. Available at https://www.eversheds-sutherland.com/en/global/insights/prepare-for-take-off.
12. Ibid.
13. Feldman, J., et al., "Taking flight: The Hague court of arbitration for aviation," Norton Rose Fulbright, November 2022. Available at https://www.nortonrosefulbright.com/en-za/knowledge/publications/cc118ff0/taking-flight-the-hague-court-of-arbitration-for-aviation.
14. Netherlands Public Prosecution Service, "Aviation expertise centre of the PPS North Holland launched and ambitions announced," 28 March 2024. Available at https://www.prosecutionservice.nl/organisation/public-prosecution-office-north-holland/news/2024/03/28/aviation-expertise-centre-of-the-pps-north-holland-launched-and-ambitions-announced.
15. See The Instruction for Criminal Investigation and Prosecution of Civil Aviation Occurrences Registration number: 2020A001. Available at https://skybrary.aero/sites/default/files/bookshelf/5855.pdf.
16. Ibid.
17. Netherlands Public Prosecutions Service, "Network of European aviation prosecutors," 29 May 2024. Available at https://www.prosecutionservice.nl/organisation/public-prosecution-office-north-holland/news/2024/05/29/network-of-european-aviation-prosecutors.
18. Netherlands Public Prosecutions Service, "PA fine for the pilot: Higher punishment due to lack of learning effect," 9 September 2021. Available at https://www.prosecutionservice.nl/latest/news/2021/09/09/a-fine-for-the-pilot-higher-punishment-due-to-lack-of-learning-effect.
19. Netherlands Public Prosecutions Service, "Multiple unruly passengers and drone pilots convicted," 27 April 2024. Available at https://www.prosecutionservice.nl/organisation/public-prosecution-office-north-holland/news/2024/03/27/multiple-unruly-passengers-and-drone-pilots-convicted.
20. Netherlands Public Prosecutions Service, "A higher fine and flying disqualification for pilot refused to cooperate in alcohol test," 21 April 2022. Available at https://www.prosecutionservice.nl/organisation/public-prosecution-office-north-holland/news/2022/04/21/a-higher-fine-and-flying-disqualification-for-pilot-refused-to-cooperate-in-alcohol-test.

7 The Way Forward

7.1 INTRODUCTION

The runway excursion accident involving Jeju Airlines Flight 2216, which resulted in the tragic loss of life when the aircraft hit a barrier at the end of the runway and was viewed by millions worldwide, the Azerbaijan Airlines Flight 8243 loss of control in flight following its shoot-down by Russian military activity, the US midair collision in Washington D.C., and the unimaginable events surrounding the Air India Flight AI 171 accident in June 2025, when it crashed into the top floor of a doctors' hostel, have brought global attention to aviation safety standards and raised more questions about blameworthiness and accountability – especially at a time when the aviation industry boasts a continuously improving and impressive safety record.

The gradual shift in accountability and blameworthiness, holding front-line operators, pilots, ATC, and engineers criminally prosecuted after an accident based on evidence obtained from, inter alia, the accident investigation report and crucial safety data, to the accountability of senior managers and organizations, as is evident from the Concorde accident in 2000, the Helios accident in 2005, the AF 447 accident in 2009, and the Boeing 737 MAX accidents in 2018 and 2019. This new judicial approach, where courts are increasingly examining organizational corporate culture, the effective implementation of an SMS, and the second pillar of safety risk management – encompassing elements of hazard identification, safety risk assessment, and mitigation – is now becoming established, as we discuss below. Before discussing this significant judicial shift, it is essential to understand the significant role that an SMS has in managing safety in the current aviation environment.

The effective implementation of a Safety Management System, improved regulatory oversight, technological advancements, and enhanced aviation training have all played significant roles in improving aviation standards and reducing fatalities. The Japan Airlines Flight JL516 runway incursion collision with a Japan Coast Guard DHC-8 in 2024, where the newest Airbus model, the A350, one of the first commercial aircraft made with composite carbon fiber materials, appeared to withstand the initial impact and fire relatively well and helped save those onboard, demonstrates ongoing improvements in aircraft manufacturing designs and materials. Better training with advanced aircraft simulators, including cabin mock-ups, where complex emergencies are practiced in realistic environments, and the introduction of competency-based and evidence-based training have elevated the skills and competencies of aviation professionals in handling complex emergencies, improved safety standards, and reduced fatalities following serious incidents and accidents. In the case of Southwest Airlines Flight 1380 on 17 April 2018, the crew managed to safely land the 737-700 aircraft following an engine failure when a fan blade and parts of the

DOI: 10.1201/9781003724872-7

engine cowling and engine air inlet cowl had separated. The cowl fragments damaged the fuselage and subsequently damaged a window and its frame, resulting in decompression of the aircraft. The flight crew successfully landed the aircraft and handled a double emergency in a manner attributed to their high standard of training, crew resource management, experience, and airmanship.

In addition, the effective implementation of SMS during the last twenty years can be considered to be the cornerstone of improvements in aviation safety standards, leading the aviation industry from being reactive in managing safety risks to establishing highly effective processes, policies, and procedures that proactively and predictively identify, assess, and mitigate safety risks and emerging concerns, such as inter alia, runway incursions, runway excursions, onboard fires, flying over restricted zones, midair collisions, and Global Positioning System (GPS) jamming and spoofing.

7.2 SAFETY MANAGEMENT SYSTEM

ICAO Annex 19 Safety Management Systems (SMS), now in its 2nd edition (2016), contains provisions applicable to safety management functions related to, or in direct support of, the safe operation of aircraft and highlights the importance of safety management at the State level across multiple aviation domains.[1] As a proactive strategy to improve safety performance by systematically addressing safety risks and achieving acceptable safety performance in their civil aviation systems, States are required to establish a State Safety Program (SSP). Guidance material on safety management principles and concepts, State Safety Programme (SSP), and Safety Management System implementation are contained in the ICAO Safety Management Manual (SMM) (Doc 9859), now in its 4th edition of 2018.

A SMS, defined by ICAO (2013) as "a systematic approach to managing safety, including the necessary organizational structures, accountabilities, policies, and procedures"[2] is based on four pillars, namely, (a) safety policy, (b) safety risk management, (c) safety assurance, and (d) safety promotion, and the following twelve elements as specified in Appendix 2, which outlines the framework for the minimum requirements for a SMS implementation and maintenance.

1. Safety policy and objectives
   - 1.1 Management commitment
   - 1.2 Safety accountability and responsibilities
   - 1.3 Appointment of key safety personnel
   - 1.4 Coordination of emergency response planning
   - 1.5 SMS documentation
2. Safety risk management
   - 2.1 Hazard identification
   - 2.2 Safety risk assessment and mitigation
3. Safety assurance
   - 3.1 Safety performance monitoring and measurement
   - 3.2 The management of change
   - 3.3 Continuous improvement of the SMS

4. Safety promotion
   4.1 Training and education
   4.2 Safety communication[3]

The EASA requirements for a Safety Management System (SMS) are integrated into the Management System (MS) framework, which encompasses the core elements of the ICAO SMS as outlined in Appendix 2 to ICAO Annex 19. This promotes an integrated approach to managing an organization. Additional safety management components can be integrated into the existing management system, rather than creating a separate framework for those components. This encourages organizations to include safety management and risk-based decision-making in their activities. The EASA Management System focuses on the essentials for safety management and aviation organizations must:

> clearly define accountabilities and responsibilities; establish a safety policy and the related safety objectives; implement an occurrence reporting system that meets the requirements defined in Regulation (EU) No 376/2014; implement internal safety reporting procedures in line with "just culture" principles; ensure the identification of aviation safety hazards posed by its activities, ensure their evaluation, and the management of associated risks, including: taking action to mitigate the risks, and verifying the effectiveness of each action taken to mitigate the risks; monitor compliance, while considering any additional requirements that are applicable to the organization; keep its personnel trained, competent, and informed about significant safety issues; and document all the MS key processes.[4]

The ICAO Safety Management Manual (SMM) states that the systematic identification of hazards and other safety deficiencies may be more beneficial for safety management than error reporting alone. It notes a significant difference between hazard reporting, which is said to be predictive and should be objective and neutral, and error reporting, which is said to be reactive and may incriminate the reporter or the reported, potentially leading to blame and punishment.[5] The safety policy of a State or organization should encourage safety reporting and also "define the line between acceptable performance (often unintended errors) and unacceptable performance (such as negligence, recklessness, violations or sabotage), and provide fair protection to reporters."[6] Effective safety reporting, a cornerstone of safety management, relies upon voluntary error and hazard reporting by people.

Various SMS evaluation tools highlight the significance of an SMS in enhancing safety standards and assisting aviation organizations and authorities to implement and assess the effectiveness of their SMS. For example, the Safety Management International Collaboration Group (SMICG) Safety Management System Evaluation Tool, now in its second edition, evaluates the overall effectiveness of the SMS based on both compliance and performance, through a series of indicators aligned with ICAO Annex 19 and ICAO Safety Management Manual (Doc 9859), and is organized by the ICAO SMS Framework.[7] The EASA Management System Assessment Tool (MSAT) provides support for assessing management systems during initial certification and continuing oversight, and may also be used by organizations to self-assess the effectiveness of their management systems or those of their subcontracted organizations.[8] Furthermore, complying with international safety standards such as the IATA Operational Safety Audit (IOSA) Program requires an effective SMS. The risk-based IOSA (RBI) Program enhances the effectiveness of the audit by shifting to a risk-based approach, which focuses on safety risks, while maintaining a baseline of safety. It includes a maturity assessment that introduces a more structured and comprehensive way of providing airlines with an evaluation of their relevant safety systems and programs, and assists in identifying steps to improve their operational safety.[9] This proactive, risk-based safety management approach is not just a regulatory obligation but also a fundamental responsibility and legal duty.

In most of the criminalization cases discussed, especially the earlier ones that were covered in our first book, the parties at the sharp end - pilots, ATCs, and engineers - were prosecuted for their alleged acts, omissions, and violations that were found to have caused or contributed to the accident resulting in loss of life, injury, or damage. More recently, legislative amendments across several jurisdictions, as discussed in Chapter 2, reflect a global trend toward increased accountability for organizations and senior managers. The focus has shifted to how managers, senior managers, post holders, and CEOs perform their duties and responsibilities, which are increasingly becoming the subject of judicial review.

In accordance with Annex 19, aviation service providers are legally obligated to a) identify the accountable executive who will be accountable on behalf of the organization for the implementation and maintenance of an effective SMS; clearly define lines of safety accountability throughout the organization, including a direct accountability for safety on the part of senior management; identify the responsibilities of all members of management and employees with respect to the safety performance of the organization; document and communicate safety accountability, responsibilities, and authorities throughout the organization; and define the levels of management with authority to make decisions regarding safety risk tolerability.[10] One of the main focal points of the SMS is to develop an organizational mindset from top to bottom, from senior management to employees, of a commitment to safety, safety improvement, and safety reporting.

The core objective of an SMS is to proactively identify and mitigate risks, thereby reducing the likelihood and severity of incidents and accidents. Anticipating potential safety risks, conducting an effective risk assessment, and implementing effective corrective measures undoubtedly enhance safety. However, it can be argued that the quality and safety management systems aimed at proactively assessing and managing safety risks across all aviation organizations could lead to increased criminal prosecutions if lapses or failures in these systems are identified, potentially resulting in legal liability and accountability.

Effectively implementing an SMS calls for the creation of a database of corporate policies, risk assessment, mitigating controls and measures, and policies and decision-making. A hazard risk register is a document that identifies potential hazards, assesses their likelihood and impact, and outlines the mitigation strategies and risk controls, namely, the specific procedural, technological, or training measures that have been determined as appropriate for managing those risks. The advantages of an airline sharing its safety hazard registers, de-identified safety data, and risk controls include, inter alia, enhancing aviation safety throughout the aviation industry by sharing information related to safety risks, disseminating lessons learnt from incidents, risk management and other strategies; safety managers are identified as leaders and the organization as one that fosters a safety culture and this is in line with having a just culture where safety is a shared responsibility; trust is cultivated through the transparency, which accountable executives and passengers value, while also providing a competitive advantage; costs can be reduced by sharing effective, proven controls and measures.

The decision to share these documents is a complex one. Aviation safety managers and accountable executives must balance the benefits of transparency with potential risks. Sharing safety risk data could be exploited by competitors and may compromise a company's competitive edge. It could also damage an airline's or airport's reputation and be sensationalized by the media. More critically, sharing hazard risk registers might expose an organization to legal and regulatory scrutiny, as well as potential liability.[11]

The ICAO definition of safety is "The state in which the possibility of harm to persons or of property damage is reduced to, and maintained at or below, an acceptable level through a continuing process of hazard identification and safety risk management."[12] The definition itself encompasses a determination of hazard identification and risk management to reach an acceptable level of safety, which is a decision based on one's evaluation of facts, possibilities, and probabilities.

The core of SMS is the safety risk management (SRM) process, which encompasses gathering data related to potential hazards, the measures to mitigate them, updating and evaluating the effectiveness of those measures, and ranking them according to whether they are acceptable, acceptable with mitigation, or unacceptable. The designated accountable executive of the airport, airline, or other aviation organization has both the "ultimate responsibility and accountability" for the implementation and maintenance of the SMS and "full control of the human and financial resources required to implement and maintain" it.

Applying the elements of negligence, a person or entity responsible for identifying a risk but failing to mitigate it may be held liable in negligence to those injured or damaged. However, if the involved individual or aviation organization can demonstrate that it reasonably determined the risk of a particular hazard occurring and its potential consequences, and that it then took mitigating measures reasonably expected to reduce the risk of such a hazard occurring to an acceptable level, any potential liability could be minimized. Having said that, it is essential to note the legal complexity and possible inconsistencies that can arise when a judge or jury must determine whether aviation professionals' and organizations' actions were reasonable in those circumstances, and whether they are therefore not negligent in discharging their duties and responsibilities.[13]

A risk assessment involves the risk assessment matrix concepts of severity and probability, the meanings of which are globally agreed upon. However, each airline, airport, or other aviation organization determines its own scale for severity and probability and then decides on its own specific levels of risk tolerance. Does this not lead to a scenario where, in litigation after a serious accident, plaintiffs might call upon aviation experts to give evidence on the accuracy of the tolerance level determined or the effectiveness of mitigating actions or corrective measures imposed to reach an acceptable level or a judge who is often unaware of the technicalities and complexities of the aviation industry to decide on these matters which could result in criminal charges or the prosecution of senior managers?

Under the SMS, a Management of Change (MOC) is a mandatory component that ensures organizational changes do not compromise safety performance. It is a structured process for identifying, assessing, and controlling safety risks associated with modifications in aviation operations. Proposed changes, ranging from minor procedural amendments to significant organizational changes, are systematically evaluated before implementation, ensuring safety risks are identified, assessed, and mitigated appropriately. Central to a MOC is proactive risk management, which addresses safety concerns by conducting a thorough risk assessment during the planning stage. Key elements of an effective MOC process include: identifying the changes, determining the scope and potential impact of proposed modifications; a risk assessment to evaluate potential safety implications using systematic methodologies, mitigating the risk by developing and implementing controls to address identified hazards; implementation planning by creating detailed procedures for change execution; and monitoring and review by establishing mechanisms to track effectiveness and identify unforeseen consequences.

Systematically evaluating proposed modifications and implementing appropriate risk controls enables aviation organizations to effectively and safely adapt to the ever-changing, rapidly developing aviation industry. However, every step in the MOC can potentially indicate a failure, a breach of one's duties and responsibilities, and may incur civil and/or criminal penalties.

When the World Health Organization (WHO) declared the COVID-19 outbreak a pandemic on 11 March 2020, the aviation industry entered sudden, unexpected, unplanned, and unprecedented challenges threatening the viability of aviation organizations, which also greatly impacted safety and operational standards. The Safety Management System and the effective implementation of hazard identification and enhanced safety risk assessment processes, with the guidance material provided by ICAO, EASA, and other aviation organizations, provided support to airlines, airports, maintenance and ground handling, and other aviation organizations to develop and effectively implement risk assessments during the COVID-19 crisis. The safety risk assessment for the carriage of cargo in the passenger cabin allowed several airlines to continue operations and have some financial revenue at a time when passenger operations came to a standstill. The safety risk assessment for assessing flight crew competencies and the revalidation of crew licenses due to travel restrictions and the inaccessibility of simulators demonstrated how complex situations were mitigated through the successful implementation of effective mitigating controls. In this context, as a post holder in an airline, one of the authors notes that the implementation of the risk assessments conducted to carry cargo and the assessment of the flight crews' competencies raised significant liability and accountability concerns among the post holders who had the responsibility to sign those risk assessments.

The question of potential liability and accountability for the airline and its post holders who had signed the risk assessments conducted in the event of a flight crew incorrectly applying rejected takeoff procedures that resulted in a runway excursion and subsequent fatalities needs to be considered.

7.2.1 Legal Complexities

The complexities and continuous challenges faced by senior managers, post holders, and those who are assigned the responsibility of conducting, signing, and implementing risk assessments and the associated mitigating controls inevitably result in tensions and friction when they are faced with the "tolerability dilemma." The "tolerability dilemma" is a term the authors introduce to describe a specific situation when individuals responsible for a risk assessment are faced with a risk assessment that has a high tolerability risk score. A risk assessment is a complex process that typically involves, among other elements, subjectivity, human limitations, and personality dynamics.

For example, an airline starting operations to a specific airspace and airport that had been closed for years, with navigational facilities destroyed by civil war, contaminated fuel limiting refueling, occasional military strikes in the city and airport vicinity, drone operations, and ongoing conflicts in the country – along with political and commercial pressures to begin operations – illustrates a highly complex risk assessment that creates an intense "tolerability dilemma."

This scenario raises several questions to consider. Would obtaining the consent of the Civil Aviation Authority and confirmation from the insurance company that the risk assessment mitigations have been implemented serve as a waiver and a valid defense against personal and organizational liability following an accident or security event at that airport? What are the potential legal consequences for the post-holders and the accountable manager who signed the risk assessment and approved the start of the operation?

Another example to be considered is with regard to major technical issues that are being faced following the introduction to service of the fuel-efficient, new generation engines installed on the A320-Neo and Boeing 737 MAX aircraft. Safety data analysis indicates an increase in the number of engine in-flight shutdowns (IFSD) associated with several technical issues. Several service bulletins (SB) and airworthiness directives (ADs) have been issued by the engine manufacturers and civil aviation authorities to address these technical issues and the associated risks. However, operators are required to conduct their own safety risk assessments to ensure that the SBs and ADs are correctly implemented, and also to identify hazards related to, among other things, their specific operation, crew training needs, and human factors. The duty to conduct such a complex safety risk assessment and the mitigation controls deemed necessary may significantly increase maintenance and operational costs, potentially resulting in the grounding of aircraft, which could impact the airline's strategic development and financial performance. The "tolerability dilemma" and potential exposure to legal liability and accountability following an accident as a result of an engine in-flight shutdown, as well as the internal considerations regarding the impact on the operation and the financial viability of the airline, will be at the forefront of the aviation managers and professionals who have the duty and responsibility to conduct the safety risk assessment.

The authors emphasize the need for enhancement in SMS training, particularly advanced training in risk assessment for senior managers. The training should provide an understanding of fundamental legal principles and concepts, such as gross negligence and how these concepts are applied, as well as awareness of subjective elements within a safety risk assessment, human limitations, personality dynamics, and leadership styles. The authors also recommend that additional research be conducted regarding the personality and team dynamics of the managers and post holders assigned to perform the safety risk assessments, which may have a profound impact not only on the individual but also on the organization itself.

Following the Concorde accident in 2000, the safety risk assessments related to several hazards identified in the final accident investigation report played a central role in the prosecution's case and significantly influenced the court's decision. The landmark court ruling examining the extent and depth of the risk assessment process, the use of experts to assess the risk evaluations and the effectiveness of mitigation controls, as well as the judiciary's assessment of the actions taken to mitigate risks, further linked the safety management system, hazard identification, risk assessment process, and the assigned duties, responsibilities, and accountabilities of individuals in maintaining safety standards as part of the judiciary's evaluation when determining blameworthiness and apportioning accountability.

The Concord decision discussed in Chapter 2 has established a judicial precedent where the courts scrutinized the safety risk assessments performed by the organizations and senior managers. In our first book, we submitted that this shift, where a court assesses the effectiveness of the risk assessment and mitigating action, fundamental elements of a SMS, could result in a fear of legal ramifications, and this fear could result in an emerging Legally Defensive Safety Management (LDSM) culture within aviation. The judicial and legislative developments discussed in our book highlight the tensions among managers within organizations when implementing a SMS, discharging their duties and responsibilities, and their concerns about possible legal liability and accountability.

If an LDSM approach is adopted within the aviation industry, senior management could take a defensive approach toward safety to protect themselves and the organization from criminal liability instead of aiming to continuously monitor and improve safety.

The legal complexities surrounding the Air France 447 accident and the landmark trial that began in October 2022, involving Airbus SAS as the manufacturer of the A330 aircraft and Air France as the aircraft's operator, along with their legal representatives facing criminal charges of involuntary manslaughter, have sent shockwaves through the aviation industry.

Central to the case is the legal question of when the adequacy of the risk assessment performed and the mitigating actions taken by both organizations in handling the identified hazards related to the aircraft pitot tubes and the investigation of the recurring unreliable airspeed and stall incidents can transition to a criminal act or gross negligence. The AF 447 legal proceedings could play a significant role in establishing a legal precedent and provide guidance as to how a court will apply principles of negligence when assessing the effectiveness of the SMS and risk assessments.

The BEA accident investigation report and a review of the history of previously reported incidents of unreliable airspeed and incorrect angle of attack (AOC) related warnings due to the icing of the pitot tubes raise several legal questions about Airbus and Air France's mitigation of the known and foreseeable risks arising from the malfunctioning pitot tubes. To successfully find the defendants Airbus and Air France guilty of the charges, the prosecutor had to prove, inter alia, that both organizations' risk assessments and mitigations against the known hazards from the defective A330 pitot tubes and the number of reported incidents related to this critical aircraft system constituted gross negligence, and that there was a causal link between any negligent acts or omissions and the accident.

In implementing their SMS, both Airbus and Air France faced the hazard of pitot tube icing under certain meteorological conditions, causing unreliable airspeed indications on the aircraft's primary flight displays (PFDs). Their risk assessment with regard to the severity of unreliable airspeed, especially at high altitude, and the probability outcome, taking into consideration the frequency of such incidents, and the risk assessment evaluation outcome, and especially the implemented mitigating controls, was crucial to establishing gross negligence.

It should be noted that at the end of the first trial, which was from October to December 2022, the defendants were acquitted in April 2023. The court did establish negligence and "acts of imprudence" on the part of both parties; however, it found that there was not a strong enough causal link between their failures and the accident to find the companies guilty of involuntary manslaughter. The court found that the defendants' negligence was not a direct cause of the accident and that the pilots' error, particularly their failure to recover from the stall, was an intervening cause that broke the chain of causation.

While we have no access to the court transcript or the legal arguments submitted by both parties, it can be argued that a robust risk assessment should have identified the weaknesses in the flight crew's understanding and their ability to recover from a stall following an unreliable speed event. It should have included human factors elements and proactively enhanced training. By not doing so, a latent condition was allowed to exist, which eventually resulted in an accident and loss of life.

The public prosecutor of the Paris Appeal Court appealed the decision. In 2024, the Appeal Court overruled the acquittal of both defendants and ordered a new trial. The 8-week Appeals trial which commenced on 29 September and ended on 26 November 2025 re-examined whether the defendants' negligence could be directly linked to the accident. If the Appeals Court considers that it was the alleged negligence in performing a risk assessment that created the conditions where pilot error was not merely a possibility, but a probability, it could result in a decision that the crew's actions would not be considered an intervening cause breaking the chain of liability, but a systemic failure of the organization's SMS and risk assessment for which the defendants may be liable. Such an outcome could have a profound impact on the aviation industry and set a critical precedent in how SMS and risk assessments are performed.

It can thus be said that there is a shift from identifying the parties responsible for or contributing to an accident to identifying post holders who have performed risk assessments and assessing whether any shortcomings or failures could amount to gross negligence. It can also be argued that this shift is a shift in accountability, as organizations may be liable for underestimating the probability and severity of risks, failing to implement adequate and sufficient mitigations, and for not measuring the effectiveness of the mitigation controls they have implemented. For aircraft manufacturers and airlines, it can be said that the regulatory requirement to perform in-depth, proactive, and predictive safety risk assessments and ensure effective implementation of mitigation controls to identified hazards and risks is a legal duty of care that could be assessed by a court of law to determine liability and accountability.

The final ruling by the French Appeal Court will be decisive and will pave the way forward in how courts will apply the high standards of the duty of care and hold aviation organizations accountable for the way their SMS is being implemented and how their safety risk assessments are being performed. An acquittal of Airbus and Air France will set a very high standard of proof required in complex aviation accidents regarding causation.

The legal ramifications after the AF 447 and the Boeing 737 MAX accidents illustrate how organizations and post holders could be faced with criminal charges for failing to effectively exercise their duties, responsibilities, and accountabilities under the SMS and failing to mitigate known risks in accordance with the severity and probability of risks that are known or should have been mitigated.

Reviewing the aftermath of the two Boeing 737 MAX accidents in 2018 and 2019, resulting in 346 fatalities, highlights a significantly different approach to the criminalization of individuals and organizations after aviation accidents. The MAX 737 accidents are related to manufacturing system malfunctions, flight crew training, and the way Boeing introduced the MCAS system. The failure to provide an adequate description of the MCAS system and the classification of this system as one that does not require additional and specific flight crew training are similar to the AF 447 accident. However, the difference in the subsequent legal proceedings and outcome is profound and demonstrates the divergence in how different jurisdictions approach aviation accidents and accountability.

In the aftermath of the Boeing 737 MAX accidents, it appeared that the top management of Boeing prioritized profits, meeting deadlines, and retaining its market share above safety and quality. This was the result of the organizational culture, which stems from the 1997 merger with McDonnell Douglas Corporation and the gradual move from being an engineering company to a company that prioritized profits and return on investment. When Airbus introduced the A320-neo in 2010, offering greater fuel efficiency and upgraded operational systems without requiring additional flight crew training, it threatened Boeing's market share and profitability. In response, Boeing decided to design an upgrade of the Boeing 737 rather than develop a new medium-sized aircraft. To achieve the same level of competitive fuel efficiency, Boeing selected the CFM LEAP-1B engine for the 737 MAX aircraft. This larger engine had to be installed higher and further forward on the wing, and the nose landing gear had to be extended. These changes significantly altered the aerodynamic characteristics of the 737 MAX aircraft, resulting in a high aircraft pitch-up tendency that increased the aircraft's angle of attack and also increased the risk of a stall. Boeing responded by mitigating the risk through upgrades to the MCAS system, which would allow 737-MAX pilots to fly the aircraft under a single type certification rating and without requiring any additional flight crew training.[14]

Following a simulation test in 2012, Boeing was aware that the MCAS system could, in the worst-case scenario, result in a catastrophic loss of control if the crew did not respond within 10 seconds to the activation of the MCAS system. The system was designed so that, after 60 seconds of MCAS activation, it would induce a full nose-down trim to counter the impending stall of the aircraft. Without adequate knowledge of the system and any flight crew training, the flight crews of Lion Air and Ethiopian Airlines were unable to respond to the MCAS activation and the resulting nose-down trim.[15]

If these accidents had occurred in France, the French prosecutors would have followed the same arguments, and by referring to Boeing's SMS and risk assessment regarding the introduction of the MCAS, Boeing could have faced similar criminal charges of involuntary manslaughter. In the US, Boeing pleaded guilty to conspiracy to defraud the US, agreed to pay a penalty, and to strengthen its compliance program under a plea agreement reached with the Department of Justice to avoid a criminal trial. The contradiction in how different jurisdictions' legal systems and their laws were applied to the two manufacturers and the consequences to both individuals and the organizations is concerning.

The manufacturing and certification standards, the operation of aircraft and their airworthiness requirements, the implementation of an SMS, and the investigation of aviation accidents are clearly specified on an international level by the ICAO Annexes, guidance material, and the regulations of States' civil aviation authorities. This lays down the legal and regulatory requirements that all ICAO member states shall comply with. However, when judicial authorities assess the level of compliance to determine negligence, gross negligence, and accountability, severe inconsistencies arise that create uncertainty and fear among organizations and individuals regarding their legal liability.

The authors acknowledge the sovereignty of States and the diverse legal systems; however, we suggest that an international forum, such as an Aviation Court, would provide greater consistency, certainty, and a fairer, more just outcome in future criminal cases involving complex aviation accidents and serious incidents. A fundamental prerequisite for effectively implementing an organization's SMS is the commitment by the senior management and the entire organization to its safety policy and culture, corporate ethics, and values. The commitment is driven by the safety leadership of the organization's top management, including the CEO, COO, and other key post holders, with primary regulatory responsibility assigned to the organization's designated accountable executive. The Boeing 737 MAX congressional hearings severely criticized the erosion of the organization's safety culture and its commitment to safety and quality standards, as it prioritized profitability and shareholders' interests and sought to avoid Airbus gaining a competitive advantage.

A safety culture has a direct impact on positive safety performance and enhances aviation safety across the entire aviation industry. It would be interesting and equally concerning to see how a court would assess an organization's safety policy and culture in light of evidence of non-compliance with the safety policy and an erosion of the organization's safety culture, as well as corporate legal requirements.

If a safety culture is examined from a legal perspective, the web of defendants in criminal litigation in the aftermath of an aviation accident could expand, increasing the criminalization of aviation professionals and organizations charged with unintentional negligence and/or manslaughter, whether as individuals or as corporations. The global trend in corporate criminalization is to accept safety culture as a variable term that determines organizational blameworthiness and accountability.

ICAO recognizes that an effective SMS requires organizations to have a just culture, defined as "an atmosphere of trust where people are encouraged and even rewarded for providing safety-related information, but which also clearly delineates the difference between acceptable and unacceptable behavior."

Aviation professionals fearing criminal liability and accountability might not openly share valuable safety information, which will impede aviation safety. Taking into account the developments in many jurisdictions that are enacting and/or amending, modernizing, and improving laws related to corporate manslaughter holding senior managers and executives, as well as organizations accountable for injury or death after an aviation accident, as highlighted in our book, one has to consider the impact that an SMS may have on the liability and accountability of senior managers and organizations. If organizations fear exposure and retrospective scrutiny by the criminal justice system, openly reporting and sharing of safety data gathered through SMS will decline, lessons learnt will be minimized, and safety will be impeded. As is very aptly stated, "This remains one of the greatest challenges to the effectiveness of SMS across commercial aviation and other industries at the operator, national, and international level."[16]

Our analysis of the cases discussed, where aviation professionals have been prosecuted based on their "negligence," a legal term denoting varying degrees of negligence, and based on States' national criminal laws, suggests that a just culture may not always result in unintended errors not being criminalized. There have been significant developments regarding the implementation of a just culture within the framework of a SMS. The authors recognize and fully support the initiatives and tremendous progress made during the last few years within the ambit of the Eurocontrol Just Culture Task Force (JCTF). As the notion of just culture varies greatly and is linked to local cultures and national laws, there is a need to expand the understanding of how these principles are implemented across all jurisdictions.

In today's rapidly changing aviation environment, safety, security, geopolitical, and financial challenges need to be effectively managed for aviation organizations to survive. This requires adopting an enhanced approach to manage the constant changes and ensure safety and operational standards are maintained. In this complex, highly competitive aviation environment, organizations need to constantly examine their processes and performance strategies through their Management of Change Safety Risk Assessment (MOC SRA). Organizations need to effectively adapt and adjust to the rapid changes through an effective and well-implemented MOC SRA process that captures hazards and effectively assesses and mitigates risks. Constant change must be accepted as the new reality in aviation. Ineffective implementation of these processes can increase not only the risk of serious accidents or incidents but also the chances of facing legal consequences and criminal charges in today's environment, where the web of defendants has expanded from pilots, ATCs, and engineers to include senior managers and post holders, as well as corporate liability and accountability.

7.3 CONCLUSION

In addition to the challenges faced regarding the admissibility of accident investigation reports and sensitive safety data into a court of law, the development of courts assessing corporate safety cultures, senior managers' corporate and safety leadership, and the effective implementation of a SMS with laser-sharp focus on the hazard identification process and the risk assessments conducted creates a new judicial approach in dealing with blame and accountability following an aviation accident. Society will always continue to demand justice after an aviation accident involving injury, loss of life, and property damage. Aviation organizations and aviation professionals, from top to bottom, should be aware of this shift and ensure that they discharge their duties, responsibilities, and accountabilities, and adhere to regulatory requirements and industry best practices, but also, and more importantly, do so in accordance with the strictest legal standards set by the courts, irrespective of the jurisdiction in which they operate.

These legal developments and the risk of legal liability raise significant concerns within aviation organizations, including CEOs, COOs, post holders, senior managers, and operational staff, and create tension when it comes to handling complex daily operational hazards and risks. Considering that financial performance and profitability of aviation organizations in today's highly competitive global aviation environment can influence CEOs and senior managers' approval to implement costly mitigation controls required by the safety risk assessments conducted, especially when they prioritize profitability over safety, recent legal developments – where courts examine corporate decisions and the risk assessment process – can be viewed as a positive safeguard in protecting the traveling public and maintaining aviation safety standards.

We end the book with the same sentiment we expressed in the introduction, borrowing from and paraphrasing the famous preamble of the 1944 Chicago Convention, that:

> WHEREAS the future development and safety and operational standards of international civil aviation could be improved through an effective implementation of a robust and mature safety management system, positive safety reporting based on a safety corporate culture, and values and lessons learned from accident and incident investigations can significantly help to create and preserve a just culture environment and

understanding among the nations and peoples of the world, aviation organizations and aviation professionals with regard to criminalization of aviation accidents, yet its abuse can become a threat to general aviation safety; and

WHEREAS it is desirable to avoid friction and to promote cooperation between aviation organizations and professionals and nations and peoples, upon which the balance between safety and society's demand for accountability can be achieved.

THEREFORE, the authors, having agreed on certain principles and information available to us, hereby present to the aviation industry our book to contribute to the further development of the aviation industry in a safe and orderly manner, and that international air transport services may be established based on equal opportunity, operated soundly and economically, safely, and when needed, are justly evaluated.

NOTES

1. ICAO, Annex 19 – Safety Management. Available at https://store.icao.int/en/annex-19-safety-management.
2. Ibid., Annex 19, Chapter 1. Definitions, at page 1-1.
3. Ibid., Annex 19, Appendix 2.
4. EASA, "Safety management system and management system – The integrated approach." Available at https://www.easa.europa.eu/en/domains/safety-management/safety-management-system-sms.
5. ICAO SMM Doc 9559, at 2.8.19.
6. Ibid., 2.8.22.
7. SMICG, Safety Management System Evaluation Tool, 1 April 2019. Available at https://skybrary.aero/bookshelf/safety-management-system-sms-evaluation-tool-v2 SM ICG, Safety Management.
8. EASA, Management System Assessment Tool, 1 September 2023. Available at https://www.easa.europa.eu/en/document-library/general-publications/management-system-assessment-tool.
9. IATA, IOSA and the Risk-Based Approach. Available at https://www.iata.org/en/programs/safety/audit/iosa/about-iosa/.
10. ICAO Annex 19, Safety Management System, at 1.2 Safety accountability and responsibilities.
11. Howell, C., "Sharing aviation SMS hazard risk registers: Safety vs. competition," 14 August 2025. Available at https://aviationsafetyblog.asms-pro.com/blog/sharing-aviation-sms-hazard-risk-registers-safety-vs.-competition.
12. International Civil Aviation Organization's (ICAO) Safety Management Manual (SMM) Doc 9859.
13. Ibid.
14. Lengyel, D.M. et al., "Examining risk management failures: The case of the Boeing 737 MAX program," 2023. ISSN 1937-7916 2023, Vol. 8, No. 1, Available at www.dau.edu.
15. Ibid.
16. FSF, "Accident investigator group sign criminalization resolution," 13 January 2010. Available at https://flightsafety.org/accident-investigator-group-sign-criminalization-resolution/.

8 Cases of Prosecution of Aviation Professionals and Organizations

8.1 INTRODUCTION

A chronological overview and at times, extensive discussion, of cases in which pilots, ATCs, engineers, managers, CEOs, and other aviation professionals, as well as aviation organizations that were either criminally charged or convicted subsequent to an aviation accident, is presented. Cases discussed in our first book, up to 2010, that have had legal developments are discussed first, before going on to cases from 2010 to July 2025. Every effort was made to compile a comprehensive collection of cases and information related to legal proceedings and data from the relevant criminal courts; however, we acknowledge the limitations in accessing such information.

8.2 AIR FRANCE CONCORDE FLIGHT 4590, CHARLES DE GAULLE AIRPORT, FRANCE (25 JULY 2000)

In November 2012, a French Appeals court overturned the involuntary manslaughter charges against Continental Airlines, which merged with United Airlines two years ago, saying that it had no criminal wrongdoing in the accident.

The Appellate Court also overturned the conviction of a Continental mechanic who was accused of wrongly using titanium to construct a replacement piece known as a wear strip for the DC-10 and of improperly attaching the strip to the aircraft, resulting in its falling onto the runway. The ruling did not challenge the lower court's finding that linked the metal strip from the Continental aircraft to the chain of events that caused the accident and the death of all 109 passengers and crew on board, and the four people on the ground, but said that the criminal manslaughter charge was unjustified. The French accident investigators concluded that a small strip of metal that fell off from the Continental DC-10 had punctured a tire of the Concorde as it took off. The tire disintegrated in seconds, sending rubber debris into the fuel tanks, leading to the chain of events that caused the crash.

In addition, the court also upheld a lower court's order in 2010 that the company pay civil damages of €1 million (approximately $1.3 million) to Air France to compensate the French carrier for damage to its image. Air France was not a defendant in the case, but it joined as a civil party claiming that it should be compensated for the damages that it had paid to the relatives of the deceased. This case is an important

DOI: 10.1201/9781003724872-8

case that set a precedent, as it is the first case in France where a court held that someone can be held responsible in civil law for an accident without also having criminal responsibility.[1]

8.3 HAPAG-LLOYD FLIGHT 3378, VIENNA-SCHWECHAT AIRPORT (12 JULY 2000)

On 12 July 2000, Flight 3378 with 143 passengers and eight crew members was on a scheduled flight from Chania, Greece, to Hanover, Germany. Problems were encountered when fully raising the right-hand main landing gear, and the crew decided to continue with the gear down and to continue to Munich. As the calculated spare fuel at Munich decreased, the crew then decided to divert to Vienna-Schwechat Airport instead. As they approached Vienna, it appeared that there was not enough fuel on board, and the engines stopped, at approximately 12 nm short of the runway, at about 4,000 feet. The crew managed to restart one engine for a short period of time, and they managed to reach the airport. The aircraft landed in the grass about 500 m from the runway and slid for another 600 m before coming to rest. The left main gear broke off, and the No. 1 engine and wing sustained substantial damage.

The Austrian Air Accident Investigation Board conducted the investigation. The final report found that the causes of the accident were[2], inter alia, continuing the flight with a landing gear problem until the engines failed due to fuel shortage and the crew not complying with the company's rules on fuel reserves, caused by several human factors, with extreme workload and stress being the important factor, failure to develop alternative strategies to deal with the fuel problem, failure to comply with a fuel warning and the decision to continue the flight to Vienna International Airport and not to divert to Zagreb Airport which was closer. The report also identified that the manufacturer had inadequate and misleading documentation for this specific case and that the aviation companies had inadequate documentation for abnormal checklist landing gear up indication and a lack of review of the fuel needs by the Operations Division.

About six months after the incident, the captain left his employment at the charter airline. He was charged with dangerous encroachment of air traffic. The public prosecutor sought a one-year prison sentence and a fine of €10,000. In May 2004, the judge found the captain guilty and imposed a six-month suspended sentence.[3]

8.4 JAPAN AIRLINES BOEING 747, FLIGHT 907 AND MCDONNELL DOUGLAS DC 10 FLIGHT 958, NEAR COLLISION, YAIZU, JAPAN (31 JANUARY 2001) – UPDATE

On 31 January 2001, two Japan Airlines aircraft were involved in a near-collision. Flight 907, which was scheduled to fly from Haneda Airport, Japan, to Naha Airport, Okinawa, narrowly avoided a midair collision with Flight 958, which was en route from Gimhae International Airport, South Korea, to Narita International Airport, Japan. The Tokyo Metropolitan Police and the Land, Infrastructure and Transport

Ministry investigated the incident.[4] The investigation found that the incident was the result of errors made by two air traffic controllers, namely, the air traffic controller trainee and the trainee supervisor. The trainee air traffic controller mistakenly instructed Flight 907, instead of Flight 958, to descend to avoid a collision between the two aircraft. The trainee controller did not notice the incorrect flight number called out by the controller. Neither controller picked up the mistake when the pilot of Flight 907 repeated the same number and the instruction. Flight 907 then proceeded to descend, contrary to the instruction to gain altitude shown on the traffic alert and collision avoidance system (TCAS). When Flight 907 approached Flight 958, which followed the instruction on its system to descend, Flight 907 nose-dived to avoid a collision. Fifty-seven passengers on Flight 907 were injured.

In March 2004, prosecutors indicted the two air traffic controllers for professional negligence. They both pleaded guilty and argued that the pilots of the aircraft should be held responsible for the incident. In 2006, the court ruled that they were not guilty, as they could not have foreseen the accident, and that the mistake in the flight numbers did not have a causal relationship with the accident. The court said that it would be "unsuitable" to prosecute the controllers and the pilots in this case.

The Tokyo District Public Prosecutor's Office filed an appeal with the Tokyo High Court. The Tokyo High Court found both the air traffic controllers guilty and sentenced one to 18 months in prison and the other to 12 months, with both sentences suspended for three years. It is reported that they are the first air traffic controllers to have been prosecuted for being criminally responsible for a near-collision incident. Both air traffic controllers appealed.

In December 2010, the Supreme Court of Japan upheld the decision of the Tokyo High Court, stating that even if the pilot of Flight 907 followed the TCAS alert and avoided the near collision, there was a relation of cause and effect between the air traffic controllers' mistaken wording and instructions and the near collision.[5]

8.5 HELIOS AIRWAYS BOEING 737, FLIGHT 522, GRAMMATIKO, GREECE (14 AUGUST 2005)

On 14 August 2005, Helios Airways Boeing 737, on its way to Prague, via Athens, crashed into the mountainside of Grammatiko, north of Athens, killing all 121 passengers and crew on board the aircraft. The official accident investigation was conducted by the Greek Air Accident Investigation and Aviation Safety Board (AAIAB).

In December 2008, one hundred and nineteen charges of manslaughter and causing death through a reckless, careless and dangerous act were filed in the Nicosia District Criminal Court against the Chairman of the Board of Directors and CEO of Helios, the Chief Pilot, the General Manager of Helios, the Operations Manager, and the airline, Helios Airlines. The company, "Helios Airways," was renamed "Ajet" and the Cyprus Government detained Ajet's aircraft and froze the company's bank accounts. In February 2010, the Greek judicial authorities, despite the fact that four individuals, as well as Helios Airlines as a legal entity, were already on trial at the Nicosia Criminal Court, proceeded with charges against the same individuals but included the two engineers. It is the first case in which criminal trials in two jurisdictions were initiated against aviation professionals subsequent to an air accident.

In Cyprus, in December 2011, all the defendants (the four individuals and the defunct Helios Airways) were acquitted. The Cyprus Criminal Court held that there was no prima facie evidence to justify the charges of manslaughter and reckless endangerment against the defendants on the grounds that they had employed "unsuitable and inadequate" pilots. The court said that the evidence showed that both pilots' competence was satisfactory. In a three to two decision, the court said that the prosecution failed to establish any causal association between the defendants and the negligence they were charged with for the fatal accident, and that there was no proof that the accused had violated any of their duties, and/or that the violation of their duties was the cause of the damage. The Attorney General filed an appeal against the acquittal.[6] The Supreme Court upheld the appeal and ordered a new trial to commence against the four defendants who were acquitted.

In Greece, in December 2011, the chief executive officer, the flight operations manager, the former chief pilot, as well as the chief engineer were charged with manslaughter. In April 2012, all four defendants were found guilty and sentenced to 10 years' imprisonment, and they remained free on bail pending an appeal.

In February 2013, the Court of Appeals in Athens convicted three of the four defendants. Their 10-year sentence was confirmed, but the defendants were given the option to buy out their sentence for approximately €75,000 each. The defendants paid the amount and were set free. The chief engineer, the fourth defendant, who had checked the aircraft before the doomed flight, was found not guilty.[7] After the ruling by the Athens Supreme Court, the Cyprus Supreme Court set aside the new trial.

8.6 BELL 206 HELICOPTER, PAPUA NEW GUINEA (20 APRIL 2006) – UPDATE

A pilot of a Bell 206 helicopter became caught in inadvertent Instrument Meteorological Conditions (IMC) and crashed in the highlands of Papua New Guinea on 20 April 2006. Three of the six passengers were killed in the crash, and the pilot was rendered a quadriplegic. The pilot blamed his employer, Hevilift Ltd (Hevilift), for failing to warn him of the risk of a fast-forming cloud and failing to provide appropriate instruments.

He sued his employer for damages for negligence and breach of his contract of employment, alleging that Hevilift failed to warn him that in the mountainous regions of Papua New Guinea, cloud can form and move very quickly, giving rise to a greater than ordinary risk to unintentionally enter into or be enveloped by cloud and that it failed to provide him with a helicopter equipped for flight in such circumstances.

The defendant claimed that the plaintiff pilot was not a competent pilot, that he knew, or ought to have known, not to fly where he knew he was likely to encounter fog, that the cloud did not develop so quickly that a helicopter may have been unavoidably enveloped by it and that in breach of his contract, he flew deliberately into cloud despite a forewarning of the fog and being advised of an alternative landing site. In addition, the defendant alleged contributory negligence on the part of the pilot and claimed a set-off.

In November 2016, the Court found that, as a business regularly operating helicopters in that area, Hevilift should have been aware of the phenomenon that clouds could form rapidly in the late afternoon and that it should have implemented a local regime for the monitoring of weather and the diverting of flights when prescribed weather conditions were forecast or present. The court thus held that Hevilift was liable to its employee pilot for failing to warn him of a foreseeable risk of rapid cloud formation and that it was in breach of its duty of care in not providing the flight instruments and training. No contributory negligence was found on the part of the plaintiff pilot.[8]

Hevilift appealed in 2018. In the appeal, the court's findings as well as the award of damages were challenged. In addition, the appeal argued that the lower court should not have accepted the evidence of the meteorologist with regard to the speed of cloud formation. Heavilift did not provide its own expert evidence at trial and instead relied on evidence provided by other experienced pilots flying in that region. At the court of first instance, evidence was given by an expert meteorologist that the cloud cover that the pilot had experienced at the time of the crash could occur almost instantaneously, as the region was prone to this fast formation of cloud because of the steep topography, increased temperature, rainfall, and humidity of the area. However, this was challenged in the appeal on the grounds that the expert had not personally inspected the region. The Queensland Court of Appeal ruled that the respondent's evidence from an experienced pilot and aviation company manager did not directly contradict the meteorologist's conclusions. The appeal was dismissed.[9]

8.7 GOL AIRLINES BOEING 737 FLIGHT 1907/ EXCEL AIRE EMBRAER LEGACY 600, BRAZIL MID-AIR COLLISION (29 SEPT 2006) – UPDATE

In June 2007, a Brazilian federal judge indicted the two American Embraer pilots and four Brazilian-based air traffic controllers for exposing an aircraft to danger. In 2008, the charges of negligence against the pilots were dropped, and the charge of malpractice was kept. In addition, all charges were dropped against two of the controllers, and charges against two other controllers were reduced. The judge also suggested that charges be brought against a fifth controller who was based in São José dos Campos, Embraer's departure point.

In 2010, four ATCs were acquitted by a military court, but a fifth one was convicted and sentenced to 14 months' imprisonment for failing to take action when he noted that the Embraer's anti-collision system was off. He did not go to prison, pending his appeal. In May 2011, the court acquitted the controller of the charges of harming Brazil's air transport safety and sentenced another controller to 3 years and 4months of community service. [10]

The pilots were acquitted of all but one of the six charges, namely, failure to observe cockpit warnings that the transponder and anti-collision system were turned off for nearly an hour, and they were sentenced in absentia to 4 years and 4 months in a semi-open prison. He then commuted the sentence to community service. In October 2012, the Brazilian federal court upheld, in absentia, the conviction of the two pilots and ruled that the pilots must serve 3 years and 1 month in the USA, under an open system allowed by Brazilian law.[11] The pilots appealed, and in 2015, the Brazilian Supreme Court rejected their appeal against their conviction and prison sentence, ordering them to return to Brazil from the United States.[12] Brazil and the USA do have an extradition agreement in place; however, it is improbable that the pilots would be extradited to Brazil to serve their sentence or that the sentence would be enforced in the USA.

8.8 TAM AIRLINES A320 FLIGHT 3054, CONGONHAS AIRPORT, SÃO PAULO, BRAZIL (17 JULY 2007) – UPDATE

On 17 July 2007, TAM Linhas Aéreas Airlines A320 Flight 3054, a scheduled domestic passenger flight, departed from Porto Alegre at 17:19 local time destined for São Paulo/Congonhas. The approach to runway 35L of Congonhas occurred uneventfully. The aircraft was operating with the number 2 engine reverser deactivated. The runway was wet and slippery, according to information provided by the Tower to the crew. After the touchdown, which occurred at night-time at 18:54 local time, the aircraft did not slow down as expected. The aircraft veered to the left, overran the runway, crossed over, and hit a fuel service station and the airlines air cargo service building. All 181 passengers, 6 crew members, and a further 12 people on the ground were killed. During an extensive criminal investigation that lasted 16 months, charges of involuntary manslaughter and breach of air transport safety, which could result in imprisonment of up to 12 years, were being investigated against ten government and TAM officials. They were the President and Director of the Brazil Civil Aviation agency (ANAC) at the time of the accident, the former president of Brazil's airport authority, Infraero, and two heads of TAM's flight safety and flight operations division, three ANAC officials who managed the airport's infrastructure and safety operations, and two Infraero employees based at the Congonhas Airport.

In 2011, the Brazilian Federal Public Ministry laid criminal charges against the director of the Brazilian National Civil Aviation Agency (ANAC) at the time of the disaster, two former TAM directors, namely, the director of flight safety and the vice president of operations for allegedly neglecting air transportation safety and that they had endangered safety by allowing the aircraft to land on a runway that was unsafe due to a faulty drainage system. The resurfaced runway was authorized for use twenty days before the accident, before cutting grooves that allowed water to drain off excess rainwater.

The trial commenced in São Paulo in 2013. In 2014, the charges against the vice president of operations were dropped due to insufficient evidence. In addition, a secondary charge against the director of ANAC of documentary falsehood was dismissed.[13] In May 2015, the São Paulo federal judge acquitted the former director of Brazil's National Civil Aviation Agency, TAM Airlines' former vice president of operations, and TAM's former safety director. [14]

8.9 REGIONAL, FOKKER 100 F-GMPG, PAU UZEIN AIRPORT, FRANCE (25 JANUARY 2007)

On 25 January 2007, a Fokker aircraft with 50 passengers and four crew members on board took off from Charles de Gaulle, Paris, and flew to Pau Uzein, France. The aircraft, which was to fly back to Paris as Air France Flight 7775, overshot the runway at Pau following an aborted takeoff. When the captain decided to abort the takeoff, engine power was reduced, and the Fokker contacted the ground, near the end of the runway, ran 340 m, and collided with the perimeter fence. After crossing a road, the left main landing gear struck the cabin of a truck, killing the driver. Both main landing gears were sheared off as the aircraft struck a slope and continued into a field, where it came to rest.

The accident investigation was conducted by the French BEA which concluded that

> the accident resulted from a loss of control caused by the presence of ice contamination on the surface of the wings associated with insufficient consideration of the weather during the stopover, and by the rapid rotation pitch, a reflex reaction to a flight of birds.

BEA also noted as one of the contributing factors that there was "limited awareness within the [French] aviation community regarding the risks associated with the icing on the ground and changes in the performance of the aircraft involved in this phenomenon."[15]

A criminal investigation led to the pilot and the airline being charged with homicide and unintentional injuries. In January 2012, five years after the accident, the pilot in command and the company, Regional Air Force, a subsidiary of Air France, were found guilty of manslaughter and unintentional injury. The pilot was sentenced to a six-month suspended sentence. In addition, the company was fined €20,000 and would also have to pay compensatory damages to the relatives of the deceased truck driver and to the passengers who were injured in the accident. The judges concluded that the aircraft's loss of lift originated from the formation of ice on the wings, but that the pilot in command had not performed the required de-icing prior to takeoff, instead relying on the pre-flight inspection he carried out, during which he did not observe any ice. The court also stated that the pre-flight inspection was carried out very briefly and cursorily, and that the pilot was thus negligent in the conduct of pre-flight and pre-takeoff checks, and that he was also imprudent in his consideration of the risk of icing. The court noted that it did take into account the fact that the pilot had recovered control of the aircraft and managed to avoid a crash with more severe consequences and additional loss of life as well as the fact that the BEA noted that there was "limited awareness within the [French] aviation community regarding the risks associated with the icing on the ground and changes in the performance of the aircraft involved in this phenomenon," but that this did not negate the pilot's negligence.

With regards to the company, the court concluded that it had "culpable negligence in the training and the control of the qualification of its aircrew." It did not provide its pilots with updated information, stressing the importance of conducting a final visual check from inside the aircraft in icing conditions.[16]

8.10 ATLASJET MCDONNELL DOUGLAS MD-83 FLIGHT 4203, ISPARTA, TURKEY (30 NOVEMBER 2007)

On 30 November 2007, an MD-83 operating for Atlasjet Airlines as Flight 4203 with seven crew and 50 passengers, scheduled to fly from Istanbul to Isparta, was destroyed in an accident when it impacted a mountain while the crew were flying a VOR/DME approach to Isparta Airport, killing everyone on board. The investigation into the accident found that the EGPWS had failed repeatedly (86 times in the past 235 flights) and that it had been installed on another aircraft before being installed on the aircraft in question ten days prior to the accident. Additionally, the investigation concluded that both flight crew members appeared to be inexperienced and lacked adequate training.[17]

Following the criminal investigation in Turkey, 20 people were criminally prosecuted in a trial that commenced in 2009 in the Isparta High Criminal Court. In 2015, eight were found guilty and 12 were acquitted. The general manager of World Focus Airlines, the company's training manager, and an AtlasJet manager were sentenced to 11 years and 8 months each on charges of negligent homicide. The maintenance director of World Focus Airlines received a prison sentence of 5 years and 10 months, and two pilots received 2 years and 6 months each for false testimony. The former Director General of Civil Aviation and the deputy Director General each received prison terms of 1 year and 8 months after being convicted of misconduct in office.[18]

In addition, consolidated wrongful death, product liability, and negligence actions were filed by the representatives of 32 of the 57 decedents who died in the accident in Chicago, Illinois, against The Boeing Company (Boeing) and McDonnell Douglas Corporation (McDonnell), the designers and manufacturers of the airplane, and defendant Honeywell International Inc. (Honeywell), the designer and manufacturer of the airplane's enhanced ground proximity warning system. The defendants moved to dismiss the case on the grounds of forum non conveniens, arguing that the case should be heard in the Republic of Turkey, or alternatively, in Washington. The circuit court denied the defendant's motion to dismiss the case on the grounds of forum non conveniens, and they appealed. In 2012, the Second Division Court affirmed the lower court's decision.[19]

8.11 AIR MOOREA DHC-6 TWIN OTTER FLIGHT QE1121, FRENCH POLYNESIA (9 AUGUST 2007)

On 9 August 2007, a DHC-6 aircraft scheduled to fly a public transport flight between Moorea and Tahiti Faa'a, French Polynesia, with a pilot and 19 passengers on board, struck the sea, broke up and sank. The flight with an average duration of 7 minutes is typically performed under VFR at a cruise altitude of 600 feet. The aircraft took off normally, climbed normally to an altitude estimated at between three and four hundred feet, the pilot retracted the flaps, adjusted the engine parameters, and then lost pitch control of the airplane after the failure of the elevator pitch-up control cable. The aircraft dived suddenly and struck the surface of the sea about seven hundred meters from the coastline. Everyone was killed in the accident.[20] According to the accident report, there was one minute and eight seconds between engine power-up and the end of the audio recording. Fourteen bodies, some aircraft debris, including parts of the right main gear and seat cushions, were recovered during the rescue operations. A few days later, a fifteenth body was recovered during operations to recover the flight recorder, both engines, the instrument panel, the front part of the cockpit, including engine and flaps controls, the flaps jackscrews and the tail section. Five bodies were not recovered.

The French Accident Investigation Bureau, the BEA, conducted the official accident investigation. The report outlines the following causes and contributing factors:

> 3.2 Causes: The accident was caused by the loss of airplane pitch control following the failure, at a low height, of the elevator pitch-up control cable at the time the flaps were retracted. This failure was due to the following series of phenomena: Significant wear on the cable in line with a cable guide; An external phenomenon, most likely jet blast, which caused the failure of several strands; The failure of the last strand or strands under in-flight loads on the elevator control system. The following factors may have contributed to the accident: The absence of information and training for pilots on a loss of pitch control; The operator's failure to carry out some special inspections; The failure by the manufacturer and the airworthiness authority to fully take into account the wear phenomenon; The failure by the airworthiness authorities, airport authorities and operators to fully take into account the risks associated with jet blast; The rules for replacement of stainless steel cables on a calendar basis, without taking into account the activity of the airplane in relation to its type of operation. [21]

In a civil action, the deceased's relatives sought compensation of $US 24 million. The French Polynesian lower court awarded slightly less than $US 2 million in compensation, and they appealed. In 2018, the French Polynesian Court of Appeals ruled that compensation in the amount of $US 3.3 million had to be paid to the families of the deceased.[22]

Ten years later, in November 2017, the High Court ruled that the authorities would proceed with the criminal trial and charged six former employees of Air Moorea, the former head of French Polynesia's civil aviation administration, as well as the airline itself, with involuntary criminal manslaughter.

The trial commenced in the criminal court in Papeete on 9 October 2018. The judge found five of the former employees, including the former manager, as well as the head of the government's air safety unit, guilty. The head of the civil aviation was found not guilty. The criminal court sentenced the five former airline employees to prison sentences of up to three years, including the former manager of Air Moorea.[23] The parties appealed their verdict, and one of the defense lawyers stated that for there to be a fair and impartial case, the appeal should be heard outside French Polynesia because a dispassionate trial would be difficult. The request was rejected.[24]

The appeal was heard in January 2020, and the Appeal Court confirmed the sentence of the former manager of Air Moorea and the former head of the government's air safety unit, who were given a three-year prison sentence, of which 18 months were suspended. The sentence of the airline's former technical director, who was also sentenced to a three-year prison sentence, of which two years were suspended, was also confirmed. Another Air Moorea employee was sentenced, and two defendants were acquitted on appeal. The airline was fined.[25]

8.12 RANS S-7S COURIER ULTRA-LIGHT SEAPLANE, CROUSE LAKE, NOVA SCOTIA, CANADA (25 SEPTEMBER 2007)

Two pilots, X and Y, both Swiss nationals, met in Switzerland, where X gave a presentation on flying seaplanes in Canada. Y was an experienced pilot with more than 13,500 flight hours, but was unfamiliar with seaplanes. Since X purported to be able to provide flight training to obtain a Canadian seaplane endorsement, Y decided to travel to Canada to learn from X how to fly a seaplane. X and Y agreed on the remuneration of C$100 per flight hour, including fuel and the instructor fees. On 23 September 2007, X and Y made several training flights in a Rans S-7S Courier ultra-light seaplane around Crouse Lake in Nova Scotia. On September 25, they continued their flight training in the same aircraft and planned to take off from Crouse Lake, fly a circuit and land back on the lake. Shortly after takeoff, while turning onto the downwind leg, the aircraft suddenly descended and struck the ground. Y was killed and X suffered serious injuries. No criminal charges were brought in Canada; however, the Swiss prosecutor alleged that X committed the crimes of death by criminal negligence as well as fraud under Articles 117 and 146 of the Criminal Code of Switzerland, and criminal charges were filed against X.[26]

On 15 May 2014, the Bern Oberland District Court found X guilty of negligent homicide and fraud, and he was sentenced to a suspended custodial sentence of two years and a monetary penalty. Y's widow was awarded compensatory damages and damages for her pain and suffering. Both X and the prosecution appealed, and on 10 August 2015, the Bern Appellate Court confirmed the first instance decision but slightly increased the monetary penalty.

X appealed to the Supreme Court. The Supreme Court made its judgment based on facts as established by the Bern Appellate Court, namely that on the accident flight, the Rans S-7S Courier seaplane's engine had a sudden loss of power, which resulted in an aerodynamic stall and loss of control at low altitude. Since the engine showed no signs of a pre-existing defect, it was concluded that one of the two pilots had inadvertently moved the throttle lever into the idle position, possibly while retracting the flaps. It was established that there was not much space in the cockpit and that the flaps lever was located under the seats.

Based on the facts, therefore, either X or Y had inadvertently pulled the throttle lever into the idle position, which then directly resulted in the aircraft's crash and Y's death. The court submitted that if X pulled the throttle, that act would have led to Y's death and that in that event, X acted recklessly or negligently as he should have known that the aircraft quickly loses power when the throttle lever is idle. A reasonably skilled and prudent pilot would have ensured that no loss of power occurred, or at the very least, a reasonably skilled pilot would immediately have spotted the problem and pushed the lever to the fully open position again, and X failed to do so. On the other hand, the court submitted that if Y moved the throttle lever, it was relevant that X assumed the responsibilities of a flight instructor, although he was not adequately trained to do so. A properly trained flight instructor would have known that the aircraft poses a risk of a student pilot inadvertently moving the throttle into the idle position while retracting the flaps, and would therefore have taken appropriate precautionary measures by informing and supervising the student. A properly trained instructor would also have reacted immediately and pushed the throttle lever back into the fully open position in the event of an inadvertent power loss, and X failed to do so.

On 25 February 2016, the Supreme Court dismissed the appeal. It held that in either of the two scenarios, irrespective of who moved the throttle, X caused Y's death through negligence or recklessness within the meaning of Article 117. In addition, the court found that X was guilty of fraud according to Article 146, because he falsely pretended to be a flight instructor and induced Y to travel to Canada, thereby causing financial damage.[27]

8.13 SPANAIR FLIGHT JK 5022, BARAJAS AIRPORT (20 AUGUST 2008) – UPDATE

An MD-82 crashed just after takeoff from Barajas Airport in Madrid, resulting in 154 fatalities and 18 survivors. The accident report indicates that the wing flaps failed to move into the required configuration, and the alarm system that would usually alert pilots failed to activate. Both the technical report which was conducted by the Civil Aviation Accident and Incident Investigation Committee (CIAIAC) and the criminal investigation report concluded that the accident resulted from a chain of events; however, two causes were prominent, namely, the serious errors on the part of the pilots who forgot to activate the flaps and slats on the wings, which were necessary for takeoff, and a technical error in the failure of the plane's TOWS alarm system to alert the pilots of their error.

As a result of the criminal investigation, which was opened by the Court of Instruction of Madrid in August 2008, five employees of Spanair were provisionally charged with 154 counts of involuntary manslaughter and 18 counts of causing injury. The two mechanics were charged with failing to properly repair the malfunctioning Ram Air Temperature (RAT) probe, which had caused the plane to return to the apron just an hour before the accident. The mechanics disconnected the fuse that powered the probe, saw that the temperature went down, and dispatched the plane according to the Minimal Equipment Manual, which stipulates that such repairs on malfunctions can be deferred for up to 10 days. The judicial report placed greater emphasis on this and, taking a stricter view of this error than the CIAIAC report, concluded that the mechanics dispatched the plane incorrectly, without identifying the problem. The report also blamed three Spanair managers for not properly instructing the two mechanics in how to deal with the RAT malfunction, including the maintenance shift boss working that day, and the heads of Spanair's maintenance and service divisions. Spanair technicians who had also investigated the accident concluded that Boeing, which merged with McDonnell Douglas in 1997, as the owner of the manufacturer of the plane, was liable. Spanair stated that the pilots were correctly prepared but admitted that they lacked discipline in the cockpit and that the pilots were distracted in the cockpit as a result of, inter alia, a third person being in the cockpit. In 2011, the injured passengers and the relatives of the deceased filed lawsuits in the California federal court against Boeing, alleging that the aircraft was defective. However, before the court could consider the case, it had to decide whether the USA was the correct forum to hear the case or whether, under the doctrine of forum non conveniens, it should be dismissed to be tried in the Spanish courts. The court rejected the plaintiffs' argument that it would be a financial disadvantage and economic burden to have the trial in Spain, as contingency fee agreements are not permitted in Spain, and said that it would be cheaper for the plaintiffs to obtain witness testimony in Spain. The court held that Spain would be the appropriate forum and dismissed the case.[28]

On completing the criminal investigation in December 2011, the criminal judge considered that only the two Spanair ground engineers should stand trial. The prosecutor asked for prison sentences of two-and-a-half to four years, and the revocation of their professional licenses for a period of three to six years. The victims and claimants sued Spanair in separate civil proceedings.

In September 2012, in the appeal to Madrid's Audiencia Provincial, the court referred to both the final reports on the accident from the Civil Aviation Accident and Incident Investigation Committee. The court held that the deceased pilots were solely to blame for the accident. The court stated that shortly after take-off, the crew lost control of the aircraft as a result of a stall as they did not have the correct plane configuration for take-off (by not deploying the flaps and slats, following a series of errors and omissions), coupled with the absence of any warning of the incorrect configuration. The crew did not recognize the indications of stall and did not correct the situation after take-off, and – by momentarily retarding the engine power and increasing the pitch angle – brought about a deterioration in the flight condition. The crew did not detect the configuration error because they did not correctly use the checklists to select and check the position of the flaps and slats during flight preparation. The court further held that the mechanics did not receive proper training and that there was no criminal case to answer. The charges against the two Spanair mechanics were dismissed, and the criminal investigation was closed.[29]

8.14 ITEK AIR BOEING 737 FLIGHT 6895, KYRGYZSTAN (24 AUGUST 2008) – UPDATE

The accident occurred on 24 August 2008, and in September, the pilot was arrested even before the technical investigation into the accident was completed. The trial, which took place in the Pervomaisky District Court of Bishkek, lasted more than a year. On 28 December 2009, both pilots were found guilty of a crime under Article 208, part 3 of the Criminal Code, namely, violating traffic safety and air transport operation rules. The captain was sentenced to 5 years and 2 months, and the copilot, who was taken into custody in the courtroom, to 5 years. Itek Air stopped flying in 2010. It is reported that from August 2011, both pilots were released and went to Russia.[30]

8.15 CESSNA 182, NAPA AIRPORT, SAN MATEO COUNTY, CALIFORNIA, USA (5 AUGUST 2009)

On 5 August 2009, the pilot of a Cessna 182 took off from Napa Airport on a solo flight. As the Cessna climbed from the runway, it turned in the wrong direction and collided with high terrain just north of the airport, killing the pilot. The pilot was killed on impact, his body was ejected, and the aircraft exploded and burned. The accident was investigated by the National Transportation Safety Board, which held that the accident had occurred as a result of pilot error, in that when he encountered poor weather, he became confused, failed to follow the correct instrument departure procedure, and his disorientation led to the collision with the terrain. An instructor who had flown with the deceased pilot a few days before the accident, who found that he was proficient in the Napa departure procedure and otherwise meticulous in his flying, felt it was unlikely that the deceased would become confused and turn in the wrong direction. The deceased's wife and his adult children sued the Cessna's mechanic, alleging that he was negligent in the maintenance of the aircraft, had failed to inspect the aircraft, and had made misrepresentations that led to the deceased's wrongful death.

Civil proceedings for compensation were filed in the Superior Court of San Mateo County. The plaintiffs alleged that the mechanic had performed maintenance on the aircraft without properly recording the work in the aircraft's logs and that he had performed undocumented repairs on the pilot's seat a few weeks before the crash. Expert evidence showed that as the pilot climbed away from the runway, his seat suddenly and unexpectedly slid to its full aft position and jammed. As his hands and feet could not reach the aircraft's controls, the aircraft flew off course and out of control. He then unbuckled his seatbelt so that he could go on his knees up to the aircraft's control wheel. Before he could regain control, the aircraft crashed.[31]

On 26 February 2016, after a seven-day trial, the jury found the mechanic guilty of negligence and that his negligence was a substantial factor in causing the deceased pilot harm and awarded the plaintiffs a total of $13.36 million in damages. The amount of $1.76 million for past economic damages, $1.1 million for future economic damages, $7 million for past non-economic damages, and $3.5 million for future non-economic damages was awarded. As a result of the verdict, the Federal Aviation Administration instituted proceedings to revoke the mechanic's licenses.[32]

8.16 AIR FRANCE AIRBUS A330 FLIGHT 447, ATLANTIC OCEAN (1 JUNE 2009) – UPDATE

On 1 June 2009, AF447, a scheduled passenger flight from Rio de Janeiro, Brazil, to Paris, France with 216 passengers and 12 crew, stalled and crashed into the Atlantic Ocean. All 228 persons on board the aircraft died. After many attempts to locate the wreckage and nearly two years later, on 2 April 2011, pieces of wreckage, including an engine, landing gear, fuselage, and wing parts, were located on the floor of the Atlantic Ocean. The Flight Data Recorder was found and brought to the surface on 1st May, and the Cockpit Voice Recorder on 2 May 2011.

The official investigation was conducted by the French Civil Aviation Safety Investigation Authority, the Bureau d'Enquêtes et d'Analyses pour la sécurité de l'aviation civile (BEA), which found that the accident was caused by icing of the pitot tubes and the pilot's incorrect reaction to this. The final report, published in July 2012, states that the accident was caused by, inter alia, an obstruction of the Pitot probes by ice crystals during cruise, something which was known but misunderstood by the aviation community at the time of the accident; temporary inconsistency between the airspeed measurements, which probably occurred after the obstruction of the Pitot probes by ice crystals, which caused the autopilot disconnection and the reconfiguration to alternate law; inappropriate control inputs by the pilots that destabilized the flight path; the lack of any link by the crew between the loss of indicated speeds called out and the appropriate procedure; the late identification by the pilot not flying of the deviation from the flight path and the insufficient correction applied by the pilot flying; the crew not identifying the approach to stall, their lack of immediate response and the exit from the flight envelope; and the failure by the crew to diagnose the stall situation and then a lack of inputs that would have made it possible to recover from it.[33]

Civil compensation claims were filed by the relatives of the deceased in the United States of America; however, the courts dismissed the claims, stating that, as France was still an available forum, the U.S. courts were forum non conveniens.[34]

Air France and Airbus were criminally investigated from 5 June 2009, and they were charged with manslaughter in 2011. Prosecutors argued that the charges against Airbus should be dropped, but that Air France should be charged with manslaughter and negligence based on the ground that it was allegedly aware of technical problems with a key airspeed monitoring instrument on the aircraft but did not train the pilots to resolve them.

The case against Airbus was dropped in July 2019. In September 2019, the charges against Air France were dropped. However, in 2021, a public prosecutor in Paris requested that Airbus and Air France be tried in a court, and in April, the court decided that there would be a trial. The trial commenced on 10 October 2022, and both companies pleaded not guilty. The court said that it was impossible to convict the two companies, as, even though it found that Airbus and Air France had committed "acts of imprudence," there was not a strong enough link of causality between their failings and the accident to hold the companies responsible for the charge of involuntary manslaughter.[35]

At the end of the two-month trial, on 7 December 2022, prosecutors announced that they would not seek a conviction of either Airbus or Air France as they could not prove their guilt, and recommended acquitting both companies. Much to the disappointment of the relatives of the deceased, both Airbus and Air France were acquitted of the manslaughter charges. Rarely does a prosecutor appeal an acquittal; however, in April 2023, the public prosecutor of the Paris Appeals Court announced that he would appeal the decision.[36] In 2024, the Appeal Court overruled the acquittal of both defendants and ordered a new trial. The 60-day appeal trial commenced on 29 September and ended on 26 November 2025. The verdict is expected to be given in 2026.

8.17 POLISH AIR FORCE TUPOLEV TU-154M, SMOLENSK, RUSSIA (10 APRIL 2010)

On 10 April 2010, a Tupolev Tu-154M VIP passenger aircraft operated by the Polish Air Force was scheduled to fly from Warsaw, Poland, to Russia for ceremonies honoring Polish officers killed in 1940 during World War II. The aircraft crashed on approach to Smolensk Air Base, near the city of Smolensk, Russia, in poor visibility. The plane was carrying four flight crew members, three cabin crew members, 88 passengers, and one security officer on board, all of whom were Polish citizens. All 96 passengers, including the Polish President, his wife, the Deputy Minister of Foreign Affairs, the Chief of the General Staff, Commanders-in-Chief, the President of the Polish National Bank, as well as several Members of Parliament, senators, and prominent figures, were killed. The aircraft was completely destroyed.

Shortly after the crash, the President of Russia, Dmitry Medvedev, announced that a special commission, supervised by Prime Minister Vladimir Putin, would be established to investigate the accident.[37] The Prosecutor General of Russia started a criminal case to investigate possible violations of safety rules in accordance with the Russian Criminal Code. In addition, Poland also initiated a criminal investigation.

The investigation into the accident was conducted by the Russian Interstate Aviation Committee (IAC) in accordance with ICAO Annex 13. Poland also set up its own committee to investigate the crash. The Russian IAC concluded that the immediate cause of the accident was the failure of the crew to take a timely decision to proceed to an alternate airdrome, although they had not been timely informed on the actual weather conditions at Smolensk Airdrome that were significantly lower than the established airdrome minima; descent without visual contact with ground references to an altitude much lower than minimum descent altitude for go-around (100 m) to establish visual flight, as well as no reaction to the numerous Terrain Awareness and Warning System (TAWS) warnings, which led to controlled flight into terrain, aircraft destruction, and death of the crew and passengers. According to the conclusions made by the pilot-experts and aviation psychologists, the presence of the Commander-in-Chief of the Polish Air Forces in the cockpit until the collision had exposed psychological pressure on the PIC's decision to continue descent under conditions of unjustified risk, with a dominating aim of landing by any means. The report goes on to state that the systematic causes of the accident were significant shortcomings in the organization of flight operations, flight crew preparation, and arrangement of the VIP flight in the special air regiment. The separate investigation conducted by the Polish Committee for Investigation of National Aviation Accidents concluded that the immediate cause of the accident was the descent below the minimum descent altitude at an excessive rate of descent in weather conditions that prevented visual contact with the ground and the delayed execution of the go-around procedure, which led to an impact on a terrain obstacle resulting in the separation of a part of the left wing with aileron and consequently to the loss of aircraft control and eventual ground impact.[38]

This was a high-profile accident with VIP persons on board, and there were allegations that the accident was not caused by pilot error but that it was a deliberate, political act. The deceased President's twin brother, who became the leader of Poland's nationalist ruling party, Law and Justice, claimed that the crash was a political assassination and has blamed the crash on negligence by Donald Tusk's government, which was critical of his brother. Tusk was the Prime Minister of Poland at the time of the accident and a political rival for many years.[39] He was President of the European Council, and his second term ended on 30 November 2019.

In 2015, the Law and Justice party won the parliamentary elections, and the new conservative government appointed the chair of the Polish Parliamentary Committee of Investigation as the defense minister. He announced that Poland would sue Russia as Moscow was still, at that time, withholding the wreckage.[40] In February 2016, the investigation into the crash was officially reopened.[41] As part of the renewed investigation, six years after the accident, the remains of the deceased Polish president were exhumed on 14 November 2016.[42]

The Russian report attributed the entire responsibility for the accident to the crew members. In contrast, the Polish investigators concluded that Russian air traffic control also shared some responsibility by transmitting incorrect information to the crew regarding the aircraft's position, and that the deficiencies at Smolensk Airport contributed to the crash. In addition, Poland questioned the independence and neutrality of the Russian Interstate Aviation Committee. On 11 April 2018, the Committee for re-investigating the crash, appointed by the Polish Government, published a new preliminary report in which it concluded that the aircraft was destroyed in the air as a result of several explosions.[43]

Russia kept custody of the wreckage, and in November 2015, Poland announced it would sue Russia to hand over the wreckage to the Polish authorities.[44] In 2017, the investigative committee set up by the Polish government requested experts from the British Ministry of Defence's Forensic Explosives Laboratory to join the investigation and examine the wreckage of the aircraft for traces of explosives.[45] Even though copies of the flight data recordings and some material evidence had been given to the Polish authorities, eight years after the crash, the Russian Federation still had custody of the wreckage, the black boxes with the original flight data recordings, and other evidentiary material. In 2018, the Parliamentary Assembly of the Council of Europe issued a resolution calling on the Russian Federation to inter alia, hand over the wreckage to the Polish authorities without any further delay and to adequately protect the wreckage in a manner agreed with Polish experts until the evidence is handed over. It also called on the Russian and Polish law enforcement authorities to fully cooperate in establishing any possible criminal responsibility and to expeditiously make any evidence available at the request of the other State.[46]

A number of the deceased's relatives sued officials in Tusk's government of the time, including the head of his office, alleging that they had failed to ensure the safety of the flight. Five former Polish officials were charged with negligence during the preparation of the presidential flight. They were the former Prime Minister's chief of staff, two officials who worked at his office, and two employees of the Polish embassy in Moscow. The charge alleges that the former chief of staff failed to report that the military airfield in Smolensk was not on the list of international airports suitable for the VIP plane to land at. He denied the allegations, saying that he helped organize Tusk's flight to Smolensk three days before the crash, but had not been in charge of the presidential flight.[47] In April 2018, Tusk appeared before a three-judge panel at the Provincial Court in Warsaw and testified that he had no role or influence in the preparation of his or the President's flights.[48]

On 13 June 2019, the provincial court in Warsaw found the then chief of staff for former Polish Prime Minister Donald Tusk guilty of negligence in that he had exposed the late president to danger by allowing a hazardous flight to a rudimentary Russian airport. He was given a 10-month suspended sentence. The official who was involved in preparing the flight was also found guilty and sentenced to a six-month suspended sentence.[49]

In May 2022, a Polish court ordered the arrest of the Russian air traffic controller accused by Polish prosecutors of intentional actions that caused the plane crash. Criminal proceedings commenced in March 2015 when Polish prosecutors charged the two Russian air traffic controllers with manslaughter resulting in the deaths of 96 people. In 2017, the charges were changed as prosecutors alleged that "the suspects, by knowingly allowing the plane to descend and make a conditional trial approach to landing, had anticipated a catastrophe and consented to it." In addition, the person who had been giving orders to the flight manager was also charged. The prosecutors said that the new charges were made after further analysis of the recordings from the air traffic control tower at Smolensk and from the cockpit of the Tupolev aircraft. The charges were not presented to the accused. The Polish authorities state that "the Russian Federation has refused to respond to Polish requests to deliver summonses, claiming alleged threats to its national interest."[50]

8.18 AIR INDIA BOEING 747 FLIGHT 812, MANGALORE, INDIA (22 MAY 2010)

On 22 May 2010, a passenger flight from Dubai to Mangalore crashed on landing at Mangalore International Airport and overshot the runway, resulting in the death of 152 of the 160 passengers and all 6 crew members. This accident had the most fatalities with the Boeing 737 Next Generation aircraft until the accidents involving the Boeing 737 MAX-8 aircraft. Mangalore airport has a table-top runway and is designated as a critical airfield by the Directorate General of Civil Aviation (DGCA), the rules of which stipulate that only the Captain can pilot the aircraft during take-off and landing, as the landing requires heightened awareness and a very precise landing approach. The Captain had landed 16 times in the past, and the First Officer (FO) had operated as a co-pilot on 66 flights at this airport. On 3 June 2010, the Government of India appointed the Former Vice Chief of Air Staff as the head of the Court of Inquiry to investigate the accident, and the final report was submitted five months later. The report stated that the cause of the accident was the Captain's failure to discontinue the unstabilised approach and his persistence in continuing with the landing, despite three calls from the FO to go around and several EGPWS warnings.[51]

The pilot's son called for the accident investigation to be reopened, alleging that the accident investigation report, which found his father negligent, did not consider the inadequate safety measures at Mangalore Airport. He stated that the aircraft caught fire after crashing into the instrument landing system at the end of the runway and that he believed that the positioning of the system there, which is contrary to international aviation regulations, was partly to blame for the accident.[52]

With regards to the civil action and the compensation payments to the deceased's relatives, Air India is said to have paid 1.15 billion rupees (approx. USD76.4 million) in compensation claims according to the Air Carriages Act, but families have sought compensation in accordance with the Montreal Convention (MC) 1999, of which India is a member. On 20 July 2011, based on a petition filed by one of the victims, the Kerala High Court ruled that Air India was liable to pay a no-fault liability based on the MC 1999 and that the amount would be over and above any other compensation that the petitioners were entitled to.[53] Air India appealed, and on 25 August 2011, the division bench stayed the single bench order on compensation. On 5 September 2011, the Kerala High Court ordered Air India to pay an interim compensation.[54] In 2012, the Supreme Court issued a notice to the country's government and Air India to find out why it had not paid the minimum compensation to the surviving victims and the relatives of the deceased. Air India appointed the Nanavati Commission, which negotiated with victims' relatives, and in some cases, they were settled.

Thirty months after the accident, the recommendations made by the investigation committee, which included lengthening the runway at Mangalore airport and having the Directorate General of Civil Aviation (DGCA) conduct observation flights to Mangalore between midnight and 6:00 a.m. as often as possible, had not been implemented. In January 2013, an implementation committee was formed to monitor the recommendations. In addition, a Mangalore-based trust, the 812 Foundation, acting on behalf of the deceased, filed a petition in the Karnataka High Court, which was heard on 15 January, demanding that criminal charges for negligence be filed against the Airport Authority of India, Air India, and the Director General of Civil Aviation, Mangalore. The complaint alleges that the accident was a direct consequence of the willful gross negligence by the Airport Authority of India, gross negligence on the part of Air India and the Directorate General of Civil Aviation, in addition to the pilot. The petition states that the Airport Authority did not comply with the ICAO requirements regarding the non-frangible structure at the airport, which was determined to have caused the fire. The allegation centered on the pilot's qualifications.[55]

8.19 AIRBLUE A321 FLIGHT ABQ202, ISLAMABAD, PAKISTAN (28 JULY 2010)

On 28 July 2010, Airblue A321, Flight ABQ 202, departed from Karachi International Airport and was scheduled to fly to Islamabad with 146 passengers and six crew members. The weather was poor with poor visibility. A Pakistan International Airlines (PIA) flight landed after the third attempt, and a flight from China chose not to land and returned. During the circling approach, the captain of the Airblue flight descended below Minimum Descent Altitude and lost visual contact with the airfield. After breaking off from the instrument landing system (ILS) approach, the captain ignored the tower controller's suggestion to fly a bad weather circuit. The CVR recording and flight simulation indicated that the captain decided to fly a non-standard, self-created Place Bearing Distance (PBD) based approach, which led to the aircraft straying off course. The aircraft crashed into the Margalla Hills near Islamabad-Benazir Bhutto International Airport, killing everyone aboard and destroying the plane.[56] The flight recorders, which contained the complete flight data as well as the cockpit voice recording for the entire flight duration from take-off until the crash, were found at the crash, lying in the rear fuselage.

The Pakistan Civil Aviation Authority Safety Investigation Board conducted the investigation. The report, which was released on 24 April 2012, concluded that the

> Air blue crash has been finalized as a case of Controlled Flight into Terrain (CFIT), in which aircrew failed to display superior judgment and professional skills in a self-created unsafe environment. In their pursuit to land in inclement weather, they committed serious violations of procedures and breaches of flying discipline, which put the aircraft in an unsafe condition over dangerous terrain at low altitude.

During the initial climb, the Captain started testing the knowledge of the First Officer (FO) for about an hour and a half, using harsh words and a snobbish tone, after which the FO became quiet, submissive, and did not challenge the Captain for any of his errors, breaches, and violations. The Captain did not respond to 21 EGPWS warnings related to approaching terrain and pull up, and did not take any appropriate action following calls from the FO to pull up. The report also stated that at the crucial juncture, both the ATC and the radar controllers were preoccupied with bad weather and the traffic.[57]

The Pakistan CAA report, which stated that the lack of professionalism in the cockpit and poor weather were the primary causes of the accident, was presented to the Peshawar High Court in March. In October 2013, the Peshawar High Court stated that the 61-year-old pilot was aged and not mentally alert, and that he had ignored the radar alerts that hills were ahead and that the aircraft should have gained altitude. Concluding that the cause of the accident was pilot error, the court found the pilot of Airblue Flight ABQ 202 guilty. The two judges sitting in the High Court also stated that the air traffic control tower failed to provide standard landing facilities and that the controller at the time was inexperienced in dealing with such a complex situation.[58] In addition, the High Court Chief Justice ordered Airblue to provide financial compensation to the families of the victims. It also issued directives to investigate the incident under the supervision of foreign experts, instructions to the legal heirs of the deceased to attach indemnity bonds, and to produce successor certificates for claiming compensation. The court also heard a petition filed by Pakistan Muslim League Nawaz's Marvi Memon against the Airblue administration.[59]

8.20 KATEKAVIA FLIGHT KTK57, ANTONOV 24, IGARKA AIRPORT, RUSSIA (3 AUGUST 2010)

On 3 August 2010, Katekavia Flight 57, a passenger plane, was scheduled to fly from Krasnoyarsk Cheremshanka Airport to Igarka Airport. The aircraft with four crew members and eleven passengers crashed while on final approach to runway 12 in nighttime and poor visibility conditions. The crew continued the approach below 100 m even though they had not established positive visual contact with the runway. The aircraft drifted to the right until it struck trees 477 m short of the runway and 234 m to the right of the extended centerline, slid for 140 m through trees, and a fire broke out. The aircraft was destroyed, and all eleven passengers and one of the four crew members on board were killed. The final accident report of the Russian Interstate Aviation Committee (MAK) concluded that the cause of the accident was the execution of the approach in conditions worse than the weather minima of the airfield, the aircraft, and pilot. It stated that the crew failed to take a timely decision for a missed approach when the aircraft descended below the minimum safe height in the absence of reliable visual contact with approach lights and runway lights, causing the aircraft to strike trees and the ground in controlled flight.[60]

In October 2013, the court in Krasnoyarsk, Siberia, ruled that the captain could have avoided the accident by waiting for better weather conditions instead of continuing his landing approach in poor visibility. During the trial, the pilot argued that the air traffic control service and the airport's meteorologists were responsible for the accident, alleging that they had misled the flight crew. The judge rejected his arguments, found the pilot guilty, and sentenced him to four and a half years' imprisonment. The pilot said that he would appeal the unjust verdict.[61]

8.21 DAGESTAN AIRLINES FLIGHT 372 TUPOLEV TU-154, MOSCOW DOMODEDOVO AIRPORT, RUSSIA (4 DECEMBER 2010)

Dagestan Airlines Flight 372 was a scheduled commercial flight from Moscow's Vnukovo Airport to Makhachkala, Russia, carrying 8 crew members and 163 passengers. On 4 December 2010, the aircraft skidded off the runway following an emergency landing at Domodedovo Airport. Two passengers were killed, and six crew members and 33 passengers were seriously injured. The aircraft landed hard with forces of 3.5g and 5g on a second touchdown and continued until it struck a small earthen mound beyond the end of the runway, causing it to split into three parts. The accident was investigated by the Russian Interstate Aviation Committee (IAC) and the report released on 26 September 2011 stated that the accident was caused due to the erroneous actions of the crew during the flight and approach in instrumental meteorological conditions with one engine running (out of three), which resulted in the aircraft approaching significantly to the right of the extended center line, exiting the runway after landing and colliding with an embankment. The flight engineer accidentally shut off a fuel pump while transferring fuel, resulting in fluctuating fuel flow, which led to unusual altitude and engine readings before the outer two engines shut down. The crew decided to divert to Domodedovo Airport. The report states that the crew had not used all available options to deal with the loss of engine power and had not followed procedures for landing with two nonfunctional engines. The report also noted that the crew had not received sufficient training to deal with the situation.[62]

The Russian authorities classified the investigation as a criminal investigation. The spokesperson for the Investigative Committee stated that Russia's Chief Prosecutor had taken special control of the investigation. The pilot was charged with violating the traffic safety rules and operating an air transport article in accordance with Article 263, Part 3 of the Russian Criminal Code, which carries a prison sentence of up to seven years' imprisonment.[63]

The pilot pleaded not guilty to the charges and insisted that he had acted correctly throughout the flight. On 22 January 2015, the Domodedovo City Court of the Moscow Region found that the pilot had violated safety rules of transportation and air travel and that his negligence had led to the death of two persons. He was given a suspended sentence of 3 years and was then amnestied and released from the punishment.[64]

8.22 YAK 42 FLIGHT 9633, YAROSLAVI AIRPORT, RUSSIA (7 SEPTEMBER 2011)

On 7 Sep 2011, a Yakovlev 42 with 45 passengers and crew was scheduled to fly members of the Lokomotiv Yaroslavl hockey team to a match in Minsk, Belarus. The aircraft crashed on take-off from Yaroslavl Tunoshna Airport, Russia, killing 44 people. The flight engineer who traveled in the passenger cabin was the only survivor. The Russian Interstate Aviation Committee (IAC), which investigated the accident, found that several pilot errors caused the accident. The crew incorrectly calculated the V1 speed to be 190 km/h instead of 220 km/h; the co-pilot had medical issues, he had leg coordination disturbances and deep sensibility disorders of lower extremities - blood tests revealed traces of the medicine phenobarbital in his blood, which has a negative impact on the nervous system, and degraded his performance; both the captain and the co-pilot had previously flown the YAK-40 aircraft which had a different method of braking and one of the two pilots had probably held his feet on the pedals during take-off in a similar manner used in the YAK 40 aircraft and that he inadvertently activated the brakes while pulling the controls to lift the nose for take-off, preventing the aircraft from gathering enough speed.

In addition, they stated that there were at least four factors that had contributed to the accident, namely: the absence of control over the crew's preparation for flight, the pilots' failure to follow standard take-off procedures, poor coordination between the crew during the take-off, and a lack of pilot training. The crew was scheduled to undergo re-training from 5–17 September, but instead they were flying.

On 21 May 2015, a suit was filed with the Supreme Court on behalf of the relatives of the deceased to invalidate the agreement between the Russian government and the Interstate Aviation Committee (IAC) on the terms of its operation in Russia, stating that the government cannot confer the power to investigate aviation accidents to an agency other than the country's pre-trial investigation agencies, which have the authority to investigate all criminal cases, including aviation accidents, in accordance with Russia's Criminal Procedure Code.[65]

In May, the relatives' lawyer filed a suit in the Zamoskvoretsky District Court in Moscow, challenging the official conclusions of the IAC Technical Commission and asking the court to declare the findings invalid on the basis that they were contradictory, based on supposition, and contested by independent professional experts. The families of the pilots alleged that the accident investigation was conducted in violation of ICAO standards and recommended practices, and also challenged the conclusion drawn. They alleged that the finding regarding the brake pedals was not based on any legal document. The finding that the airplane stalled due to a critical angle of attack was also challenged, as the flight data recorder did not record this critical angle.[66]

In September 2012, the IAC investigators stated that both pilots had not undergone the necessary training for the Yak-42 aircraft and that they were illegally granted permission to fly, based on forged documents. In addition, they found that the Yak Service's former deputy flight director had allegedly violated flight safety rules, among other things, by permitting the crew to make a flight illegally. On 6 September 2012, criminal charges were filed against him.[67] He pleaded not guilty and stated that the accident was caused by poorly placed cargo, as the team's luggage had not been weighed before departure in violation of the relevant rules. He faced seven years' imprisonment if found guilty. The trial, which took place in a district court in Yaroslavi, commenced on 3 December 2014 and ended in September 2015.

On 21 September 2015, in a verdict that took nearly 20 hours to pronounce, he was found guilty of violating Part 3 of Article 263 of the Russian Criminal Code, governing the safe operation of aircraft, resulting in the manslaughter of more than two people, and was sentenced to five years' imprisonment. The Court then went on to order his release under the 2015 V-Day amnesty.[68]

At the end of the criminal trial, the Russian Investigative Committee spokesman stated that, in addition to the errors made by the crew during departure, the crew was cleared for the flight by the operator, Yak Service airline, with flagrant violations of flight safety regulations. He said that the former Yak Service Deputy General Director for Flight Operations was prosecuted for violating flight safety and aircraft operation rules. Specifically, he failed to provide professional training for pilots, regularly recalled them from training courses, and illegally cleared them for flights before their training was over. In addition, he did not analyze data from flight recorders, which registered the mistakes made by the deceased captain in his previous flights.[69]

8.23 SWISS INTERNATIONAL AIRLINES SWISS INTERNATIONAL AIRLINES FLIGHT SWR132 AND SWR202W NEAR COLLISION, ZURICH AIRPORT (15 MARCH 2011)

On 15 March 2011, Swiss International Airlines Airbus SWR 1326, an A320 aircraft, received clearance to taxi to the take-off position on runway 16. While taxiing to the take-off position, the air traffic control officer of the aerodrome control cleared the aircraft for take-off. The crew acknowledged this clearance and initiated their take-off roll. At approximately the same time, another A320 Swiss International Airlines Airbus, SWR 202W, which was waiting in the take-off position on runway 28, received clearance for take-off. The crew acknowledged this clearance and immediately initiated their take-off roll. During the take-off roll, the crew of SWR 202W noticed SWR 1326, which was converging from the right on runway 16, and immediately initiated an aborted take-off. The Swiss Transportation Safety Investigation Board found that the serious incident was

> attributable to the fact that the air traffic control officer concerned gave take-off clearance to an aircraft on runway 28, although another aircraft on runway 16, to which he had given take off clearance shortly before, was still on its take-off roll. The result was that an inadvertent convergence of these aircraft occurred, involving a high risk of collision.[70]

The prosecution charged the controller who had cleared the two aircraft to take off from two crossing runways under Article 237 of the Criminal Code, which penalizes anyone who wilfully or negligently endangers public transport, including air transport, and thereby "causes danger to the life and limb of other people." Anyone found guilty could face a prison sentence or a fine. The prosecution alleged that he had negligently disrupted public transport and endangered people. The Bulach District Court held that the collision risk had been insufficiently high and acquitted the controller. The prosecution appealed the judgment.

The High Court of the Canton of Zurich ruled that the controller was guilty, as his conduct resulted in a severe and real collision risk which endangered the passengers and crew of both aircraft, and that this amounted to negligence. The controller was given a monetary penalty. The defense appealed to the Supreme Court against the conviction.

On 29 October 2019, four months after the conviction, the Supreme Court acquitted the controller, stating that Article 237 of the Criminal Code requires an actual risk, not a potential or hypothetical risk, and that the court should examine what actually happened, not what could have happened. As such, as no actual collision risk existed, the controller was not guilty under Article 237 of the Criminal Code.[71]

8.24 DARWIN AIRWAYS SAAB 2000 FLIGHT DWT 124/ SPORTCRUISER INCIDENT, ZURICH (22 AUGUST 2012)

On 22 August 2012, a Darwin Airline Saab 2000, scheduled to fly from Zurich, Switzerland, to Genoa, Italy, was departing while a private Sportcruiser was on final approach with the intention of conducting a touch-and-go. On 11 September 2012, the Swiss BFU initiated an investigation into the incident, describing it as a close encounter between a VFR aircraft attempting a touch-and-go on Runway 16 and an IFR aircraft departing from Runway 28. The final report, released on 24 September 2014, states that the minimum separation between the aircraft was reduced to 205 m laterally and 75 feet vertically and that the probable causes were the air traffic controller giving a takeoff clearance on runway 28 to a commercial aircraft while a light aircraft was on its approach to runway 16 and the incorrect assessment of the situation by the air traffic controller (which was determined to be a direct causal factor). The following factors were identified as systemic factors which contributed to the serious incident: the inadequate risk assessment by air traffic control; a complex training flight was taking place at a time when the volume of traffic was increasing and at medium complexity; visual approaches were rarely carried out on runway 16; and the TCAS fitted in the commercial aircraft did not provide any information to the crew on the ground about other aircraft, and this restricted their situational awareness.[72]

The air traffic controller on duty was criminally charged, and in March 2019, the Bulach District Court found him guilty of negligent disruption of public transport within the meaning of Article 237 of the Criminal Code.

Criticizing the court's decision, Skyguide stated that Switzerland is one of the few states that has chosen to depart from international standards and recommendations and the Annexes to ICAO with regard to the use of the final Annex 13 technical report to commence court proceedings. IFATCA and ECA state that the 1942 penal code binds the Swiss court system in these cases in a way that is contrary to aviation safety. They call for a review of the regulations to be more consistent with other States and International standards, and to incorporate the principles of just culture into their legal system.[73]

In November 2017, Darwin Airline filed for insolvency, and a day later, the Swiss Federal Office of Civil Aviation revoked Darwin Airline's operating certificate due to financial reasons.[74]

8.25 ASIANA AIRLINES BOEING 777 FLIGHT 214, SEOUL, SOUTH KOREA (6 JULY 2013)

On 6 July 2013, Asiana Airlines Flight 214 with 291 passengers and 16 crew members left Incheon International Airport, Seoul, South Korea, en route to San Francisco, USA, and crashed on final approach to San Francisco. Seven seconds before impact, one of the crew members made a call to increase speed. Four seconds before impact, the stick shaker sounded, and 1.5 seconds before impact, one of the crew members made a call for a go-around. The throttles were advanced, and the engines appeared to respond normally. The main landing gear and rear fuselage then struck a sea wall, and the tail section broke off. The aircraft ballooned, yawed left, spun 360 degrees, and then came to rest to the left of the runway. A post-impact fire occurred when a fuel tank ruptured inboard of the No. 2 engine, spilling fuel on the hot engine, causing it to ignite. Three passengers were killed and 48 were injured. Impact forces and the ensuing fire destroyed the aircraft. Evacuation was delayed for about 90 seconds, which was attributed partly to the pilot's command not to initiate an immediate evacuation, as well as disorientation and confusion. The National Transportation Safety Board investigated the accident. The final report stated that the probable cause of this accident was the flight crew's mismanagement of the airplane's descent during the visual approach, the unintended deactivation of automatic airspeed control by the pilot flying, the flight crew's inadequate monitoring of airspeed, and the flight crew's delayed execution of a go-around after they became aware that the airplane was below acceptable glidepath and airspeed tolerances.[75]

One of the passengers, a 16-year-old Chinese passenger who was ejected from the aircraft and was lying on the tarmac covered in flame-retardant foam, was accidentally hit by a fire truck that was rushing to the scene. In October, the prosecuting authorities announced that he could not be held criminally responsible and would not be prosecuted.[76]

Many lawsuits were filed in the aftermath of the accident. In July 2015, passengers filed a lawsuit against Asiana Airlines in a California federal court, alleging that the errors, omissions, and improper crew training had caused the accident and sought a minimum of $5 million for bodily and mental injuries as well as economic damages.[77] A further 83 passengers filed a lawsuit against Boeing, alleging a possible failure of the auto-throttle system.[78]

In August 2013, four plaintiffs filed a complaint against Boeing and Asiana Airlines, with five causes of action, namely:

> First, Boeing inadequately designed, manufactured, distributed, and/or sold the aircraft that crashed on 6 July 2013 with several defects, including a faulty auto-throttle control system, inadequate auto-throttle warnings, ineffective low-speed warnings, and/or lap-only seat belts in sections of its aircraft:
>
> Second, Boeing failed to adequately train, notify, monitor, supervise, and/or update pilots to fly the Boeing 777-200ER; and/or warn Asiana of concerns Boeing knew or should have known about the unfitness of Asiana pilots to fly the Boeing aircraft;

> Third, Aisana negligently operated, maintained, controlled, equipped, and/or piloted the fateful aircraft, including failing to provide passengers in economy class with the same robust seat restraint systems as those in business class;
>
> Fourth, Asiana failed to properly hire, train, and/or monitor its pilots to ensure they had the required skill and experience to safely land their aircraft at all airports in which they did business. This accident and its aftermath should never have occurred. It was a by-product of reckless inattention by the Asiana pilots in combination with dangerous shortcomings with auto flight modes and low airspeed warning systems incorporated into the Boeing aircraft;
>
> Fifth, at all [relevant] times, the Boeing 777-200ER was defective, dangerous, unsafe, and not airworthy by reason of Defendant Boeing's defective manufacture, design, warning systems, inspections, testing, service, and/or maintenance[79]

Over 100 injured passengers sued Asiana Airlines and reached settlements. The relatives of the girl who was hit by the fire truck sued the city of San Francisco, and they reached a settlement agreement. In September 2017, the last passenger reached a confidential settlement with the airline for physical, mental, and emotional damages as well as hospital and rehabilitation costs.[80]

In February 2014, the U.S. Department of Transportation fined Asiana Airlines $500,000 for their poor emergency response, in that they, inter alia, took five days to contact the victims and the victims' families, did not keep them updated, and the required hotline was initially turned into an automated reservations line.[81]

A week after the accident, the pilots who were on board the aircraft flew back to Seoul, Korea.[82] The pilot who was flying the aircraft had ten years of experience and was undergoing training on the Boeing 777. He had completed 8 flight legs and 33 hours 31 minutes before the accident flight. The pilot monitoring and trainer had 12,307 total flight hours, including 9,045 hours as PIC and 3,208 hours in the 777.[83] It is reported that the pilots feared that they would be criminally prosecuted when they returned to South Korea.[84]

8.26 RYANAIR, BOEING B737 FLIGHT FR058 AND TAP AIR PORTUGAL A319, UNINTENTIONAL CONVERGENCE, NAPF, LUCERNE (12 APRIL 2013)

On 12 April 2013, a Ryanair Boeing 737 and a TAP Air Portugal A319 unintentionally infringed the prescribed minimum separation in the upper airspace in the Swiss area of Toggenburg. This occurred as a result of a misunderstanding between the flight crew of the Ryanair flight and the Air Traffic Control Centre of Zurich that initially remained undetected. After a warning issued by the ground-based Safety Net, the Air Traffic Controller (ATC) detected the hazardous situation and issued the necessary instructions. The potential collision was avoided by the Safety Net. No one was injured, and there was no damage to property.

In April 2019, the Federal Criminal Court in Bellinzona sentenced the ATC on duty to a heavy fine for negligent disruption of public transport. The ATC filed a complaint to the Federal Supreme Court appealing against the ruling of the court at first instance, and on 4 July 2019, this was rejected by the Federal Court in Lausanne, which confirmed the sentence. This case is said to have set a precedent in Swiss Aviation as it is the first time in Switzerland that an air traffic controller had been convicted with legal effect. The ATC's employment had not been affected. Skyguide, the Swiss Air Navigation Service Provider, was supporting him.[85]

It is important to note that the air traffic control safety nets recognized the convergence of the two aircraft and the system, working as it was supposed to, assisted in preventing a potential disaster. It is also essential to note that, in this case, the air traffic controller and one of the pilots involved filed an Air Safety Report (ASR) and reported the incident openly and honestly, which resulted in both an internal and external investigation,[86] and contrary to the principles of just culture, which enable aviation professionals to report mistakes without fearing disciplinary consequences unless they were willful violations or committed deliberately, or negligently, the ATC was subjected to judicial proceedings.

8.27 HELIDUBAI AIRBUS HELICOPTER FLIGHT EC-130B4, ATLANTIS PALM HOTEL HELIPORT, DUBAI (22 JANUARY 2014)

On 22 January 2014, the aircraft, operated by Helidubai, attempted to depart from the Atlantis Palm hotel heliport for a positioning flight to the Dubai International Airport, but it impacted the heliport during departure. The aircraft had already operated six passenger tourist flights to the Dubai Air Wing fixed operating base before the positioning flight. There were no passengers on board, and both the pilot and the helicopter landing officer were injured.[87] The accident was investigated by the Air Accident Investigation Sector of the UAE General Civil Aviation Authority, which concluded that the accident was caused by the intentional entry into a continuous left-hand pedal turn, which rapidly increased the rotation rate of the aircraft, leading to an unstable condition that resulted in a loss of control in-flight and impact with the heliport; spatial disorientation; the pilot's inability to determine the cause of the induced turn rate and apply the corrective actions; and the collective was lowered resulting in an uncontrolled descent onto the heliport. The contributing factors were found to be the unforced skills-based errors by the handling pilot, poor pilot judgment in handling the intended maneuver, the acceleration of the inertia reel, and the lack of a requirement for a flight data monitoring system, which can detect safety occurrences and trends when monitored effectively.[88] In this case, even though the report concludes that the pilot flew in a negligent and reckless manner, no further action was taken.

8.28 RAF VOYAGER, FLIGHT ZZ333, AFGHANISTAN, BLACK SEA (9 FEBRUARY 2014)

On 14 February 2104, the Voyager Flight ZZ333 was flying to Camp Bastion Airfield, Afghanistan, from RAF Brize Norton with 189 passengers and 9 crew members for their Christmas holidays. Approximately five hours after take-off, the captain dropped his personal camera between his seat armrest and his side controller. Shortly afterwards, he adjusted the position of his seat, and this resulted in the sidestick deflecting completely forward. The co-pilot was out of the aircraft at that moment but was able to re-enter the cockpit. The aircraft went into a steep descent and nose-dived 33,000 feet within 27 seconds. The aircraft had lost 4,400 feet in 27 seconds, at a rate of descent of approximately 15,800 feet per minute, before recovering to a straight and level flight. Passengers and crew were thrown toward the cabin roof as a result of the negative "G" forces, resulting in twenty-five passengers and seven crew being injured. The aircraft was diverted to Incirlik Airbase in southern Turkey. Many passengers suffered long-term psychological injuries, including adjustment disorders, post-traumatic stress disorder (PTSD), and the fear of flying. Passengers who were injured have filed civil claims in the UK High Court claiming compensation for damages suffered, including for post-traumatic stress.

In 2017, the pilot appeared before a Court Martial facing criminal charges for negligently performing a duty, perjury, and making a false record.

A Service Inquiry investigated the incident, and the Report, published in March 2015, was the basis of the criminal proceedings against the pilot. The Report found that the pitch-down command was the result of the Captain's personal digital camera inadvertently hitting his side stick, which obstructed the left armrest and the side-stick unit when the Captain's seat was moved forward. As a result, the autopilot was disconnected, causing the aircraft to nose-dive. The Captain had taken 77 photographs during the flight, using his personal camera on the flight deck, including just minutes before the incident occurred. The Final Inquiry Report also confirms that the co-pilot was away from the flight deck for approximately 18 minutes before the incident occurred.[89]

8.29 MALAYSIA AIRLINES BOEING 777, FLIGHT 370 (MH370), SOUTH CHINA SEA (8 MARCH 2014)

On 8 March 2014, Malaysia Airlines MH370, a scheduled passenger plane with 227 passengers and 12 crew members flying from Kuala Lumpur, Malaysia, to Beijing, China, disappeared over the South China Sea. The last radio contact was approximately 38 minutes after take-off when the Kuala Lumpur Radar controller instructed the flight to contact the radio frequency of Ho Chi Minh Air Traffic Control Centre, Vietnam. Approximately two seconds later, the aircraft was observed on the radar screen of the Kuala Lumpur Radar controller as it passed over waypoint IGARI, and nine seconds later, the radar label for MH370 disappeared from the radar screen. The transponder was switched off.[90] A Joint Investigation Team was formed by Malaysia, which included experts from Malaysia, China, the United Kingdom, the United States, and France.[91] A parallel criminal investigation was also launched. One of the largest in aviation history, the search, locate, and recovery operations conducted by various countries, including Australia, Malaysia, and China, were unsuccessful. Parts of the wreckage were discovered off the eastern coast of Tanzania and South Africa, but the wreckage, as well as the bodies of the victims, have not been found. In January 2017, the official search of the southern Indian Ocean by Australia, Malaysia, and China was called off. In January 2018, the search for the missing aircraft by an American company on behalf of Malaysia was called off.[92] Shortly afterwards, the investigation into the aircraft's disappearance was classified as a criminal investigation. Many conspiracy theories emerged, including, inter alia, that the pilot in command had deliberately brought down the aircraft, that there was a fire on board, that it was a cyber-attack, that it was flown to the U.S. military base in Diego Garcia, or that it was shot down.[93]

On 5 July 2017, the Dutch Foreign Ministry announced that the joint investigation team from Australia, Belgium, Malaysia, the Netherlands, and Ukraine would continue with any subsequent criminal prosecution and that the criminal trial would be heard in the Dutch courts under Dutch law. This was a significant development as the victims came from 17 different countries on five continents.[94] As of 2018, France was the only country still conducting a judicial inquiry. Two investigating magistrates continued their investigation on behalf of a French national who lost his wife and two teenage children in the disappearance of the aircraft.[95]

In accordance with Part XII of the Malaysian Civil Aviation Regulations 1996, the Malaysian Minister of Transport established an independent international investigation team to investigate the disappearance of the aircraft. The investigation team was made up of 19 Malaysians and 7 Accredited Representatives of 7 safety investigation authorities from the following 7 countries, namely, the UK Air Accidents Investigation Branch (AAIB), the Australian Transport Safety Bureau (ATSB), the French Bureau d'Enquêtes et d'Analyses pour la Sécurité de l'Aviation civile (BEA), the Chinese Civil Aviation Administration of the People's Republic of China (CAAC), the American National Transportation Safety Board (NTSB), the Indonesian National Transportation Safety Committee (NTSC), and the Transport Safety Investigation Bureau (TSIB) of Singapore. On 9 April 2014, the Malaysian Ministry of Transport released a Preliminary Report which contained a Safety Recommendation to ICAO regarding in-flight tracking of large commercial aircraft. On 8 March 2015, the 1st Interim Statement and Factual Information Report was released, outlining the factual information available at that time. The 2nd Interim Statement was released on 8 March 2016, the 3rd one on 8 March 2017, and the 4th on 8 March 2018.[96]

The final report of 495 pages was released on 2 July 2018, concluding that it could not be certain what happened to MH370. The report identifies several shortcomings after the plane diverted from its planned flight path, in that the air traffic controllers on duty at the time did not notify Chinese authorities when the aircraft failed to make contact with them, and they did not initiate emergency procedures, which delayed the search and rescue. The report states that Malaysian Air Traffic Control failed to follow official procedures and emergency protocols on six occasions.[97]

The report found that MH370 turned back, and that it was not due to any technical issues. It concluded that the aircraft was turned back under manual control, and not under the autopilot. It further states that it could not establish whether the two subsequent changes in direction were made under manual control or autopilot, or whether the aircraft was flown by anyone other than the pilots. The report dismissed several conspiracy theories about the aircraft and the pilot's alleged suicide mission. It ruled out any mechanical problems and the theory that the plane was hijacked remotely, but it also stated that it could not rule out the possibility of unlawful interference from a third party.[98]

Relatives of more than 100 of the deceased from the United States, Australia, China, India, and Malaysia filed proceedings in America for wrongful death and product liability against the carrier, its insurer Allianz SE, and Boeing Co. On 21 November 2018, a U.S. District Judge dismissed their claims, stating that the trial should be heard in Malaysia and not in the United States.[99]

In July 2019, French investigators stated that the flight data suggested that someone was behind the control stick when the plane broke up in the Indian Ocean and that, without drawing any conclusions, their investigation revealed that an 89 kg load was added to the cargo list after the plane took off, that one of the containers was overloaded without any explanation and that there were different, inconsistent versions of the passenger list.[100]

8.30 MAULE M-5 FOUR-SEATER PLANE, CLARENCE RIVER, EWINGAR, NEW ZEALAND (12 APRIL 2014)

On 12 April 2014, a pilot in a Maule M-5 four-seater plane left Casino Airport and flew to Lismore Airport to refuel. He picked up a friend of his and his 11-year-old daughter. The pilot was flying low, approximately 16 to 25 meters, over the Clarence River. The aircraft struck power cables, stalled, and crashed upside down into the river. The pilot and the father freed themselves and got out of the aircraft, and tried to free the daughter. When they managed to get her out of the aircraft, she could not be resuscitated, and she died from her cervical spine injury. The father suffered cuts, burns, a fractured shoulder, and fractured vertebrae. The pilot was very remorseful and suffered depression as well as post-traumatic stress disorder.

The pilot was charged with manslaughter, operating an aircraft recklessly to endanger the life of a person, operating an aircraft recklessly to endanger a person or property, and flying an aircraft below 500 feet. The trial commenced in the Lismore District Court, and he received a 15-month suspended sentence. The judges ruled that the original 15-month suspended sentence was "manifestly inadequate" and the pilot was sentenced to two years imprisonment, which was to be served in the community under the strict supervision of an intensive correction order if assessed as suitable. The court also noted that the pilot had paid the father over $300,000 as compensation and that he was also being sued for nervous shock.[101]

The Appeal Court found the sentencing judge appeared to have confused specific deterrence with general deterrence; a particularly important consideration when dealing with dangerous flying. Justice Davies said,

> The Crown submitted that there was a significant body of evidence before the sentencing judge that low flying was a highly dangerous activity and of the high prevalence of wire-strike aviation accidents. In my opinion, general deterrence is a significant matter where an offence is committed in relation to the flying of an aircraft.[102]

8.31 MALAYSIA AIRLINES BOEING 777, FLIGHT 17 (MH17), HRABOVE, UKRAINE (17 JULY 2014)

On 17 July 2014, MH 17, a scheduled passenger flight with 283 passengers and 15 crew members en route from Amsterdam, the Netherlands, to Kuala Lumpur, Malaysia, was shot down while flying over eastern Ukraine, killing everyone on board. Contact with the aircraft was lost when the aircraft was over an area that was controlled by pro-Russian rebels, at about 50 km from the Ukraine-Russian border, flying 1000 feet above airspace that the Ukrainian authorities had classified as restricted because of ongoing fighting. The aircraft broke apart in midair, scattering debris over a large area. The center section of the fuselage and parts of the horizontal and vertical stabilizers were found near Hrabove, approximately 40 km from the border. The cockpit and lower nose section were located approximately 6.5 km west-southwest of Hrabove. Two doors and parts of the fuselage were found about 8 km west of Hrabove. Days before the shooting down, two Ukrainian Air Force aircraft were shot down in the region.

On the day of the accident, the National Bureau of Air Accidents Investigation of Ukraine (NBAAI) commenced the investigation. On 23 July 2014, it delegated the official investigation to the Dutch Safety Board. On 9 September 2014, a preliminary report was released. On 13 October 2015, the final report, which found that the crash was caused by the detonation of a 9N314M-type warhead launched from the eastern part of Ukraine using a Buk missile system, was released. The report also states that Ukraine clearly had sufficient reason to close the airspace over the eastern part of Ukraine as a precaution before 17 July 2014, and that none of the parties involved recognized the risk posed to overflying civil aircraft by the armed conflict in the eastern part of Ukraine.

Parallel to the Dutch Safety Board investigation, a criminal investigation was launched in the Netherlands, led by the Public Prosecution Service, and is said to be the largest criminal investigation in Dutch history. In November 2014, Belgium, Ukraine, Australia, and Malaysia joined the Dutch investigation.[103] The Chief Dutch Prosecutor said that evidence showed that Russia had provided the missile launcher as the Buk came from the Russian army's 53rd Anti-Aircraft Missile Brigade and that it was transported from Russia the day the aircraft was shot down. In July 2019, nearly five years after the shooting down of the aircraft, the Joint Investigation Team announced that three Russian nationals and one Ukrainian would be charged with causing the crash of the aircraft, which led to the death of all those on board and the murder of the 298 persons for allegedly facilitating the transport of the missile used to shoot down the jet from Russia into Ukraine.[104] The trial started on 9 March 2020 at the Hague District Court, and as the defendants were not present at the trial, the case was heard in absentia.[105] On 17 November 2022, two Russian nationals and a Ukrainian were found guilty in absentia of the murder of the 298 people on board Flight MH1 and were sentenced to life imprisonment and ordered to pay over €16m in compensation to the victims. A third Russian national was acquitted.[106]

8.32 TRANSASIA ATR-72 FLIGHT GE222, TAIWAN (23 JULY 2014)

A TransAsia Airways ATR-72, a passenger plane with 54 passengers and four crew, departed from Kaohsiung International Airport, scheduled to fly to Magong Airport, Penghu Islands, Taiwan. The aircraft was destroyed when it crashed into buildings during its approach to land, killing forty-eight passengers and the four crew members. The flight had been delayed because of poor weather due to a typhoon. The Taiwanese Aviation Safety Council investigated the accident, and the report was published in January 2016.[107] The report outlines 46 findings related to probable causes, risks, and other findings. It concludes, inter alia, that:

> The cause of this accident was the result of controlled flight into terrain, that is, an airworthy aircraft under the control of the flight crew was flown unintentionally into terrain with limited awareness by the crew of the aircraft's proximity to terrain. The crew continued the approach below the minimum descent altitude (MDA) when they were not visual with the runway environment, contrary to standard operating procedures. [108]

The report also concluded that "The discrepancies between the reported runway visual range (RVR) and automated weather observation system (AWOS) RVR confused the tower controllers about the reliability of the AWOS RVR data; the controller did not provide the weather information to the flight crew in accordance with ATMP due to ATC considering the RVR was unreliable."[109] In addition to the pilots flying below the minimum descent altitude and overconfidence of the pilot, the report also outlined a number of contributory and other safety factors relating to the flight crew of the aircraft, TransAsia's flight operations and safety management processes, the poor communication of weather information to the flight crew, coordination issues at Magong airport, and the regulatory oversight of TransAsia by the Civil Aeronautics Administration (CAA). Investigators found it was common for pilots to make routine violations and that non-compliance with standard operating procedures was tolerated at the airline.

In April 2016, two air traffic controllers were charged. The two pilots who died in the accident were also blamed. The prosecutors stated that both the pilots and the two ATCs were negligent in their duties, and the ATCs would be charged with criminal negligence, which carries a maximum prison sentence of five years.[110] In June 2017, the two ATCs were acquitted. The Penghu district court acknowledged that errors were made, but stated that the accident was ultimately caused by the errors made by the deceased pilots, who were flying below the minimum altitude required in poor visibility due to a procedural mistake common among TransAsia's pilots at the time.[111]

8.33 DASSAULT FALCON 50EX BUSINESS JET COLLISION WITH SNOW-REMOVAL MACHINE – MOSCOW VNUKOVO AIRPORT (26 OCTOBER 2014)

On 20 October 2014, a Dassault Falcon 50EX business jet, scheduled to fly to France from Moscow, collided with a snow-removal machine while gathering speed to take off from Moscow's Vnukovo Airport in poor visibility. The three crew members and the only passenger on board, the chief executive officer of the French oil company, Total SA, died in the accident. At the time of the accident, two snowplows were working under the supervision of a supervisor who sat in a car in the area. The supervisor lost sight of one of the snowplows, which entered the runway at the time the Falcon 50 was cleared for takeoff. When the aircraft commenced the take-off, the crew observed a "car" crossing the runway. Takeoff was continued, and the aircraft lifted off the runway at a speed of about 134 knots. After 1030 meters, the right wing and right-hand main landing gear impacted the snowplow. The airplane rolled, inverted, and came down 250 meters further on and was then engulfed in flames.[112] The technical investigation was conducted by the Russian Accident Investigation Board, the MAK Interstate Aviation Committee (IAC). Investigators from the French accident investigation board, the BEA (as the state of registration). Advisers from Unijet, the plane's operator, and Dassault Aviation will also assist in the investigation.[113]

In February 2015, the results of the preliminary report were handed to the French BEA technical commission. The report states that the snowplow driver and his supervisor both tested positive for alcohol in their blood two hours after the accident. The driver was allegedly behaving awkwardly and had gotten lost on the runway just before the incident. The supervisor had failed to report to airtraffic controllers that the whereabouts of the vehicle had been unknown for 15 minutes before the aircraft took off.[114] The report also establishes that the accident was caused by several mistakes made by several different services.[115]

A criminal investigation into the accident was conducted to consider possible violations of aviation safety rules, causing multiple deaths through negligence. The driver of the snow cleaning vehicle was detained within 48 hours of the accident and then formally charged with being under the influence of alcohol at the time of the accident, drunk, and for violating safety regulations. It is alleged that the doctor who should have checked the pulse and blood pressure of the snowplow crew only looked them over, as a more thorough examination would have taken more time and caused flight delays.

It is important to note that the reports indicate that the trainee controller was unaware that there were maintenance vehicles on both runways and that it was only her second night shift.[116] The Judge, Valentina Levashova, agreed with the prosecutors that the accused supervisor dispatcher could disappear, destroy evidence, threaten witnesses, and cohort with co-workers, which would hamper investigations.

In October 2105, three people were arrested. The Moscow Basmanny Court ruled that the driver of the snowplow, the air traffic control supervisor at the time of the accident, and the chief airfield service engineer of Vnukovo airport service, who was responsible for snow removal, be placed into custody. The trainee controller who gave the signal to the pilot to take off on the runway and the chief of flights at the Vnukovo air navigation control center were placed under house arrest.[117]

All five accused were then indicted for committing a crime by contravening Russian Criminal Code Article 263 Part 3, namely, violation of aircraft safe air traffic and aircraft operation rules that resulted in the death of two or more people through negligence. Breaching aviation safety rules and causing multiple deaths through negligence could result in imprisonment of up to seven years.[118] It is reported that the Russian prosecutors forwarded the case materials to their French colleagues in late January 2015.[119]

The airport's general director and the deputy general director resigned after the accident, and other managerial staff were dismissed.[120] In September, all those who were detained were released from custody as the maximum time allowed for their detention had expired.[121] In January 2016, the charges against the trainee controller were dropped as the investigators concluded that she had acted correctly on the night of the accident and that there was no element of crime in her actions.[122] The airport engineer responsible for snow removal and snow removal vehicles, and for coordinating their movement via intercom on the day of the accident, pleaded guilty to failing to properly organize the snow removal and to violating instructions. He said that he had seen the snowplow driver detour from the approved route, that he tried to speed and catch up to him, but that it was too late. He did not try to notify the traffic controller of the problem, nor did he call the driver or the chief engineer via intercom.[123]

8.34 AIRASIA AIRBUS A320, FLIGHT QZ8501, JAVA SEA BETWEEN SURABAYA, INDONESIA AND SINGAPORE (28 DECEMBER 2014)

On 28 December, Air Asia Flight QZ8501 with 156 passengers and six crew members was a scheduled passenger flight en route from Surabaya, Indonesia, to Singapore. Thirty-six minutes after taking off, the aircraft contacted Jakarta ATC and informed them that the flight was deviating to the left of the planned route to avoid the clouds and requested to climb to flight level 380. As this was not possible at that time due to traffic, they were cleared to climb to flight level 340. That was the last communication with the aircraft. Five minutes later, Jakarta radar cleared the aircraft to climb to 380, but there was no response to the ATC's several attempts to contact the pilot. The aircraft crashed into the Java Sea between Surabaya and Singapore, killing everybody on board. No distress signal was sent. At the end of the search in March, only 116 bodies were recovered. On 30 December, pieces of debris and bodies were recovered from the sea. The Flight Data Recorder (FDR) and Cockpit Voice Recorder (CVR) were retrieved on 12 and 13 January 2015, and the main fuselage was recovered on 14 January. The CVR captured a number of warnings, including a stall warning during the final minutes of the flight.[124] The official investigation was conducted by Indonesia's National Transportation Safety Committee, the KNKT (Komite Nasional Keselamatan Transportasi). The final report released on 1

December 2015 stated that a fault in the plane's rudder control system, together with the pilot's error, contributed to the accident. The investigation revealed that there was a crack in a tiny electronic module, which caused the system to send repeated warning alerts to the pilots. The pilots responded by resetting the system, resulting in the autopilot being disengaged. The aircraft rolled to the left, and the pilots struggled to right the plane, which then stalled and crashed into the Java Sea. The report found that the maintenance crew had previously known about the problem, which occurred 23 times in 2014, and that resetting the system was one of several methods that were used to address the problem. The report also states that although AirAsia was licensed to fly the Surabaya to Singapore route on four days of the week, it did not have permission to fly that route on the day of the accident.[125]

France initiated a criminal investigation to consider possible manslaughter charges. In addition, the relatives of the deceased co-pilot, a French national, filed a lawsuit against AirAsia for endangering the lives of others by scheduling the flight on the day of the accident without having permission to fly on that day.[126]

In September 2016, a lawsuit was filed in Illinois, USA, against the manufacturer, Airbus, alleging that the aircraft was "defective and unreasonably dangerous." In December 2016, the case was dismissed, and the lawsuit was dropped.[127] On 20 January 2015, a 37-year-old British aircraft engineer who felt that he was responsible for the accident committed suicide. His wife told the inquest that he had become obsessed with an irrational fear that he was to blame and became very depressed.[128]

8.35 EUROCOPTER HELICOPTERS LQ-CGK/LQ-FJQ COLLISION, LA RIOJA, ARGENTINA (9 MARCH 2015)

On 9 March 2015, a helicopter LQ-CGK collided in midair with another helicopter, near Villa Castelli in La Rioja province, Argentina, during the filming of a French TV survival show, "Dropped." The passengers, eight French nationals, three of whom were well-known sports personalities, and the two Argentinian pilots were killed. The helicopter had planned to make passenger and equipment transport flights from the city of Villa Castelli to Quebrada del Yeso, as agreed by the Secretary of Tourism of the Government of the Province of La Rioja and the producer of Adventure Line Production. The day before the accident, the support of another helicopter (LQ-FJQ) from the Aviation Administration of Santiago del Estero had been requested. After the take-off, both aircraft made a low-altitude flight over the take-off site. Approximately 2 minutes after take-off, and to the west of the starting point, the aircraft crashed into the ground. A fire ensued, and both pilots and the eight passengers were killed. The accident was investigated by the Argentine Civil Aviation Accident Investigation Board (Junta de Investigación de Accidentes de Aviación Civil, JIAAC). The investigation revealed that on the day of the accident, each aircraft had made three flights. At the end of the flight, the pilot of the LQ-CGK helicopter, who was responsible for coordinating the task, informed the LQ-FJQ pilot that they would make an additional flight with passengers on board LQ-CGK and a team of photographers and sound engineers on board LQ-FJQ to film the flight. The pilots of both helicopters and the production Company staff conducted a briefing about the task to be done, which consisted of, after take-off, making a 360° heading change turn, a passage over the location of the take-off site for filming from the ground, as well as the flight to the intended destination. The report, published on 17 December 2015, concluded that the in-flight collision was caused by the combination of the following factors: The location of the filming helicopter (LQ-FJQ) from the outside in the path of both aircraft that significantly limited the visual contact of the pilot who had to move forward in flight in order to film the target (LQ-CGK); lack of a formal assessment of the safety risks for an unusual operation (filming and flight in proximity), which prevented the identification and analysis of the dangers inherent to that operation and the adoption of mitigation actions; deficiencies in the operation planning that led to the accident, including the failure of observing the "see and be seen" concept or an evasive maneuver if visual contact is lost between both aircraft; lack of formal procedures in accordance with the nature of the operations performed; the use of aircraft whose public identification prefix does not imply providing logistics and aerial support for filming of a completely private nature; and the ambiguity in the observance of regulations related to air operations of public aircrafts.[129]

On 10 March 2015, prosecutors in France opened a manslaughter investigation into the accident.[130] In 2017, the mother, wife, and two children of the cameraman who died in the accident lodged a claim with the Social Security Court (TASS) of the Hauts-de-Seine claiming damages from his employer, SAS Adventure Line Productions (ALP). The company denied having any liability. In April 2018, three years after the accident, TASS found that the accident, which occurred during his employment, was due to the inexcusable fault of the cameraman's employer, SAS Adventure Line Productions, the production company of the show "Dropped." The company was ordered to pay the family €120,000 and to repay the primary health insurance fund almost €400,000 in annuity increases.[131] In a second case, the Court of Social Security Affairs (TASS) of Lyon also ruled that the company pay the widow, son, parents, and brother of another cameraman who was killed, the sum of €120,000 in damages plus interest. The company has denied liability and has appealed both decisions. It should be noted that the TASS no longer exists as, from 1 January 2019, it has merged with the High Court Tribunal, the Tribunal de Grande Instance. Proceedings brought by relatives of other victims are pending. It is important to note that in both of the proceedings, the TASS relied on the conclusions of the final accident investigation report issued by the Argentinian JIAAC.

Two criminal proceedings were commenced in Argentina and France. In Paris, the company and its production director were placed under the status of assisted witness, currently escaping prosecution. In proceedings in TASS de Paris, relatives of the deceased journalist are claiming €400,000 in compensation; however, the decision was postponed, pending the outcome of criminal proceedings.[132]

On 26 February 2019, the person who was in charge of security during the filming was indicted for murder. The examining magistrate alleges that he was not careful with regard to the qualifications, the skills, and the state of health of the pilots on board the two helicopters. The accused submits that he cannot be held as he does not have pilot training or knowledge of aviation regulations, and cannot be responsible for the recruitment of pilots who, on the day of the accident, were not authorized to fly in formation. He also states that, as someone has to be blamed, he is being singled out as the scapegoat.[133] Relatives of the deceased insist that the company, ALP, should also be indicted.

In civil proceedings, the Company has been found liable for its "inexcusable fault" by the Hauts-de-Seine court and ordered to pay compensation to the families of the second cameraman and another victim. A second court decision of the Lyon Social Security Tribunal ruled that the company was liable for compensatory damages of €120,000 to the widow, son, parents, and brother of the first cameraman. The courts relied on the final accident investigation report of the Argentinian Jiaac, which concluded that the fatal accident at work was a result of the inexcusable fault of the Company, ALP.[134] The Company appealed.

8.36 GERMANWINGS A320 FLIGHT AU9525, FRENCH ALPS (24 MARCH 2015)

On 24 March 2015, a Germanwings A320 passenger flight with 154 passengers and six crew members departed from Barcelona, Spain, and was scheduled to land in Düsseldorf, Germany. When the aircraft reached the cruising altitude, the captain told the co-pilot that he was leaving the cockpit and asked him to take over the radio communications. When he was alone in the cockpit, the co-pilot intentionally modified the autopilot settings to order the airplane to descend. He locked the cockpit door and kept it locked during the descent, despite the many requests to be let in via the keypad, the cabin interphone, and the knocks on the door. He did not respond to the civil or military air traffic controllers' calls. The aircraft continued to descend until it impacted the terrain in the French Alps. Everybody aboard the plane was killed, and the aircraft was completely destroyed. The investigation into the accident was conducted by the French Civil Aviation Safety Investigation Authority, the Bureau d'Enquêtes et d'Analyses pour la sécurité de l'aviation civile (BEA). The German BEA, as well as the U.S. FBI, assisted with the investigation. The final report by the French BEA, published on 13 March 2016, confirmed the findings made in the preliminary report. It concluded that the collision with the ground was a result of the deliberate and planned action of the co-pilot, who decided to commit suicide while alone in the cockpit. It goes on to state that the process for medical certification of pilots, particularly self-reporting in the case of a decrease in medical fitness between two periodic medical evaluations, failed in preventing the co-pilot, who was experiencing a mental disorder with psychotic symptoms, from exercising his license as a pilot.[135]

The investigation report states:

> The co-pilot had been flying for Germanwings since June 2014 and was the holder of a class 1 medical certificate that was first issued in April 2008, which had been revalidated or renewed every year. Since July 2009, this medical certificate had contained a waiver because of a severe depressive episode without psychotic symptoms

> that had lasted from August 2008 until July 2009. This waiver stated that it would become invalid if there were a relapse into depression. In December 2014, approximately five months after the last revalidation of his class 1 medical certificate, the co-pilot started to show symptoms that could be consistent with a psychotic depressive episode. He consulted several doctors, including a psychiatrist, on at least two occasions, who prescribed antidepressant medication. The co-pilot did not contact any Aero-Medical Examiners (AME) between the beginning of his decrease in medical fitness in December 2014 and the day of the accident.[136]

In February 2015, a private physician diagnosed a psychosomatic disorder and an anxiety disorder and referred the co-pilot to a psychotherapist and psychiatrist. On 10 March 2015, the same physician diagnosed a possible psychosis and recommended psychiatric hospital treatment. A psychiatrist prescribed antidepressants and sleep aid medication in February and March 2015. Neither of those health care providers informed any aviation authority, nor any other authority, about the co-pilot's mental state. These physicians issued several sick leave certificates, but not all of them were forwarded to Germanwings.

After the crash, many civil lawsuits were filed by relatives of the deceased. Some of the civil actions include the following: relatives who sued the Lufthansa Group, which owns the low-cost Germanwings airline, as well as the Lufthansa training school in the US. In April 2016, a lawsuit for punitive damages was filed against the Airline Training Center Arizona (ATCA) in Goodyear, Arizona, which belongs to the Lufthansa Group, where the co-pilot had undergone his training. They claimed that the school had an obligation to investigate the co-pilot's medical history, that it had ignored a reference to his mental health problems, that he should have been disqualified because of the signs of psychological abnormalities, and that more stringent mental health screenings could have prevented the tragedy. They alleged that the flight school and Lufthansa failed to prevent the crash by not supervising the medical condition of the co-pilot adequately. Initially, plaintiffs filed the suit against Lufthansa Airline Training Center in the Arizona District Court, but the case was dismissed on the grounds of forum non conveniens. The court then sent the case to the German courts in 2017 to hear the matter.[137] In concluding that a German court should hear the matter, they stressed that 70 of the victims listed in the lawsuit were from Germany, the flight school had agreed to cooperate with the courts in Germany, and that the public interest in the case was greater in Germany than in Arizona. The court also stressed that if the set conditions attached to its decision were not met, the plaintiffs could return to the courts in America. It is important to note that the Arizona court had accepted the plaintiffs' argument that the flight school shared responsibility for assessing whether the co-pilot was suitable for the training program. The court ruled that the plaintiffs had sufficiently argued that ATCA knew or should have known about [the co-pilot's] mental health problems.[138] Strict privacy laws related to doctor-patient confidentiality in Germany, preventing his doctors from disclosing his mental health problems, were cited; however, it was argued that a US company was not precluded from inquiring further into his background.[139]

With regards to the reporting of a pilot's medical condition, in Canada, for example, the law regarding the reporting of pilot medical conditions is clearly stated in Section 6.5 of the *Aeronautics Act.*[140] The Act requires that any physician who believes on reasonable grounds that a patient is a pilot, an air traffic controller, or other holder of a Canadian aviation document, who has a medical condition that is likely to constitute a hazard to aviation safety, must inform a medical adviser designated by the Minister of Transport forthwith. In addition, it explicitly states that no legal, disciplinary, or other proceedings can be brought against a physician for anything done in compliance with the reporting requirement. Canadian Aviation Regulations require a pilot to ground him or herself if they suffer from an illness that could impair their ability to exercise their flying privileges.[141] The laws in Canada are intended to encourage self-reporting of medical issues, protect doctors from violating confidentiality, and enhance aviation safety.[142]

An additional reason for filing the legal proceedings in Arizona, USA, was with regard to the compensation amounts. Relatives of the deceased felt that the compensation voluntarily paid by Lufthansa was too low. As compensation awarded by the USA courts is generally substantially higher than that awarded by courts in Germany, they filed the suits in the USA. The class action suit sought a payment of at least $75,000 per victim, as well as additional compensation of €30,000 for pain and suffering from the Germanwings parent company, Lufthansa. The courts also had to consider who was responsible for monitoring his mental health: the German state, Lufthansa, and/or the flight school. In September 2021, more than six years after the crash, judges at the Higher Regional Court in Hamm upheld the lower Essen Regional Court decision and rejected the appeal lodged by several relatives who had demanded additional compensation. The plaintiffs' lawyers argued that if the airline's doctors had discharged their duties adequately and effectively, they would have recognized the severe mental illness on the part of the co-pilot, and his flying license would have been withdrawn. Disagreeing with this point, the judges upheld the "very clear reasoning" for the lower court's verdict. They considered that the medical supervision of pilots was a sovereign task of the state and that federal authorities, namely the Federal Aviation Office (LBA), had the responsibility for checking pilots' airworthiness. As such, it was not the airline's parent company's duty, and therefore, Lufthansa was not the correct addressee for the claims for damages. They also held that the claims for damages were not sufficiently substantiated.[143]

In another lawsuit filed in Germany in 2016, a man who lost his daughter and grandson sued the co-pilot's doctor for not reporting his mental problems, the Lufthansa doctors, and German aviation authority officials. The plaintiff alleged that confidentiality should not have applied in this case, as the doctor knew that he was a pilot with mental problems and that the doctor should have notified the airline and the regulators. It is interesting to note that the head of Germany's doctors' association also criticized Lufthansa for allowing Lubitz to fly and blamed both the airline and the regulators for not monitoring his mental state more carefully. He stated, "As doctors, we find it appalling that both the Federal Aviation Authority and Lufthansa knew that this pilot had records of severe depression but underwent no particular checks."[144] A relative who lost his daughter, her partner, and his grandson filed a criminal complaint against the co-pilot's parents, alleging that they should have prevented him from flying.[145]

Relatives of the only two American victims filed a wrongful death lawsuit in the U.S. District Court in Alexandria, Virginia. They alleged that, as they had purchased their international tickets for England and Spain through United Airlines and had departed on a United flight from Dulles International Airport in Virginia, they based their claim on the Montreal Convention, which has been ratified by both the USA and Germany. Being part of a global airline alliance, United, Lufthansa, and Germanwings passengers can book international flights through each other's websites. The Montreal Convention permits legal proceedings to be filed in the country in which a carrier is domiciled or headquartered, where the contract of carriage was made, or where the plaintiff resides. They argued that, as United Airlines is headquartered in Chicago, they had purchased their tickets in Virginia, their principal and permanent place of residence; and because United's schedule provided Dulles International Airport as the start and finish of the international trip, the U.S. courts had jurisdiction to hear the matter. Their legal action alleged negligence on the part of Germanwings in that as carriers taking revenue from U.S. customers while holding themselves as having the highest levels of safety, the defendants owed the passengers of Germanwings Flight 9525 a duty of utmost care and the vigilance for the safe transport of passengers, and to ensure that its fleet is maintained and operated to the highest degree of safety and care. They alleged that the

> defendants, together negligently, carelessly and recklessly breached their duty of care to passengers by failing to maintain, operate, maneuver, handle, control, equip, manage, and pilot Germanwings Flight 9525, and by failing to properly and safely train, educate, prepare, inform, alert, monitor, guide, or tutor its pilots, crew, and other personnel to operate a passenger aircraft.

In addition, they argued that

> the defendants did not have known policies in place that would have timely and safely responded to or prevented emergency situations, including an unaccompanied, solitary, crew member in the cockpit. As a direct and proximate result of the defendants' gross negligence, [the passengers] suffered unspeakable horrors before their lives were tragically cut short.[146]

In November 2019, four relatives of the 35 deceased Spanish passengers who were aboard the flight sued the parent company Lufthansa for negligence in the Barcelona Courts, alleging, inter alia, that:

(i) Lufthansa granted Lubitz a pilot's license shortly after having suffered severe depression with suicidal tendencies in 2008, and during 2008 and 2015, the airline did not require him to go for any psychiatric evaluation, and shortly before the plane crash, he presented three casualties that were not sufficiently investigated, given his background.
(ii) They should have been aware of his illness and raised the alarm after three incidents at work; and

(i) Lufthansa "failed to do its job" by not subjecting Lubitz to psychiatric tests and should never have declared him fit to fly.

The lawsuit also names Germanwings and the insurance company, Allianz Global, as defendants. The claimants are seeking to raise the damages in accordance with the 1999 Montreal Convention, which allows claimants who allege negligence of the carrier to seek more than the 113,100.00 SDR for which the carrier is strictly liable. To avoid liability, Lufthansa has the burden to prove that it was not negligent.[147]

In November 2021, six years after the crash, after an inquest in the death of one of three British passengers on board Germanwings Flight 9525, the coroner confirmed that the death was an "unlawful killing."[148]

Criminal investigations were conducted in both France and Germany. In June 2015, a French prosecutor formally opened a criminal inquiry and appointed three investigative judges to examine any possible charges of involuntary manslaughter and investigate whether the airline or any individuals had any responsibility for failing to monitor the psychological health of the co-pilot adequately.[149] In January 2017, the German prosecutors closed the investigation. They said that there would be no further criminal investigation, as only the co-pilot was responsible for the crash. As no third party was involved, there would not be any criminal prosecutions.[150] This also dismissed any suspicion of negligence on behalf of the doctors who examined Lubitz.

In 2022, seven years after the crash, French judicial authorities in Marseille concluded that the co-pilot's suicidal act was not foreseeable. They stated that "No one could have acted beforehand to avoid the incident of 24 March 2015," and that "No serious fault, nor any deliberate violation of a duty of care or safety imposed by law or regulation could be blamed on Germanwings, Lufthansa (its parent company) or its managers or employees." In addition, they closed the case against any doctors who may have been aware of Lubitz's medical situation in the months leading up to the crash.[151]

8.37 AIR CANADA A320 FLIGHT AC624, HALIFAX STANFIELD INTERNATIONAL AIRPORT (CYHZ), NOVA SCOTIA (29 MARCH 2015)

An Air Canada A320 aircraft, which departed from Toronto Pearson International Airport scheduled to fly to Halifax Stanfield International Airport with 133 passengers and five crew members on board, sustained substantial damage when it suffered a landing accident. While conducting a non-precision approach, the aircraft severed power lines and then struck the snow-covered ground about 740 feet before the runway threshold. The aircraft then continued airborne through the localizer antenna array, hit the ground twice more before sliding along the runway, and impacted the ground 225 meters short of the runway. All passengers exited the aircraft within five minutes after it came to a stop. Twenty-five people, including both pilots, were injured and taken to the hospital.[152] The Transportation Safety Board of Canada conducted the investigation into the accident, and the final report was released in May

2017. It concluded that the primary cause of the accident was Air Canada's crew procedures, as in accordance with the airline's Standard Operating Procedures (SOPs), the crew selects Flight Path Angle Guidance Mode. Once the aircraft passes through the final approach fix, the pilots are no longer required to monitor the aircraft's altitude or make any adjustments to the flight path angle. This procedure was contrary to the flight crew operating manuals of Air Canada or Airbus. Following the SOPs, when the crew selected flight path angle guidance mode and passed through the final approach fix, they stopped monitoring their altitude and distance from the runway and did not adjust the flight path angle. As a result, they failed to notice that the aircraft had descended below the vertical descent angle flight profile and dropped below the minimum safe altitude. In addition, the limited visibility also hindered the crew's ability to perceive the impending impact. The Air Canada SOPs were revised after the accident. [153]

After the accident, a class-action lawsuit was filed against Air Canada, Airbus, the Halifax International Airport Authority, NAV Canada, which provides navigation services at Canadian airports, Transport Canada, the attorney general of Canada, as well as the pilots, alleging that their negligence caused the accident. The plaintiffs sued for damages for the physical and psychological harm they alleged they suffered as a result.[154]

The certification of a class action-lawsuit filed on behalf of the passengers was challenged by federal lawyers who argued that Transport Canada could not be sued because it had no direct relationship with the passengers on board Flight 624, did not owe a duty of care to the passengers aboard, and that as they are regulators, they do not have any responsibility over the operational issues and that they should therefore be exempt from the lawsuit. The other defendants did not oppose the certification of the class action.[155]

The lawsuit alleged that Transport Canada breached its duty of care by failing to monitor the airport's compliance with safety requirements adequately and by choosing not to install an ILS for the relevant runway. It also alleged that the Halifax International Airport Authority was liable because it failed to clear the runway properly and did not replace an older-style navigation system with a more advanced instrument landing system (ILS).[156]

On 30 March 2017, Air Canada filed a lawsuit in the Nova Scotia Supreme Court against Airbus, alleging their negligence in failing to identify shortcomings of the Airbus A320. It alleged inter alia, that the manufacturer did not advise that, in certain conditions, the plane's flight path angle could be affected by external forces and did not provide adequate and/or accurate information as to how pilots should correct a deviation in the flight path in circumstances where manual intervention was required. The airline stated that the flight crew correctly configured the aircraft for landing, including entering the correct flight path angle into the flight computer, and therefore, the aircraft should have intercepted the threshold to the runway at an altitude of 50 feet. Air Canada claimed damages sustained by the aircraft and other expenses related to the accident.[157]

During the class proceedings, Airbus, joined by the airport authority and Nav Canada, moved for an order to require the Transportation Safety Board of Canada

(TSB) to hand over the audio of the cockpit voice recording. The TSB refused to do so, claiming a statutory privilege over the materials, and asked the court to deny the order.

The Nova Scotia Supreme Court judge stated that in the specific circumstances of the case, the public interest in the administration of justice outweighed the importance attached to the statutory privilege protecting the cockpit voice recorder and ordered the Transportation Safety Board of Canada to release the CVR. The application judge ordered disclosure subject to confidentiality conditions. As a result, the TSB was required to produce a copy of the CVR and transcript for counsel's use only in the class litigation.[158]

The TSB appealed. On 16 April 2021, dismissing the appeal, the Court of Appeal upheld the lower court's authorization of the conditional release of the contents of the CVR to the parties to a class action. The Appeal Court unanimously affirmed the earlier decision that the public interest in the proper administration of justice outweighed the statutory privilege attached to the CVR.[159]

A 45-day trial was set for 26 January 2026. The lawsuit seeks compensation for the passengers on the flight named from multiple defendants, including Air Canada, Nav Canada, Halifax International Airport Authority, Airbus S.A.S., the Attorney General of Canada (on behalf of Transport Canada), and the two pilots involved.[160]

8.38 HAWKER HUNTER G-BXFI, SHOREHAM AIRSHOW, UK (22 AUGUST 2015)

On 22 August 2015, a Hawker Hunter aircraft, which was performing a maneuver at the Shoreham Airshow, which involved both a pitching and rolling component, failed to complete the loop maneuver and crashed on the A27, Shoreham Bypass, where vehicles and pedestrians were standing by at the junction with the Old Shoreham Road. The aircraft broke into four main sections. Fuel and fuel vapor released from the fuel tanks ignited. Eleven road users and bystanders were killed, and thirteen people, including the pilot, were injured in the accident. The UK AAIB investigated the accident. The pilot was interviewed seven times during the investigation. The final report, which was published on 3 March 2017, found that the accident was caused by pilot error. The report states that the maneuver

> commenced from a height lower than the pilot's authorized minimum for aerobatics, at an airspeed below his stated minimum, and proceeded with less than maximum thrust. This resulted in the aircraft achieving a height at the top of the maneuver less than the minimum required to complete it safely, at a speed that was slower than normal. Although it was possible to abort the maneuver safely at this point, it appeared that the pilot had not recognized that the aircraft was too low to complete the downward half of the maneuver. An analysis of human performance identified several credible explanations for this, including: not reading the altimeter due to workload, distraction, or visual limitations such as contrast or glare; misreading the altimeter due to its presentation of height information; or incorrectly recalling the minimum height required at the apex.[161]

The report also states that the investigation determined the guidance regarding the minimum height to commence aerobatic maneuvers was unclear and not consistently applied, and that other pilots did not always verify or correctly perceive that the required height had been achieved at the apex of maneuvers. In addition, the training and assessment procedures in place at the time of the accident did not fully prepare pilots for conducting relevant escape maneuvers in the Hunter aircraft.[162]

In addition to the technical investigation conducted, the Sussex police initiated their own investigation into the accident. As part of their investigation, the police applied to the High Court to gain access to the interviews that the AAIB conducted with the pilot as well as the results of tests, which the AAIB refused to hand over. Sussex Police applied to the High Court for copies of the interviews, as well as the results of tests on aspects of the accident, and video recordings obtained from the two action cameras that were in the aircraft and subsequently recovered from the wreckage. In September 2016, the High Court denied access to the interviews and test results, but the footage from the onboard video cameras was handed over to the Chief Constable of the Sussex police.[163]

In March 2018, the pilot was charged with eleven counts of manslaughter by gross negligence and one count of endangering an aircraft in contravention of the 2009 Air Navigation Order.[164] The pilot pleaded not guilty on 15 May 2018, and proceedings were postponed until the trial commenced again on 16 January 2019. The trial lasted for seven weeks. On 8 March 2019, after seven hours of deliberation, the jury found him not guilty.[165]

8.39 METROJET AIRBUS A321 FLIGHT 9268, SINAI, EGYPT (31 OCTOBER 2015)

On 31 October 2015, a Metrojet aircraft, Flight 9268, an international passenger flight operated by Russian airline Kogalymavia (branded as Metrojet), which took off from Sharm El Sheikh International Airport, Cairo, Egypt, and was scheduled to fly to Pulkovo Airport, Saint Petersburg, Russia, was destroyed in an accident above northern Sinai. All 224 persons on board were killed. The Egyptian Aircraft Accidents Investigation Directorate conducted the investigation. On 13 December 2015, the investigation team issued the preliminary report. The report was submitted to ICAO and the Accredited Representatives of the States participating in the investigation, namely, Russia, the State of Operator, France, the State of Design, Germany, the State of Manufacturer, Ireland, the State of Registration, and the USA, the State of Engine Manufacturer. The report included the 19 articles, which are typically part of the accident investigation report, as well as the information that was available at that time. On 31 October 2016, the preliminary report was published.

Both the Egyptian and Russian authorities launched a parallel criminal investigation. The technical investigation under ICAO Annex 13 coordinated with the Egyptian and Russian judicial authorities and various other Russian teams, including a team specializing in metallurgy and representatives of insurance companies. The interim report states that Criminal Evidence Experts examined samples of the wreckage under the instruction of the General Prosecutor. In addition, the investigation committee received a report issued by the Federal Security Service of the Russian Federation. The report was then submitted to the General Prosecutor, in accordance with Article 108 of the Egyptian Civil Aviation Law, as it included some suspects of criminal acts. The Accredited Representatives of the States participating in the investigation, as well as the judicial authorities, were present when a surface layout process for the wreckage was carried out at the storage area at Cairo Airport in an attempt to identify the area of the first disintegration point of the aircraft fuselage and its propagation. Photos from the crash scene show a main impact zone of the forward fuselage and wings, and the engines and the tail section of the aircraft were found away from the main wreckage.

The wreckage was scattered over a wide area more than 13 km in length.[166] Investigators reported that they believed the aircraft broke apart in the air.

On 17 November 2015, the Russian security services stated that their investigation had concluded the crash was the result of a terrorist act. Traces of explosives were found in the wreckage. They submitted that an improvised homemade explosive device having the power equivalent of up to 1.5 kilograms of Trinitrotoluene (TNT) was detonated. As a result, the aircraft blew up in the air. This was consistent with the significant scattering of the fuselage parts of the aircraft. Russia offered a US$50 million reward for further information.[167] Subsequent to the crash, all CCTV footage was examined, and all airport personnel involved in handling the aircraft, its passengers, and baggage were interrogated. Several airport staff were detained for questioning, some of whom were suspected of assisting the person(s) who planted the bomb on the aircraft. Two employees suspected of leaving a baggage-scanning machine unattended for an extended period while passengers were boarding the aircraft were sought. It is reported that no arrests were made.[168] In November 2015, the Russian Defence Minister announced that the Islamic State of Iraq and the Levant (ISIL) branch operating on the Sinai Peninsula, the so-called Vilayat Sinai terrorist group, was responsible for blowing up the plane.[169] Shortly after that announcement, on 18 November 2015, the Islamic State released a photo in the online magazine Dabiq of the purported improvised bomb. The photo showed a Schweppes soft drink can containing an explosive charge, a military-grade detonator, and a switch.[170] On 29 January 2016, an Egypt Air mechanic who is a cousin of an ISIS fighter was arrested on suspicion of planting the bomb on board the aircraft. Security officials who spoke on condition of remaining anonymous are reported to have said that the mechanic is believed to have put the bomb on board after his cousin had given him the bomb in a handbag. In addition, a baggage handler at the airport and two airport policemen who were also suspected of helping were also reportedly arrested.[171]

8.40 FLYDUBAI BOEING 737 FLIGHT FZ981, ROSTOV-ON-DAM, RUSSIA (19 MARCH 2016)

On 19 March 2016, Flydubai FZ981, which took off from Dubai, UAE, with seven crew and 55 passengers, crashed during a second approach attempt to land in bad weather at Rostov-On-Don Airport in Southern Russia. The first landing approach was aborted, and the aircraft went into a holding pattern for approximately two hours before making a second attempt. After aborting the second landing attempt, the aircraft climbed sharply during the go-around procedure, descended rapidly, and then crashed onto the runway. The aircraft was destroyed, and there were no survivors.

On the day of the crash, an investigative commission was established by the Russian Interstate Aviation Committee (IAC) to investigate the accident, with representatives from inter alia, the NTSB, FAA, the Boeing Company, AAIS, the Flydubai airline, and France, where the aircraft's designer and manufacturer is headquartered. The final report issued in November 2019 concluded that the

> accident occurred during the second go around, due to an incorrect aircraft configuration and crew piloting, the subsequent loss of Pilot in Command's (PICs) situational awareness at night in Instrument Meteorological Conditions (IMC), which resulted in a loss of control of the aircraft and the aircraft impacting the ground.[172]

The report further states that,

> the contributing factors were most probably:
>
> - the presence of turbulence and gusty wind classified as wind shear, resulting in the need to perform two go-arounds;
> - the lack of psychological readiness (not go-around minded) of the PIC to perform the second go-around;
> - the loss of the PIC's leadership in the crew after initiating the go-around and his "confusion" that led to the impossibility of transitioning from "approach with landing" to "go-around";
> - the absence of the instructions of the maneuver type specification at the go-around callout in the aircraft manufacturer documentation and the airline OM;
> - the crew's uncoordinated actions during the second go-around; the failure of the PIC to create the pitch required to perform a go-around and maintain the required climb profile while piloting aircraft unbalanced in forces;
> - the PIC's insufficient knowledge and skills on the stabilizer manual trim operation; the psychological incapacitation of the PIC that resulted in his total spatial disorientation, did not allow him to respond to the correct prompts of the F/O;
> - the absence of the criteria of the psychological incapacitation in the airline OM, which prevented the first officer from the in-time recognition of the situation and undertaking more decisive actions;
> - the possible operational tiredness of the crew as, at the time of the accident, the crew had been proceeding the flight for 6 hours, of which 2 hours under intense workload that implied the need to make non-standard decisions; in this context the fatal accident occurred at the worst possible time in terms of the circadian rhythms, when the human performance is severely degraded and is at its lower level along with the increase of the risk of errors.[173]

In addition, a criminal investigation into the accident was conducted by the Russian Federation Investigative Committee General Directorate for Major Investigations, which said that the accident was caused by crew error, technical failure, adverse weather conditions, and other factors.[174] In April 2016, relatives of a number of the deceased passengers filed a lawsuit against Boeing seeking compensation of US$5 million per passenger on the flight.[175]

8.41 ROBINSON R22, NEAR LINDIS PASS, NEW ZEALAND (30 APRIL 2016)

On 30 April 2016, a Robinson R22 helicopter took off from Athol, in Southland, New Zealand, to Mt Algidus Station, in Canterbury, with two people on board, the pilot and his business partner, who were contracted to work at the Station as part of their earthmoving business AgWorks. The helicopter was co-owned by the pilot and his nephew. Approximately one hour after taking off, the helicopter reached the mountains around the Lindis Pass area. As a result of heavy clouds and reduced visibility, the pilot decided to descend, and he brought the helicopter to a hover. The helicopter was overloaded and could not maintain the hover. The compromised balance and reduced visibility resulted in the pilot losing spatial awareness, and the helicopter struck the side of the hill. Both initially survived the crash, but the passenger died at the scene of the accident, and the pilot, who suffered serious injuries, later recovered.

Charges were brought against the pilot by the Civil Aviation Authority. The pilot was charged with five charges under the Health and Safety at Work Act (HSWA) 2015. This was the first case where someone was prosecuted as an "officer" under the HSWA. The charges carry a maximum of up to five years' imprisonment and/or a fine of $600,000. The trial was held in the Queenstown District Court. On 30 October 2019, the pilot was convicted of two charges, both under s47 of the Act, namely that, as an officer of AgWorks, and as a worker of that business, he, without reasonable excuse, engaged in conduct that exposed the deceased to the risk of death or serious injury, and was reckless as to that risk. The judge sentenced him to four months' community detention, 350 hours' community service, and ordered him to pay $100,000 in reparations. He was also fined $10,000 and ordered to pay the $10,000 court costs.[176] He appealed the convictions, and the Civil Aviation Authority appealed the quantum of the damages awarded as consequential losses for the victim's family. In December 2020, the High Court dismissed both the appeals.

8.42 EGYPT AIR A320 FLIGHT 804, MEDITERRANEAN SEA (19 MAY 2016)

On 19 May 2016, Egypt Air Flight 804, which took off from Paris Charles de Gaulle Airport with 10 crew members and 56 passengers flying to Cairo, Egypt, crashed into the Mediterranean Sea, killing everybody on board. Greek military radar showed that the aircraft suddenly took a 90-degree left turn, followed by a 360-degree turn in the opposite direction as it descended from FL370 to FL150 before disappearing off radar. The flight data recorder and cockpit voice recorder were recovered from the seabed on 16 June 2016 and sent to the French civil aviation accident bureau, the Bureau d'Enquêtes et d'Analyses pour la Sécurité de l'Aviation civile (BEA) for decoding. As the State of Registration, Egypt conducted the official accident investigation. The Egyptian authorities found, inter alia, that the aircraft systems sent Aircraft Communications Addressing and Reporting System (ACARS) messages indicating the presence of smoke in the toilets and the avionics bay. In addition, several pieces of debris retrieved from the accident site showed signs of having been exposed to high temperatures and contained traces of soot. In December 2016, when the Egyptian accident investigators reported that traces of explosives had been found on several victims, the crash was deemed to be the result of a criminal act, and the case was transferred to the Egyptian Attorney General. The judicial authorities took over the investigation.[177]

In July 2018, the BEA confirmed that the Aircraft Communications Addressing and Reporting System (ACARS) messages indicated smoke in the cabin as well as a fault in the flight control unit minutes before crashing. Contradicting the Egyptian authorities, the BEA stated that "the most likely hypothesis is that a fire broke out in the cockpit while the aeroplane was flying at its cruise altitude and that the fire spread rapidly, resulting in the loss of control of the aeroplane."[178]

The BEA reported that it was frustrated that more progress had not been made in the accident investigation, that its proposals concerning further work on the debris and recorded data were not followed up, and that technical elements of the investigation already collected by Egypt, including those provided by the BEA, are "protected by the Egyptian judicial investigation." It further stated that

> The BEA's Egyptian counterpart did not publish the final report, which would have allowed the BEA to set out its differences of opinion as authorized by the international provisions. The BEA considered that it was necessary to have the final report to have the possibility of understanding the cause of the accident and to provide the aviation community with the safety lessons which could prevent future accidents.[179]

The French prosecution authorities opened a manslaughter investigation and stated that the case was being treated as a criminal matter, rather than a terrorist act.[180] The three investigating judges found that the aircraft was not safe to fly on that fateful day, as there were maintenance and safety lapses in the preceding five flight days, which were largely ignored. The report states that "The plane should have been checked during its four previous flights and should not have left Cairo after the appearance of repeated faults that were not reported by successive teams." The report determined that the day before the crash, there were nearly twenty alerts sent via the ACARS system, some of which signaled an electrical problem that could lead to a fire, but the airline had not addressed the alerts. The pilots on those flights did not file any safety reports, and the EgyptAir ground technician stated that neither the airline nor the pilots notified him of these issues. Investigators also questioned whether the EgyptAir technician in Paris who inspected the plane was qualified to service aircraft in Europe.[181]

Despite a prior September 2014 agreement between the French justice system and the BEA to cooperate when investigating aviation accidents, there was significant conflict between the two authorities in the aftermath of the MS 804 accident. The judicial authorities had been attempting to gain access to the data retrieved from the black boxes for approximately 2 years. The French BEA refused to hand over a copy of the data to the French prosecution authorities. They argued first, that they had decrypted the black boxes and given the data to the Egyptian authorities and then had erased all the data; second, that in accordance with international law it was up to the Egyptian authorities to provide the data to the judicial authorities (which they did not do) and; third, the cooperation agreement between the BEA and the French judiciary only applied if the BEA was the authority conducting the investigation. In October 2018, the premises of the BEA were raided by the judicial authority, where they found a backup copy of the data. The BEA said they were not aware that an automatic backup had been made.[182]

8.43 EMIRATES EK 521, BOEING 777 FLIGHT 521, DUBAI, UAE (3 AUGUST 2016)

Emirates Airlines Boeing 777 Flight EK521, an international passenger flight, took off from Thiruvananthapuram, India, scheduled to fly to Dubai, UAE with 18 crew and 282 passengers on board. During an attempted go-around at Dubai Airport, the aircraft impacted the runway. Everyone on board survived, and 24 passengers suffered injuries. An airport firefighter died during the rescue operations. The General Civil Aviation Authority of the UAE (GCAA) Air Accident Investigation Sector investigated the accident. The interim report, issued in August 2017, found that the pilot attempted to take off again after briefly touching down, and that the aircraft ultimately hit the runway as its landing gear was still retracting. The final report issued on 6 February 2020 states that the causes of the accident are:

> (a) During the attempted go-around, except for the last three seconds prior to impact, both engine thrust levers, and therefore engine thrust, remained at idle. Consequently, the Aircraft's energy state was insufficient to sustain flight. (b) The flight crew did not effectively scan and monitor the primary flight instrumentation parameters during the landing and the attempted go-around. (c) The flight crew were unaware that the autothrottle (A/T) had not responded to move the engine thrust levers to the TO/GA position after the Commander pushed the Takeoff/Go-Around (TO/GA) switch at the initiation of the FCOM- Go-around and Missed Approach Procedure. (d) The flight crew did not take corrective action to increase engine thrust because they omitted the engine thrust verification steps of the FCOM- Go-around and Missed Approach Procedure.[183]

On 15 August, the passengers who were injured filed a civil motion in the Circuit Court of Cook County, Illinois, in the USA against Boeing, claiming compensation for injuries they allege that they had suffered when the aircraft fell violently back to the ground during the landing maneuver. They are suing Boeing for an alleged design defect in the cockpit switch used by pilots when taking off or attempting a go-around. On 26 September, Boeing filed a motion to dismiss the suit based on forum non conveniens, alleging that the matter had to be heard in the UAE as the evidence related to the crash, including testimony from the airline and airport, which was in the UAE, was necessary to both parties. The plaintiffs responded that much of the evidence was already publicly available and that evidence from other relevant jurisdictions, particularly the UK, would be easier to obtain in a U.S. court than in a court in Dubai, as the UAE does not recognize the 1970 Hague Convention on the Taking of Evidence Abroad.

The judge, balancing the private and public interests in the case, ruled against Boeing and dismissed the appeal, stating that the arguments submitted by Boeing in favor of dismissal were not persuasive and that the passengers, who are not residents in the USA, have the right to sue Boeing in the USA.[184]

8.44 CHINA EASTERN AIRLINES FLIGHT MU5643, NEAR COLLISION AT SHANGHAI AIRPORT, CHINA (10 OCTOBER 2016)

On 10 October 2016, a China Eastern Airlines A320 Flight MU5643, which took off from Shanghai Hongqiao Airport for a domestic flight to Tianjin, China, with 147 passengers, was involved in a serious runway incursion incident during take-off from Shanghai Hongqiao Airport. After the aircraft was cleared for takeoff and as it was accelerating down runway 36L, an Airbus A330 entered the active runway via another taxiway. The China Eastern Airbus A330 had just landed on the runway after a flight from Beijing and had reportedly been cleared to taxi to the terminal. It left the runway, crossed the taxiway, and entered the active departure runway. The crew assessed that they would not be able to stop in time to avoid a collision and selected TOGA thrust and continued their takeoff. They rotated the aircraft and managed to climb over the A330 with a separation of 19 m before landing safely at its destination airport. China's Civil Aviation Authority, CAAC, initiated an investigation. On 12 October 2016, it stated that preliminary results suggest a serious incident was caused by air traffic controllers at Hongqiao Airport who had issued clearances to both aircraft, causing the conflict. The report stated that "The air traffic controllers on the control tower were to blame for the 'serious accident symptoms,' who forgot the planes' movements and gave wrong orders to the pilots."

Several disciplinary measures were imposed on 15 air traffic controllers. The licenses of the two controllers who were manning the commanding and monitoring seats were revoked, and one of the controllers was banned for life from working as an air traffic controller. Thirteen officials with the East China Air Traffic Management Bureau and the Bureau's air traffic control center and safety management department were either given Party warnings, serious warnings, had demerits recorded or faced losing their positions. The captain of the A320 was given a first-class merit and other rewards for defusing the crisis.[185]

8.45 LAMIA FLIGHT 2933 COLUMBIA (28 NOVEMBER 2016)

LaMia Flight 2933, a charter flight, was transporting the Brazilian Chapecoense football team from Santa Cruz de la Sierra, Bolivia, to Colombia. During a holding pattern waiting to be authorized to intercept the localizer for landing at the Colombian airport, the aircraft suffered a sequential flame-out of its 4 engines and impacted the southern slope of a mountainous terrain located 10 nm south of the threshold of the runway in nighttime and rainy weather conditions. There were 77 people on board the Avro RJ85, which was destroyed after impact. Seventy-one people died, and six survived: one crew member, three players, and two other passengers.

A recording of the CVR of the pilot repeatedly requesting permission to land because of fuel problems and of the controller explaining that another plane, which had mechanical problems, had been diverted and had priority, and instructing the pilot to wait for seven minutes was leaked to the media. Investigators also looked into the role of the captain, who was also one of the owners of LaMia, who allegedly abandoned a stop for refueling and only took the minimum amount of fuel and no extra fuel to account for any delays or diversions as he was legally required to do.[186]

The official investigation was conducted by the Colombian Aviation Accident Investigation Authority (GRIAA), which stated[187] that the cause of the accident was fuel exhaustion and that the following were contributing factors: the inappropriate planning and execution of the flight by the operator with regards to the amount of fuel required for the safe completion of the intended flight; the flame-out of the four engines as a result of fuel exhaustion; inadequate decision making on the part of the aircraft operator's company management, in terms of the implementation of operational safety in its processes; and loss of situational awareness and wrongful decision making by the flight crew, because of the fixation on continuing the intended flight with an extremely limited amount of fuel.

The report also states that contributing factors were: premature configuration of the aircraft for landing during descent in the holding pattern; latent deficiencies in the planning and execution of non-regular transportation flights by the aircraft operator related to insufficient supply of the required amount of fuel; specific deficiencies in the planning of the flight involved in the accident by the aircraft operator; lack of oversight and operational control of the flight by the operator; absence of timely calls for "priority," or declaring an "emergency" by the aircraft crew members during the flight, particularly when fuel depletion which would have alerted air traffic services to provide the necessary support; organizational and operational noncompliance by the aircraft operator in the implementation of fuel management procedures; delay in the approach caused by its late priority request, and late emergency declaration for fuel.[188]

The Bolivian DGAC suspended LaMia's air operator's certificate, and the company's two remaining aircraft were impounded. Bolivian, Brazilian, and Colombian prosecutors formed a tripartite commission to share information and cooperate in the criminal investigation of this case.[189] A week after the accident, LaMia's chief executive was detained and charged with inter alia, involuntary manslaughter. His son, the former director of DGAC's National Aeronautics Registry, was also charged with breach of duty and for allegedly using his influence to authorize the license of the plane. Criminal charges were also brought against LaMia's co-owner, who disappeared after the accident. In addition, the Bolivian authorities were also investigating the role of two other people. An official with the Bolivian flight control entity[190] and another staff member of the Civil Aviation Authority, who had allegedly seen the aircraft's flight plan before it took off from the airport and had warned that it barely had enough fuel to reach its destination in Colombia. She is said to have reported that her bosses had pressured her to change a flight report she made at the time and that, as she felt that she would not get a fair trial, she fled the country and sought asylum in Brazil. An arrest warrant has been issued for her arrest.[191]

8.46 PIPER A-28, MANCHESTER, UK (M62) CHEROKEE (9 SEPTEMBER 2017)

On 9 September 2017, a Piper Cherokee A-28 took off from Barton aerodrome in Manchester with three passengers who were a group of birdwatchers. Each passenger paid the pilot £500 to fly them to the Isle of Barra in Scotland. The fifty-two-year-old pilot had his own private license. Shortly after takeoff, the airplane crossed the M62 motorway twice before clipping trees alongside the motorway, descending and crashing into a potato field, approximately 150 meters from the motorway. The pilot broke his nose, one passenger cut his hand, another suffered whiplash and cracked his ribs, and another suffered a serious cut to the head with severe rib bruising. The accident was investigated by the Civil Aviation Authority and the Greater Manchester Police's Serious Collision Investigation Unit. Investigators found that he had failed to weigh the three passengers and their luggage before taking off and that the aircraft was 426lb over the maximum takeoff weight of 2150 lb.

The pilot was charged with violating seven offenses under the Air Navigation Order (ANO) 2016 and the Civil Aviation (Insurance) Regulations, namely: recklessly endangering the safety of an aircraft or persons in an aircraft; recklessly endangering the safety of persons or property; conducting a public transport flight without an Air Operator Certificate; acting as a pilot without holding an appropriate license; flying outside the flight manual limitations; flying without insurance; and flying without the aircraft flight manual. He pleaded guilty to these charges.

The pilot had several previous convictions. In May 2013, an aircraft, which was operated and insured by the pilot and hired out to a pilot, crashed at Caernarfon in Wales, killing one passenger and seriously injuring two others. In 2014, he was prosecuted after a Piper PA plane owned by his company had crashed in the Swiss Alps, killing the pilot and a passenger. A Swiss inquiry blamed pilot error for the accident, but the investigation revealed that the plane was not airworthy, and the pilot was fined £333. As a result of not having an airworthiness certificate, the insurance was invalid, and the company lost its £25,000 value. In 2008, he was accused of wrongdoing after the plane he owned crashed off the coast of Blackpool, killing the inexperienced pilot and the 81-year-old co-pilot. In 1997, he was fined £1,500 for false representation. His business collapsed in 2001 owing £1.15 million, but it is thought that he set up another company.[192]

In November 2019, the Manchester Crown Court found him guilty, and he was sentenced to three and a half years for violating the ANO.[193] In addition, the pilot was also charged with fraud and making a false declaration to obtain insurance. The police's investigation found that shortly before he took out the insurance policy for the aircraft, he had been declined insurance from another firm. As he had previously operated under another name, the records for that operation should have been disclosed.

An aviation expert witness testimony for the Crown Prosecutor stated that the pilot had failed in his responsibilities as pilot in command and was grossly negligent. The judge described him as someone with a cavalier attitude toward aviation and who deliberately lied to achieve a financial advantage, resulting in reduced premiums. He was sentenced to an additional 22 weeks in prison, to be served concurrently with his three-and-a-half-year sentence.[194]

8.47 CUBANA DE AVIACIÓN BOEING 737 FLIGHT 972, HAVANA, CUBA (18 MAY 2018)

Global Air Flight 972, a scheduled domestic flight from José Martí International Airport, Havana, Cuba, to Frank País Airport in Holguín, Cuba, with 107 passengers and six crew on board, crashed on take-off from Havana-José Martí International Airport, Cuba, broke up, and burst into flames about 19 km from the Havana city center. The Boeing aircraft operated by Mexican airline Damojh Aerolíneas, operating as Global Air, on behalf of Cubana, flew from Havana to Santiago de Cuba and back to Havana on the day of the accident. There was one survivor. Initially, three passengers survived the accident, but one survivor died on May 21, and a second died on May 25. The official investigation was conducted by the Cuban CEIAA (Comisión De Investigación De Accidentes E Incidentes De Aviación), which found that there were 62 passengers in the forward cabin when it had a capacity for 54. The weight in the cargo compartments was incorrect, and the crew calculated the fuel weight at take-off to be about 99,900 lb. However, it was just over 104,000 lb. The center of gravity was listed as 17.4% of the mean aerodynamic chord, but the recalculation by the investigators found it to be at 28.5%, which was very close to the permissible operating limit of 29%. Additionally, the stabilizer trim setting was off by more than two units. Even though the weight and center of gravity were technically within the aircraft's capabilities, the investigators determined that the balance miscalculation and the position of the trim resulted in unstable behavior of the plane and made piloting the aircraft difficult.[195]

The final report published on 12 September 2019 states that the most probable cause of the accident was the collapse of the aircraft, as a consequence of its entry into abnormal positions immediately after the separation of the landing gear from the runway surface during take-off, which led to the loss of control due to a chain of errors, with a preponderance in the human factor. The contributing factors were the inconsistencies in crew training, gross errors in calculating the weight and balance, and low operational standards during the flight.[196]

In August 2018, even before the final accident investigation report was issued, relatives of 3 passengers who died in the accident filed a lawsuit in the Cook County Circuit Court in Chicago, USA, claiming compensation from Global Air (Aerolineas Damojh) alleging that they did not fulfill their legal duty as the operator to ensure its pilots were adequately trained and that they had trained the pilots in a negligent and reckless manner.[197]

8.48 AEROVIAS DE MÉXICO (AEROMÉXICO) EMBRAER ERJ-190 FLIGHT 2431, DURANGO INTERNATIONAL AIRPORT (31 JULY 2018)

The Aeroméxico Flight 2431 operated by Aeroméxico Connect, a domestic scheduled passenger flight, took off from Durango International Airport bound for Mexico City, and crashed on takeoff from Durango. During the take-off roll, there were notable changes in airspeed and wind direction. Shortly after becoming airborne, the plane encountered sudden wind shear caused by a microburst. The aircraft lost speed and altitude and impacted left of the runway, left wing first. Both engines were detached, and the aircraft then came to rest approximately 380 m beyond the runway. The post-impact fire completely destroyed the aircraft. All 103 passengers survived, but many suffered serious injuries.

The Mexican Directorate General of Civil Aeronautics conducted the official investigation. The final report issued seven months later in February 2019 stated that the probable cause of the accident was the impact against the runway caused by loss of control of the aircraft in the final phase of the take-off run by low altitude wind shear that caused a loss of speed and lift. Contributing factors included errors from the pilots, namely a decrease in situational awareness of the flight crew when the commander was performing unauthorized instructional tasks without being qualified to provide flight instruction and to assign co-pilot and pilot flying duties to an uncertified and unlicensed pilot; failure to detect variations in the indicator displayed by the airspeed indicator on the PFD during the take-off run; and a lack of adherence to sterile cabin procedures and operational procedures. In addition, errors on the part of the air traffic control were also identified in that there was a lack of adherence to procedures, a failure to provide information on important variations in wind direction and speed, value of visibility existing at the time of take-off and significant meteorological conditions, and a lack of supervisory personnel in the tower at the time of the accident.[198]

The authors were not able to find any reports of any criminal charges against the airline, the crew, or the air traffic controllers. Civil proceedings against the airline were filed in the Cook County Circuit Court in Chicago by many of the passengers who were injured, seeking compensation. They allege inter alia that the airline was negligent in that the pilot failed to execute a proper takeoff maneuver and that the aircraft took off in unsafe weather conditions, which the airline did not monitor. The judge issued an order to the airline to "preserve, protect, and produce" the cockpit voice recorder, the black box, and any other communications between the pilot, air traffic control, ground control, and airline staff.[199]

8.49 LION AIR BOEING 737 MAX 8 FLIGHT 610, JAVA SEA (29 OCTOBER 2018)

Lion Air Flight 610, a scheduled domestic flight with 181 passengers and eight crew, operated by Lion Air, took off from Jakarta-Soekarno-Hatta International Airport, Indonesia, and approximately 13 minutes later, crashed into the Java Sea, killing everyone on board. It was the first major accident involving the new Boeing 737 MAX series aircraft, which was introduced in 2017. The investigation was conducted by the Indonesian National Transportation Safety Committee (NTSC), officially called the KNKT (Komite Nasional Keselamatan Transportasi), and a final report was published in October 2019. The flight data recorder was located on 1 November, at a depth of 105 feet, and the CVR was recovered on 14 January 2019. The following are listed as factors that contributed to the accident:[200]

1. During the design and certification of the Boeing 737-8 (MAX), assumptions were made about flight crew response to malfunctions which, even though consistent with current industry guidelines, turned out to be incorrect.
2. Based on the incorrect assumptions about flight crew response and an incomplete review of associated multiple flight deck effects, MCAS's reliance on a single sensor was deemed appropriate and met all certification requirements.
3. MCAS was designed to rely on a single AOA sensor, making it vulnerable to erroneous input from that sensor.
4. The absence of guidance on MCAS or more detailed use of trim in the flight manuals and in flight crew training, made it more difficult for flight crews to properly respond to uncommanded MCAS.
5. The AOA DISAGREE alert was not correctly enabled during Boeing 737-8 (MAX) development. As a result, it did not appear during flight with the mis-calibrated AOA sensor, could not be documented by the flight crew and was therefore not available to help maintenance identify the mis-calibrated AOA sensor.
6. The replacement AOA sensor that was installed on the accident aircraft had been mis-calibrated during an earlier repair. This mis-calibration was not detected during the repair.
7. The investigation could not determine that the installation test of the AOA sensor was performed properly. The mis-calibration was not detected.
8. Lack of documentation in the aircraft flight and maintenance log about the continuous stick shaker and use of the Runaway Stabilizer NNC meant that information was not available to the maintenance crew in Jakarta nor was it

available to the accident crew, making it more difficult for each to take the appropriate actions.

9. The multiple alerts, repetitive MCAS activations, and distractions related to numerous ATC communications were not able to be effectively managed. This was caused by the difficulty of the situation and performance in manual handling, NNC execution, and flight crew communication, leading to ineffective CRM application and workload management. These performances had previously been identified during training and reappeared during the accident flight.

In the aftermath of the accident, relatives of the deceased passengers filed wrongful death lawsuits in the Cook County Circuit Court in Chicago against Boeing for their alleged negligence. They allege that the aircraft and the 737 MAX 8 flight operations manual (FOM) were defective and unreasonably dangerous in that inter alia, the aircraft's anti-stall system, the Maneuvering Characteristics Augmentation System (MCAS), was defective. The aircraft and the FOM lacked proper and adequate instructions and warnings regarding the design and functions of its MCAS system, the possible consequences resulting from that, and how to correct a malfunctioning MCAS system.[201] This case is discussed in greater detail in Chapter 4.

8.50 PIPER MALIBU N264DB, ENGLISH CHANNEL, UK (21 JANUARY 2019)

On 21 January 2019, a Piper Malibu single-engine propeller plane with a pilot and one passenger took off from Nantes, France, to go to Cardiff and crashed into the sea. The passenger on board was the football player, Emiliano Sala, who had gone to say goodbye to his teammates from the French club Nantes as he had recently been transferred to Cardiff City. The search operation recovered the body of the passenger in the wreckage on 6 February 2019, 13 days after the crash. A further search of the wreckage and surroundings did not reveal any evidence of the pilot.

In accordance with ICAO Annex 13, as the aircraft was lost in international waters, the State of Registration, namely the USA, had the responsibility to investigate the accident. The NTSB, however, delegated the investigation to the State of Operator, and therefore, the UK AAIB investigated the accident. The AAIB was assisted by the French Bureau d'Enquêtes et d'Analyses pour la Sécurité de l'Aviation Civile (BEA), the NTSB in the USA, and the Junta de Investigación de Accidentes de Aviación Civil (JIAAC) in Argentina.

The preliminary report the AAIB published on 25 February 2019 states that the

> aircraft was extensively damaged, and the main body of the aircraft was in three parts held together by electrical and flying control cables. The engine had disconnected from the cockpit area, and the rear section of the fuselage had broken away from the forward section adjacent to the trailing edge of the wing. The outboard section of both wings, tail plane and fin were missing [ ]. In the days following the accident, two seat cushions, an armrest and possible skin from the fuselage washed up along the coast of the

> Cotentin Peninsula, France. A seat cushion also washed up in Bonne Nuit Bay on the north coast of Jersey.[202]

It also determined that neither the pilot nor the aircraft had the required licenses or permissions to operate commercially. The pilot had a private pilot's license (an EASA PPL, issued by the CAA in the UK, and an FAA PPL, issued on the basis of his EASA PPL), but he was not rated for night flights, and he did not hold a commercial license required for charter operations. The investigation also revealed that the aircraft was registered in the USA through an American trust to which ownership was transferred. In 2011, the aircraft was imported to the UK when it was acquired by a UK company, Southern Aircraft Consultancy Inc., and it was that company that was responsible for the operation and maintenance of the aircraft, ensuring it was maintained in accordance with applicable regulations and met all airworthiness requirements. The aircraft was managed by a third party.[203]

In June 2019, during an ongoing criminal investigation, a British pilot who allegedly arranged for a colleague to fly the return trip from France was arrested on suspicion of manslaughter by an unlawful act. He was later released pending the conclusion of the investigation. The private pilot is said to have previously worked with an agent connected to the footballer's transfer to Cardiff.

On 13 March 2020, the AAIB published its final report, concluding that the pilot had lost control of the aircraft as it crossed the English Channel in poor weather conditions at night, and states that the

> investigation identified the following causal factors:
>
> 1. The pilot lost control of the aircraft during a manually-flown turn, which was probably initiated to remain in or regain Visual Meteorological Conditions (VMC).
> 2. The aircraft subsequently suffered an in-flight break-up while manoeuvring at an airspeed significantly in excess of its design manoeuvring speed.
> 3. The pilot was probably affected by carbon monoxide (CO) poisoning.[204]

In October 2020, the UK Civil Aviation Authority proceeded with a criminal prosecution against the British pilot who was allegedly responsible for arranging the flight. Criminal charges under the Air Navigation Order were filed, alleging that the flight was an illegal commercial operation and that he had acted in a reckless/negligent manner likely to endanger the aircraft.[205]

8.51 ETHIOPIAN AIRLINES BOEING 737 MAX 8, FLIGHT 302, NEAR BISHOFTU, ETHIOPIA (10 MARCH 2019)

The Ethiopian Airlines Boeing 737 MAX 8, a scheduled international passenger flight, took off from Addis Ababa-Bole Airport with eight crew and 149 passengers on board, destined for Jomo Kenyatta International Airport in Nairobi, Kenya. Approximately six minutes after take-off, the aircraft crashed. All 157 people on board were killed. This was the second accident involving the Boeing 737 MAX 8, and shortly after the accident, the 737 MAX series was grounded by airlines and regulators globally.

The Ethiopian Airplane Accident Investigation Bureau (EAIB) issued a preliminary report on 4 April 2019, which states that

> Shortly after take-off, the Angle of Attack sensor recorded value became erroneous and the left stick shaker activated and remained active until near the end of the flight. In addition, the airspeed and altitude values from the left air data system began deviating from the corresponding right side values. Due to flight control problems, the Captain was unable to maintain the flight path and requested to return back to the departure airport. The crew lost control of the aircraft which crashed South-East of Addis Ababa near Ejere village.[206]

On 23 December 2022, the EAIB issued its final accident report[207] stating that:

> 3.2 Probable cause of the accident
>
> Repetitive and uncommanded airplane-nose-down inputs from the MCAS due to erroneous AOA input, and its unrecoverable activation system which made the airplane dive with the rate of -33,000 ft/min close to the ground was the most probable cause of the accident.
>
> 3.3 Contributing Factors
>
> 1. The MCAS design relied on a single AOA sensor, making it vulnerable to erroneous input from the sensor;
> 2. During the design process, Boeing failed to consider the potential for uncommanded activation of MCAS, but assumed that pilots would recognize and address it through normaluse of the control column, manual electric trim, and the existing Runaway Stabilizer NNC. The OMB and Emergency AD issued after the Lion Air accident included additional guidance but did not have the intended effect of preventing another MCAS-related accident;
> 3. While Boeing considered the possibility of uncommanded MCAS activation as part of its FHA, it did not evaluate all the potential alerts and indications that could accompany a failure leading to an uncommanded MCAS;
> 4. The MCAS contribution to cumulative AOA effects was not assessed;
> 5. The combined effect of alerts and indications that impacted pilot's recognition and procedure prioritization were not evaluated by the Manufacturer;
> 6. Absence of AOA DISAGREE warning flag on the flight display panels (PFD);
> 7. The B737 MAX Crew difference CBT training prepared by Boeing and delivered to Pilots did not cover the MCAS system;
> 8. Failure by the manufacturer to design simulator training for pilots with regards to safety critical systems like MCAS with catastrophic consquences during undesired activation.
> 9. The manufacturer failed to provide procedures regarding MCAS operation to the crew during training or in the FCOM;
> 10. Failure by the manufacturer to address the safety critical questions raised by the airline which would have cleared out crew confusion and task prioritization.[208]

The only individual to be criminally prosecuted after the two Boeing 737 MAX accidents is the former Chief Technical Pilot, who was charged and indicted for deceiving the Federal Aviation Administration's Aircraft Evaluation Group in connection with their evaluation and certification of the 737 MAX, and scheming to defraud Boeing's customers for Boeing's profits. It was alleged that he abused his position of trust by intentionally withholding critical information from the FAA and that he provided materially false, inaccurate, and incomplete information about the MCAS. It was also alleged that this resulted in depriving airlines and pilots of knowing crucial information about an essential part of the aircraft's flight controls, that the aircraft manuals and related pilot-training materials did not make any reference to the MCAS, and that Boeing's U.S.-based airline customers did not have all the relevant information when making their decisions to buy the 737 MAX airplanes.[209]

He was charged with two counts of fraud involving aircraft parts in interstate commerce in that he, on two separate occasions, knowingly and with the intent to defraud, made and used a materially false writing, entry, certification, document, record, data plate, label, and electronic communication concerning the MCAS and four counts of Wire Fraud in that he

> knowingly, and with the intent to defraud, having devised and intended to devise a scheme and artifice to defraud, and to obtain money and property by means of materially false and fraudulent pretenses, representations, and promises, did transmit and cause to be transmitted, by means of wire communication in interstate commerce, writings, signs, signals, pictures, and sounds for the purpose of executing such scheme and artifice

and for the purpose of executing and in furtherance of the aforementioned scheme and artifice to defraud, and to obtain money and property by means of materially false and fraudulent pretenses, representations, and promises, [he] "knowingly transmitted and caused to be transmitted certain interstate wire communications, with each transmission as set forth in the table below forming a separate count."[210] If convicted, he could have faced a maximum penalty of 20 years in prison on each count of wire fraud and 10 years in prison on each count of fraud involving aircraft parts in interstate commerce. However, in March 2022, a federal jury acquitted him of all charges.

On March 11, the first government regulator, the Civil Aviation Administration of China, grounded the MAX aircraft, followed by many others. On the same day, the FAA initially publicly reaffirmed the airworthiness of the aircraft, but on 13 March, it grounded the aircraft after it became aware of new evidence pointing to the similarities between the two MAX 737 accidents. By 18 March, all 387 airplanes were grounded by 59 airlines. The U.S. Congress and federal agencies then commenced an investigation into the FAA certification process of the MAX, with particular scrutiny of the FAA delegating the authority to Boeing to approve the aircraft. In April 2019, Boeing admitted that the MCAS had, in fact, played a key role in both accidents. In April 2019, the Indonesian Transportation Safety National Committee (NTSC) concluded in its final accident investigation report that problems with airplane design, certification, maintenance, and flight crew actions contributed to the Lion Air accident. The FAA then revoked Boeing's authority to issue airworthiness certificates for individual MAX airplanes in November 2019.[211]

The MAX 737 aircraft was grounded for 20 months before the FAA approved the aircraft to return to service. Orders increased to approximately 750 in 2021, 700 in 2022, and nearly 1,000 in 2023.[212] However, in January 2024, a panel covering an unused emergency exit blew off a MAX during an Alaska Airlines flight over Oregon, raising safety concerns once again at Boeing and prompting the Justice Department to open a new investigation into the Boeing Company (see Chapter 4).

8.52 AEROFLOT, SUKHOI SUPERJET-100 FLIGHT 1492, SHEREMETYEVO AIRPORT, MOSCOW, RUSSIA (5 MAY 2019)

Aeroflot Flight 1492 took off from Sheremetyevo Airport's runway on a scheduled passenger flight to Murmansk, Russia, with 5 crew members and 73 passengers. As the aircraft was climbing, it suffered an electrical failure and returned to Sheremetyevo airport for an emergency landing. The aircraft overflew the runway threshold, touched down hard, and bounced to a height of about 2 m. After two seconds, the aircraft landed again on the nose landing gear and bounced to a height of 6 m. The third landing of the aircraft occurred at a speed of 140 knots with a vertical overload of at least 5g, causing a rupture of the wing structure and fuel lines. A fire erupted and flames engulfed the rear of the aircraft while an evacuation was being carried out. The flight attendant seated at the rear of the aircraft and 40 passengers lost their lives in the accident. The Russian Interstate Aviation Committee (IAC) investigated the accident. The interim report released on 14 June 2019 provides factual information but does not make any conclusions.

In addition to the technical investigation, the Russian authorities commenced a criminal investigation to determine if there were any violations of the rules of safe movement and exploitation of air transport. In October 2019, prosecutors filed criminal charges against the captain for violating traffic safety rules resulting in the negligent death of two or more people on the flight, seeking the maximum prison sentence of seven years if found guilty.[213]

Prosecutors submitted that "After the decision was made to return to the airport of departure, (he) made, without observing the procedure for operating the aircraft, a very rough landing, allowing the aircraft to 'bounce,'" and "As a result, the main landing gear collapsed and the aircraft structure was destroyed with a spill and ignition of the fuel."[214] He pleaded not guilty to the charges, but on 20 June 2023, he was found guilty and sentenced to six years' imprisonment and banned from operating an aircraft for three years. He said that he would file an appeal.[215]

8.53 UKRAINE INTERNATIONAL AIRLINES BOEING 737, FLIGHT 752, TEHRAN, IRAN (8 JANUARY 2020)

Ukraine Airlines Flight 752, a scheduled international passenger flight from Tehran to Kiev, with 9 crew members and 167 passengers, crashed near Sabashahr 7 minutes after taking off from Tehran Imam Khomeini International Airport. The aircraft disintegrated and everyone on board was killed. On 11 January, Iran issued a statement that the aircraft was accidentally shot down by two surface-to-air missiles belonging to the Iranian Revolutionary Guard Aerospace Force.[216] The accident was officially investigated by the Islamic Republic of Iran Civil Aviation Organization Aircraft Accident Investigation Board, which issued preliminary reports on 9 January 2020 and on 21 January.

On 17 March 2021 the final report[217] which states that the accident was caused by

> The air defense's launching two surface-to-air missiles at Flight PS752, UR-PSR aircraft, the detonation of the first missile warhead in proximity of the aircraft caused damage to the aircraft systems, and the intensification of damage led the aircraft to crash into the ground and explode instantly[218]

and that it is likely that the second missile "did not affect the aircraft" and that it "had maintained its structural integrity by the time it crashed into the ground and exploded." The report also states that

> The mitigating measures and defense layers in risk management proved to be ineffective due to the occurrence of an unanticipated error in threat identifications and ultimately failed to protect the flight safety against the threats caused by the alertness of defense forces."

Ukraine's Vice Prime Minister and the Transportation Safety Board of Canada have openly criticized the report.

On 30 December 2020, Iran unilaterally announced that it had allocated $150,000 for each victim's family. Ukraine, however, stated that compensation should be settled after the causes of the crash were established. In Canada, five plaintiffs who were surviving family members and/or estate representatives of six deceased passengers sued the Islamic Republic of Iran, the IRGC, its military commander, the Iranian Armed Forces, and the Iranian supreme leader Ali Khamenei for compensation.

Before considering the issue of compensation, the judge had first to determine whether the action by the Iranians fell under specific exceptions that would lift the immunity that foreign states have from the jurisdiction of any court in Canada. In accordance with Canada's State Immunity Act, foreign states are immune from the jurisdiction of any Canadian court, unless a civil cause of action against a foreign state that is identified as a supporter of terrorism for acts or omissions amounting to terrorism offenses under the Canadian Criminal Code can be established. Iran was listed as a supporter of terrorism under Canada's State Immunity Act since 2012. In May 2021, the judge of the Ontario Superior Court of Justice, in the case Zarei v Iran,[219] concluded that the shooting down of Flight 752 by the defendants, the Islamic

Republic of Iran, was an act of terrorism and constitutes terrorist activity in accordance with the State Immunity Act and the provisions of the Canadian Criminal Code. The Iranian defendants were served with the plaintiffs' claim by the Canadian Minister of Foreign Affairs, but as they did not file a defense and did not appear in court, the court issued a default judgment. Iran's foreign ministry reacted by stating that the court's verdict was political.

With regard to the compensation claimed, the plaintiffs sought five types of damages.[220] The surviving family members of the deceased claimed damages for loss of care, guidance, and companionship, damages for intentional infliction of emotional distress and aggravated damages (namely, additional damages for mental distress). They also sought damages for the pain and suffering experienced by the deceased passengers and punitive damages. In a decision released on 31 December 2021, the judge, in the first case that a court in Canada had to consider the amount of damages to be awarded for loss of life caused by a terrorist act, awarded the plaintiffs damages in the amount of C$107 million.[221] A further legal obstacle for the plaintiffs is the enforcement of the judgment and how they will receive the compensation awarded to them.

In 2023 a court in Iran sentenced 10 armed forces personnel to prison over the shooting down of Ukraine International Airlines Flight PS752. The unit's commander was sentenced to 13 years for being an accessory to manslaughter and disobeying orders. The air defense unit's commander had been sentenced to 10 years in prison for firing missiles without authorization and three years for being an accessory to manslaughter. Nine other unnamed personnel with varying ranks were sentenced to between one and three years, including two who handled the missile system.[222]

8.54 SIKORSKY S-76B HELICOPTER, CALABASAS, CALIFORNIA (26 JANUARY 2020)

On 26 January 2020, a Sikorsky S-76B helicopter carrying a pilot and eight passengers collided with hilly terrain near the city of Calabasas, California. The helicopter, operated by Island Express Helicopters Inc., was on an on-demand passenger visual flight rules (VFR) flight which took off from John Wayne Orange County Airport, Santa Ana, California, bound for Camarillo Airport, Camarillo, California. The passengers, who were going to a basketball tournament, were Kobe Bryant (a well-known NBA player), his daughter, who was going to play in the tournament, one of her teammates, and her mother, a head baseball coach who was traveling with his wife and their daughter, and a basketball coach. All the passengers and the pilot were killed, and the helicopter was destroyed on impact and by the ensuing fire.[223]

The National Transportation Safety Board, together with the assistance of the Federal Aviation Administration, Island Express Helicopters, Sikorsky, and the National Air Traffic Controllers Association, investigated the accident.[224]

The NTSB released a preliminary report on their investigation, which includes facts but does not provide any conclusions. An audio recording of an exchange between the pilot and air traffic controllers revealed that the helicopter was flying under special visual flight rules. This is an air traffic control authorization that allows the pilot to fly in weather conditions worse than those permitted for standard visual flight rules and less than the standard visual flight minimum of 1,000-foot ceiling with three miles visibility. While the pilot was waiting for the approval for the special VFR, he circled for approximately 12 minutes until air traffic controllers approved his request. The pilot requested "flight following," which means that the flight is tracked by radar and that controllers maintain regular contact with the aircraft, allowing them to assist with navigation. The air traffic controller replied that the helicopter was flying too low to allow for that, and that about four minutes later, the pilot advised that they were climbing to avoid a cloud layer. The controller then asked the pilot what he intended to do, but there was no reply.[225]

The lead investigator stated that it was a high-energy-impact crash and that the helicopter did not have a Terrain Awareness and Warning System, as it was not required to have this by law. She noted that 15 years ago, the NTSB had recommended to the FAA that all existing and new U.S.-registered turbine-powered rotocrafts certificated for six or more passenger seats be equipped with a Terrain Awareness and Warning System. This was not implemented, and the NTSB then closed the recommendation in 2014.[226]

A civil lawsuit for wrongful death was filed in the Los Angeles County Superior Court by the wife of Kobe Bryant and mother of their 13-year-old daughter, who also died in the accident, against Island Express Helicopters, its holding company and the heirs of the deceased pilot. She sought an unspecified amount of general and punitive damages, alleging 28 counts of negligence and breach of duty. Specifically, that the defendants failed to exercise "ordinary care in piloting the subject aircraft" and in "providing proper and safe aircraft services," and that they had authorized the operation in a negligent, careless or reckless manner. The suit alleged that the pilot failed to: properly monitor and assess the weather prior to takeoff, abort the flight when he knew of the cloudy conditions; keep a safe distance between the helicopter and natural obstacles; and that he improperly flew the helicopter by visual orientation under limited-visibility conditions that require instrument-guided navigation.[227]

8.55 PEGASUS AIRLINES BOEING 737 FLIGHT 2193, SABIHA GOKCEN INTERNATIONAL AIRPORT, ISTANBUL (5 FEBRUARY 2020)

On 5 February 2020, Pegasus Flight 2193, a scheduled domestic passenger flight from Izmir to Istanbul with six crew and 183 passengers on board, suffered a runway excursion after landing at the Sabiha Gokcen Airport, Istanbul, Turkey. Three passengers were killed, and the other people on board were injured. The pilots, reported to be a Turkish national and a South Korean, were also injured and taken to the hospital for treatment.[228] A thunderstorm was passing the airport as the flight arrived at Sabiha Airport. When the aircraft was cleared for landing, there was a 19-knot tailwind, and as the wind was shifting, the controller reported to a flight on the ground that it was to expect a runway change for departure. The Pegasus flight touched down but failed to come to a complete stop on the runway. It overran the runway, went down an embankment, and broke into three pieces. The aircraft came to rest about 20 m below runway elevation, and a fire broke out. Data obtained from Flightradar24 suggests that the aircraft was steered to the left at the end of the runway, most probably because there was an antenna array just past the stopway.[229]

In addition to the official technical investigation, a criminal investigation was also launched. Prosecutors questioned the pilot after he had been released from the hospital and reportedly took statements from air traffic control staff, airport employees, and the pilots of two other planes that aborted landings shortly before the Pegasus flight landed. In February 2020, a court ordered the arrest of the pilot on charges of involuntary manslaughter and causing injury.[230]

In March, after spending two weeks in the hospital, where he was being treated for injuries sustained in the accident, the captain was released under house arrest. When interviewed by the Chief Public Prosecutor, the captain pointed out many of the circumstances surrounding the accident and the contributory factor, including the fact that his co-pilot, who was a Dutch citizen, did not speak Turkish, which was the language being spoken with air traffic control. The crew received a last-minute change of runway due to weather, and shortly after that, the aircraft was struck by lightning. The pilots were then informed that the flight before them had decided not to land, but that the pilot had determined the 14-knot tailwind was within the airline's limit of 15 knots. As he was concerned about the lightning strike, he chose to land the aircraft. When the main gear was on the runway, the aircraft did not decelerate. He said that the co-pilot had not warned him of this and that when he noticed this after six seconds, the crew began applying manual brakes. At that time, the aircraft was picking up speed from an increasing tailwind, according to a preliminary report to the prosecutors by the Turkish Transport and Infrastructure Ministry. It was this delay in braking that was central to the criminal prosecution, according to Turkish news reports. The poor runway conditions, no drainage for the rainwater, and the fact that the runway did not have an overrun arresting bed at its end were also raised by the captain when he was outlining the "chain of faults" in his request to be released from custody into home confinement.[231]

8.56 PAKISTAN INTERNATIONAL AIRLINES (PIA) A320, FLIGHT 8303, JINNAH INTERNATIONAL AIRPORT, KARACHI, PAKISTAN (22 MAY 2020)

On 22 May 2020, an A320 Pakistan International Airlines (PIA) Flight 8303, a scheduled domestic flight, took off from Allama Iqbal International Airport, Lahore, scheduled to fly to Jinnah International Airport in Karachi with 91 passengers and 8 crew members on board. After a failed attempt to land and while on a second approach to land, the aircraft crashed in a densely populated residential area of Karachi, a few kilometers from the runway. All those on board, except two passengers, died in the accident. Eight people on the ground were injured, one of whom later died. A total of 12 houses and multiple cars suffered significant damage due to the accident. The Pakistan Aircraft Accident Investigation Board (AAIB) investigated the accident, with Airbus, the French BEA, and the American NTSB assisting. The flight data recorder and the cockpit voice recorder were recovered and taken to the BEA for decoding.

On 24 June 2020, the Pakistan AAIB released a preliminary report on the accident. The report states that the actions of the crew, combined with communication failures with air traffic control, contributed to the accident. The investigation found that the Captain was "overconfident" and extracts from the CVR indicated that the pilots were distracted as they were talking about the COVID-19 pandemic.[232]

The report's Preliminary Findings state that the controller at Karachi East Area Control cleared the flight for the arrival procedure and advised that an ILS approach for runway 25L was expected. The flight was later cleared at the pilot's discretion to report direct to the waypoint MAKLI, descend to FL100, and later re-cleared the aircraft for FL50. The aircraft changed over to the Karachi Approach controller and was cleared to descend to 3000 feet before reaching MAKLI. The aircraft ended up higher than the required descent profile, and to manage the descent and lose the additional height, the OPEN DES[233] mode was selected via the FCU[234], both autopilots were disengaged, and speed brakes were extended. Karachi Approach inquired, "confirm track mile comfortable for descend" and later advised to take an orbit so that the aircraft could capture the required descent profile. No orbit was executed, and the effort to intercept the glide slope and ILS localizer was continued. The FDR indicated the action of lowering the landing gears at 7221 feet at around 10.5 nautical miles from runway 25L. Karachi Approach advised repeatedly (twice to discontinue the approach and once cautioned) about excessive height, but the flight continued the approach. The landing approach was not discontinued. However, the FDR shows that the landing gears were raised at 1740 ft, followed by retraction of the speed brakes (at a distance slightly less than 05 nautical miles from runway 25L). At this time, the aircraft had intercepted the localizer as well as the glide slope. Flaps 1 were selected at 243 knots IAS, the landing gears and speed brakes were retracted. Over-speed and EGPWS warnings were then triggered.

Since the approach to land was continued, Karachi Approach, instead of changing over the aircraft to the Tower controller, contacted Karachi Tower by phone to request landing clearance. The Tower controller confirmed clearance to land without observing the abnormality that the landing gears were not extended. Karachi Approach then cleared the aircraft to land. At 500 ft, the FDR indicates the landing gear retracted, slat/flap configuration 3, an indicated airspeed (IAS) of 220 knots, descent rate 2000 ft/min. According to the FDR and CVR recordings, several warnings and alerts, such as overspeed, landing gear not down, and ground proximity alerts, were disregarded. The landing was undertaken with the landing gears retracted. The aircraft touched the runway surface on its engines. The flight crew applied reverse engine power and initiated a braking action. Both engines scrubbed the runway at various locations, causing damage to both. The Tower controller observed the gear-up landing and contacted the Karachi Approach controller by phone. Subsequently, Karachi Approach did not relay this to the flight crew. The landing was discontinued, and a go-around was executed.

The flight crew radioed that they were going around and requested another ILS approach to runway 25L. The controller instructed the flight to turn left heading 110 and climb to 3000 feet. Four minutes later, the flight reported that both engines failed one by one. Ram Air Turbine (RAT) was deployed to power the essential systems. FDR data recording stopped during this timeframe (as per the designed limitation). The aircraft was unable to maintain the required height. The pilots then declared an emergency that both engines were lost and transmitted a "Mayday Call." The aircraft crashed about 1340 meters short of the runway. The aircraft broke up, and a large post-impact fire erupted.[235]

The final investigation report dated 20 April 2023 was issued in February 2025. The primary and contributory causes were listed as:[236]

> Aircraft made Gears Up landing where both Engines' nacelle made contact with R/W. Both Engines were damaged causing loss of Engine Oil and lubrication which resulted in failure of both Engines during Go-Around.2 Non-adherence to SOPs and disregard of ATC instructions during the event flight.3 Lack of communication between the ATC and the flight crew regarding Gears Up landing particularly once aircraft was on the R/W.Contributing Causes 1 Ineffective implementation of FDA programme.2 FDA regulatory oversight programme was ineffective in producing sufficient and timely improvement.3 Lack of clear and precise regulations to restrict flying while fasting.4 Inadequate level of CRM application during the event flight.

After the preliminary report was issued, PIA suspended 150 of its 434 pilots over alleged license fraud. The Pakistani aviation minister reported to Parliament that 262 of Pakistan's 860 active, licensed pilots had been found to have fraudulently obtained their licenses as they had paid others to sit the exams for them.[237] In addition, the European Union Aviation Safety Agency (EASA) imposed a ban on PIA from operating to Europe, which lasted until 2024, when the ban was lifted. EASA said the lifting of the ban "marks the end of a long process initiated in 2020," during which the PCAA's oversight capabilities were found to have fallen below acceptable levels.[238]

Many relatives were not satisfied with the preliminary report and petitioned the Sindh High Court, seeking an independent inquiry into the accident. The high court suspended the proceedings, stating that the final report should be released first.[239] Relatives were also unsatisfied with the final report findings, which left crucial details undisclosed and raised concerns. In addition, tragically, the bodies of the deceased passengers were allegedly handed over to the wrong relatives. In February 2024, one of the relatives who claimed that the body of his relative, a Lebanese citizen, along with belongings crucial to the family, was reportedly misplaced, initiated legal action in the Sindh High Court claiming clarification and restitution. He stressed during the proceedings that he was not seeking financial compensation but only wished to obtain clarity and retrieve the lost belongings. The court issued notices to PIA, the Civil Aviation Authority (CAA), and others involved in the case, demanding detailed responses from all the parties.[240]

In May 2020, the Sindh High Court heard a petition concerning the non-implementation of the Pakistan Airline Pilots' Association (PALPA) flight safety regulations during the fatal crash, which claimed 97 lives. The two-member bench issued a directive seeking the record of the staff assigned to the control tower and ordered the PIA and the federal government to submit a detailed response. The CAA's lawyer presented the list of staff at the control tower at the time of the accident. The Chief Justice questioned the CAA regarding the actions taken by those responsible for overseeing the aircraft's landing. They responded that the individuals concerned were immediately removed from active duty. The Court noted its dissatisfaction with that and replied that merely removing them from duty was insufficient, as many lives were endangered, and that 97 people had died in the accident. The court remarked that those present at the control tower were responsible for the crash, as they had permitted the aircraft to land without the landing gear, to which the CAA's lawyer replied that PIA was ultimately responsible. When the court again inquired about the number of controllers at the tower, the lawyer responded that the court had the list and that there were two people in the control tower. When the court tried to establish if there were any backup staff, the lawyer replied by describing the control room, saying that it was a small room where radar and other equipment were installed. The judge then rebuked him, saying that he was misleading the court with his answers. The judge ordered PIA and the federal government to submit their detailed written reply within a week.[241] In October 2024, the Court expressed its displeasure over the CAA for only naming the names of two controllers and filing an incomplete report about the controllers, and directed it to file a complete inventory of individuals in traffic control and safety oversight within a week. The Court also noted that PIA and the federation were put on notice, and that PIA had requested adjournments, while the federation still had to file its comments.[242]

8.57 AIR INDIA EXPRESS BOEING 737, FLIGHT IX1344, KOZHIKODE-CALICUT AIRPORT, INDIA (7 AUGUST 2020)

On 7 August 2020, Air India Express Flight 1344, an international scheduled flight departing from Dubai, UAE, to Kozhikode, Calicut, India, with 184 passengers and 6 crew members on board, suffered a runway incursion while landing at the airport, after the plane twice attempted to land in heavy rain. The flight was a repatriation flight taking back Indian citizens as a result of the COVID-19 pandemic. The aircraft overflew the airport, performed a teardrop approach to runway 28, which was then discontinued. The aircraft then flew a teardrop approach to runway 10, failed to stop on the remaining runway, overshot the runway, and went down a 34 m drop-off, breaking in two. Over a hundred passengers were injured, and both the pilots and nineteen passengers were killed. The Indian Air Accident Investigation Bureau conducted the investigation. The final report was issued on 11 September 2021.

8.58 SRIWIJAYA AIR BOEING 737 FLIGHT 182, OFF THOUSAND ISLANDS, JAVA SEA, INDONESIA (9 JANUARY 2021)

On 9 January 2021, a Sriwijaya Airlines B737 took off from Jakarta-Soekarno-Hatta International Airport, Indonesia, on a scheduled domestic passenger flight to Pontianak. The aircraft with 56 passengers and 6 crew members crashed into the Java Sea four minutes after taking off. All 62 people on board were killed.

Flight 182 was scheduled to depart at 13:40. The poor weather at the airport, heavy rainfall, and low clouds due to a thunderstorm in the vicinity delayed the departure for approximately 38 minutes. The flight data recorder was recovered during the search. The official accident investigation was conducted by the Indonesian National Transportation Accident Committee (KNKT) with the assistance of the NTSB, USA. The Ministry of Transportation stated that there was an abnormality during the flight. During the aircraft's climb to 29,000 feet after having taken off on a standard instrument departure, it went off course to the northwest. There was no response to the ATC's query about the deviation, and a few seconds later, the aircraft dropped off the radar.[243] A preliminary investigation suggested that the aircraft's engines were still operating at the time of impact.

8.59 LATAM AIRLINES FLIGHT 2213, AIRBUS A320 NEO, PERU (18 NOVEMBER 2022)

On 18 November 2022, Flight 2213, a LATAM Airlines Airbus A320 Neo, departed on a scheduled domestic passenger flight from Lima to Juliaca, Peru, with 6 crew members and 102 passengers on board. As the aircraft was taking off from Jorge Chávez International Airport, it collided with a fire engine that was crossing the runway. During the take-off roll, several fire engines were positioned across the runway, performing a planned emergency exercise that crossed the active runway in front of the aircraft that was accelerating for take-off. The No.2 engine of the aircraft impacted the fire truck, the right gear collapsed, and a fire broke out. The aircraft came to a stop on the runway, about 1600 m past the point of impact. All 102 people on board were evacuated. Two firefighters were killed. A third firefighter was injured and died from his injuries seven months after the accident. Forty passengers were injured, and the aircraft was severely damaged. This was the first hull loss of the A320 Neo fleet.[244]

The pilots were questioned after the accident and were then arrested by the police and held in custody until the evening of the following day.[245] The International Federation of Air Line Pilots' Associations (IFALPA) released a statement condemning the arrest of the pilots, stating,

> The flight crew of LATAM 2213 were also placed under arrest and held in custody in Lima up until last night. The Federation considers this situation unacceptable. Holding individuals in custody who are already under intense psychological pressure due to an accident is extremely detrimental to flight safety and can only hinder the investigation. Further, it shows a complete disregard for the Positive Safety Culture principles

> laid out by Annexes 13 (Aircraft Accident and Incident Investigation) and 19 (Safety Management) to the Convention on International Civil Aviation. It may also lead the public to conclude that the accident resulted from the flight crew's intentional acts, rather than technical issues or a string of errors originating from multiple factors.[246]

It also condemned the fact that the pilots were questioned just after the accident and that they were not provided with immediate medical care and professionally evaluated by qualified medical personnel to determine whether they were mentally and physically fit to be investigated at that time and provide accurate information to the investigators. It called upon Peru to adhere to and fully implement ICAO's positive safety culture principles.[247]

The investigation was conducted by the Commission for the Investigation of Aviation Accidents (CIAA), with assistance from the French Bureau of Enquiry and Analysis for Civil Aviation Safety (BEA). On 2 October 2023 the final report was released, stating that the probable cause of the accident was the collision of the aircraft during the takeoff run with a rescue vehicle that entered the runway without explicit authorization from the control tower while conducting a response time exercise from the new aeronautical fire station at Jorge Chavez International Airport. The report states that the chain of events was caused by a lack of joint planning, poor coordination, and the failure to use standardized communication and phraseology according to ICAO regulations.[248] The final report highlights a series of organizational and communication breakdowns that led to the accident, from meetings and telephone conversations in the days, hours, and minutes preceding the chain of events that resulted in the accident.

8.60 YETI AIRLINES ATR-72, FLIGHT 691, POKHARA INTERNATIONAL AIRPORT, NEPAL (15 JANUARY 2023)

On 15 January 2023, Yeti Airlines Flight 691, a scheduled domestic flight, with 68 passengers and four crew on board, took off from Kathmandu's Tribhuvan International Airport to fly to Pokhara International Airport. While on final approach to runway 12 at Pokhara International Airport, the aircraft crashed on the bank of the Seti River and partially ended up in a deep gorge, 2 km northwest of the airport. All 72 persons on board were killed.

Two Captains operated the flight; one Captain was in the process of obtaining aerodrome familiarization for operating into Pokhara International Airport, and the other Captain was an instructor pilot. The Captain, being familiarized, who was occupying the left-hand seat, was the Pilot Flying, and the instructor pilot, occupying the right-hand seat, was the Pilot Monitoring. The Government of Nepal constituted an Aircraft Accident Investigation Commission to investigate the accident with the assistance of French, American, Canadian, and Singaporean investigators.

The Aircraft Accident Investigation Commission released its final report on 28 December 2023.[249] The most probable cause of the accident was stated to be the "inadvertent movement of both condition levers to the feathered position in flight, which resulted in feathering of both propellers and subsequent loss of thrust, leading to an aerodynamic stall and collision with terrain. The contributing factors to the accident were:

> 1. High workload due to operating into a new airport with surrounding terrain and the crew missing the associated flight deck and engine indications that both propellers had been feathered.
>
> 2 Human factor issues such as high workload and stress that appears to have resulted in the misidentification and selection of the propellers to the feathered position.
>
> 3 The proximity of terrain requiring a tight circuit to land on runway 12. This tight circuit was not the usual visual circuit pattern and contributed to the high workload. This tight pattern also meant that the approach did not meet the stabilised visual approach criteria.
>
> 4 Use of visual approach circuit for RWY 12 without any evaluation, validation and resolution of its threats which were highlighted by the SRM team of CAAN and advices proposed in flight procedures design report conducted by the consultant and without the development and approval of the chart by the operator and regulator respectively.
>
> 5 Lack of appropriate technical and skill based training (including simulator) to the crew and proper classroom briefings (for that flight) for the safe operation of flight at new airport for visual approach to runway 12.
>
> 6 Non-compliance with SOPs, ineffective CRM and lack of sterile cockpit discipline."[250]

In the aftermath of the accident, there were calls for a criminal investigation alleging that a "serious crime and mass murder had taken place."[251] In June 2023, the Tourism Ministry accused the Director General of the Civil Aviation Authority of negligence, violating government policy, misusing his position and failing in his duty, and was told to provide clarification on nine points related to the accident within seven days. Referring to five aircraft incidents and accidents on his watch, including two major disasters during his time as Director General, the Ministry accused him of consistently failing to ensure aviation safety. The note stated:

> As serious incidents and accidents continue to happen, the country is suffering losses, and serious questions are being raised about Nepal's aviation safety. As an accountable executive for the state safety programme, why shouldn't we charge you that you failed to fulfil your responsibility to make aviation safety effective?[252]

Inter alia, he was asked to explain why he had permitted a Himalaya Airlines Airbus A320 to land under visual flight rules at Pokhara International Airport during its inauguration on January 1, despite the airport not having been tested. The note said, "As the head of the regulatory body, why and how did you conduct such an extremely negligent act that adversely affects flight safety?" Other cases of neglect were highlighted, such as when the civil aviation body, which serves as both the regulator and service provider, had flown many journalists, government officials, and other dignitaries on a test flight, described as a demonstration flight, during the opening of the Bhairahawa airport on 16 May 2022.[253] It was reported that several experts had stated that the civil aviation body was misusing its authority, but no official report was issued due to concerns about potential retaliation. It was alleged that the new Pokhara International Airport was inaugurated under pressure to meet the project deadline, without adequate preparations, and against the flight calibration recommendation that aircraft should not land from the west, which Flight 691 had tried to do. In addition, flight procedures were not published, and airlines had little information regarding airport procedures and data.

Importantly, mention was also made of the requirements of a "safety management system" and that the required evaluation was not carried out, neither by the civil aviation regulator, as service provider, nor by the airlines.

A lawyer on behalf of the relatives of one of the Russian passengers killed in the accident stated that, together with leading US and EU-based law firms, he would file a case in the French court against the ATR 72 manufacturer, Yeti Airlines, and the Civil Aviation Authority of Nepal.[254]

In 2025, aiming to enhance aviation safety and aligning with international standards, two bills, the Nepal Air Service Authority Bill 2081 and the Civil Aviation Authority of Nepal Bill 2081, to restructure the Civil Aviation Authority of Nepal, were forwarded by Nepal's House of Representatives to be discussed at a parliamentary committee. The two bills, under discussion for decades, aimed at separating their dual roles and establishing two distinct entities, one for regulatory oversight and another for service provision, including air traffic management and airport operations, with a focus on enhancing accountability and aviation safety in Nepal.[255]

8.61 EMBRAER LEGACY 600 BUSINESS JET, NEAR KUZHENKINO IN TVER OBLAST, RUSSIA (23 AUGUST 2023)

On 23 August 2023, an Embraer Legacy 600 jet with seven passengers and three crew members departed Moscow's Sheremetyevo Airport on a flight to Saint Petersburg-Pulkovo Airport. Approximately 27 minutes later, the aircraft burst into flames and crashed in a field near Kuzhenkino, Tver Region, Russia, killing all ten persons on board. As one of the passengers was Yevgeny Viktorovich Prigozhin, head of the Wagner Group, a Russian state-funded private military organization, there was much speculation as to the cause of the accident and suggestions of political motivations. The official accident investigative body, the Interstate Aviation Committee (IAC), announced that it would not conduct the investigation and that the main investigation federal authority, the Investigative Committee of Russia (ICR), would conduct the investigation, with the governor of the Tver Oblast region in charge. A criminal investigation was also launched under Article 263 of Russia's criminal code, which deals with violations of safety and air transport operation rules.[256]

8.62 JAPAN AIRLINES AIRBUS A350 FLIGHT JAL516 AND A JAPAN COAST GUARD DE HAVILLAND CANADA DASH 8 RUNWAY COLLISION, TOKYO HANEDA AIRPORT (2 JANUARY 2024)

On 2 January 2024, two aircraft were destroyed in a runway collision at Tokyo's Haneda airport. Japan Airlines Flight 516 was a scheduled domestic passenger flight from New Chitose Airport near Sapporo, Japan, to Haneda Airport in Tokyo, with

367 passengers and 12 crew members on board. A Japan Coast Guard De Havilland Canada Dash (DHC-8) aircraft, which was on a relief mission to transport supplies after the 2024 Noto earthquake, which had occurred the day before, was on the runway. While landing, after touchdown, the A350 collided with the Coast Guard DHC-8 aircraft. The nose section of the A350 suffered severe damage, and the aircraft slid over the runway for about 1700 meters, swung to the right, and came to a stop next to the runway. A fire erupted, destroying both aircraft. Five of the six crew on board the DHC-8 died in the collision, and only the captain survived, having suffered severe burns. Within 18 minutes, everyone on board the A350 evacuated safely and survived with minor injuries to several passengers. This was the first accident resulting in severe damage to an A350 aircraft.

The official technical investigation was conducted by the Japan Transport Safety Board, which is a division of the Ministry of Land, Infrastructure, Transport and Tourism (MLIT). The French BEA, together with Airbus, as well as UK investigators from the A350 engine, Rolls-Royce, the Canadian Transportation Safety Board, and the A350 engine manufacturer, technical advisers from the Dash 8's manufacturer De Havilland Canada, the engine manufacturer Pratt & Whitney, Canada, and the NTSB, assisted in the investigation. A transcript of the air traffic control communication, covering the last 4 minutes and 27 seconds before the crash, was released by the MLIT on 3 January. This showed that the air traffic controllers cleared the A350 aircraft to land on the runway and that the Coast Guard aircraft was instructed to hold short of the runway at a holding point on the taxiway, and that this instruction was read back correctly. However, in a statement contradicting the transcript, the captain of the Coast Guard DHC-8 aircraft said that he had been cleared for take-off.

The Tokyo Metropolitan Police Department launched an investigation into the accident to consider possible professional negligence resulting in death and injury.[257]

8.63 ALASKA AIRLINES, FLIGHT 1282, BOEING 737 MAX 9, PORTLAND INTERNATIONAL AIRPORT, PORTLAND, USA (5 JANUARY 2024)

On 5 January 2024, Alaska Airlines Flight 1282 was a scheduled US domestic flight with 171 passengers and six crew members that took off from Portland International Airport in Portland, Oregon, to go to Ontario International Airport in Ontario, California. Approximately 6 minutes into the flight, the left mid exit door plug of the Boeing 737 MAX 9, which had not been bolted in place, blew out, resulting in a rapid and uncontrolled decompression. The aircraft returned to Portland for an emergency landing without any further incident, and all persons on board deplaned at the gate. Seven passengers and one flight attendant received minor injuries. The accident was investigated by the NTSB, which published a preliminary report on 6 February 2024.[258] It invited qualified parties, including Alaska Airlines, Air Line Pilots Association, Association of Flight Attendants, Federal Aviation Administration, the Boeing Company, Spirit AeroSystems, and the International Association of Machinists Union, to participate in the investigation. Specialized groups were formed in the areas of Operations, Structures, Materials/Metallurgy, Systems, Survival Factors/Cabin Safety, Flight Recorders, and Manufacturing Records/Human Performance.[259]

According to the Captains' statement, the flight crew heard a loud bang while the aircraft was climbing at about 16,000 ft, and their ears popped. His head was pushed into the heads-up display, and his headset was pushed up, nearly falling off his head. The first officer said that her headset was removed entirely due to the rapid outflow of air from the flight deck. Both flight crew said they immediately put on their oxygen masks and that the flight deck door was blown open.[260] The force of the depressurization ripped the shirt off a teenage boy seated in row 26A, and the oxygen masks fell.[261] The seatback of 26A, as well as the headrests in seats 26A and 26B, next to the blown-out hole in the fuselage, were torn off. Paneling and window trim in several rows extending from the point of failure were damaged, and passengers seated near the hole moved to seats closer to the front.[262]

The investigation team located the left plug mid-exit door (MED) plug and recovered it from the backyard of a private residence. The plug and associated hardware were shipped to the NTSB's Materials Laboratory for examination.[263] The preliminary report includes details regarding the accident MED plug, which Spirit AeroSystems Malaysia manufactured in March 2023, and was received at Spirit AeroSystems Wichita in May. The MED plug was then installed and rigged on the fuselage before being shipped to Boeing on 20 August 2023. The fuselage arrived at Boeing's Renton, Washington, facility on 31 August 2023.[264]

The preliminary report states that the manufacturing/human performance group did a complete records review from the time the aircraft left the Boeing factory up to the time of the accident, and that they found no evidence that the left MED plug was opened after leaving Boeing's facility.[265] In other words, the investigation revealed that four bolts, intended to secure the door plug, were missing at the time of the accident, and that Boeing records showed evidence that the plug had been reinstalled with no bolts before initial delivery of the aircraft. The four bolts were not installed on the aircraft when it was delivered from the factory.

The preliminary report highlighted areas that would be investigated further during the investigation, such as Boeing's SMS and Spirit AeroSystems' ongoing development of its voluntary SMS program, the FAA's involvement in the manufacturers' development of their respective SMS programs, and the level of oversight applied to each.[266]

Boeing was once again faced with intense scrutiny and multiple inquiries and investigations from regulators, lawmakers, and customers in response to this serious incident, which is discussed in greater detail in Chapter 4.

8.64 AZERBAIJAN AIRLINES FLIGHT 8243, EMBRAER ERJ-190AR, NEAR AKTAU AIRPORT, KAZAKHSTAN (25 DECEMBER 2024)

On 25 December 2024, Azerbaijan Airlines Flight 8243 was a scheduled international passenger flight from Heydar Aliyev International Airport in Baku, Azerbaijan, to Kadyrov Grozny International Airport near Grozny, Russia. The Embraer ERJ-190AR crashed near Aktau Airport, Kazakhstan, after having declared an emergency. There were 62 passengers and five crew on board. Two cabin crew and 27 passengers survived the crash. The Russian Federal Agency for Air Transport (Rosaviatsiya) stated that during that morning, the situation in the vicinity of Grozny airport was 'very difficult' as Ukrainian military drones were reported to be carrying out attacks in the cities of Grozny and Vladikavkaz. It stated that as a result, the airspace was closed. The timeframe of the closure in relation to flight 8243 was not stated. In addition, there was dense fog in the area. Meteorological data from 05:02 UTC indicated an overcast cloud deck at 800 feet, with a visibility in fog of 3,500 meters. Rosaviatsiya goes on to state that the aircraft made two attempts to land at Grozny, which were unsuccessful. The flight was then offered other airports for diversion, and the flight crew decided to proceed to Aktau Airport. Flightradar24 ADS-B data stopped at 04:25 UTC and reappeared at 06:07 UTC when the flight showed up over the Caspian Sea, squawking 7700 (emergency). Altitude and speed data are available from 05:14 UTC, showing fluctuating altitude and speed as the aircraft heads to Aktau Airport. According to local media, Kazaeronavigatsiya stated that the flight crew had reported problems controlling the aircraft.[267] Approximately 40 minutes after takeoff, as the aircraft entered Russian airspace and neared Grozny, the crew reported losing GPS navigational aids due to jamming.[268]

The preliminary report issued was cautiously worded and did not specify what had caused the extensive damage to the plane, including its stabilizers, hydraulics, and trim systems. It states that the cockpit voice recorder identified the sound of two impacts within 25 seconds and that two minutes later, the pilot reported to air traffic control that he thought the plane had suffered a bird strike. The report also included photographs showing that the port side of the tail section was punctured with numerous holes and fragments described as "foreign metal objects" removed from the left stabilizer and hydraulic system. Azerbaijan's President said in December that the aircraft had been damaged by accidental shooting from the ground in Russia, allegedly from a Russian surface-to-air missile. Moscow did not confirm this. The Russian President issued an apology for the "tragic incident" in Russian airspace and said that a criminal case had been opened to determine the cause and circumstances of the accident.[269]

8.65 JEJU AIRLINES, FLIGHT 2216, BOEING 737-800, MUAN INTERNATIONAL AIRPORT, MUAN COUNTY, SOUTH JEOLLA PROVINCE, SOUTH KOREA (29 DECEMBER 2024)

On 29 December 2024, at approximately 04:30 local time, a Jeju Air passenger flight departed from Suvarnabhumi International Airport, Thailand, bound for Muan International Airport, South Korea, carrying 175 passengers and six crew members on board the Boeing 737-800. At 08:54:43, the ATC tower of Muan International Airport cleared the aircraft for landing on runway 01. While approaching the runway at 08:57:50, the tower advised the crew to be cautious of bird activity. Both the

CVR and FDR recordings stopped at 08:58:50. The aircraft made a gear-up landing on runway 19, slid past the end of the runway, and collided with the ILS localizer antenna array that was installed in a concrete platform. The aircraft disintegrated and burst into flames. The tail separated near the beginning of the vertical stabilizer and remained relatively intact. All 175 passengers and four crew members were killed. Two crew members were seriously injured. After a few seconds (time converted from CVR waveform), the aircraft made an emergency declaration (Mayday x 3) due to a bird strike during a go-around. As it was flying over the left side of runway 01, it turned right and approached runway 19 to land after aligning with the runway centerline. The aircraft belly-landed without its landing gear deployed, overran the runway, and crashed into the embankment, including the installed localizers, bursting into flames. The pilots identified a group of birds while approaching runway 01, and a security camera filmed the aircraft coming close to a group of birds during a go-around. An examination of both engines found feathers and bird blood stains on each, which were later identified as belonging to Baikal Teals. [270]

The investigation is ongoing and is being conducted by the South Korean National Aviation and Railway Accident Investigation Board (ARAIB) with the assistance of other bodies, including the US NTSB, Boeing, and the French Bureau d'Enquêtes et d'Analyses pour la Sécurité de l'Aviation Civile. A preliminary report was issued on 27 January 2025. On 7 January, the director of the ARAIB resigned and the Transport Minister announced that several former and current senior officials were removed from the investigation and all of its activities to avoid any conflict of interest.[271]

This is the deadliest accident involving a Boeing 737 Next Gen aircraft, the deadliest one involving a Boeing aircraft since the Lion Air Flight 610 accident[272] and the deadliest accident involving a South Korean airliner since the 1997 Korean Air Flight 801 crash in Guam, and to be the deadliest accident on South Korean territory, surpassing the 2002 Air China Flight 129 accident, which killed 129 people.[273] It is the first accident of Jeju Air, one of South Korea's largest low-cost carriers, which was established in 2005.[274]

Videos of the accident show that the pilots performed what seems to be a text book belly landing, even though it was much faster than usual, as there were no flaps deployed. Belly landings typically do not result in such a catastrophe as airports usually have long runways followed by runoff areas, and any infrastructure at the end of the runway, such as ILS aerials, is generally at ground level and designed to cause minimal damage to an aircraft. Boundaries such as a fence or a bank of earth are usually soft and help absorb an impact. However, accident videos show the aircraft landing on the runway, sliding along its whole length, and off the end of the runway into the runoff area, where it collided with the ILS aerials, just before the aircraft broke into fragments and exploded into a ball of flame. It was only the tail section of the aircraft that remained intact from the L2 and R2 doors to the rear. The ILS aerials were mounted on a large concrete block, which was in the path of the aircraft that was still traveling at a significant speed. [275]

Focus shifted to examining the airport's concrete barrier and the position of the localizer, which revealed that they did not comply with international ICAO standards and local standards, and whether regulatory compliance would have mitigated the severity of the accident and increased the survivability rate of those on board the aircraft.

Findings showed that Muan International Airport did not meet safety standards for installing a localizer, the antenna system that emits radio signals to guide aircraft toward the center of the runway, and an essential landing guidance system. The airport's operational manual, published on May 9 by Korea Airports Corporation (KAC), revealed that Muan International Airport failed to comply with the runway end safety area (RESA) regulations of the Ministry of Land, Infrastructure and Transport's "Standards for Safe Operation of Airports." The manual specifies the requirements for airport facilities, emergency operation plans, and safety management systems. Under those guidelines, the airport must maintain a safety area of 240 meters from the runway's end, but the localizer was installed just 202 meters from the southern end and 199 meters from the northern end. The Korea Airports Corporation specifically noted that the airport had a RESA that fell 38 meters short in one direction and 41 meters in the other. Airport officials responded that modifications and any corrective actions would be considered during the airport's second-phase expansion. It also noted that the localizer's installation point at Muan airport did not meet recommended standards. At the airport, the localizer was embedded in a 2- to 3-meter-high mound, protruding approximately 7 cm above the surface and reinforced with concrete. Many experts argue that placing the localizer like that increases the risk of aircraft damage.[276] Some aviation experts go so far as saying that there is no justification for the localizer to be there, and that having it there is "verging on criminal."[277]

After the accident, South Korea's then-acting president said that immediate action must be taken if the investigation was to uncover any issues with the Boeing aircraft model. All Boeing 737-800 aircraft operated by the South Korean carriers were subjected to a special inspection, which focused on the landing gear.[278]

On 22 January 2025, the transportation ministry announced that the existing concrete barriers used for navigation at seven Korean airports would be replaced with structures that are easier to break, localizers would be upgraded, and safety zones at the end of some runways would be extended to a minimum of almost 790 feet.[279]

The police commenced a separate parallel investigation into the accident. They released a statement saying that they intended to "swiftly and rigorously determine the cause and responsibility for this accident in accordance with the law and principles." On 2 January, the Jeonnam Provincial Police Agency conducted a search and seizure operation at three locations: Muan airport, the Jeju Air office in Seoul, and a regional aviation office. In addition, the investigation resulted in imposing a travel ban on two individuals, including the chief executive of Jeju Air.[280]

On 21 January 2025, the former president of the Korea Airports Corporation was found dead in his home. He was the president of KAC, a government-owned company that operates more than a dozen airports, including Muan, from 2018 to 2022, and was in office at the time of the accident. Police do not suspect any criminal activity leading to his death and have called it an apparent suicide.[281] In May 2025, 72 relatives of those who died in the accident filed a criminal complaint against 15 people, including South Korea's transport minister and the airline's CEO, alleging professional negligence and violations of the Serious Accidents Punishment Act and the Aviation Safety Act. Government officials, airline officials, and airport staff responsible for construction, supervision, facility management, and bird control were also named in the complaint. The families believe "the disaster wasn't a simple accident, but a serious civil disaster caused by negligence in mitigating risks." The complaint focuses on possible failure to act by air traffic control in not responding appropriately and on the reinforcement of the mound at the end of the runway, and raises questions regarding the sharp pivot the pilot made before attempting to land, the aircraft's engine maintenance, and why the flight recorder stopped working four minutes before the crash.[282]

8.66 MIDAIR COLLISION PSA AIRLINES BOMBARDIER CRJ700 AIRPLANE AND SIKORSKY UH-60 MILITARY HELICOPTER, RAEGAN AIRPORT, WASHINGTON D.C., USA (29 JANUARY 2025)

On 29 January 2025, approximately 2048 eastern standard time (EST), a Sikorsky UH-60L, operated by the U.S. Army under the callsign PAT25, and an MHI (Mitsubishi Heavy Industries) RJ Aviation (formerly Bombardier) CL-600-2C10 (CRJ700), N709PS, operated by PSA Airlines as flight 5342, collided in flight approximately 0.5 miles southeast of Ronald Reagan Washington National Airport (DCA), Arlington, Virginia, and impacted the Potomac River in southwest Washington, District of Columbia. All 60 passengers and the four crew members on board the airplane and the three crew members aboard the helicopter were killed. Both aircraft were destroyed.[283]

8.67 AIR INDIA, FLIGHT AI171, BOEING 787-8 DREAMLINER, AHMEDABAD INTERNATIONAL AIRPORT (AMD), INDIA (12 JUNE 2025)

Air India Flight AI171, a Boeing 787-8 Dreamliner, was scheduled to fly from Ahmedabad Airport, India, to Gatwick Airport, UK, with 229 passengers and 12 crew on board. Thirty-two seconds after taking off from runway 23, the aircraft crashed following a loss of thrust at approximately 08:09 UTC. Of the 242 occupants, one passenger survived. Nineteen people on the ground were killed. A further 67 people were seriously injured. The aircraft was destroyed due to impact with five buildings on the ground and subsequent fire. The wreckage, from the first impact point until the last identified aircraft item, was distributed in an area of approximately 1,000 feet by 400 feet. This is the first fatal accident and hull loss involving a 787 since 2011, when the type entered service.

The India Air Accident Investigation Bureau is conducting the investigation into the accident with the assistance of accredited representatives and technical advisers from Boeing, GE, and the Federal Aviation Administration from the USA and the UK AAIB. A preliminary report was released on 8 July 2025. According to the preliminary report, at 08:07:33, the aircraft was cleared for take-off from Runway 23, and at 08:09:05, a MAYDAY call was transmitted by one of the pilots while the aircraft continued to lose altitude. The main gear then impacted the top floor of a hostel building for doctors, where a restaurant was situated. The tail section then impacted the roof and became detached. As the remainder of the aircraft continued its path, it burst into flames upon impact, with the front of the aircraft striking a residential hostel that housed undergraduate and postgraduate student doctors. The mid-section was scattered across a garden and adjoining road. The first point of impact was located approximately 1.5 km southwest of the runway end.[284]

The aircraft was equipped with two enhanced airborne flight recorders (EAFRs), a flight data recorder, and a cockpit voice recorder, collectively referred to as the black box. On 13 June, the first was recovered from the mess hall rooftop, and the second from the crash debris on 16 June. The data extracted revealed that the accident was caused by both engines losing thrust after their fuel control switches moved from RUN to CUTOFF a few seconds after liftoff. No cause for the switch movement was given.

The preliminary report states that the co-pilot was the pilot flying, and the pilot in command was the pilot monitoring for the flight from Ahmedabad Airport to Gatwick Airport. According to the report, the aircraft achieved the maximum recorded airspeed of 180 knots at about 08:08:42 UTC, and immediately thereafter, the Engine 1 and Engine 2 fuel cutoff switches transitioned from RUN to CUTOFF position one after another with a time gap of 01 seconds. Thereafter, engines N1 and N2 began to decrease from their take-off values as the fuel supply to the engines was cut off. In the cockpit voice recording, one of the pilots is heard asking the other why he cut off the engine. The other pilot is heard replying that he did not do so. [285] The report does not clarify which pilot said what. Both fuel switches were turned back on, but the aircraft was too low to recover.

The release of the preliminary report, specifically that the pilot questioning why fuel cutoff switches were transitioned from "run" to "cutoff," raised many questions. It was also widely criticized for indicating that the fuel cutoff switches were likely to have been deliberately moved by one of the pilots. The Indian Commercial Pilots' Association has condemned what it called a "reckless and unfounded insinuation of pilot suicide," saying that the crew "acted in line with their training and responsibilities under challenging conditions and the pilots shouldn't be vilified based on conjecture."[286]

If any further evidence supports this theory, the Air India A1171 crash is likely to be investigated as a criminal act if it is deemed similar to the 1997 SilkAir, 1999 EgyptAir, and 2015 Germanwings cases.

Germanwings Flight 9525 has been discussed earlier. The following provides a brief outline of the conclusion reached from the accident investigations following the 1997 SilkAir and 1999 Egyptair crashes. The official investigation into the 1997 Silk Air crash by the Indonesian National Transport Safety Committee was inconclusive, as they concluded that they were unable to determine the cause of the crash.[287] The NTSB, on the other hand, determined that the crash was most likely the result of deliberate flight-control inputs that were most likely made by the captain.[288] The official criminal investigation by the Singapore Police Force found "no evidence that the pilot, copilot, or any crew member had suicidal tendencies or a motive to deliberately cause the crash of the aircraft."[289]

The investigation into the 1999 EgyptAir crash was led by the NTSB, at the request of the Egyptian government, with the participation of the Egyptian Civil Aviation Authority (ECAA). The NTSB's final report, issued on 21 March 2002, concluded that the probable cause of the crash was the relief first officer's actions, but it could not determine the reason for those actions.[290] The conclusion by the ECAA was that "the Relief First Officer did not deliberately dive the airplane into the ocean," and that mechanical failure was "a plausible and likely cause of the accident."[291]

The Air India accident has also added to a longstanding debate regarding the pros and cons of installing video camera monitoring in the cockpit. Those in favor of having cockpit video cameras argue that cockpit video camera monitoring of pilots' actions can complement voice and flight data recorders, which accident investigators already use, and can fill in any gaps. An example in support of this is the "invaluable" video footage, which led the Australian Transport Safety Bureau to determine the cause of a Robinson R66 helicopter that broke up in midair in 2023, killing the pilot. The video footage clearly showed that "the pilot was occupied with non-flying related tasks for much of this time, specifically, mobile phone use and the consumption of food and beverages."[292] In the wake of the 1999 EgyptAir accident, the Chairman urged the Federal Aviation Administration to require commercial airliners to be equipped with cockpit image recorders.[293]

On the other hand, arguments against installing video cameras in cockpits include, inter alia, privacy issues, confidentiality, and potential misuse of the video footage, such as for example, disciplinary measures or sensationalism. Pilot unions such as the Air Line Pilots Association (ALPA) and Allied Pilots Association (APA) argue that the CVR and FDR already provide enough information to determine what caused an accident, and that current systems should be enhanced to record higher-quality data, instead of installing video cameras.[294]

NOTES

1. Clark, N., "French court overturns convictions in Concorde crash," The New York Time, 29 November 2012. Available at http://www.nytimes.com/2012/11/30/business/global/french-court-overturns-conviction-in-concorde-crash.html?_r=0.
2. Flugunfalluntersuchungsstelle of the Austrian Federal Office for Transport (Bundesanstalt für Verkehr, BAV GZ. 85.007/0001-FUS/2006, 21 March 2006. Available at http://versa.bmvit.gv.at/uploads/media/A310_GZ._85007_vom_12._Juli_2000_2_01.pdf.
3. MacKenzie, C., "Pilot lands suspended prison sentence after Vienna crash," Flightglobal, 18 May 2004. Available at https://www.flightglobal.com/pilot-lands-suspended-prison-sentence-after-vienna-crash/54459.article.
4. Schaefer, G., "Japanese police pursuing possibility of negligence in planes' near collision," 3 February 2001. Available at http://www.stripes.com/01/feb01/ed020301i.html.
5. Umeda, S., "Japan: Air traffic controllers found guilty," 1 December 2010. Available at http://www.loc.gov/law/foreign-news/article/japan-air-traffic-controllers-found-guilty/.

6. Hazou, E., "AG to appeal Helios ruling," Cyprus Mail, 23 December 2011. Available at https://web.archive.org/web/20111224054828/http://www.cyprus-mail.com/helios/ag-appeal-helios-ruling/20111223.
7. Psyllides, G., "The downing of Flight 522," Cyprus Mail, 9 August 2015. Available at https://cyprus-mail.com/2015/08/09/the-downing-of-flight-522/.
8. Nilsson, B., "Employer liable for fatal helicopter crash," 12 December 2016. Available at https://www.bnlaw.com.au/page/Insights/Insurance_Alerts/Employer_s_Liability/Employer_liable_for_fatal_helicopter_crash/.
9. Brooks, M., and Donaldson, K.L., "Hevilift Limited v Towers [2018] QCA 89-Don't push it Land It"- Employer liable to pilot for a failure to warn of a weather phenomenon, 12 June 2018. Available at https://hwlebsworth.com.au/hevilift-limited-v-towers-2018-qca-89-employer-liable-to-pilot-for-a-failure-to-warn-of-a-weather-phenomenon/ See Hevilift Limited v Towers [2018] QCA 89, Appeal No 13091 of 2016 SC No 180 of 2009, available at https://archive.sclqld.org.au/qjudgment/2018/QCA18-089.pdf.
10. Associated Press, "Brazil court upholds US pilots' conviction in 2006 airliner crash, but no jail time given," 15 October 2012. Available at https://www.foxnews.com/world/brazil-court-upholds-us-pilots-conviction-in-2006-airliner-crash-but-no-jail-time-given.
11. Boadle, A., "Brazil upholds U.S. pilots' convictions in 2006 air disaster," Reuters, 16 October 2012. Available at http://www.reuters.com/article/2012/10/16/uk-brazil-crash-retrial-idUSLNE89F01420121016.
12. Associated Press, "Brazil's top court rejects US pilots' appeal in 2006 crash," 16 October 2015. Available at https://www.ksl.com/article/36978552/brazils-top-court-rejects/us-pilots-appeal-in-2006-crash.
13. Fausto, M., "STJ anula acusação de 'falsidade documental' contra ex-diretora da ANAC," 12 November 2014. Available at https://politica.estadao.com.br/blogs/fausto-macedo/stj-anula-acusacao-de-falsidade-documental-contra-ex-diretora-da-anac/.
14. Gallo, R., "Federal court acquits two defendants of criminal responsibility in TAM's accident," 5 May 2015. Available at https://www1.folha.uol.com.br/internacional/en/brazil/2015/05/1624849-federal-court-acquits-two-defendants-of-criminal-responsibility-in-tams-accident.shtml.
15. Aviation Safety Network, "French pilot: 6 months suspended sentence in accident case," 11 January 2012. Available at https://news.aviation-safety.net/2012/01/11/french-pilot-6-months-suspended-sentence-in-accident-case/.
16. Elisa Artigue-Cazcarra, E., "Pilote et compagnie déclarés coupables," 3 January 2012. Available at https://www.sudouest.fr/2012/01/03/pilote-et-compagnie-declares-coupables-594918–4621.php.
17. Ranter, H., "Accident criminalization," Aviation Safety Network, 3 April 2017. Available at https://aviation-safety.net/database/record.php?id=20071130-0.
18. Hurriyet Daily News, "Senior manager, top civilian aviation officials convicted over passenger plane crash," 7 January 2015. Available at http://www.hurriyetdailynews.com/senior-managers-top-civil-aviation-officials-convicted-over-passenger-plane-crash-.aspx?pageID=238&nID=76599&NewsCatID=.
19. Yavuz Arik, Administrator, et al., v. The Boeing Company, et al., 2011 IL App (1st) 100750-U Second Division, 10 January 2012. Available at https://courts.illinois.gov/R23_Orders/AppellateCourt/2012/1stDistrict/1100750_R23.pdf.
20. BEA, Report Accident on 9 August 2007 off the coast of Moorea (French Polynesia) to the DHC6-300 registered F-OIQI operated by Air Moorea, December 2008. Available at https://reports.aviation-safety.net/2007/20070809-0_DHC6_F-OIQI.pdf.
21. Ibid., 3.2 at pages 68–71.

22. RNZ, "Compensation awarded to families of Air Moorea crash victims," 7 September 2018. Available at https://www.rnz.co.nz/international/pacific-news/365959/compensation-awarded-to-families-of-air-moorea-crash-victims.
23. RNZ, "Jail terms for Air Moorea staff over 2007 crash," 23 January 2019. Available at https://www.newsie.co.nz/news/137924-jail-terms-air-moorea-staff-over-2007-crash.html.
24. RNZ, "Air Moorea crash appeal case to go to court in Tahiti," 10 May 2019. Available at https://www.rnz.co.nz/international/pacific-news/404272/jail-terms-sought-over-air-moorea-crash.
25. RNZ, "Air Moorea crash: Appeal court confirms jail sentence," 24 January 2020. Available at ttps://www.rnz.co.nz/international/pacific-news/408093/air-moorea-crash-appeal-court-confirms-jail-sentences.
26. Machler, B., "Seaplane pilot found guilty of manslaughter," 9 November 2016. Available at http://www.lexology.com/library/detail.aspx?g=9cb07f79-f354-4318-9a5d-832b413438d7&utm_source=Lexology+Daily+Newsfeed&utm_medium=HTML+email+-+Body+-+General+section&utm_campaign=Lexology+subscriber+daily+feed&utm_content=Lexology+Daily+Newsfeed+2016-11-11&utm_term=.
27. Federal Court, Criminal Law Department, 6 B_1341/2015, Judgment of 25 February 2016. Available at https://www.bger.ch/ext/eurospider/live/de/php/aza/http/index.php?highlight_docid=aza%3A%2F%2F25-02-2016-6B_1341-2015&lang=de&type=show_document&zoom=YES&.
28. Danko, M., "US court dismissed all Spanair Flight 5022 crash lawsuits," Aviation Law Monitor, 7 April 2011. Available at https://www.aviationlawmonitor.com/2011/04/lawsuits-1/us-court-dismisses-all-spanair-flight-5022-crash-lawsuits/.
29. Hernandez, J.A., "Prosecutor seeks prison for Spanair crash mechanics," ElPais, 22 August 2011. Available at https://elpais.com/elpais/2011/08/22/inenglish/1313990445_850210.html.
30. Aktalov, A., "Convicted pilots of crashed plane in 2008 are free," Knews, 24 August 2011. Available at https://knews.kg/2011/08/24/osujdennyic-pilotyi-razbivshegosya-v-2008-godu-samoleta-nahodyatsya-na-svobode/.
31. Brinkerhoff, N., "Jury faults mechanic in fatal American Canyon plane crash," Napa Valley Register, 3 March 2015. Available at https://napavalleyregister.com/community/eagle/news/local/jury-faults-mechanic-in-fatal-american-canyon-plane-crash/article_419687b8-7fd1-5195-8ae3-291598923026.html.
32. Superior Court of San Mateo County, San Mateo, "Family claimed Cessna crash due to mechanic's negligence," Verdict Search, 26 February 2015. Available at https://verdictsearch.com/verdict/family-claimed-cessna-crash-due-to-mechanics-negligence/.
33. Ibid., at 3.2 Causes of the accident.
34. Goodridge, J., and Brow, A., "United States: Air France Flight 447 – Breyer decision round 2: United States still forum non conveniens," Clyde & Co, 9 February 2012. Available at http://www.mondaq.com/unitedstates/x/163854/Aviation/Air+France+Flight+447+Breyer+Decision+Round+2+United+States+Still+Forum+Non+Conveniens.
35. RFI, "Prosecutor to appeal acquittal of Airbus, Air France in Rio-Paris crash case," 28 April 2023. Available at https://www.rfi.fr/en/france/20230428-french-prosecutor-to-appeal-acquittal-of-airbus-air-france-in-rio-paris-crash.
36. RFI, "Prosecutor to appeal acquittal of Airbus, Air France in Rio-Paris crash case," 28 April 2023. Available at https://www.rfi.fr/en/france/20230428-french-prosecutor-to-appeal-acquittal-of-airbus-air-france-in-rio-paris-crash.

37. Lenta.ru, "Investigation of the circumstances of the death of the President of Poland entrusted Putin," 10 April 2010. Available at https://lenta.ru/news/2010/04/10/comission/.
38. Interstate Aviation Committee Air Accident Investigation Commission Final Report Tu-154M tail number 101, Republic of Poland, at p.182. Available at https://reports.aviation-safety.net/2010/20100410-0_T154_101.pdf.
39. Scislowska, M., "Polish court: Ex: aide negligent in presidential plane crash," AP News, 13 June 2019. Available at https://apnews.com/d90454a2e68041c99e8a5525d8cacc61.
40. Poland to sue Russia over withholding 2010 plane crash wreckage, 10 November 2015. Available at https://www.reuters.com/article/us-poland-russia-smolensk/poland-to-sue-russia-over-withholding-2010-plane-crash-wreckage-idUSKCN0SZ2B920151110.
41. BBC, "Smolensk air crash: Poland re-opens investigation," 4 February 2016. Available at https://www.bbc.com/news/world-europe-35498400.
42. The Guardian, "Poland exhumes president Lech Kaczyński's remains," 14 November 2016. Available at https://www.theguardian.com/world/2016/nov/14/poland-exhumes-presidents-lech-kaczynski-remains.
43. Parliamentary Assembly Resolution 2246 (2018), "The crash of Polish Air Force Tu-154M transporting the Polish State delegation, on 10 April 2010 on the Russian Federation's territory," 12 October 2018. Available at http://assembly.coe.int/nw/xml/XRef/Xref-XML2HTML-en.asp?fileid=25191&lang=en.
44. Josek, P., "Poland to sue Russia over withholding 2010 plane crash wreckage," Reuters, 10 November 2015. Available at https://www.reuters.com/article/us-poland-russia-smolensk/poland-to-sue-russia-over-withholding-2010-plane-crash-wreckage-idUSKCN0SZ2B920151110.
45. Day, M., "MoD experts to investigate Polish leader's plane crash blamed on 'Russian aggression,'" The Telegraph, 27 February 2017. Available at https://www.telegraph.co.uk/news/2017/02/27/mod-experts-investigate-polish-leaders-plane-crash-blamed-russian/.
46. Parliamentary Assembly Resolution 2246 (2018), "The crash of Polish Air Force Tu-154M transporting the Polish State delegation, on 10 April 2010 on the Russian Federation's territory," 12 October 2018. Available at http://assembly.coe.int/nw/xml/XRef/Xref-XML2HTML-en.asp?fileid=25191&lang=en.
47. RT., "New investigation into crash that killed Polish president aimed at ex-PM Tusk – former minister," 31 March 2016. Available at https://www.rt.com/news/337931-smolensk-crash-tusk-blamed/.
48. TRT World, "EU's Tusk testifies in Poland over president's plane crash," 23 April 2018. Available at https://www.trtworld.com/europe/eu-s-tusk-testifies-in-poland-over-president-s-plane-crash-16952.
49. Scislowska, M., "Polish court: Ex-aide negligent in presidential plane crash," AP News, 13 June 2019. Available at https://apnews.com/d90454a2e68041c99e8a5525d8cacc61.
50. Tiles, D., "Polish court orders arrest of Russian air traffic controller over Smolensk crash," 20 May 2022. Available at https://notesfrompoland.com/2022/05/20/polish-court-orders-arrest-of-russian-air-traffic-controller-over-smolensk-crash/.
51. Report on Accident to Air India Boeing 737-800 Aircraft VT-AXV on 22 May 2010 at Mangalore, by the Court Air Marshal BN Gokhale, PSVM, AVSM, VM (Retd), Former Vice Chief of Air Staff, Indian Air Force, New Delhi, 31 October 2010. Available at http://dgca.nic.in/accident/reports/VT-AXV.pdf.
52. Rahman, F., "Pilot's son fights to clear his father's name over fatal Air India crash," The National, UAE, 2 January 2012. Available at https://www.thenational.ae/news/uae-news/pilots-son-fights-to-clear-his-fathers-name-over-fatal-air-india-crash.

53. See, for example, S. Abdul Salam et al., v. Union of India and National Aviation Company of India Ltd, Kerala High Court, WP(C) No. 32550 of 2010(P). Available at https://indiankanoon.org/doc/65803078/.
54. Kochi, DC, "Give Rs 10 lakh to Mangalore crash victim: HC tells Air India," Deccan Chronicle, 6 September 2011. Available at https://www.webcitation.org/65NAwa1wl ?url=http://www.deccanchronicle.com/channels/cities/kochi/give-rs-10-lakh-mangalore-crash-victim-hc-tells-air-india-759.
55. Madan, K., "Flight 812: Two years of tears." Last update 15 September 2018. Available at https://gulfnews.com/world/asia/india/flight-812-two-years-of-tears-1.102597.
56. Aviation Safety Network. Available at https://aviation-safety.net/database/record.php ?id=20728-0.
57. Investigation Report Air Blue Flight Abq-202 A-321 Reg Ap-Bjb Pakistan Crashed On 28 July 2010 At Margalla Hills Islamabad. Available at https://www.caapakistan.com .pk/Upload/SIBReports/SIB-337.pdf.
58. Shah, N., "Airblue disaster: PHC cites 'pilot error' for Margalla Hills air crash," The Express Tribune, 4 October 2013. Available at https://tribune.com.pk/story/613359/airblue-disaster-phc-cites-pilot-error-for-margalla-hills-air-crash/.
59. Webdesk, "Pilot guilty in Airblue crash: PHC," The Express Tribune, 3 October 2013. Available at https://tribune.com.pk/story/612978/pilot-guilty-in-airblue-crash-phc/.
60. Aviation Safety Network, 2010 Database. Available at https://aviation-safety.net/database/record.php?id=20803-0.
61. Ria Novosti, "Russian pilot gets jail sentence over fatal airliner crash," Sputnik News, 2 October 2013. Available at https://sputniknews.com/russia/20131002183900066 -Russian-Pilot-Gets-Jail-Sentence-Over-Fatal-Airliner-Crash/.
62. Flightglobal, "Tu-154 crew battled power loss after switching of fuel pump," 26 September 2011. Available at https://www.webcitation.org/6201YvgM8?url=http:// www.flightglobal.com/news/articles/tu-154-crew-battled-power-loss-after-switching -off-fuel-pump-362508/.
63. Sputnik News, "Russia's Tu-154 jet breaks into pieces killing 2, injuring over 80," 4 December 2010. Available at https://sputniknews.com/russia/20101204161629703/.
64. Stenin, A., "The Moscow Region Court found the aircraft commander guilty of the death of two people," Russian Legal Information Agency. 23 January 2015 Ria Novosti, 23 January 2015. Available at http://www.rapsinews.ru/judicial_news/20150122 /273008484.html.
65. RAPSI, Russian Legal Information Agency, "Families of Lokomotiv hockey team killed in air crash file lawsuit," 21 May 2015. Available at http://rapsinews.com/judicial _news/20140521/271374859.html.
66. ANS, "MAK investigation findings of Yaroslavl Yak-42 accident challenged in court," 2 February 2012. Available at https://news.aviation-safety.net/2012/02/02/mak-investigation-findings-of-yaroslavl-yak-42-accident-challenged-in-court/.
67. Earle, J., "Charges filed in hockey jet tragedy," Moscow Times, 6 September 2012. Available at https://themoscowtimes.com/articles/charges-filed-in-hockey-jet-tragedy -17593.
68. TASS, "Sole person blamed for death of ice hockey team in 2011 plane crash amnestied," 23 September 2015. Available at https://tass.com/society/823040.
69. Interfax, "Russian Investigative Committee ends inquiry into ice hockey plane crash," 7 October 2014. Available at http://rbth.com/news/2014/10/07/russian_investigative _committee_ends_inquiry_into_ice_hockey_plane_crash_40414.html.
70. Swiss Accident Investigation Board, Final Report no. 2136 of the Swiss Accident Investigation Board SAIB, 6 March 2012. Available at https://www.skybrary.aero/ bookshelf/books/2221.pdf.

71. Frankhauser, A., "Supreme Court acquits air traffic controller," Proton Legal LLC, International Law Office, 8 January 2020. Available at https://www.internationallawoffice.com/Newsletters/Aviation/Switzerland/Proton-Legal-LLC/Supreme-Court-acquits-air-traffic-controller?utm_source=ILO+Newsletter&utm_medium=email&utm_content=Newsletter+2020-01-08&utm_campaign=Aviation+Newsletter and see Judgment 6B_332/2019.
72. Hradecky, S., "Incident: Darwin SAAB 2000 at Zurich on Aug 22nd 2012, close encounter with touch and go on crossing runway," 9 September 2012, updated 24 September 2014. Available at http://avherald.com/h?article=455b97eb.
73. Eurocockpit, "Two Air Traffic Controllers in Switzerland convicted," 14 December 2008. Available at https://www.eurocockpit.be/news/two-air-traffic-controllers-switzerland-convicted.
74. Polek, G., "Switzerland's Darwin airline ceases operations," 28 November 2017. Available at https://www.ainonline.com/aviation-news/air-transport/2017-11-28/switzerlands-darwin-airline-ceases-operations.
75. NTSB, Descent Below Visual Glidepath and Impact With Seawall Asiana Airlines Flight 214 Boeing 777-200ER, HL7742 San Francisco, California, NTSB/AAR-14/01 PB2014-105984, 6 July 2013. Available at https://www.ntsb.gov/investigations/AccidentReports/Reports/AAR1401.pdf.
76. South China Morning Post, "No prosecution for death of Chinese teen who survived Asiana air crash," 20 October 2013. Available at https://www.scmp.com/news/world/article/1335409/no-prosecution-death-chinese-teen-who-survived-asiana-air-crash.
77. Dye, J., "Passengers eye legal action against Boeing, Asiana over crash," 17 July 2013. Available at https://www.reuters.com/article/us-usa-crash-asiana-lawsuit/passengers-eye-legal-action-against-boeing-asiana-over-crash-idUSBRE96G01V20130717.
78. Kim, V., and Mather, K., "83 Asiana victims file legal papers against Boeing, cite malfunction," 16 July 2013. Available at https://www.latimes.com/local/lanow/la-me-ln-asiana-passengers-sue-boeing-in-asiana-crash-20130716-story.html.
79. Copy of complaint: US District Court, Northern District of California Case#CV133684 (Filing only), 9 August 2013. Available at https://www.cpmlegal.com/media/cases/149_File%20Endorsed%20Complaint.pdf.
80. Thanawala, S., "Final lawsuit settled in deadly San Francisco plane crash," 25 September 2017. Available at https://www.insurancejournal.com/news/west/2017/09/25/465377.htm.
81. Associated Press, "Asiana Airlines penalized $500K for not assisting families after crash," 25 February 2015. Available at https://www.cbsnews.com/news/asiana-airlines-penalized-500000-for-failing-to-assist-family-members-after-crash/.
82. Washington Post, "Pilots of crashed Asiana plane return to S. Korea," 14 July 2013. Available at https://www.bangkokpost.com/world/359799/pilots-of-crashed-asiana-plane-return-to-s-korea.
83. NTSB report, op cit at 1.5 Personnel Information.
84. Pasztor, A., "Asiana pilots fear criminal charges in San Francisco crash," Wall Street Journal, 15 July 2015. Available at https://www.wsj.com/articles/SB10001424127887323664204578608040691727544.
85. IFATCA, "The Swiss Justice System is setting new unheard-of standards for the Aviation industry," 5 July 2019. Available at https://www.ifatca.org/category/regions/page/3/.
86. Skyguide, "Federal Court rejects appeal by air traffic controller – conviction legally binding," 4 July 2019. Available at https://www.skyguide.ch/en/events-media-board/news/#p95885-95887-95888.

87. GCAA, "Accident Investigation Final Report No AIFN/0002/2014," Air Accident Investigation Sector General Civil Aviation Authority The United Arab Emirates, UAE, 28 December 2016. Available at https://www.gcaa.gov.ae/en/ePublication/admin/iradmin/Lists/Incidents%20Investigation%20Reports/Attachments/97/2014-AFIN022014-%20FINAL%20REPORT.pdf.
88. Ibid., at 3.3 |Causes.
89. Withey, C., RAF Voyager ZZ333 Incident: Deadline for civil claims looms on 9 February 2017 as criminal proceedings due to start, Bolt Burdon Kemp, 30 January 2017. Available at http://www.boltburdonkemp.co.uk/news-blogs/military-claims-blog/raf-voyager-zz333-incident-deadline-civil-claims-looms-9-february-2017-criminal-proceedings-.
90. The Malaysian ICAO Annex 13 Safety Investigation Team for MH37, Safety Investigation Report Malaysia Airlines Boeing B777-200ER (9M-MRO) 8 March 2014 MH370/01/2018, 02 July 2018. Available at https://reports.aviation-safety.net/2014/20140308-0_B772_9M-MRO.pdf.
91. Riegler, P., Malaysia Reorganizes Flight 370 Investigation, Appoints Independent investigator,' 6 April 2014. Available at http://www.frequentbusinesstraveler.com/2014/04/malaysia-reorganizes-flight-370-investigation-appoints-independent-investigator/.
92. Fleig, S., "The search for MH370 has ended. Here are the theories behind the plane's disappearance," USA Today, 23 May 2018. Available at https://www.usatoday.com/story/news/2018/05/23/mh-370-search-wraps-up-theories-disappearance/637414002/.
93. Conspiracies, MH370 Conspiracy Theories: Missing Malaysian Flight, 12 April 2017. Available at https://www.conspiracies.net/mh370-conspiracy/.
94. Madge-Wyld, T., "Netherlands chosen to hear Flight MH17 prosecutions," 6 July 2017. Available at https://gettingthedealthrough.com/aviation/article/5683/netherlands-chosen-to-hear-flight-mh17-prosecutions.
95. Apen-Sadler, D., "MH370 investigators discover 'mystery load weighing 200lb' was added to the cargo flight list AFTER take-off," Daily Mail, 16 July 2019. Available at https://www.dailymail.co.uk/news/article-7251795/amp/MH370-French-investigators-discover-mystery-200lb-load-added-flight-list-off.html.
96. Safety Investigation Report Malaysia Airlines Boeing B777-200ER (9M-MRO) 08 March 2014, Issued on 02 July 2018 MH370/01/2018. Available at https://reports.aviation-safety.net/2014/20140308-0_B772_9M-MRO.pdf.
97. Safety Investigation Report Malaysia Airlines Boeing B777-200ER (9M-MRO) 08 March 2014, Issued on 02 July 2018 MH370/01/2018. Available at https://reports.aviation-safety.net/2014/20140308-0_B772_9M-MRO.pdf.
98. Ibid.
99. The Strait Times, "US judge dismisses litigation over missing Malaysia Airlines flight MH370," 24 November 2018. Available at https://www.straitstimes.com/asia/se-asia/us-judge-dismisses-litigation-over-missing-malaysia-airlines-flight-mh370.
100. The Week, MH370: mysterious 89kg load "added to cargo flight list after take-off," 17 July 2019. Available at https://www.theweek.co.uk/mh370/57641/mh370-malaysia-airlines-missing-plane.
101. Calcino, "Pilot faces jail term after 11yo girl's death in plane crash," 29 November 2016. Available at https://www.sunshinecoastdaily.com.au/news/pilot-faces-jail-term-after-11yo-girls-death-in-pl/3117181/.
102. Ibid.
103. Dutch Safety Board, Crash of Malaysia Airlines Flight MH17, 13 October 2015.
104. Seamons, K., "5 years after MH17 was shot down, murder charges," 19 June 2019. Available at https://www.newser.com/story/276736/5-years-after-mh17-was-shot-down-4-charged.html.

105. Corder, M., "4 charged for shooting down Flight MH17, trial to begin March 2020," 19 June 2019. Available at https://www.thequint.com/news/world/suspects-charged-for-shooting-down-flight-mh17-trial-to-begin-march-2020.
106. Rankin, J., "Three men found guilty of murdering 298 people in shooting down of MH17," 17 November 2022. Available at https://www.theguardian.com/world/2022/nov/17/three-men-found-guilty-of-murdering-298-people-in-flight-mh17-bombing.
107. Aviation Safety Council Taipei, Taiwan Aviation Occurrence Report 23 July 2014 TransAsia Airways Flight GE222 ATR72-212A, B-22810, January 2016. Available at https://reports.aviation-safety.net/2014/20140723-0_AT75_B-22810.pdf.
108. Ibid., at 1.4 Conclusion at page 301.
109. Ibid., at 2.4 Conclusions at page 307.
110. Straitstimes, "Taiwan charges 2 air traffic control officers over deadly 2014 TransAsia plane crash that killed 49," 15 April 2016. Available at https://www.straitstimes.com/asia/east-asia/taiwan-charges-2-air-traffic-control-officers-over-deadly-2014-transasia-plane-crash.
111. Yahoo news, "Taiwan acquits two over deadly 2014 TransAsia crash," 2 June 2017. Available at https://sg.news.yahoo.com/taiwan-acquits-two-over-deadly-2014-transasia-crash-062841890.html.
112. Aviation Safety Network, Preliminary accident description. Available at http://aviation-safety.net/database/record.php?id=20020-0.
113. Aerospace. Available at http://aerospace-ds.com/pub/?p=381.
114. Spinella, P., "Russia's inquiry into oil exec's deadly jet crash handed over to France," The Moscow Times, 26 February 2015. Available at http://www.themoscowtimes.com/news/article/russia-s-inquiry-into-oil-exec-s-deadly-jet-crash-handed-over-to-france/516628.html.
115. Russian Legal Information Centre, RAPSI, "Several services guilty of air crash that killed Total CEO – Report, 26," February 2015. Available at http://rapsinews.com/news/20150226/273230958.html.
116. Russian Legal Information Centre, RAPSI, ibid.
117. Russia Beyond the Headlines, *Trainee Air Traffic Controller Indicted in Total CEO Plane Crash, Says Investigative Committee,* 29 October 2014. Available at http://rbth.co.uk/news/2014/10/29/trainee_air_traffic_controller_indicted_in_total_ceo_plane_crash_says_in_40987.html.
118. Stewart, W., "Russia charges 'drunk' snowplow driver who caused plane crash that killed Total oil boss," MailOnline, 31 October 2014. Available at http://www.dailymail.co.uk/news/article-2816095/Russia-charges-drunk-snowplough-driver-caused-plane-crash-killed-Total-oil-boss.html#ixzz3SxEBHl40.
119. Russian Legal Information Centre, RAPSI, op cit.
120. Sputnik International, op cit.
121. TASS, *All People Featured in October 2014 Falcon Jet Crash Released from Moscow Custody*, 22 September 2015. Available at http://tass.ru/en/society/822943.
122. TASS, Investigators drop charges against one of Falcon crash suspects-lawyer, 14 January 2016. Available at http://tass.ru/en/society/849755http://tass.ru/en/society/849755.
123. Russian Legal Information Agency, (RAPSI), *Vnukovo Airport Engineer Pleads Guilty in Total CEO Plane Crash Case-report*, 27 August 2015. Available at http://www.rapsinews.com/judicial_news/20150827/274481242.html.
124. KNKT, Komite Nasional Keselamatan Transportasi, PT. Indonesia Air Asia Airbus A320-216, Karimata Strait, Republic of Indonesia, 2015. Available at https://reports.aviation-safety.net/2014/20141228-0_A320_PK-AXC.pdf.
125. Ibid.

126. Malay Mail, "QZ8501: French judge to probe crash, possible 'manslaughter,'" Malay Mail Online, 31 January 2015. Available at https://www.malaymail.com/news/malaysia/2015/01/31/qz8501-french-judge-to-probe-crash-possible-manslaughter/831211.
127. Tan, A., "Airbus sued by AirAsia crash families over defective systems," 30 June 2015. Available at https://www.bloomberg.com/news/articles/2015-06-30/airbus-sued-by-airasia-crash-families-claiming-defective-systems.
128. Carter, G., "AirAsia plane crash: British aircraft engineer killed himself over 'irrational' obsession he was to blame for deadly disaster," 22 May 2015. Available at https://www.mirror.co.uk/news/uk-news/airasia-plane-crash-british-aircraft-5741712.
129. JIAAC, Final report by the Argentine Civil Aviation Accident Investigation Board (Junta de Investigación de Accidentes de Aviación Civil, JIAAC) regarding the AS350 helicopters LQ-CGK and LQ-FJQ accident on 9 March 2015 in Villa Castelli, La Rioja province. 17 December 2015. Available at https://jiaac.gob.ar/files/88–15.pdf.
130. Le Point, La société de production de l'émission a été condamnée pour « faute inexcusable » et devra indemniser la famille d'un caméraman mort dans l'accident de 2015, 25 April 2018. Available at https://www.lepoint.fr/justice/accident-d-helicoptere-en-argentine-la-production-de-dropped-condamnee-25-04-2018-2213345_2386.php.
131. Le Point, La société de production de l'émission a été condamnée pour « faute inexcusable » et devra indemniser la famille d'un caméraman mort dans l'accident de 2015, 25 April 2018. Available at https://www.lepoint.fr/justice/accident-d-helicoptere-en-argentine-la-production-de-dropped-condamnee-25-04-2018-2213345_2386.php.
132. Le Point, "La société de production a été condamnée pour « faute inexcusable » après l'accident en Argentine qui avait coûté la vie à 10 personnes en 2015," 27 September 2018. Available at https://www.lepoint.fr/faits-divers/accident-d-helicoptere-2e-condamnation-pour-la-production-de-dropped-27-09-2018-2258468_2627.php.
133. Venance, L., "'Dropped': Five years after the crash, a man discreetly indicted," LePoint.fr, 7 February 2020. Available at https://www.lepoint.fr/justice/dropped-cinq-ans-apres-le-crash-un-homme-mis-en-examen-discretement-07-02-2020-2361666_2386.php.
134. LePoint, Helicopter accident: 2nd conviction for the production of "Dropped," 27 September 2018. Available at https://www.lepoint.fr/faits-divers/accident-d-helicoptere-2e-condamnation-pour-la-production-de-dropped-27-09-2018-2258468_2627.php.
135. Bureau d'Enquêtes et d'Analyses pour la sécurité de l'aviation civile (BEA), Final Report on Accident on 24 March 2015 at Prads-Haute-Bléone (Alpes-de-Haute-Provence, France) to the Airbus A320-211 registered D-AIPX operated by Germanwings, at 3.2, March 2016. Available at https://www.bea.aero/uploads/tx_elyextendttnews/BEA2015-0125.en-LR_03.pdf.
136. Ibid.
137. See Manuel Bandres Oto, et al v Airline Training Center Arizona, Incorporated, Arizona District Court, Case 2:16-cv-01027 cited in Karner, E., Steininger, B.C., (eds), "European Tort Law 2017." Available at wurmnest-goemann-yb-2017-european-tort-law.
138. DW, "Lawsuit over Germanwings crash dismissed," 28 March 2017. Available at https://www.dw.com/de/us-gericht-weist-klage-zu-germanwings-absturz-ab/a-38175224.
139. Janjevic, D., "Arizona flight school was in the 'best position to prevent Germanwings crash," DW, 6 June 2016. Available at https://www.dw.com/en/arizona-flight-school-was-in-the-best-position-to-prevent-germanwings-crash/a-19199058.
140. Canda Aeronautics Act (R.S.C., 1985, c. A-2). Available at https://laws-lois.justice.gc.ca/eng/acts/A-2/FullText.html.
141. Canadian Aviation Regulations (SOR/96-433), s Section 404.06 Available at https://laws-lois.justice.gc.ca/eng/regulations/sor-96-433/; https://laws-lois.justice.gc.ca/eng/regulations/sor-96-433/.

142. Foster, S., "The aftermath of Germanwings" Alexander Holborn, 27 April 2017. Available at https://www.ahbl.ca/wp-content/uploads/2017/04/Shaun-Foster-Wings-article.pdf.
143. Dame, F., "Court rejects compensation claim after Germanwings crash," 1 October 2021. Available at https://www.dailyfinland.fi/europe/23800/Court-rejects-compensation-claim-after-Germanwings-crash#google_vignette.
144. Janjevic, D., "Father of Germanwings crash victim sues pilot's doctor," 6 June 2016. Available at https://www.dw.com/en/father-of-germanwings-crash-victim-sues-pilots-doctor/a-19310507.
145. Dean, S., "Grieving man who lost three relatives – Including his baby grandson – in Germanwings crash sues the pilot's parents because they didn't stop him from flying," 20 July 2016. Available at https://www.dailymail.co.uk/news/article-3698928/Grieving-man-lost-three-relatives-Germanwings-crash-sues-pilot-s-PARENTS-didn-t-stop-flying.html.
146. Baum Hedlund Aristei & Goldman PC, "Baum Hedlund files Germanwings crash lawsuit for two Americans killed," 30 January 2017. Available at https://www.wisnerbaum.com/blog/2017/january/baum-hedlund-files-germanwings-crash-lawsuit-for/.
147. Cosculluela, F., "Victims of the Germanwings accident sue Lufthansa for 'negligence,'" ElPeriodico, 26 November 2019. Available at https://www.elperiodico.com/es/sociedad/20191126/germanwings-juicio-lufthansa-7751811.
148. Campbell, J., "Hull man, 28, killed by 'psychotic' pilot who flew airliner into mountain," Hull Live, 8 November 2021. Available at https://www.hulldailymail.co.uk/news/hull-east-yorkshire-news/inquest-hears-how-hull-man-6177512.
149. Clark, N., "France opens Germanwings crash criminal inquiry," New York Times, 11 June 2015. Available at https://www.nytimes.com/2015/06/12/world/europe/germanwings-crash-criminal-inquiry-planned-by-france.html.
150. Jordans, F., et al., "Prosecutors close Germanwings crash inquiry," Courthouse News Service, 9 January 2017. Available at https://www.courthousenews.com/german-prosecutors-close-germanwings-crash-inquiry/.
151. Euronews, "Germanwings: France closes manslaughter investigation into 2015 plane crash," 3 September 2022. Available at https://www.euronews.com/2022/03/09/germanwings-france-closes-manslaughter-investigation-into-2015-plane-crash.
152. Aviation Investigation Report A15H0002 Collision with terrain Air Canada Airbus Industrie A320-211, C-FTJP Halifax/Stanfield International Airport Halifax, Nova Scotia 29 March 2015, Transportation Safety Board of Canada. Available at http://www.bst-tsb.gc.ca/eng/rapports-reports/aviation/2015/A15H0002/A15H0002.pdf.
153. Ibid.
154. Ball & Bonholtzer, Class Action Lawsuit Filed In Air Canada Crash, 30 April 2015. Available at https://www.pasadenalaw.com/blog/2015/04/class-action-lawsuit-filed-in-air-canada-crash.shtml.
155. McDonald, M., "Transport Canada challenging Halifax plane crash lawsuit," The Canadian Press, 13 December 2016. Available at https://www.cbc.ca/news/canada/nova-scotia/lawsuit-certification-air-canada-halifax-airport-supreme-court-1.3892153.
156. Ibid.
157. Thomson, Aly., "Air Canada lawsuit accuses Airbus of negligence in Halifax crash landing," The Canadian Press, 30 March 2017. Available at https://atlantic.ctvnews.ca/air-canada-lawsuit-accuses-airbus-of-negligence-in-halifax-crash-landing-1.3347468.
158. Campbell, F., "Court orders TSB to hand over cockpit recording from 2015 crash at Halifax airport," The Guardian, 21 November. Available at https://www.theguardian.pe.ca/news/canada/court-orders-tsb-to-hand-over-cockpit-recording-from-2015-crash-at-halifax-airport-378861/.

159. *Canada (Transportation Safety Board) v. Carroll-Byrne*, 2021 NSCA 34, Nova Scotia Court Of Appeal, Docket CA 49503516 April 2021. Available at https://decisia.lexum.com/nsc/nsca/en/item/495674/index.do.
160. Canadian Press, "2026 trial date set for class-action lawsuit over Air Canada crash landing in 2015," 21 May 2024. Available at https://atlantic.ctvnews.ca/more/2026-trial-date-set-for-class-action-lawsuit-over-air-canada-crash-landing-in-2015-1.6895014.
161. AAIB. Report on the accident to Hawker Hunter T7, G-BXFI near Shoreham Airport 22 August 2015, 3 March 2017. Available ahttps://assets.publishing.service.gov.uk/media/58b9247740f0b67ec80000fc/AAR_1-2017_G-BXFI.pdf.
162. Ibid.
163. BBC, "Police refused access to Shoreham pilot interviews," 28 September 2016. Available at https://www.bbc.com/news/uk-england-sussex-37495884].
164. BBC, "Shoreham air crash: Pilot Andy Hill to be charged over deaths," 21 March 2018. Available at https://www.bbc.com/news/uk-england-43494430.
165. Davies, G., "Shoreham disaster families say they have been 'let down by the justice system' as pilot is cleared," The Telegraph, 8 March 2019. Available at https://www.telegraph.co.uk/news/2019/03/08/shoreham-airshow-trial-pilot-andrew-hill-cleared-manslaughter/.
166. Directorate of Aircraft Accident Investigation, Arab Republic of Egypt Ministry of Civil Aviation, Interim Statement Russian Aircraft crash at Sinai on 31-10-2015 Aircraft type Airbus A321 Registration EI-ETJ Operated by Kogalymavia Airline Ltd, 31 October 2016. Available at http://www.aviation-accidents.net/report-download.php?id=658.
167. Russia Today, "Plane crash in Sinai a terrorist attack – Russian Security Service," 17 November 2015. Available at https://www.rt.com/news/322393-russian-plane-crash-terrorist-attack/.
168. Hassan, A.H., "Exclusive: Egypt detains two airport staff over Russian air crash – Security sources," Reuters, 17 November 2015. Available at https://www.reuters.com/article/us-egypt-crash-bomb-arrests/exclusive-egypt-detains-two-airport-staff-over-russian-air-crash-security-sources-idUSKCN0T60VM20151117.
169. Ria Novosti, Шойгу: группировка "Вилаят-Синай" причастна к теракту на борту A321 (in Russian), 24 November 2015. Available at https://ria.ru/20151124/1327758468.html.
170. Mezzofiore, G., "Isis claims 'Schweppes can bomb' blew up Russian Metrojet flight 9268 in Egypt's Sinai – Dabiq." 18 November 2015. Available at https://www.ibtimes.co.uk/isis-claim-schweppes-can-bomb-blew-russian-metrojet-flight-9268-egypts-sinai-dabiq-1529374.
171. Bacchi, U., "Egypt Air mechanic who is cousin to Isis fighter \'among 4 arrested\' over Russian plane bombing," International Business Times, 29 January 2016. Available at https://www.ibtimes.co.uk/egypt-air-mechanic-who-cousin-isis-fighter-among-4-arrested-over-russian-plane-bombing-1540834.
172. Interstate Aviation Committee Air Accident Investigation Commission Final Report-Boeing 737-8KN A6-FDN Fatal Accident. Available at https://mak-iac.org/upload/iblock/1e8/report_a6-fdn_eng.pdf.
173. Ibid.
174. Nechepurenko, I., "Wind given as possible cause of fatal plane crash in Russia," New York Times, 19 March 2016. Available at https://www.nytimes.com/2016/03/20/world/europe/plane-from-dubai-crashes-at-russian-airport-killing-62.html.
175. Goryaev, O., "Boeing companies recalled Rostov plane crash," Kommersant, 13 April 2016. Available at https://www.kommersant.ru/doc/2962159.

176. Williams, G., "Prosecution in fatal helicopter crash a 'message' to owners," Otago Daily Times, 1 November 2019. Available at https://www.nzherald.co.nz/business/prosecution-in-fatal-helicopter-crash-a-message-to-owners/ZBNWN5VPB6RZZD3TZSAHSPT2LU/.
177. FSF Editorial Staff, "BEA pushes Egypt for continuation of EgyptAir Flight 804 crash investigation," 6 July 2018. Available at https://flightsafety.org/egyptair-804-crash-update/.
178. BBC, "EgyptAir flight MS804: What we know," 7 July 2018. Available at https://www.bbc.com/news/world-middle-east-36330879.
179. FSF Editorial Staff, "BEA pushes Egypt for continuation of EgyptAir Flight 804 crash investigation," 6 July 2018. Available at https://flightsafety.org/egyptair-804-crash-update/.
180. Chazan, D., "EgyptAir 'black box' repaired as France opens manslaughter investigation," Telegraph, 28 June 2016. Available at http://www.telegraph.co.uk/news/2016/06/28/egyptair-black-box-repaired-as-france-opens-manslaughter-investi/.
181. Vérier, V., "EgyptAir crash: The plane should never have taken off," LeParisien, 2 April 2019. Available at http://www.leparisien.fr/faits-divers/crash-d-egyptair-l-avion-n-aurait-jamais-du-decoller-02-04-2019-8044764.php.
182. Vérier, V., "EgyptAir crash: The prestigious Bureau of Investigation and Analysis searched," LeParisien, 2 April 2019. Available at http://www.leparisien.fr/faits-divers/crash-d-egyptair-le-prestigieux-bureau-d-enquetes-et-d-analyses-perquisitionne-02-04-2019-8044938.php.
183. GCAA Air Accident Investigation Sector Accident – Final Report – AAIS Case No: AIFN/0008/2016, Emirates Boeing 777-31H, Accident, Runway Impact during Attempted Go-Around. Available at https://www.gcaa.gov.ae/en/epublication/pages/investigationReport.aspx.
184. Smith, N., "Court rules passengers have right to sue Boeing in US over Emirates crash," 1 November 2018. Available at https://gettingthedealthrough.com/aviation/article/6435/court-rules-passengers-right-sue-boeing-us-emirates-crash.
185. Jian, Y., "Airport officials lose licenses after near miss," Shanghai Daily, 22 October 2016. Available at https://archive.shine.cn/metro/society/Airport-officials-lose-licenses-after-near-miss/shdaily.shtml.
186. The Guardian, "Colombia plane crash: Leaked audio shows pilot said he ran out of fuel," 1 December 2016. Available at https://www.theguardian.com/world/2016/nov/30/colombia-plane-crash-pilot-out-of-fuel-chapecoense-brazil.
187. Grupo de Investigación de Accidentes e Incidentes de Aviación (GRIAA), Colombia, Final Report Accident COL-16-37-GIA Fuel Exhaustion AVRO 146-RJ85, Reg. CP 2933 29 November 2016 La Unión, Antioquia – Colombia, 16 August 2017. Available at http://www.aerocivil.gov.co/autoridad-de-la-aviacion civil/investigacion/listado%20de%20accidentes%202016/Final%20Report%20-%20ACCIDENT%20CP2933%20-%20English%20Version.pdf.
188. Ibid.
189. Latin American Herald Tribune, "Lamia chief appears in court after being charged with manslaughter," 8 December 2016. Available at http://www.laht.com/article.asp?ArticleId=2426800&CategoryId=14919.
190. Ibid.
191. BBC, "Colombia plane crash: Second Bolivian suspect charged," 10 December 2016. Available at https://www.bbc.com/news/world-latin-america-38277788.

192. Aldersley, M., "Cavalier pilot, 52, whose light aircraft 'fell out of the sky' after he overloaded it with three birdwatchers to make an £800 profit is jailed for three and a half years," Daily Mail, 15 March 2019. Available at https://www.dailymail.co.uk/news/article-6815601/Cavalier-pilot-52-jailed-three-half-years.html.
193. News Team, "Pilot found guilty of seven charges after accident," 21 February 2019. Available at https://www.flyer.co.uk/pilot-found-guilty-of-seven-charges-after-accident/.
194. Fahey, R., "Pilot who crashed his aircraft after greedily overloading it with birdwatchers gets new jail term for failing to tell insurers his planes had already been in three fatal crashes," Daily Mail, 5 October 2019. Available at https://www.dailymail.co.uk/news/article-7540913/amp/M62-crash-pilot-sentenced-three-half-years.html.
195. Kaminski-Morrow, D., "Cuban probe details balance errors behind fatal 737 crash," 12 September 2019. Available at https://www.flightglobal.com/safety/cuban-probe-details-balance-errors-behind-fatal-737-crash/134291.article.
196. Ibid.
197. Whitefield, M., "First lawsuits in Cuban plane crash that killed 112 have been filed — in a U.S. court," 6 September 2018. Available at https://www.miamiherald.com/news/nation-world/world/americas/cuba/article217856645.html.
198. Aviation Safety Network, 31 July 2018. Available at https://aviation-safety.net/database/record.php?id=20731-0.
199. Woolley, R., "US passengers sue Aeroméxico over Durango crash," 9 August 2018. Available at https://gettingthedealthrough.com/aviation/article/6284/us-passengers-sue-aeromexico-durango-crash.
200. KNKT, Aircraft Accident Investigation Report PT. Lion Mentari Airlines Boeing 737-8 (MAX); PK-LQP Tanjung Karawang, West Java Republic of Indonesia 29 October 2018, Conclusions, page 215, October 2019. Available at http://knkt.dephub.go.id/knkt/ntsc_aviation/baru/2018%20-%20035%20-%20PK-LQP%20Final%20Report.pdf.
201. See for example Aprilia v. Boeing - Complaint (FILED 11.21.18), Dorothy Brown Circuit Clerk Cook County, Il 20181012614, 21 November 2018. Available At https://www.scribd.com/document/394193368/Aprilia-v-Boeing-Complaint-FILED-11-21-18#from_embed.
202. AAIB Bulletin S1/2019 SPECIAL, AAIB, 25 February 2019. Available at https://assets.publishing.service.gov.uk/media/5c73c02bed915d4a3d3b2407/S1-2019_N264DB_Final.pdf.
203. Ibid.
204. AAIB, Report on the accident to Piper PA-46-310P Malibu, N264DB 22 nm north-north-west of Guernsey on 21 January 2019, UK AAIB, 13 March 2020. Available at https://assets.publishing.service.gov.uk/media/5f451f768fa8f51f7faa8d4e/AAR_1 2020_N264DB_IIi_res.pdf.
205. Alcock, C., "UK CAA prosecutes pilot for alleged illegal charter flight," Ainonline, 16 October 2020. Available at https://www.ainonline.com/aviation-news/business-aviation/2020-10-16/uk-caa-prosecutes-pilot-alleged-illegal-charter-flight.
206. Ethiopian Aircraft Accident Investigation Preliminary Report Ethiopian Airlines Group B737-8 (MAX) Registered ET-AVJ 28 NM South East of Addis Ababa, Bole International Airport 10 March 2019, Report No. AI-01/19. Available at https://reports.aviation-safety.net/2019/20190310-0_B38M_ET-AVJ_PRELIM.pdf.
207. EIAB, ET_302__B737-8MAX_ACCIDENT_FINAL_REP No. AI-01/19, 23 December 2022. Available at https://bea.aero/fileadmin/user_upload/ET_302__B737-8MAX_ACCIDENT_FINAL_REPORT.pdf.
208. Ibid., pp. 255–256.

209. U.S. Department of Justice, "Former Boeing 737 MAX chief technical pilot indicted for fraud thursday' press release," 14 October 2021. Available at https://www.justice.gov/opa/pr/former-boeing-737-max-chief-technical-pilot-indicted-fraud.
210. See United States District Court For The Northern District of Texas Fort Worth Division United States of America V. Mar.Ka. Forkner, Indictment, No 421-CR-268-0, 14 October 2021. Available at https://www.justice.gov/opa/press-release/file/1442191/dl.
211. German, K., "2 years after being grounded, the Boeing 737 Max is flying again," CNET, 9 July 2021. Available at https://www.cnet.com/tech/tech-industry/boeing-737-max-8-all-about-the-aircraft-flight-ban-and-investigations/.
212. Koenig, D., and Richer, A.D., "Sweetheart deal': Families of 737 Max crash victims not satisfied by Boeing guilty plea," Associated Press, 8 July 2024. Available at https://www.csmonitor.com/USA/2024/0708/boeing-guilty-plea-737-Max-crashes.
213. O'Leary, A., "Pilot of doomed Russian plane that crashed killing 41 could face seven years in jail," 3 October 2019. Available at https://www.mirror.co.uk/news/world-news/pilot-doomed-russian-plane-crashed-20392862.
214. Papachristou, L., and Daniel, F.J., "Russian pilot sentenced to six years in prison over 2019 crash that killed 41," Reuters, 20 June 2023. Available at https://www.reuters.com/world/europe/russian-pilot-sentenced-six-years-prison-over-2019-crash-that-killed-41-2023-06-20/.
215. IZ RU, "Society Court sentences pilot of SSJ-100 that burned down at Sheremetyevo to 6 years in penal colony," (translated from Russian) 20 June 2023. Available at https://iz.ru/1531575/2023-06-20/sud-prigovoril-k-6-godam-kolonii-poseleniia-pilota-sgorev-shego-v-sheremetevo-ssj-100.
216. Johnson, R.F., "Ukraine International Airlines demands full investigation into Iran 737 shootdown," AIN, 11 January 2020. Available at https://www.ainonline.com/aviation-news/air-transport/2020-01-11/ukraine-international-airlines-demands-full-investiga-tion-iran-737-shootdown.
217. PS752 Accident Investigation- Final Report I.R.IRAN AAIB. Available at https://reports.aviation-safety.net/2020/20200108-0_B738_UR-PSR.pdf.
218. see 6.2. Accident Causes and Contributing Factors Cause of the Accident, p. 135, ibid.
219. Zarei v Iran, 2021 ONSC 3377.
220. Martins, C., and Wong, A., "Ontario court awards C$107 million against Iran for Ukraine International Airlines crash," WeirFoulds, LLP., 2 February 2022. Available at https://www.lexology.com/commentary/aviation/canada/weirfoulds-llp/ontario-court-awards-c107-million-against-iran-for-ukraine-international-airlines-crash?utm_source=Lexology%2bDaily%2bNewsfeed&utm_medium=HTML%2bemail%2b-%2bPro%2bEmbed%2b-%2bGeneral%2bsection&utm_campaign=Lexology%2bsubscriber%2bdaily%2bfeed&utm_content=Lexology%2bDaily%2bNewsfeed%2b2022-02-03.
221. Zarei v Iran, 2021 ONSC 8569.
222. Gritten, D., "Ukraine plane: Iran court jails 10 over downing of flight PS752," 17 April 2023. Available at https://www.bbc.com/news/world-middle-east-65298216.
223. NTSB, Aircraft Accident Investigative Update. Available at https://pmcdeadline2.files.wordpress.com/2020/02/kobe-crash-premilinary-investigation-wm.pdf.
224. Ibid.
225. Pedersen, E., "Kobe Bryant crash: NTSB's preliminary report finds no evidence of engine failure but doesn't speculate on cause – Read it here," 7 February 2020. Available at https://deadline.com/2020/02/kobe-bryant-crash-1202843161/.
226. Ibid.
227. Gorman, S., "Widow of NBA great Kobe Bryant sues helicopter operator for fatal crash," 24 February 2020. Available at https://www.reuters.com/article/us-people-kobe-bryant-lawsuit-idUSKCN20I23U.

228. Sfgate, "Pilot in Istanbul airport crash earlier this month arrested," 24 February 2020. Available at https://www.sfgate.com/news/crime/article/Prosecutors-seek-pilot-s-arrest-over-Istanbul-15079818.php.
229. Aviation Safety Network, 5 February 2020. Available at https://aviation-safety.net/database/record.php?id=20205-0.
230. France24, "Turkey probes pilots over deadly plane crash," 2 June 2020. Available at https://www.france24.com/en/20200206-turkey-probes-pilots-over-deadly-plane-crash.
231. Negroni, C., "Pilot in fatal pegasus crash released to house arrest," 24 March 2020. Available at https://christinenegroni.com/pilot-in-fatal-pegasus-crash-released-to-house-arrest/.
232. Agence France-Presse, "Pakistan plane crashed after pilots distracted by coronavirus fears," 25 June 2020. Available at https://www.theguardian.com/world/2020/jun/25/pakistan-plane-crashed-after-pilots-.
233. OPEN DES mode is then Open Descent Mode specifically designed for IDLE thrust.
234. A Flight Control Unit (FCU) is part of the system architecture for automatic flight functions of certain aircraft.
235. AAIB, Pakistan, "Accident of PIA Flight Pk8303 Airbus A320-214 Reg No Ap-Bld crashed near Karachi airport on 22-05-2020: Preliminary report: Crash of PIA AP-BLD 22 May 2020," June 2020. Available at https://www.caapakistan.com.pk/Upload/SIBReports/AAIB-431.pdf.
236. ASN, Investigating Agency: Pak CAA. Available at https://asn.flightsafety.org/wikibase/319173.
237. Hashim, A., "Pakistan airline suspends 150 pilots over alleged licence fraud." Al Jazeera, 26 June 2020. Available at https://www.aljazeera.com/news/2020/6/26/pakistan-airline-suspends-150-pilots-over-alleged-licence-fraud.
238. Casey, D., "EASA lifts Pakistan International Airlines flight ban." Aviation Week, 29 November 2024. Available at https://aviationweek.com/air-transport/safety-ops-regulation/easa-lifts-pakistan-international-airlines-flight-ban.
239. The New Indian Express, "Pakistan court suspends plea seeking independent probe into PIA plane crash," 30 May 2020. Available at https://www.newindianexpress.com/world/2020/May/30/pakistan-court-suspends-plea-seeking-independent-probe-into-pia-plane-crash-2150086.html.
240. Times of Karachi, "Sindh High Court demands answers in PIA plane crash case," 26 February 2024. Available at https://timesofkarachi.pk/sindh-high-court-demands-answers-in-pia-plane-crash-case/.
241. The Tribune, "Court seeks answers for 2020 PIA crash," 11 October 2024. Available at https://tribune.com.pk/story/2502086/court-seeks-answers-for-2020-pia-crash.
242. The Dawn, "CAA earns judges' ire after filing 'incomplete' list of officials responsible for PIA 2020 crash," 11 October 2024. Available at https://www.dawn.com/news/1864448.
243. Detikcom Team, "This is the chronology of the fall of Sriwijaya Air SJ182: Had lost contact," DetikNews, 9 January 2021. Available at https://www.msn.com/id-id/berita/nasional/pesawat-sriwijaya-air-sj-182-sempat-keluar-jalur-menuju-arah-barat-laut/ar-BB1cBK1Z.
244. Ranter, H., "ASN Aircraft accident Airbus A320-271N CC-BHB Lima-Jorge Chávez International Airport (LIM)." Available at https://aviation-safety.net/database/types/Airbus-A320neo/losses.
245. Niles, R., "Pilots jailed after firetruck accident," AVweb, 24 November 2022. Available at https://www.avweb.com/aviation-news/pilots-jailed-after-firetruck-accident/.
246. IFALPA, "Global pilots on LATAM Airlines Flight 2213," 20 November 2022. Available at https://www.ifalpa.org/news/global-pilots-on-latam-airlines-flight-2213/.

247. Ibid.
248. Comisión De Investigación De Accidentes De Aviación Del Perú Informe Final Accidente De Aviación N° 008-2022, Ciaa-Accid-008-2022, Airbus A320n Cc-Bhb, Latam Airlines Perú S.A. Available at https://cdn.www.gob.pe/uploads/document/file/5209692/INFORME%20FINAL%20ACCIDENTE%20DE%20AVIACI%C3%93N%20N%C2%B0%200082022.pdf?v=1696022058.
249. Aircraft Accident Investigation Commission Final Report of 9N-ANC (ATR 72-212A, MSN: 754) aircraft operated by Yeti Airlines Pvt. Ltd occurred at Pokhara (at the bank of Seti River - Gharipatan), Kaski District, Nepal, on 15 January 2023, submitted to the Government of Nepal Ministry Of Culture, Tourism And Civil Aviation 28/12/2023 (2080/09/12 B.S.). Available at https://www.tourism.gov.np/files/1/9N-ANC%20FINAL%20Report.pdf.
250. Ibid., pages 6–7.
251. Prasain, S., "Civil aviation boss hauled up over Yeti Airlines crash," The Kathmandu Post, 28 June 2023. Available at https://kathmandupost.com/money/2023/06/28/civil-aviation-boss-hauled-up-over-yeti-airlines-crash.
252. Ibid.
253. Ibid.
254. Ibid.
255. Fiscal Nepal, "Nepal's aviation reform advances: two bills to split CAAN sent to parliamentary committee," 18 May 2025. Available at https://www.fiscalnepal.com/2025/05/18/20429/nepals-aviation-reform-advances-two-bills-to-split-caan-sent-to-parliamentary-committee/#:~:text=The%20Nepal%20Air%20Service%20Authority,a%20regulator%20and%20service%20provider.
256. Armstrong, K., "What we know about Russia plane crash that reportedly killed Prigozhin," BBC News, 27 August 2023. Available at https://www.bbc.com/news/world-europe-66596127.
257. Kyodo News, "JAL jet collides with coast guard plane at Tokyo airport, 5 dead." Available at https://english.kyodonews.net/news/2024/01/0b3984aaa764-urgent-japan-airlines-aircraft-catches-fire-at-haneda-airport-jal.html#google_vignette.
258. NTSB Accident Investigation Preliminary Report of DCA24MA063. Available at https://www.ntsb.gov/investigations/Documents/DCA24MA063%20Preliminary%20report.pdf.
259. Ibid., p. 2.
260. Ibid., p. 3.
261. O'Kane, C., and Van Cleave, K., "A teen on the Alaska Airlines flight had his shirt ripped off when the door plug blew. A stranger tried to help calm him down," CBS News, 9 January 2024. Available at https://www.cbsnews.com/news/alaska-airlines-flight-door-plug-jack-teenager-shirt-passenger-kelly-bartlett/.
262. Case #: 24-2-00824-1 KNT, filed 2024 Jan 11 02:24 PM King County Superior Court Clerk E-Filed. Available at https://drive.google.com/file/d/1uhzdjYcsvxPF7i4Lv0SibcDnSeHxlvCN/view.
263. NTSB, Opcit., p. 9.
264. Opcit., p. 6.
265. Opcit., p. 18.
266. Opcit., p. 18.
267. Aviation Safety Network, Database: Azerbaijan Airlines, Wednesday 25 December 2024. Available at https://asn.flightsafety.org/wikibase/468275.
268. AIID Kazakhstan.

269. Bagirov, N., et al., "Crashed Azerbaijani plane was riddled with holes after incident over Russia, report says," Reuters, Updated 5 February 2025. Available at https://www.reuters.com/world/asia-pacific/kazakh-report-says-plane-dec-25-crash-probably-damaged-by-external-objects-2025-02-04/.
270. ARAIB, Aviation and Railway Accident Investigation Board, Aviation Accident Preliminary Report HL8088 (B737-800) belly landing, runway overrun and crash to embankment. Available at https://HL8088%20Preliminary%20Report(1)%20(1).pdf.
271. Korean Times, "Former, current gov't officials excluded from Jeju Air crash probe to ensure fair investigation," 7 January 2025. Available at https://www.koreatimes.co.kr/southkorea/law-crime/20250107/former-current-south-korean-government-officials-excluded-from-jeju-air-crash-probe-to-ensure-fair-investigation.
272. Sang-Hun, C., et al., "Anger and agony in South Korea after plane crash-lands, killing 179," The New York Times, 29 December 2024. Available at https://www.nytimes.com/2024/12/29/world/asia/what-to-know-south-korea-plane-crash.html.
273. Sang-Hun, C., et al., "What to know about South Korea's worst plane crash in decades," 29 December 2024. Available at https://www.nytimes.com/2024/12/29/world/asia/what-to-know-south-korea-plane-crash.html.
274. Jin-kyu, K., and Shin, H., "179 dead in South Korea's worst plane crash," Barron's. Agence France-Presse, 28 December 2024. Available at https://www.barrons.com/news/plane-with-181-on-board-crashes-in-south-korea-killing-29-43bace9a.
275. Harding, N., "OPINION: Nobody on Jeju Air Flight 2216 should have died," 1 January 2025. Available at https://ukaviation.news/opinion-nobody-on-jeju-air-flight-2216-should-have-died/.
276. Hee-hun, Y., and Su-hyeon, P., "Exclusive: Muan Airport fails to meet safety regulations on localizer setup," Chosun, 31 January 2025. Available at https://www.chosun.com/english/national-en/2024/12/31/TJNGK4NVE5GUXPFT372LB4CS5E/.
277. Parmente, T., "South Korea: Expert says concrete wall plane crashed into is 'verging on criminal,'" Sky News, 30 December 2025. Available at https://news.sky.com/story/south-korea-expert-says-concrete-wall-plane-crashed-into-is-verging-on-criminal-13281432.
278. TRT, "South Korean police raid Jeju Air office after deadly plane crash," 2 January 2025. Available at https://www.trtworld.com/asia/south-korean-police-raid-jeju-air-office-after-deadly-plane-crash-18249592.
279. Wood, J., "Jeju air crash latest analysis," 22 January 2025. Available at https://www.airlineratings.com/articles/jeju-air-crash-latest-analysis.
280. TRT, op cit.
281. Yu Young, J., and Sang-Hun, C., "Ex-executive who oversaw South Korean airport renovations is found dead," New York Times, 22 January 2025. Available at https://www.nytimes.com/2025/01/22/world/asia/south-korea-crash-executive-dead.html.
282. Young, J.Y., "Relatives of Jeju air crash victims file criminal complaint," The New York Times, Seoul, 14 May 2025. Available at https://www.nytimes.com/2025/05/14/world/asia/jejuair-crash-relatives-complaint.html.
283. NTSB, Aviation Investigation Preliminary Report, Accident Number: DCA25MA108DCA25MA108. Available at https://www.ntsb.gov/investigations/Pages/DCA25MA108.aspx.
284. Government of India Ministry of Civil Aviation Aircraft Accident Investigation Bureau, Preliminary Report Accident involving Air India's B787-8 aircraft bearing registration VT-ANB at Ahmedabad on 12 June 2025, 8 July 2025. Available at https://aaib.gov.in/What%27s%20New%20Assets/Preliminary%20Report%20VT-ANB.pdf.
285. Ibid.

286. Pandey, G., "A don't vilify Air India crash crew: Indian pilots' association," BBC, 14 July 2025. Available at https://www.bbc.com/news/articles/cddzp0g5125o.
287. National Transportation Safety Committee Aircraft Accident Report SilkAir Flight Mi 185 Boeing B737-300 9v-Trf Musi River, Palembang, Indonesia 19 December 1997, 14 December 2000. Available at /https://asn.flightsafety.org/reports/1997/19971219_B733_9V-TRF.pdf.
288. SilkAir flight 185, a Boeing 737-300. Available at https://asn.flightsafety.org/asndb/324077.
289. Singapore Police Office, Police News Release: Investigation into the Police Report lodged on 25 August 1999 by the Singapore-Accredited Representative to the National Transportation Safety Committee, 14 December 2000. Available at https://web.archive.org/web/20070323224159/http://www2.mha.gov.sg/mha/detailed.jsp?artid=375&type=4&root=0&parent=0&cat=0.
290. NTSB, "Egyptair Flight 990, Boeing 767-366ER, SU-GAP, 60 Miles South of Nantucket, Massachusetts, 31 October 1999," NTSB/AAB-02/01, 13 March 2002. Available at https://www.ntsb.gov/investigations/AccidentReports/Reports/AAB0201.pdf.
291. Ibid.
292. CNN, "Air India crash rekindles debate over cockpit video recorders," Reuters, 16 July 2025. Available at https://edition.cnn.com/2025/07/16/asia/air-india-crash-cockpit-video-camera-debate-intl-hnk.
293. Ibid.
294. Ibid.

Index

For Product Safety Concerns and Information please contact our EU representative GPSR@taylorandfrancis.com Taylor & Francis Verlag GmbH, Kaufingerstraße 24, 80331 München, Germany